THE NEW INTERNATIONAL COMMENTARY
ON THE NEW TESTAMENT

F. F. BRUCE, *General Editor*

The First and Second Epistles to the

THESSALONIANS

Revised Edition

by

LEON MORRIS

WILLIAM B. EERDMANS PUBLISHING COMPANY
GRAND RAPIDS, MICHIGAN

Copyright © 1991 by Wm. B. Eerdmans Publishing Company
255 Jefferson Ave. S.E., Grand Rapids, Mich. 49503
All rights reserved

Printed in the United States of America

Library of Congress Cataloging-in-Publication Data

Morris, Leon, 1914-
The first and second Epistles to the Thessalonians /
by Leon Morris. — Rev. ed.
p.   cm.   —
(The New International commentary on the New Testament series)
Includes bibliographical references and indexes.
ISBN 0-8028-2168-5
1. Bible. N.T. Thessalonians—Commentaries.
I. Bible. N.T. Thessalonians. English. New International. 1991.
II. Title. III. Series.
BS2725.3.M68   1991
227'.8107—dc20   91-6677
                                        CIP

Scripture taken from the HOLY BIBLE: NEW INTERNATIONAL VERSION. Copyright © 1973, 1978, 1984 by the International Bible Society. Used by permission of Zondervan Bible Publishers.

CONTENTS

EDITOR'S PREFACE

When the first edition of this commentary appeared in 1959, it was introduced by Dr. Ned Stonehouse. Even then Dr. Morris was by no means unknown in the theological world. His great introduction to the doctrine of atonement, *The Apostolic Teaching of the Cross,* had been published in 1955, and he had already given evidence of his quality as a commentator on Thessalonians in the first edition of the Tyndale commentary on these epistles. Reviewing that commentary in *The Expository Times* for April 1957, Dr. Vincent Taylor expressed the wish that Dr. Morris had written "a full-scale commentary on the Greek text." If the NICNT commentary that appeared two years later was not exactly "on the Greek text," it was certainly "a full-scale commentary."

Since then Dr. Morris's literary output has continued to increase, combining high theological scholarship with rare readability. In addition to works on biblical doctrine and Christian faith and life, he has produced important commentaries on the Gospel of John (NICNT), on the Gospel of Luke (TNTC), 1 Corinthians (TNTC), and Revelation (TNTC).

This productivity has been maintained along with the demanding responsibilities of the Vice-Principalship of Ridley College, Melbourne (1954-59), the Wardenship of Tyndale House, Cambridge (1961-63), and the Principalship of Ridley College (1964-79). A well-earned retirement from public duties has meant no cessation of activity: his latest commentary, an impressive volume on Romans, won a Gold Medallion Award from the Evangelical Christian Publishers Association of America in 1989. By the spoken and written word, and not least by his personal leadership, Dr. Morris has proved himself a great contemporary Doctor of the Church.

This second edition of the Thessalonians commentary does not depart in any essential from the first edition. But Dr. Morris has given fresh and mature consideration to all the issues raised by these two primitive Christian documents. His revision takes account of nearly everything of relevance and significance that has been published during the past thirty years, not only exegetical works but also studies in early Christian sociology, such as those by R. F. Hock and, outstandingly, A. J. Malherbe. Here, in short, we have a thoroughly up-to-date and reliable commentary on 1 and 2 Thessalonians for students in the 1990s, and indeed well into the twenty-first century.

The English text on which the first editions of many of the NICNT volumes were based was the American Standard Version (ARV) of 1901. Dr. Morris has, with good reason, chosen to use the NIV for this revised edition.

F. F. BRUCE

AUTHOR'S PREFACE TO THE FIRST EDITION

When I was invited to contribute to this series I must confess to some hesitation. I was well on the way with my Tyndale Commentary on these epistles, and was not at all sure that it was expedient for one man to write twice within such a short space on the same subject. What led me to respond to Dr. Stonehouse's gentle insistence was the consideration that in my work on the preceding commentary I had gathered a mass of information that the limitations of space precluded me from using. The longer commentary gave scope for this, as did the different method. It should be made clear that this is not a longer edition of the other commentary. It is a completely new work. The approach is different (though I have not felt it necessary to differ from myself at every point).

I would like to express my appreciation for the invitation extended to me by Dr. Stonehouse to contribute to this series, and also for his kindly interest in the progress of the work. As in the case of the earlier commentary, I owe much to the commentators whose works have been before me. The footnotes bear witness to my many indebtednesses. Finally, I would like to pay tribute to my colleagues on the staff of Ridley College. They have given me constant encouragement, and have made many suggestions.

LEON MORRIS

AUTHOR'S PREFACE TO THE REVISED EDITION

In the thirty years and more since this commentary was first published there has been a good deal of interest in the letters to the Thessalonians. Books and articles have appeared and a vigorous discussion has gone on. In responding to requests to bring out a new edition I have not been unmindful of the continuing debates, and I have greatly profited from what I have read. In particular I would like to pay my tribute to the commentaries by F. F. Bruce and E. Best. I have also been greatly helped by the smaller commentaries of R. Ward, A. L. Moore, D. Whiteley, and H. Marshall. In producing this second edition I have made constant use of such works as these. I should also express my appreciation for the help of Professor Gordon Fee, who was kind enough to read the manuscript and make many suggestions.

I have not felt it necessary to abandon many of the positions I took up in the first edition, but there are many things I felt I would like to express a little differently. It is my hope that in its new form this book will give help to students of these letters.

LEON MORRIS

CHIEF ABBREVIATIONS

ARV   *American Revised Version* (1901)

AS   G. Abbott-Smith, *A Manual Greek Lexicon of the New Testament* (Edinburgh, 1954)

BAGD   *A Greek-English Lexicon of the New Testament and Other Early Christian Literature* (trans. of W. Bauer, *Griechisch-Deutsches Wörterbuch*), ed. by W F. Arndt and F. W. Gingrich, second edn. rev. and augmented by F. W. Gingrich and F. W. Danker (Chicago, 1979)

Bailey   J. W. Bailey, *The First and Second Epistles to the Thessalonians,* in *The Interpreter's Bible,* vol. 11 (New York, 1955)

Barclay   W. Barclay, *The Letters to the Philippians, Colossians and Thessalonians* (Edinburgh, ²1960)

BDF   F. Blass and A. Debrunner, *A Greek Grammar of the New Testament,* trans. and rev. R. W. Funk (Cambridge, 1961)

Bengel   J. A. Bengel, *Gnomon of the New Testament,* IV (Edinburgh, 1866)

Best   E. Best, *A Commentary on the First and Second Epistles to the Thessalonians* (London, 1977)

Bicknell   E. J. Bicknell, *The First and Second Epistles to the Thessalonians* (London, 1932)

BJRL   *Bulletin of the John Rylands Library*

Bruce   F. F. Bruce, *Word Biblical Commentary,* vol. 45, *1 & 2 Thessalonians* (Waco, 1982)

Calvin   J. Calvin, *Commentaries on the Epistles of Paul the Apostle to the Philippians, Colossians and Thessalonians* (Grand Rapids, repr. 1948)

CBSC	G. G. Findlay, *I and II Thessalonians,* in *The Cambridge Bible for Schools and Colleges* (Cambridge, 1891)
CGT	G. G. Findlay, *I and II Thessalonians,* in *The Cambridge Greek Testament* (Cambridge, 1911)
Chrysostom	John Chrysostom, *Homilies on Thessalonians* (The Nicene and Post-Nicene Fathers, 1st series, vol. XIII, Grand Rapids, repr. 1956)
Clarke	J. W. Clarke, *The First and Second Epistles to the Thessalonians,* in *The Interpreter's Bible,* vol. 11 (New York, 1955)
DB	F. C. Grant and H. H. Rowley, eds., *Dictionary of the Bible* (Edinburgh, 1963)
Denney	J. Denney, *The First and Second Epistles to the Thessalonians* (London, 1892)
Dewailly and Rigaux	*Les Épîtres de Saint Paul aux Thessaloniciens,* traduites par L.-M. Dewailly et B. Rigaux (Paris, 1954)
EB	T. K. Cheyne and J. S. Black, eds., *Encyclopaedia Biblica* (London, 1914)
ET	*The Expository Times*
EGT	W. R. Nicoll, ed., *The Expositor's Greek Testament,* 5 vols. (Grand Rapids, repr. 1979)
EQ	*The Evangelical Quarterly*
Frame	J. E. Frame, *A Critical and Exegetical Commentary on the Epistles of St. Paul to the Thessalonians* (Edinburgh, 1960)
Giblin	C. H. Giblin, *The Threat to Faith* (Rome, 1967)
GNB	*Good News Bible* (1976)
Grammatical Insights	N. Turner, *Grammatical Insights into the New Testament* (Edinburgh, 1965)
GT	*A Greek-English Lexicon of the New Testament,* being Grimm's *Wilke's Clavis Novi Testamenti;* trans., rev., and aug. by J. H. Thayer (Edinburgh, 1888)
HDB	J. Hastings, ed., *Dictionary of the Bible,* 5 vols. (Edinburgh, 1898-1904)
Hendriksen	W. Hendriksen, *New Testament Commentary: Exposition of I and II Thessalonians* (Grand Rapids, 1955)
IBNTG	C. F. D. Moule, *An Idiom Book of New Testament Greek* (Cambridge, 1953)

IDB	*The Interpreter's Dictionary of the Bible,* 4 vols. (Nashville, 1962); supplementary volume, 1976
ISBE	*The International Standard Bible Encyclopedia,* 5 vols., rev. edn., 4 vols. (Grand Rapids, 1979-1988)
JB	*The Jerusalem Bible* (1966)
JBL	*Journal of Biblical Literature*
Jewett	R. Jewett, *The Thessalonian Correspondence* (Philadelphia, 1986)
JTS	*Journal of Theological Studies*
KJV	*The King James Version*
Knox	R. Knox, *The Holy Bible, A Translation from the Latin Vulgate* (London, 1955)
LAE	A. Deissmann, *Light from the Ancient East* (London, 1927)
LB	*The Living Bible*
Lightfoot	J. B. Lightfoot, *Notes on Epistles of St Paul* (London, 1904)
LXX	The Septuagint
M, I	J. H. Moulton, *A Grammar of New Testament Greek,* I, *Prolegomena* (Edinburgh, 1906)
M, II	*Ibid.,* II, *Accidence and Word-Formation,* ed. W. F. Howard (Edinburgh, 1919)
M, III	*Ibid.,* III, *Syntax,* by Nigel Turner (Edinburgh, 1963)
M, IV	*Ibid.,* IV, *Style,* by Nigel Turner (Edinburgh, 1976)
Malherbe	A. J. Malherbe, *Paul and the Thessalonians* (Philadelphia, 1987)
Marshall	I. H. Marshall, *1 and 2 Thessalonians* (London and Grand Rapids, 1983)
Metzger	B. M. Metzger, *A Textual Commentary on the Greek New Testament* (London and New York, 1971)
Milligan	G. Milligan, *St Paul's Epistles to the Thessalonians* (London, 1908)
MM	J. H. Moulton and G. Milligan, *The Vocabulary of the Greek Testament* (London, 1914-1929)
Masson	C. Masson, *Les Deux Épîtres de Saint Paul aux Thessaloniciens* (Paris, 1957)
Moffatt	J. Moffatt, *The New Testament: A New Translation*
Moffatt, *EGT*	*The Expositor's Greek Testament,* J. Moffatt: *The First and Second Epistles to the Thessalonians* (Grand Rapids, repr. 1979)

Moore	A. L. Moore, *1 and 2 Thessalonians* (London, 1969)
MT	E. de Witt Burton, *Syntax of the Moods and Tenses in New Testament Greek* (Edinburgh, 1898; repr. 1955)
NASB	*The New American Standard Bible* (1963)
NEB	*The New English Bible* (1970)
Neil	W. Neil, *The Epistle of Paul to the Thessalonians* (London, 1950)
NIDNTT	C. Brown (ed.), *The New International Dictionary of New Testament Theology*, 3 vols. (Exeter, 1975-1978)
NIV	*The Holy Bible, New International Version* (1978)
NRSV	*New Revised Standard Version* (1990)
NTS	*New Testament Studies*
Phillips	J. B. Phillips, *Letters to Young Churches* (Melbourne, 1952)
REB	*The Revised English Bible* (1989)
Rigaux	B. Rigaux, *Les Épîtres aux Thessaloniciens* (Paris, 1956)
Robertson	A. T. Robertson, *A Grammar of the Greek New Testament in the Light of Historical Research* (London, n.d.)
Rolston	H. Rolston, *Thessalonians to Philemon* (London, 1963)
RSV	*The Revised Standard Version*, 2nd edn. (New York, 1971)
RTR	*The Reformed Theological Review*
Rutherford	W. G. Rutherford, *St. Paul's Epistles to the Thessalonians and to the Corinthians, A New Translation* (London, 1908)
SBk	H. L. Strack and P. Billerbeck, *Kommentar zum Neuen Testament aus Talmud und Midrasch* (München, 1922-1928)
Thomas	R. L. Thomas, in F. E. Gaebelein, ed., *The Expositor's Bible Commentary*, vol. 11 (Grand Rapids, 1978)
TDNT	*Theological Dictionary of the New Testament*, a translation by G. W. Bromiley of *Theologisches Wörterbuch zum Neuen Testament*, ed. G. Kittel and G. Friedrich (Grand Rapids, 1964-1976)
Trench	R. C. Trench, *Synonyms of the New Testament* (London, 1880)

Ward	R. A. Ward, *Commentary on 1 & 2 Thessalonians* (Waco, 1973)
Way	A. S. Way, *The Letters of St. Paul* (London, ⁵1921)
Whiteley	D. E. H. Whiteley, *Thessalonians in the Revised Standard Version* (Oxford, 1969)
Wilson	G. B. Wilson, *1 & 2 Thessalonians* (Edinburgh, 1975)

INTRODUCTION

I. THE FOUNDING OF THE CHURCH AT THESSALONICA

In response to the vision of the man from Macedonia Paul turned his back on Asia Minor and became the first known Christian missionary to preach in Europe. It is probable that this step did not seem so momentous to him as it does to us, for he simply passed from one province of the Roman Empire to another. But it set the course of Christianity westward. In time Europe would become Christian.

Associated with Paul were Silas, Timothy, and Luke. There may have been others, but if so, we have no knowledge of them. The little band followed Paul's usual practice of seeking out strategic centers from which the new faith might radiate out to the surrounding districts. They preached with success in Philippi, a Roman colony, and the most important town in the district adjacent to their landfall. The mission there concluded with something very similar to a riot (Acts 16:22). The preachers were scourged and imprisoned. Their jailor was dramatically converted after an earthquake in the middle of the night. In the morning Paul and Silas as Roman citizens refused to accept summary release, and the incident ends with the lordly praetors bringing the humble preachers out of their prison and requesting them to leave the city.

The preachers[1] then made for Thessalonica. They passed through Amphipolis and Apollonia (Acts 17:1), but there is no record of preaching in either center. It is clear that Paul was seized with the importance of

---

1. Paul and Silas are both mentioned as having been at Thessalonica. We do not hear of Timothy between the time Paul took him "along on the journey" from Lystra (Acts 16:1-3) and his being left at Berea with Silas when Paul went on to Athens (Acts 17:14). But the natural presumption that he had journeyed all along with Paul and Silas is strengthened by the fact that he is joined with these two in the superscriptions of both epistles to the Thessalonians.

1

Thessalonica and wished to establish the church there. This was the largest and most important city in Macedonia and the capital of the province. Its situation halfway between the Adriatic and the Hellespont and at the head of the Thermaic Gulf, coupled with its fine harbor, made it the natural outlet for the trade of Macedonia and a center where many roads met. The great Via Egnatia, the Roman highway to the East, passed through it. As Meletius said long ago, "So long as nature does not change, Thessalonica will remain wealthy and fortunate."[2] To this day it is a flourishing center.[3]

The city had a long history. In early days the hot springs had given the name Therma to the settlement alongside them. In 315 B.C. Cassander named the place Thessalonica, after his wife who was half sister to Alexander the Great. It is possible that he renamed the old city, but it seems more probable that this was a new foundation near to Therma, for Pliny the Elder speaks of the two cities as existing together. But in time Thessalonica became increasingly prosperous and swallowed up the older center. When the Romans conquered Greece they recognized the importance of the city by making it the capital of one of the four parts into which they divided Macedonia. When they later altered the system and made a single province, Thessalonica became the capital of the whole. During the first civil war the city was Pompey's headquarters, but in the second it was wise enough, or fortunate enough, to side with Antony and Octavian. When they emerged victorious Thessalonica was rewarded by being made a free city. Its rulers were called "politarchs," as Luke tells us in Acts 17:6, 8, and as we know from inscriptions. While many Romans were undoubtedly there, the city remained basically Greek. Included among the extraneous elements in the population was a strong Jewish community. The Jews had a synagogue, whereas in Philippi there was only a *proseuchē,* which probably there means an open-air place where worshippers were accustomed to meet for prayer.

Thus Thessalonica had everything we would expect to attract Paul from what we know of his missionary methods.[4] It is not at all surprising

---

2. Cited by J. B. Lightfoot, *Biblical Essays* (London, 1893), p. 255.

3. It is often said that it is called Salonica, but this is not correct. It did have that name, but it was changed back to Thessaloniki in 1937 (*The Statesman's Year Book* [1938], p. 1,002, n. 1).

4. Cf. the discussion by Roland Allen in ch. 2 of *Missionary Methods, St. Paul's or Ours?* (London, 1930). He says, e.g., "Thus at first sight it seems to be a rule which may be unhesitatingly accepted that St. Paul struck at the centres of Roman administration, the centres of Hellenic civilization, the centres of Jewish influence, the keys of the great trade routes" (p. 23).

that he made his way there soon after coming to Macedonia. As was his custom, he began by attending the synagogue and preaching there (Acts 17:2). This he did for "three Sabbath days," which sets before us the problem of the length of his stay. The impression we get from Acts 17 is that it was at the end of this period that the riot took place that ended Paul's activities in Thessalonica. But while he was in the city Paul worked hard with his hands (1 Thess. 2:7-11), which might well indicate a longer period. So also the Philippian church sent gifts to the apostle while he was in Thessalonica (Phil. 4:16). The usual interpretation of this passage is that they sent twice, but it is not probable that they would do this within the period covered by "three Sabbaths." Allowing for some days before the first Sabbath and after the third, this would give us rather less than a month.

Most commentators find a solution to the difficulty in thinking that the three Sabbaths refer to the period of Paul's activities in the synagogue. After that the apostle continued his mission, preaching elsewhere, and he may have been in the city as long as six months.[5] This may be so. The chronology of Paul's life is difficult, and there are many points about which we cannot be certain. But it seems that the period may well have been just short of a month, as Acts tells us.[6] In the first place, the preaching was in the nature of a short campaign; it was not a prolonged affair.[7] It is clear from the epistles that, while Paul had given

5. This is Ramsay's estimate; see *St. Paul the Traveller and the Roman Citizen* (London, 1930), p. 228. G. Ogg thinks of a period "considerably longer" than two or three weeks, but he does not say how much longer (*The Chronology of the Life of Paul* [London, 1968], pp. 121-22).

6. Frame accepts a period "not longer than three weeks," though he allows for the possibility of a longer stay (p. 7). Bicknell prefers to think of Paul as spending "a few weeks" on "a direct mission to the heathen" after his three Sabbaths' preaching in the synagogue (p. xiii).

7. "St. Paul and Silas must not be compared to men who preach to a heathen population tolerably well satisfied with its creed, or seek to convince minds which are not especially interested, and do not share in the general point of view of the missionaries, but rather to 'revival preachers' such as Wesley or Whitefield, who understood and were understood by their hearers, and had a definite message for a clearly felt want. For such men three weeks is long enough for anything; certainly it is long enough to create a considerable body of fervent believers among men who are dissatisfied with their own position—and that is exactly what the God-fearers were" (K. Lake, *The Earlier Epistles of St. Paul* [London, 1919], p. 65). Cf. also Ward, "Many evangelists have known what happens when their work 'snowballs.' Crowds beget crowds, and when the tides of the Spirit are running high, converts beget converts" (p. 8).

a good deal of teaching, there was much that he had not been able to say. In the second place, Paul may well have had to go to work even if his stay was only about a month. We have no reason for thinking that he was a man of means, and to have a month without income is a luxury that not all can afford. In the third place, it is not at all certain that the Philippian passage means that the friends at Philippi sent help to him twice. The expression may well mean "both [when I was] in Thessalonica and more than once [when I was in other places] you sent . . ." (see the commentary on 1 Thess. 2:18). Even if it does mean "twice," it is not at all beyond the bounds of possibility that this should take place within a month, though admittedly unlikely. In the fourth place, Acts gives careful information about the circumstances of Paul's preaching in places like Corinth, Ephesus, and Rome. It tells us in each case when he turned from the Jews to the Gentiles. It is not impossible that this was over-looked at Thessalonica, but Luke's method makes this unlikely.

It seems, then, that we cannot say with certainty how long Paul and his companions preached in the city. But it was certainly a short period and may have been as little as about a month. The preaching was strikingly successful. From Acts we learn that it centered on the necessity for the Christ to suffer and to rise from the dead, and on the identity of Jesus with this Christ. "Some" Jews were converted, as were "a large number" of "God-fearing" Greeks and "not a few" of the chief women (Acts 17:4).[8] The largest group among the converts was thus derived from the Gentiles who had attached themselves loosely to the synagogue. These people were dissatisfied with the moral laxity and the intellectual absurdity of polytheism, and in their search for something better many turned to Judaism. At this time they were to be found attending Jewish synagogues in most places. It was among this group that Christianity everywhere found its most ready adherents. In this new faith they found the satisfying monotheism and the lofty morality that attracted them to Judaism, without the intense nationalism, the legalism, and the ritual requirements that they found so uncongenial. In Thessalonica, as in other places, this group gave the gospel a ready welcome. Nothing is said, either in Acts or the Thessalonian epistles, about the social class of the converts, except that some of the "prominent women" believed (Acts

8. There is evidence that women occupied a position of greater prominence in Macedonia than was common in the ancient world (Ramsay, *St. Paul the Traveller,* p. 227). So also J. B. Lightfoot cites inscriptions on monuments erected in honor of women by public bodies and other relevant data (*Saint Paul's Epistle to the Philippians* [London, 1908], pp. 55-56).

4

17:4). But from Paul's stress on manual labor, and from the fact that he does not find it necessary to warn the Thessalonians about the perils of riches, we might fairly deduce that most of them were from the lower classes. Not all were, however, for we may justly reason that someone must have been wealthy enough to own a house big enough for the church to meet in.

In recent times scholars have given attention to the way Paul would have evangelized the Gentiles, and this is relevant, for "you turned to God from idols" (1 Thess. 1:9) is not a description of converts from the synagogue. Abraham J. Malherbe points out that this may well have been done in working among households. He draws attention to the *insula,* "a type of apartment house that served the vast majority of people in the large cities of the Roman Empire." He goes on, "A typical *insula* would contain a row of shops on the ground floor, facing the street, and provide living accommodations for the owners and their families over the shop or in the rear. Also on the premises would be space for the manufacturing of goods sold in the shops and living quarters for visitors, employees, and servants or slaves." Such a household provided Paul "with a relatively secluded setting and a ready-made audience as well as a network along which his influence could spread."[9] In some such way Paul extended his influence far beyond the synagogue and made converts from among the Gentile population.

The members of the synagogue reacted to the success of the Christian mission with violence. They gathered "some bad characters from the marketplace" (Acts 17:5) and stirred up a riot. They attacked the house of a certain Jason, expecting to find the preachers there. When they were unsuccessful they dragged Jason and some of the believers before the politarchs. They accused Jason of harboring "these men who have caused trouble all over the world" (Acts 17:6), and went on to complain that they affirmed Jesus to be king. This was the kind of accusation that might well proceed from the Jews with their understanding of the royal functions of the Messiah. It may also reflect some of the second-advent preaching of the apostles. It was a very damaging accusation to be made in a free city, for the countenancing of treason

9. Malherbe, pp. 17-18. Ronald F. Hock has argued that Paul came from the upper classes rather than the lower and that his tentmaking was due to the fact that he "preferred self-sufficiency to economic dependence" (*JBL* 97 [1978], p. 560). He cites Musonius Rufus and Dio Chrysostom as upper-class men who performed menial work to sustain themselves during periods of exile.

might lead to the loss of all its privileges. That there was no substance in the allegations was plain, for the politarchs simply took security of Jason and others and released them.[10] The believers promptly sent Paul and Silas away to the next large town, Berea.

It is not easy to make out just what was implied in the taking security[11] of these men. It is usually held that Jason was no longer to shelter Paul and his company, but Acts does not say this. The big difficulty in the way of this view is that it is plain that Paul anticipated that he would return (1 Thess. 2:17-18). Therefore it does not seem possible that Jason had agreed to keep him away. It is more probable that Jason and his friends were bound over in general terms. They were to keep the peace, and in the circumstances of the moment all agreed that Paul and his companions had better leave the city quickly. This explains the sudden departure as well as Paul's expectation that he would return.

II. OCCASION AND PURPOSE OF
1 THESSALONIANS

Paul's next preaching place after Thessalonica was Berea (Acts 17:10). Here he found the Jews much less prejudiced, and when he and Silas preached in the synagogue the Bereans received their word and checked it against Scripture. As a result many Jews believed, as well as Gentile adherents of the synagogue. But the Thessalonian Jews heard what was happening, and some of them came to Berea. There they stirred up so much trouble that Paul sailed away to Athens, though his helpers, Silas and Timothy, stayed on.

Having arrived at Athens, Paul sent for Silas and Timothy to come to him quickly (Acts 17:15). But he was so stirred by the idolatry he saw that he could not wait for their arrival before preaching the gospel, both in the synagogue and in the marketplace. His preaching aroused interest and won some converts. But for the most part the cultured Athenians found the resurrection a stumbling block. At some time during

10. Why did the politarchs take notice of the Jews' accusation? E. A. Judge suggested that "the oath of personal loyalty to the Caesarian house" may lie behind it all, and further that "There may have been an imperial edict covering Jewish messianic agitation which the Thessalonian informers invoked" (*RTR* XXX [1971], pp. 5, 7).

11. Cf. MM: "The neut. ἱκανόν is common = 'bail,' 'security.'" They cite examples of its use, e.g., "unless indeed they persuade the chief usher to give security for them until the session"; "security is demanded by the tax-gatherers."

Paul's stay in Athens Timothy came to him, but Paul sent him back to Thessalonica to strengthen and encourage the believers (1 Thess. 3:2). That left him alone in Athens.

We have every reason for thinking that Paul was a discouraged man when he came to Corinth, his next port of call. Fanatical opponents had brought about his forcible ejection from three successive preaching places, in each case just when it seemed that his work would be crowned with success. After that he had gone to Athens, the cultural center of Greece, and had been met by mockery. In later days he recalled that he had arrived at Corinth "in weakness and fear, and with much trembling" (1 Cor. 2:3).

But not long after this, Silas and Timothy came to him from Macedonia (Acts 18:3), bringing news of his converts there. They told him that despite all difficulties the new believers were standing firm (1 Thess. 3:6-9). Their story was such that Paul could not but be encouraged. He saw his setbacks in their right perspective and realized afresh that God was with him, that he was indeed God's messenger, and that the blessing of God was on the work he was doing. He received new strength. Inspired by this news, he gave himself over to the vigorous proclamation of the gospel that was to mean so much to Corinth in the following days, as we gather from Luke's report: "When Silas and Timothy came from Macedonia, Paul devoted himself exclusively to preaching, testifying to the Jews that Jesus was the Christ" (Acts 18:5). Paul's first letter to the Thessalonians reflects this mood of relief and exultation. He prayed night and day that he might see these good friends and supply what was still lacking in their faith (1 Thess. 3:10). But since that was not possible he prayed for them where he was, and his prayer shows something of what he longs for God to do in and for his Thessalonian converts (1 Thess. 3:11-13). This whole letter expresses his concern for them and his joy in them.

It is not certain that Silas as well as Timothy had been to Thessalonica, but we know that Timothy had been there (1 Thess. 3:6), and that recently. One or both of these friends brought Paul news of the Thessalonian church, and 1 Thessalonians was the reaction to the need thus revealed. While in general Paul was thrilled at the progress made by this church, the report showed that these new Christians had gone astray in some matters and that they were facing some difficulties. He wrote accordingly to correct and encourage them.

It is clear from Acts that the principal opposition to the church at Thessalonica came from the implacable Jewish community in that city. They were probably able to enlist a certain amount of Gentile support, but the Jews were the mainspring of the constant opposition. One part of their campaign was a personal attack on Paul himself. They urged that he had no real love for his converts (else why did he not come back to them?). They said that he had never been motivated by a genuine concern for them, but only by the desire for personal profit. At that period there were many wandering preachers, both of philosophy and religion, who made a living by imposing on the credulity of those whom they could persuade to listen to them.[12] It was easy to impugn Paul's sincerity[13] and to class him with these familiar wandering charlatans. Should his enemies have been successful in this campaign of slander Paul would have been hopelessly discredited,[14] and the message he preached along with him.

Findlay reconstructs the calumnies of the slanderers thus: "Those so-called apostles of Christ are self-seeking adventurers. Their real object is to make themselves a reputation and to fill their purse at your expense. They have beguiled you by their flatteries and pretense of sanctity . . . into accepting their new-fangled faith; and now that trouble has arisen and their mischievous doctrines bring them into danger, they creep away like cowards, leaving you to bear the brunt of persecution alone. And, likely enough, you will never see them again!"[15] If the Thessalonians had come to accept this (and the amount of attention Paul gives it may indicate that some were being influenced), the effect on the church would have been disastrous. So Paul devoted a considerable amount of space to the refutation of such slanders. He insisted on the purity of his motives. He pointed to the way he and his companions had steadfastly refused to

12. Abraham J. Malherbe has shown that Paul's language in 1 Thess. 2 is "strikingly similar" to that of Dio Chrysostom in his references to the Cynics ("Gentle as a Nurse," *Novum Testamentum* XII [1970], pp. 201-17). It is clear that many pseudo-prophets preyed on the public with a pretense of philosophy. Cf. M. Dibelius: "Paul's mission might easily have been confused by the public with the activities of wandering speakers, mendicant philosophers, pseudo-prophets and sorcerers. Therefore the missionary's first concern had to be to dissociate himself from them by emphasising that his aims were not self-seeking" (*Studies in the Acts of the Apostles* [London, 1956], p. 156).

13. "It is clear that in the early days of the Church the device of discrediting the teachings of a prominent man by throwing doubt on his motives and conduct was perfectly understood and efficiently practised" (K. and S. Lake, *An Introduction to the New Testament* [London, 1938], p. 135).

14. All the more would this be so if, as Lake suggests, the failure of Paul and Silas to appear before the politarchs meant that the treasonable nature of Christianity had been settled by default (*Earlier Epistles*, pp. 70, 76). It would mean that some of the blame for the persecutions might plausibly be attributed to Paul.

15. Findlay, *CGT*, pp. xxxiv-xxxv.

take anything from the Thessalonians, but had worked hard day and night to support themselves. He protested his love for his converts.

In addition to the campaign of the Jews there was opposition from the Gentiles ("your own countrymen," 1 Thess. 2:14-15). Paul wrote to encourage his friends to stand fast in the face of such persecution.

Apart from these external trials, within the church some erroneous views on the second advent were causing trouble. It is clear that the converts, while they knew the essentials, were yet imperfectly informed about this doctrine. Paul wrote to give the Thessalonians that fuller information which they needed. Some of them had evidently received the impression that the Parousia was imminent. Christ would come and take them *all* to himself. But then some of them died, and that raised a problem for the survivors. Did it mean that the deceased would miss their share in the events of that great day? Did it perhaps throw discredit on the whole idea of the Parousia? Paul wrote to set their minds at rest and to give them the true teaching.

Another false inference that some of them drew from the thought of the imminence of the second coming was apparently that it was unnecessary for them to do any work.[16] This in turn meant that they had to live on the charity of their fellows and became idle busybodies. The full development of this tendency is seen in the second letter, but we find its beginnings in the first (1 Thess. 4:11-12). Paul sought to set such people on the right track.

A further aspect of the second coming seems to have concerned the possibility of knowing just when it would be. At any rate Paul thought it necessary to remind his readers that there was no knowing when it would happen (1 Thess. 5:1-3), which seems to indicate that some had been concerned about the point.

It is likely that in trying to deal with the problem the zeal of the leading members of the congregation had outrun their tact. Some of the rank and file were offended and were beginning to have a low opinion of them. Paul counseled the church at large to hold their leaders in high esteem "because of their work" (1 Thess. 5:13).

A feature of life in a Greek city of the first century was its laxity

16. Another view is that Paul has in mind "the urban poor" who were unable to find work because of the scarcity of jobs and who, when converted to Christianity, "could have appeared to outsiders to be idle beggars who exploited the generosity of the Christian community without any sense of reciprocal response to their new benefactors" (S. Russell, *NTS* 34 [1988], p. 113). There may be something in this, but I do not find the case convincing.

in sexual morality. Converts were taught that in Christ things were different, but the pressure from their environment to revert to the old, easy behavior must have been very strong. Paul accordingly includes a section encouraging them to stand firm in this matter (1 Thess. 4:4-8).

There are other indications of some measure of irregularity in the new church. Thus Paul speaks about the Holy Spirit in a way that may indicate that some had frowned on the enthusiasm[17] of members who were more Spirit-led.[18] But in the foregoing we will have most of the matters that seem to have weighed on the great apostle as he wrote to his friends. The really important thing was that he wrote in exultation of spirit, having just heard the good news of the way they were standing fast. He wrote to let them know how thankful he was. He wrote to let them know of his tender concern for them. He wrote to give them fuller information about matters in which their zeal had outdistanced their knowledge. He wrote to put them further along the Christian way that meant so much to him and to them.

A number of recent scholars, notably W. Schmithals and W. Marxsen, are of opinion that Paul was combating some form of Gnosticism, but the attempt to establish this has not been notably successful. In the first instance, the reasons for seeing Gnosticism behind this letter have not proved very cogent; all the passages urged can be satisfactorily understood quite apart from any Gnostic interpretation. Furthermore, despite the popularity in some quarters of the view that there is Gnosticism behind some of the New Testament writings, no one has been able to show that Gnosticism as such was in existence as early as this.[19] Until it can be clearly shown that Gnosticism preceded the Christian movement

17. Jewett's emphasis on the enthusiasm associated with millenarian movements is relevant (Jewett, pp. 161ff.).

18. Cf. Lightfoot: "An unhealthy state of feeling with regard to spiritual gifts was manifesting itself. Like the Corinthians at a later day, they needed to be reminded of the superior value of 'prophesying,' compared with other gifts of the Spirit which they exalted at its expense" (*Biblical Essays,* p. 264). Most, however, feel that the Thessalonian error was different. There the danger was that they might "put out the Spirit's fire" (1 Thess. 5:19). See the notes *ad loc.*

19. See the arguments of R. McL. Wilson, *Gnosis and the New Testament* (Oxford, 1968), pp. 31-59. Best finds the view unsatisfying (pp. 17-19). We should not overlook the verdict of E. Yamauchi: "In conclusion, we have seen how the imposing scholarly edifice of Reitzenstein's and Bultmann's pre-Christian Gnosticism is but little more than an elaborate multi-storied, many-roomed house of cards, whose foundations have been shaken, some of whose structures need buttressing and others have collapsed, leaving a mass of debris with but few solid timbers fit for use in reconstruction" (*Pre-Christian Gnosticism: A Study of the Proposed Evidences* [London, 1973], pp. 184-85).

it is difficult to take seriously the idea that the basic Christian writings depend on and express or oppose Gnostic concepts.[20]

Malherbe points out that in writing 1 Thessalonians Paul "created something new."[21] Letters were, of course, well known and widely used in the ancient world, but Malherbe's point is that in the letters of the time there is no parallel to Paul's pastoral purpose. Throughout 1 Thessalonians the apostle's concern for the spiritual well-being of his converts shines through, and he has considerable success in providing what was needed for the Thessalonian Christians in the unexpected difficulties they were encountering. We are so accustomed to reading the New Testament letters that we are apt to take this kind of letter for granted. But it helps us see something of Paul's achievement when we reflect that in his Thessalonian correspondence he has done something that, as far as we know, nobody else in antiquity had succeeded in doing.

III. OCCASION AND PURPOSE OF 2 THESSALONIANS

The first letter was evidently successful in doing some of the things Paul set out to do. For example, he strongly defended his personal integrity in that letter, and since there is no repetition in 2 Thessalonians we may fairly assume that his readers had taken this in. But this was not true of every point.

Thus in 1 Thessalonians Paul had had much to say about the second coming. He had stressed that this will take place suddenly. But either from misunderstanding this or for some other reason, some of the Thessalonians had concluded that the day of the Lord had already come. Paul heard of this, perhaps from the people who had delivered his letter when they returned to him, and he wrote accordingly to correct such a false impression. This second letter is largely concerned with the second coming, and Paul gives information about the Man of Lawlessness that is intended to make clear that the coming of the Lord could not be as yet.

When he first wrote, Paul knew of certain people whose second-advent speculations had led them to give up their work and live lives of

---

20. Jewett discusses a number of "models" and their applicability to the Thessalonian church (pp. 133-57). He discards them in favor of his "millenarian" model.

21. Malherbe, p. 68.

meddlesome idleness. They had not been persuaded by his short reference to their position, and accordingly he devotes considerable space to them. He points out the importance of quiet work and urges them to follow the example he and his companions had set in working for their living so that they would not be a burden on others. But he apparently feels it unlikely that all will heed him, so he gives instructions as to how the church is to treat the disobedient.

These two topics, the second coming and the idlers, are the principal topics of this epistle. As he is writing about such matters, Paul takes advantage of the opportunity to give further encouragement to the believers in their continuing difficulties, to request their prayers, and to give general counsel.

IV. THE DATE OF THE EPISTLES

1 Thessalonians was written shortly after Timothy had reached Paul (1 Thess. 3:6) and not long after he himself had left his converts (1 Thess. 2:17). Paul sent Timothy to Thessalonica from Athens (1 Thess. 3:1-2), so that Timothy would have rejoined him in Athens. From Acts 18:5 we discover that Timothy also joined him in Corinth. This meeting would be within a few months of Paul's departure from Thessalonica, and would therefore be early enough to fit in with 1 Thessalonians 2:17. There is no way of saying with absolute certainty whether the letter was written just after Timothy came to him in Athens or in Corinth, but in general the latter is more likely. The situation envisaged in the epistle must have taken a little time to develop. People died. Strange ideas about the second coming appeared. Jewish propaganda and Gentile persecution made their presence felt. Paul also speaks of the widespread reputation of the Thessalonian church (1 Thess. 1:8; cf. 4:10), and we must allow time for this to eventuate. The epistle can scarcely come after Paul's stay in Corinth, for he was there for eighteen months (Acts 18:11), but he speaks of being separated from the Thessalonians only "for a short time" (1 Thess. 2:17). A negative consideration is that there is no indication of anything happening after Paul's visit to the city; the letter has reminiscences of what happened while Paul was there (e.g., 3:1-6), but nothing later. Perhaps this is because Paul wrote too soon for anything much to have occurred. Had the time of his absence been a matter of years Paul would surely have had information about what had happened subsequent to his visit, but there is no indication of any such information. We should also bear

in mind that Silvanus was with Paul when he wrote the letter (1:1), but we have no indication that the two were together at any time after Paul's second missionary journey (he is last mentioned in Acts 18:5). A further consideration is that neither letter mentions officebearers. This does not prove an early date, but it would be consistent with a time when officebearers had not yet emerged or had not yet become important. We conclude that Paul wrote from Corinth at the time indicated in Acts 18:5.

Now it happens that one of the important dates for a determination of New Testament chronology is associated with just this period. The proconsul Gallio (mentioned in Acts 18:12) referred a question to the Emperor Claudius, and the Emperor's reply is found on an inscription at Delphi. The date given is the 12th year of Claudius's power as a tribune, and after his 26th acclamation as Emperor. His 12th year was from January 25, 52 to January 24, 53. The date of the 26th acclamation is not known exactly, but the 27th acclamation took place before August 1, 52. That means that the Emperor's decision would have been given in the months preceding this. Thus it must have been during the earlier rather than the later part of the year 52. It was the custom for proconsuls to assume their office in early summer, which makes it unlikely that Gallio began his term in 52. It does not seem possible for him to assume office, come across the difficulty, refer the question to Claudius, and receive his answer in the time. He must have been in office a year earlier, that is, in 51.[22]

Acts 18 does not say at what stage of Gallio's proconsulship Paul was brought before him, though it seems as if it was early. The great apostle was in Corinth for a period of eighteen months (Acts 18:11), but again, we do not know at what point in this period he came before Gallio. Clearly he had exercised a considerable ministry by then. Yet it was not at the very end of his time there, for he stayed in Corinth after this incident "for some time" (Acts 18:18). All in all it seems likely that Paul had been in Corinth for rather more than a year before Gallio's arrival. Probably the best we can do is to say that Gallio assumed office early in the summer of 51 and that Paul came to Corinth in the first half of the preceding year. 1 Thessalonians would thus have been written in the early part of the year 50.

---

22. Kirsopp Lake quotes and discusses the inscription and other relevant texts in *The Beginnings of Christianity*, V (London, 1933), pp. 460-64, as do G. Ogg, *The Chronology of the Life of Paul*, pp. 104-11, and J. Murphy-O'Connor, *St. Paul's Corinth* (Wilmington, 1983), pp. 141-52.

It will be obvious that this date must be taken as approximate only. To the uncertainties already noted must be added another. Proconsuls sometimes spent two years in office instead of one. Thus Gallio may have been at Corinth earlier than we have so far allowed. The date of the epistle may vary a year or two from our date, but it will scarcely vary more than that. Almost all commentators are agreed that the epistle must be dated in the early 50s.[23]

As we have already seen, there is every indication that the second letter followed within a period of weeks after the first. The same sort of situation is envisaged and the same sort of advice given. Another point confirmatory of an early date arises from the fact that Paul is recorded as visiting Macedonia, going through those parts and giving much exhortation (Acts 20:1-2). 2 Thessalonians must come before this, for it is hard to think of so similar a situation to that in 1 Thessalonians emerging again after Paul had had an opportunity of dealing with it in person. Now Corinth is the only place we know of where Silas and Timothy were with Paul during the period up to Acts 20. Thus 2 Thessalonians as well as 1 Thessalonians was written from this city. This brings the dates together. It seems impossible to assign 2 Thessalonians to any other period.

The letter is dated later by some who deny its authenticity. Thus W. Marxsen says that it was written "soon after A.D. 70,"[24] but since he cites no evidence this assertion cannot be taken seriously. N. Perrin and D. C. Duling hold that 2 Thessalonians is "a deliberate imitation of 1 Thessalonians by a member of a Pauline school," and they date it at "the stage we know from the book of Revelation, itself a text from the end of the first Christian century."[25] These authors do not even notice, let alone explain, the difficulty of reconciling this view with the fact that 2 Thessalonians was included in Marcion's canon c. A.D. 140. But it seems impossible that an inauthentic letter, not written till long after Paul's death, could have been accepted as canonical within the space of about forty years, and that even by Marcion, a man who rejected most of the New Testament books. A further problem is posed by the reference

23. C. L. Mearns thinks a date of A.D. 49 "is strongly indicated for the first letter" (*NTS* 27 [1980-81], p. 140).

24. *Introduction to the New Testament* (Philadelphia, 1968), p. 44.

25. *The New Testament: An Introduction* (New York, ²1982), pp. 208, 209. Morton Enslin is another who accepts a second-century date without bothering to discuss the letter's acceptance by Marcion (*Christian Beginnings* [New York and London, 1938], p. 244).

to the Man of Lawlessness as sitting "in God's temple" (2 Thess. 2:4). This is a more than curious statement if it was written after the temple had been destroyed and was no longer available for the Man of Lawlessness's purposes.

In recent years some have argued that the letters should be dated in the 40s (notably John Knox). The basic idea is that we should not try to reconcile these letters with what is said in Acts, but concentrate on what the letters themselves say. When we do this, it is argued, we must date the letters well before such writings as Galatians. Various dates in the 40s have been reached by this method. But Robert Jewett has shown that, even if we rely on the other Pauline letters and omit all reference to Acts, a date "in the spring of C.E. 50" is indicated.[26]

The evidence, then, is such that we should accept a date about A.D. 50 for both letters;[27] the Thessalonian epistles are among the earliest that Paul wrote. Some scholars put Galatians earlier, but none, I think, would place any of the other Pauline epistles so early. These are among the oldest Christian writings we have, and they "probably carry us closer to the time of Christ than any other written documents which have come to us in unaltered form" (Rolston, p. 8).

V. THE AUTHENTICITY OF 1 THESSALONIANS

This letter claims to be from Paul (1:1; 2:18), and it is Pauline both in language and ideas. We know from Acts that the author's associates, Silvanus and Timothy, were with Paul on his second missionary journey. The letter must be early for various reasons. Church organization is apparently in a very early stage. It is difficult to think that anyone writing after Paul's death would put out in Paul's name a statement that might be understood to mean that the Parousia would take place during the apostle's lifetime (1 Thess. 4:15). The question of the fate of believers who died before the Parousia must have been answered fairly early in the church's life. Yet it is impossible to think of anyone but Paul putting the letter out in early times.[28] How could it possibly gain a circulation

---

26. *The Thessalonian Correspondence* (Philadelphia, 1986), p. 60. Best also finds a date in the 40s untenable (pp. 11-13).

27. This date is accepted by J. A. T. Robinson (*Redating the New Testament* [London, 1976], pp. 53-54); he cites Kümmel and Best as in agreement.

28. Cf. the verdict of F. C. Burkitt: "There was plenty of pseudepigraphical literature in late-Judaism and among the early Christians, but the unauthentic docu-

while the apostle was still engaged in vigorous work, traveling among the churches and well able to denounce it? (Yet we must bear in mind that the possibility of forgery seems to be implied by 2 Thess. 2:2 and the explanation of the autograph in 2 Thess. 3:17.)

Moreover, the letter is as well attested as we could reasonably ask. It is not the kind of letter that would be quoted often, which explains its absence from the few subapostolic writings that have come down to us (though some similarities of language may be more than coincidence[29]). But it was accepted as sacred Scripture by Marcion (c. A.D. 140). It is included among the canonical books in the list given in the Muratorian Fragment (a list of the books accepted as canonical sometime after the middle of the second century, probably in Rome). And it is definitely quoted by Irenaeus (c. A.D. 180) and later writers.

It scarcely seems to be the kind of letter that would be forged. Why would anyone produce a letter like this? What would he aim to achieve thereby? The letter reads naturally as the reaction of Paul to the situation outlined in an earlier section. But it seems completely out of character as a forgery foisted on the church to serve some devious purpose of its author.

Nothing very considerable can be set over against all this. Some members of the Tübingen school regarded the epistle as inauthentic, but they stand practically alone and their reasons for rejecting it do not commend themselves. Thus we find the objection that it is not doctrinal enough, or again, that it shows too close a dependence on 1 and 2 Corinthians. These two surely cancel each other out, for the former means that it is not Pauline enough, and the latter that it is too Pauline! Neither carries conviction.

No more convincing is the suggestion that the letter cannot be an authentic writing of the apostle because there are serious discrepancies between it and Acts. For example, the epistle gives us a picture of Paul working at his trade (1 Thess. 2:7-9), and this is said to be incompatible with the statement that he preached in the synagogue at Thessalonica on three Sabbaths (Acts 17:2). We have already examined this suggestion

---

ment betrays itself by marks of a later date. Exactly the reverse is the case with the Thessalonian Letters" (*Christian Beginnings* [London, 1924], pp. 129-30).

29. Milligan, e.g., though discounting "the frequently-cited passages from the Apostolic Fathers," is of the opinion that "two passages in Ignatius, and one in the *Shepherd of Hermas* may perhaps be taken as showing acquaintance with its contents" (p. lxxii).

in considering the circumstances of the first preaching in the city, and have seen no necessary contradiction. Paul may have stayed in Thessalonica no longer than Acts indicates. Or, if we feel that a longer period is required, Acts may give us the length of his synagogue preaching. The same is true of the allegation that the two contradict each other since Acts 17:4 speaks of the converts as both Jews and Gentiles, while the letter refers to Gentiles only (1 Thess. 1:9; 2:14). So when Acts 18:5 says that Silas and Timothy came to Paul at Corinth, whereas the letter shows that Timothy was with Paul for a time in Athens (1 Thess. 3:1-2). As F. B. Clogg says, "Discrepancies of this nature prove little except that the authors of Acts and of 1 Thessalonians wrote independently of each other."[30] Neither is giving the complete story, and we must make use of both. But to say that both must in all points tell all they know is so obviously false that it needs no refutation.

We conclude, then, that there is no real reason for doubting the authenticity of this epistle.[31]

VI. THE AUTHENTICITY OF 2 THESSALONIANS

As in the case of the first epistle, there are good reasons for thinking of 2 Thessalonians as authentic. It has early attestation, for Polycarp, Ignatius, and Justin all seem to have known it, and possibly the writer of the Didache. It is found in the Marcionite canon and in the Muratorian Fragment. It is quoted by name by Irenaeus and later writers. As with 1 Thessalonians, the mention of Silvanus and Timothy as associates of the author and the obviously early date of the writing favor Pauline authorship. 2 Thessalonians emerged into church history associated unequivocally with 1 Thessalonians. It claims to have been written by Paul, and the language and theology are Pauline. It is difficult to think of a suitable motive for a forger (notice that, in addition to the opening verse, since 2 Thess. 3:17 claims to be Paul's signature, forgery is the only alternative to authenticity;[32] we cannot think of someone putting out in good faith a sample of Pauline teaching). It is difficult to think of a

---

30. *An Introduction to the New Testament* (London, ²1940), p. 21.

31. Cf. McGiffert: "If one accepts any of Paul's epistles there is no good reason for denying the authenticity of 1 Thess." (*EB,* col. 5041).

32. Cf. Whiteley, "This is an extremely blatant forgery, if it is not Pauline" (p. 11).

reason for making the letter resemble 1 Thessalonians so closely, and it is not easy to understand how a forger could have entered so fully into the mind of Paul as to produce a writing so redolent of the apostle as this one.[33] There is also the point that if we did not have 1 Thessalonians we would scarcely doubt the authenticity of 2 Thessalonians. It is rather strange to call in question an epistle that has all the hallmarks of a genuine Pauline writing on the grounds that it is similar to another Pauline writing.

For such reasons most scholars have not hesitated to accept this writing. In recent times, however, some of them have focused on certain matters that raise doubts, and a number have come to the conclusion that 2 Thessalonians does not come from the hand of Paul. The following points have been raised.

1. There is the matter that Neil puts this way: "The problem of the letter is one of accounting for the similarity to and difference from a letter written by the same hand, to the same people, only a short while before."[34] Sometimes 2 Thessalonians repeats 1 Thessalonians not only in general ideas but also in actual words. The objection is that such an outstanding man as Paul would not find it necessary to repeat himself. He would, if he had to say the same thing, say it in different words, so that deliberate imitation is a better explanation. At the same time there are differences, such as those on eschatology, which we shall notice in the next section. The contention is that the ideas are not the ideas of Paul, and that they are expressed in language that is a deliberate imitation of that of the great apostle.[35]

In the first place it must be said that the similarity to Pauline style is very close indeed. It is very difficult to envisage a forger who could imitate Paul's language so very closely. Pauline words and phrases and constructions are everywhere.[36] So are Pauline ideas. If Paul wrote

---

33. Cf. Milligan: "Not only are there abundant traces of the Apostle's characteristic phraseology and manner, as has been clearly shown by Dr Jowett and others, but the whole epistle reflects that indefinable original atmosphere which a great writer imparts to his work, and which, in this instance, we are accustomed to associate with the name of St Paul" (p. lxxx).

34. Neil, p. xxi.

35. Cf. the objection of Johannes Weiss: "the majority of critical scholars are doubtful of the genuineness of 2 Thess.; for, since they only read it in the shadow of 1 Thess., it appears to them as an insignificant and empty copy of 1 Thess." (cited by T. W. Manson, *BJRL* 35 [1952-53], pp. 436-37).

36. Cf. the lists in Rigaux, pp. 133-34.

2 Thessalonians not so very long after 1 Thessalonians, it would not be surprising if sometimes words and phrases were repeated,[37] especially if, as Neil thinks possible, he read through "the customary draft copy of his first letter before writing the second."[38] This would be the more likely in that he had to bear in mind what was written in 1 Thessalonians, because some of it had been misunderstood.

It must also be borne in mind that the extent of the resemblances is easy to exaggerate. It is natural for the openings and closings to resemble each other, and indeed for the whole structure of the letters to be similar. It is natural also for an author to come close to repeating himself when he is writing on the same subject twice within a matter of weeks or even months.[39] But the suggested parallels do not cover more than about one-third of the letters, which is strange in deliberate imitation. And even so, more or less identical language is used in different ways. For example, there are marked resemblances between the ways in which Paul describes hard manual labor in the two letters. But in the first he does it to show his love for his converts, while in the second it is to bring out the force of his example. This kind of thing is more likely to be due to a writer's free handling of familiar expressions than to slavish imitation by a forger.[40] There is, moreover, the point that the resemblances are to 1 Thessalonians. Why should a later imitator confine himself to this one letter and not make use of Paul's major writings?

The differences are no more conclusive. Thus Paul's comments on the Man of Sin (or Lawlessness) in the second letter are different from

37. Bicknell in another connection adduces a number of similarities between passages in Romans, 1 and 2 Corinthians, and Galatians, and comments: "In fact every epistle is full both of ideas and expressions to which parallels can be found in the rest. It is only natural that a writer should tend to express himself in much the same terms when dealing with similar situations. In pastoral work even the most original of teachers falls into certain habits of style and phrasing" (p. xxv).

38. Neil, p. xxiii. Frame cites Zahn as the originator of the suggestion (p. 53). McGiffert thinks that "the genuineness of the second epistle can be maintained, in fact, only by assuming that Paul had a copy of 1 Thessalonians in his possession, and that he read it over again shortly before writing 2 Thessalonians" (*EB,* col. 5045).

39. Moffatt points out that the similarities might be explained "by the hypothesis . . . that his mind was working still along the lines of thought voiced in the former epistle, when he came to write the latter." This, he says, "can be illustrated from any correspondence" (*EGT,* p. 14).

40. Cf. Frame: "Apart from the formal agreements in the main epistolary outline, the striking thing is not the slavish dependence of the author of II on I, but the freedom with which he employs the reminiscences from I and incorporates them in original ways into new settings" (p. 47).

19

anything he has to say in the first. But the difference does not amount to an incompatibility. It is no more than a person might add as a supplement to what he has already said on the subject. It is the same with other differences that are brought forward.

This combination of likeness and difference is interesting, and there may be more to it than appears at present, but the point is that it does not prove difference of authorship. Such a man as Paul was quite capable of both.

2. The eschatology of 2 Thessalonians is said to be different from that in the first letter.[41] The simplest way of putting this is to say that in the First Epistle the coming of the Lord is thought of as about to take place very soon and very suddenly. But in the Second it will be preceded by signs, like the great rebellion and the appearance of the Man of Lawlessness.

But to state this objection is virtually to refute it, for it is a commonplace in apocalyptic literature that the Lord's coming is to be sudden, and yet that it will be preceded by signs. We find this in the Gospels and Revelation, to name no other. It should also not be overlooked that Paul's warning not to be unprepared when the day comes (1 Thess. 5:1-6) may well imply a knowledge of premonitory signs.

A similar objection is that the people to whom 2 Thessalonians was written obviously knew a good deal about the Parousia, for even the teaching about the Man of Lawlessness is given them only by way of reminder, and not as communicating new information (2:5). Such people would scarcely be in ignorance of fundamental teaching on the subject (such as is given in 1 Thess. 4:13-17). But again the objection does not get us far. In the short time that he was in Thessalonica Paul could not give all the teaching on the second coming that he would have wished. Many matters were certainly left ungrasped by the Thessalonians. It is entirely natural that eager new converts should have fastened their attention on such an outstanding figure as the Man of Lawlesness without appreciating that some of their number would die before the great day. Indeed, they may well not have given this matter thought at all before the decease of some of their number forced it on their notice.

Other objections turn on the Man of Lawlessness. Thus some

41. J. A. Bailey stresses the importance of the eschatology: "The key to the purpose for which another wrote it in Paul's name is to be found in the passage which is both most striking and least dependent on 1 Thessalonians, the eschatological passage of ii.1-12" (*NTS* 25 [1978-79], p. 142).

expositors urge that this figure does not appear elsewhere in Paul and argue that therefore we cannot accept the idea as Pauline. But once more we may remark that to say this is to refute it. We cannot dismiss an idea because Paul produces it once only. For that matter it does not occur elsewhere in the New Testament. But Paul had an eager, questing mind. He is more likely to have seized on the truth concerning this being than some at least of his contemporaries. There is no real objection here.

A variant of this objection dates the origin of the idea of the Man of Lawlessness too late to put it within the time of Paul. This objection maintains that the whole idea of the Man of Lawlessness is based on the Nero redivivus myth. After Nero's death in A.D. 68 a number of people appeared claiming to be that emperor come back to life again. They were discredited, but the idea persisted that one day Nero would return and put himself at the head of the forces of evil. The myth came to have a supernaturalistic tinge. Nero was held to be demonic as well as human. Now if the portrait of the Man of Lawlessness was drawn from this myth, then obviously Paul could not have drawn it. The idea did not gain currency until after his death. But the idea of the Antichrist is far older than the Nero redivivus myth, as Bousset, for example, has shown. It goes back long before the time of Paul, and there is no reason to hold that 2 Thessalonians 2 is based on the late myth. Consequently the objection falls to the ground.

There are thus several ways of putting the argument from eschatology, but none of them is decisive.[42] The eschatological teachings in the two letters are not contradictory but complementary.

3. Some scholars think that a difference of authorship is indicated by the fact that, whereas 1 Thessalonians is warm and friendly in tone, 2 Thessalonians is cold and rather formal. But this difference is difficult to sustain. Frame points out that the vehement self-defense in the first letter accounts for a good deal of its warmth, and that if this were omitted the differences in tone "would not be perceptible."[43] Again, the coldness

---

42. Moffatt cites Baur's admission: "It is perfectly conceivable that one and the same writer, if he lived so much in the thought of the παρουσία as the two epistles testify, should have looked at this mysterious subject in different circumstances and from different points of view, and so expressed himself regarding it in different ways." Moffatt proceeds, "This verdict really gives the case away. Such variations are hardly conceivable if both epistles emanated from a later writer, but they are intelligible if Paul, living in the first flush and rush of the early Christian hope, is held to be responsible for them" (*EGT,* p. 14).

43. Frame, p. 35.

alleged in the second letter is very largely due to a few expressions. Thus Paul says, "We ought always to thank God for you, brothers," and adds, "and rightly so" (2 Thess. 1:3). But this is probably to be understood as a protestation that his praise of them in the first letter was no more than was right (see the notes *ad loc.*). Again, the objection that we meet authoritative commands (2 Thess. 3:6 and elsewhere) overlooks the fact that throughout the whole section there is an undertone of genuine brotherly warmth. Paul is very concerned to bring back into full fellowship some whose conduct had raised a barrier. But he is just as loving as he is authoritative.

Thus while admittedly 2 Thessalonians is slightly cooler in tone than the first letter, it does not seem as though the difference amounts to much. Even if we were to grant all that the objectors put forward, it would still prove very little. Writers are not always in the same mood, and we have no reason for thinking of Paul as an exception. Moreover, as we saw in the opening section, there is good reason for thinking that when he wrote 1 Thessalonians Paul was experiencing a joyful reaction after a time of discouragement. It would not be surprising if a later letter failed to reproduce such a mood, especially if it revealed that some had failed to give heed to instructions given in that first letter. Moreover, we know that Paul was in a somewhat difficult situation when he wrote the second letter (see 2 Thess. 3:2).

Thus it does not seem as though any of the objections is compelling. There is none for which an answer does not lie ready to hand. As Luke T. Johnson puts it, "it is difficult to make that case [i.e., the case for inauthenticity] convincing."[44] Other authors have also stressed the difficulties in the way of establishing inauthenticity. Holland Hendrix, for example, cites R. Jewett's view that, "While the likelihood of definitely proving the Pauline authorship of 2 Thessalonians remains at a modest level, the improbability of forgery is extremely high."[45] Hendrix goes on to point to two difficulties Jewett has brought to light: "On the one hand, an adequate theory of inauthenticity must provide a likely occasion for the forgery. On the other, the explicit avowal of Paul's signature as a practice in *all* of his letters (2 Thess. 3:17) must be rendered comprehensible as an authenticating tactic on the forger's part."[46] The positive evidence, taken with the difficulties in the way of

44. *The Writings of the New Testament* (Philadelphia, 1986), p. 266.
45. Jewett, pp. 17-18.
46. *JBL* 107 (1988), p. 765.

inauthenticity, means that we should accept this epistle as an authentic writing of Paul.[47]

VII. THE RELATIONSHIP BETWEEN THE TWO EPISTLES

Granted that the two epistles are both authentic, there are still some unusual features, such as those which have caused some scholars to doubt the authenticity of one or both. A number of ideas have been put forward in the attempt to explain them.

A. A DIVIDED CHURCH

A suggestion of Adolf Harnack that was taken up by Kirsopp Lake and others is that the church at Thessalonica was divided into two sections that met separately, a Jewish and a Gentile church. On this view 1 Thessalonians was written to the Gentile church and 2 Thessalonians to the Jewish church.[48]

In favor of this view is that it points out that Gentiles seem to be the recipients of the first letter (see, for example, the turning from idols in 1:9 and the distinction between "your own countrymen" and "the Jews" in 2:14). In the second letter, it is urged, there is a much stronger Jewish flavor, with appeals couched in Old Testament language. A second point depends on the acceptance of *aparchēn* as the true reading instead of *ap' archēs* (2 Thess. 2:13); that is, "God chose you as a firstfruit" rather than "God chose you from the beginning." The Thessalonians were not the first converts in Macedonia, nor Paul's first converts, so the term does not fit the entire church very well. But the Jews were Paul's first converts in Thessalonica, so the term might apply to them

47. Marshall has a useful survey of the recent arguments for inauthenticity and concludes: "When we examine all the arguments, then, it emerges that neither singly nor cumulatively do they suffice to disprove Pauline authorship. That 2 Th. contains some unusual features in style and theology is not to be denied, but that these features point to pseudonymous authorship is quite another matter" (Marshall, p. 45). B. S. Childs finds it "far from obvious that the pseudepigraphical hypothesis has been successful in describing a suitable hypothetical historical setting for the letter. The suggestions remain vague and hypothetical with little solid evidence on which to build" (*The New Testament as Canon* [London, 1984], p. 364).

48. For this view see Kirsopp Lake, in *ET* XXII (1910-11), pp. 131-33; his *Earlier Epistles*, pp. 83ff.; K. and S. Lake, *An Introduction to the New Testament*, 134-35.

over against the Gentiles. The case is more or less completed by drawing attention to the "all" in the closing section of the first letter (1 Thess. 5:26-27). It is felt that something must lie behind Paul's insistence that *all* be greeted and that the letter be read to *all*. The autograph (2 Thess. 3:17) was "to avoid the danger which he foresaw of one of the two parties in the Church impugning the authenticity of the other's Epistle."[49]

But this evidence is not compelling. The Jewish coloring of 2 Thessalonians is not apparent to all. Thus there is not one quotation from the Old Testament in this letter. While admittedly some of the language, particularly in the section dealing with the Parousia, is reminiscent of that in the Old Testament, it is significant that Plummer's close scrutiny of both epistles for traces of Septuagint language reveals that this is "less conspicuous" in the second letter than the first.[50] But in any case Old Testament language is not at all decisive for a Jewish destination. Paul quotes the Old Testament most frequently in Romans, a letter addressed to a church that was predominantly Gentile. Not much can be built on a variant reading, especially when, as here, competent critics (Best, for example) prefer the alternative. Again, the "all" at the end of 1 Thessalonians is not emphatic, and is capable of being explained otherwise. Paul wanted his greetings to embrace everybody and left no doubt about this (see the notes *ad loc.*). And Lake's explanation of the autograph is not at all convincing.

Thus the evidence in favor of the theory is not strong. There are also good reasons for rejecting it. The most important of these is the impossibility of thinking that Paul would have acquiesced in such a situation. He was strongly opposed to disunity within a church (cf. 1 Cor. 1:11-17) and did not hesitate to rebuke those who disturbed the unity of the churches; the absence of such a rebuke in the Thessalonian correspondence is surely significant. Again and again in his letters he speaks of the unity of those in Christ. It is impossible to understand his joy in the Thessalonians if they were divided so deeply that the two segments did not even worship together.

Quite apart from Paul's attitude there is the fact that we do not know of any church divided in this way. While there are many things about the early church that we do not know there are also many that we do. And none of them gives countenance to the idea that the early

49. K. Lake, in *ET* XXII (1910-11), p. 132.
50. A. Plummer, *A Commentary on St. Paul's Second Epistle to the Thessalonians* (London, 1918), pp. xviiff.

Christians would anywhere have accepted a situation like that posited by Harnack and Lake. We need very strong evidence to establish such a division, but the reasons we are offered are not at all convincing.

There are also some points about the epistles themselves that militate against the theory. Thus the superscriptions are practically the same, which is strange if they were intended for different groups. Harnack was driven to suppose that the words "which are of the circumcision" have been lost from the superscription of 2 Thessalonians. Then we have such curious facts as Paul's praise of the Jewish churches in a section that on this view was intended for the Gentile church (1 Thess. 2:13-16); he praises his readers for imitating the Jewish churches. This for Gentiles who would not even meet together with the Jewish Christians in their own city!

A more acceptable view is that of E. Earle Ellis, who argues that "the brothers" are "Paul's Thessalonian co-workers" (though he does not notice that the expression always lacks the article in 2 Thessalonians, and that it is more common in the first letter [19 times] than in the second [9 times]). His view is that the first letter is sent to the whole church and the second to "a group of Christian workers." He finds support for this in the reading "firstfruits" (2 Thess. 2:13), which he thinks refers to "the consecrated first-born who, like the Levites, are set apart for the work of God." He regards "the idlers" as people who receive financial support or at least meals, and thus as "Christian workers."[51] It is not easy to understand why Christian workers should be dubbed simply "idlers," and in view of the statistics of "brother" and the textual doubt about "firstfruits" I do not regard this view as having been substantiated.

Thus it appears that neither hypothesis should be accepted. There are difficulties with both, and it is simpler to accept the view that both letters were meant for the whole Thessalonian church. As they stand, neither is addressed to a group within the church but each is addressed to the whole church; there is no evidence that either ever had any other address.

B. COAUTHORSHIP

Both epistles tell us that the senders were "Paul, Silas, and Timothy." Throughout both letters "we" tends to be used rather than "I" (though there are some exceptions). It has been suggested accordingly that we

51. *NTS* XVII (1970-71), pp. 448-51.

might find a solution to our problems by thinking of one or other of Paul's helpers as being the writer of one or both of the letters, Silas usually being favored.

Now it is obvious that if we think of either Silas or Timothy as being responsible for both letters, we are in no better case than if we think of Paul as having written them both.[52] Indeed, the case is rather worse, for we are then faced with the problem of accounting for the similarity of style, language, and theology to those of other letters certainly written by Paul.

It is more plausible to think of one of Paul's helpers as having a larger place in 2 Thessalonians than in 1 Thessalonians. As we saw earlier, there is practically no disputing that Paul wrote 1 Thessalonians; what doubts there are center around the second letter. But against such a solution are three considerations. The first is the similarity of style, language, and theology. How did Silas or Timothy achieve this? The second is the statement that Paul signed the letter (2 Thess. 3:17). The third is Paul's intense personal interest in his converts. The Corinthian correspondence shows that it was his habit to deal in person with even comparatively unimportant matters. It is not easy to think of him as delegating to another the responsibility for dealing with a situation like that at Thessalonica.

Thus while this view is superficially attractive, it will not bear critical examination. The facts point us to Paul as the author of both epistles.

C. REVERSAL OF ORDER

The letters as we have them are not dated, and there is no statement in either that tells us which was written first. Traditionally the epistle we know as 1 Thessalonians has been held to be the older, but some scholars hold that many of our problems are solved if we simply reverse the order and think of 2 Thessalonians as having been written first.[53] The point is

---

52. F. C. Burkitt thinks of Silas as having drafted both letters and read them to Paul, who added 1 Thess. 2:18 and 2 Thess. 3:17 (*Christian Beginnings*, p. 132). But he does not really face the difficulty of how Silas made these two letters so very much like the letters that come from Paul.

53. T. Zahn says, "Grotius thinks that 2 Thess. was written as early as 38 A.D., before Paul visited Thessalonica, to certain Jewish Christians there" (T. Zahn, *Introduction to the New Testament*, I [Edinburgh, 1909], p. 241). See also T. W. Manson, *BJRL* 35 (1952-53), pp. 438-47; R. Gregson, *EQ* 38 (1966), pp. 76-80; J. C. Hurd, *IDB*, V, p. 901, etc.

made that 1 Thessalonians is fuller and richer in content, so that when 2 Thessalonians is held to follow it suffers by comparison, and hypotheses of copying and the like begin to appear. But if we think of 2 Thessalonians as a first letter, it is an attractive piece of work. It does not deal fully with a number of topics and thus calls for another letter that will amplify what it says and make clear points left in doubt.

A number of reasons are urged to show the priority of 2 Thessalonians. Here are some of them:

(a) 2 Thessalonians shows the church undergoing sore trials and difficulties whereas 1 Thessalonians speaks of these as past.[54]

(b) There are difficulties in the church that are mentioned in 2 Thessalonians as though the writers have just heard of them, and indeed they may have appeared but recently. But in 1 Thessalonians they are mentioned as though familiar to everyone, which points to a later stage. For example, the loafers seem to be a new development in 2 Thessalonians 3:11-15, but well known in 1 Thessalonians 5:14.

(c) Such a statement as that the Thessalonians have no need to be informed about "times and dates" (1 Thess. 5:1) is very much in point if these people have already received 2 Thessalonians 2.

(d) Paul explains his signature in 2 Thessalonians (2 Thess. 3:17), but not at the end of 1 Thessalonians. Such a statement would be needed at the end of a first letter.

(e) T. W. Manson thinks that the recurrence of "Now concerning" (1 Thess. 4:9, 13; 5:1) is significant.[55] This same formula is found in 1 Corinthians in the places where Paul is replying to a letter, each time referring to a point raised in the letter. The inference Manson draws is that Paul sent 2 Thessalonians. This letter, however, did not deal with all the difficulties in the minds of the readers. They accordingly wrote him back a letter, and 1 Thessalonians is his reply.

(f) Some members of the Thessalonian church had died when 1 Thessalonians was written. This is more likely if we allow a longer period.

(g) The organization revealed in the first letter (1 Thess. 5:12-13) requires a longer time interval than we have if 1 Thessalonians is first.

---

54. Whiteley objects, "we have no reason to believe that the *same* trials are referred to in both epistles" (p. 6).

55. He does not, however, deal with the fact that in 1 Thess. 4:13 we have not περὶ δέ but δέ . . . περί. It is at least doubtful whether this can be regarded as an occurrence of a "formula."

(h) Lyle O. Bristol thinks that the shortness of 2 Thessalonians is significant. He reasons that 1 Thessalonians is a later elaboration of the shorter epistle.[56]

(i) The postponement of the Parousia (2 Thess. 2:1-12) is what leads to the problem of the place of the dead when it comes (1 Thess. 4:13), and to the implied question "When will the Parousia come?" (1 Thess. 5:1).

These arguments, however, seem very vulnerable. So far from thinking that the trials in question were over by the time 1 Thessalonians was written, most students believe that one reason for that letter was to give the believers encouragement so that they might endure the trials before them. No real reason appears to exist for thinking that the internal difficulties were new when 2 Thessalonians was written, apart from the words, "We hear that some among you are idle" (2 Thess. 3:11). This is not really a strong argument, for the expression could just as easily follow what is said in 1 Thessalonians as precede it. It is not necessary to postulate 2 Thessalonians 2 as the background to the statement about "times and dates" (1 Thess. 5:1). On any showing Paul spoke about the Parousia and attendant happenings during his preaching while he was yet in the city, and this is sufficient to explain any reference in 1 Thessalonians. The argument about the explanation of the autograph being required in a first epistle breaks down on the fact that Paul does not explain it in any other of his epistles, which are mostly first epistles. He mentions the autograph (1 Cor. 16:21; Col. 4:18), but gives no explanation of its significance. Clearly some special reason is required in 2 Thessalonians, and Paul gives it (2 Thess. 2:2). There was a letter that purported to be from Paul, so they wondered how they could know a genuine letter when they saw one. Paul tells them.

Manson's "Now concerning" is no more conclusive. There seems to be no reason why it should not refer to matters to which Timothy drew attention in his oral report or of which Paul learned in some other way. Moreover, we do not know that it was used only as a formula in replying to a letter. It certainly is not used in that way in Mark 12:26; 13:32; John 16:11; Acts 21:25.[57] Its occurrence in 1 Corinthians does not prove that

56. *ET* LV (1943-44), p. 223. He was answered by Edward Thompson *ET* LVI (1944-45), pp. 306-7. Another who has argued for the reversal of order is J. C. West, "The Order of 1 and 2 Thessalonians," *JTS* XV (1914), pp. 66-74.

57. Chalmer E. Faw, in an article entitled "On the Writing of First Thessalonians," in *JBL* LXXII (1953), pp. 217ff., argues that the Thessalonians had sent a letter to Paul before 1 Thessalonians. He notices that the passages we have cited refer to

Paul used the expression in no other way. The deaths of some members do not call for a long period. Life is an uncertain business, and in any given group it is always possible for deaths to occur. The problem of the fate of the deceased could have arisen quite early. So with the organization. There is nothing in 1 Thessalonians that requires a lengthy period for its development. From Acts 14:23 we know that Paul appointed elders quite soon after establishing churches, and if he did that at Thessalonica that is all that is required. Moreover, there was no great interval between the two epistles, and not much could have developed in the intervening period. The argument from the shortness of 2 Thessalonians proves nothing. There is no reason why a first epistle should be shorter than a second. Moreover, 1 Thessalonians is not an elaboration of 2 Thessalonians. Where the same point is treated in both letters (for example, the loafers) the discussion is apt to be longer in 2 Thessalonians.

On the other hand, there are good reasons for thinking the traditional order to be the correct one.[58]

(a) Of the problems that occur in both letters—persecution, the second advent, and the loafers—each seems to intensify as we pass from 1 Thessalonians to 2 Thessalonians. The natural line of development seems to be in this direction and not the reverse.

(b) A letter from Paul certainly preceded 2 Thessalonians (see 2:2, 15; 3:17). If 1 Thessalonians followed 2 Thessalonians we must postulate another Thessalonian epistle now lost. It seems more natural to understand that 2 Thessalonians follows 1 Thessalonians, which letter incidentally does not mention any previous letter to its recipients.

(c) The general tone of 1 Thessalonians seems to be that called for by the situation we have outlined in an earlier section. If Paul experienced a feeling of exultation when his discouragement was removed by the good news from Thessalonica, then a letter like 1 Thessalonians is called for. The slightly cooler tone of 2 Thessalonians is explained by the interval of time and the fact that some of the converts had disregarded

---

replies to oral, not written communications. But, strangely, he does not notice that this demonstrates that the occurrence of the expression in 1 Thessalonians may just as well refer to the oral report brought by Timothy as to a hypothetical letter from the Thessalonians.

58. McGiffert thinks that the idea of the priority of 2 Thessalonians "is excluded by the literary relationship between the two epistles, which clearly points to the secondary character of the second, by the sharper tone of 2 Thess. in dealing with the disorderly (3:6f.), and by the relation of the apocalyptic passage in 2:2f. to I Thess. 4:13f." (*EB*, col. 5039, n. 2).

his injunctions. But if we reverse the order of the letters, how shall we explain these things?

(d) In similar fashion the personal reminiscences that we find in 1 Thessalonians are perfectly natural in a first letter, and need not be repeated in another missive following soon after. It is more difficult to think of a first letter as lacking in such items, and then of their appearing in a later letter. W. G. Kümmel holds that the section 1 Thessalonians 2:17–3:10 "could stand only in the first letter to the congregation," and he thinks that this "speaks decisively against the hypothesis that 1 Thessalonians is the second letter to the congregation."[59]

(e) There are some indications of a continuing growth in the spiritual stature of the Thessalonians. Thus in the first letter Paul refers to the converts as having accepted the gospel (1 Thess. 1:6; 2:13), while in the second he speaks of their faith as growing (2 Thess. 1:3). In the first he prays that their love may abound and exhorts them to abound in love (1 Thess. 3:12; 4:10) and in the second he gives thanks for their love abounding (2 Thess. 1:3). This sort of thing is not decisive, but it supports other indications that 2 Thessalonians is rightly put second.

(f) There is a small point in the teaching on eschatology. The teaching that believers will be caught up to meet the Lord (1 Thess. 4:17) is apparently new teaching. But it seems to be presupposed by the reference to "our being gathered to him," which is assumed as familiar in 2 Thessalonians 2:1.[60]

(g) The section 1 Thessalonians 2:17–3:6 seems to presuppose that this is the first letter written by Paul to this church (so Milligan, Jowett, Dewailly and Rigaux, and others).[61]

Thus sufficient reason does not seem to have been shown for rejecting the traditional order of these epistles. The evidence as we have it seems rather to indicate that the first letter in point of time was our 1 Thessalonians.

---

59. *Introduction to the New Testament* (London, 1966), p. 186.

60. On the whole question of the eschatology of the two epistles Edward Thompson remarks, "The likelihood is greater that the Apocalypse of II Thessalonians grew out of I Thessalonians rather than the reverse" (*ET* LVI [1944-45], p. 307).

61. J. Rendel Harris argued that 1 Thessalonians gives indications of a previous letter Paul sent and to which the Thessalonians had replied (*The Expositor,* 5th Series, VIII, pp. 161-80). But his arguments do not carry conviction, and in any case, he did not dispute the order of our 1 and 2 Thessalonians.

Commentary on
1 THESSALONIANS

1 THESSALONIANS 1

I. GREETING (1:1)

1 *Paul, Silas*[a] *and Timothy,*
To the church of the Thessalonians in God the Father and the
Lord Jesus Christ:
Grace and peace to you.[b]

[a]1 Greek *Silvanus,* a variant of *Silas*
[b]1 Some early manuscripts *you from God our Father and the Lord Jesus Christ*

1 Every age has had its conventions in letter writing. In our own day we begin by saluting our addressee as "Dear," and conclude with the assurance that we are "Yours faithfully" or "Yours sincerely" or the like. In the first century there was some latitude, but a letter always began with the name of the writer, followed by that of the addressee, and a greeting. Frequently there was then some pious expression, such as a thanksgiving or a prayer that the gods would keep the addressee in health.

It is important to notice that the first words of 1 Thessalonians are in the form usual at the beginning of a letter of this period.[1] What follows is not a theological treatise, but a real letter arising out of the situation in which Paul and his friends find themselves. Paul retains the conventional form, but he adapts it both to the wider context of the Christian religion and to the narrower one of the particular situation in which he is writing. The opening of this letter is the simplest Pauline form, but in it we have all the elements that we see expanded in the openings of the other epistles.

Paul begins by associating Silvanus and Timothy with himself. Silvanus was Paul's chief assistant on his second missionary journey.

1. For writing materials, procedure, etc., see Note A in Milligan's commentary, and ch. 3 of Deissmann, *LAE.*

When Paul and Barnabas quarreled over Barnabas's suggestion that John Mark should accompany them on a second visit to the churches they had founded, they separated. Paul chose Silvanus (or Silas, as Luke calls him; despite *NIV* Paul always calls this man Silvanus) as his helper. This man came under notice previously as one of the two who took the decisions of the Council of Jerusalem to Antioch (Acts 15:22, 27). He is called one of the "leaders among the brothers" (Acts 15:22) as well as a prophet (Acts 15:32). He seems to have worked harmoniously with Paul throughout the missionary journey, and Paul later recalled his faithful preaching (2 Cor. 1:19). Among other places, he had, of course, preached at Thessalonica, and this accounts for his association with Paul in the greeting to the church that had come into being as a result of the mission there. After the second missionary journey Silvanus may be mentioned once more, namely, as Peter's amanuensis in the writing of 1 Peter (1 Pet. 5:12; it is not certain that this is the same Silvanus).

Timothy was the son of a Greek father and a Jewish mother. He was not circumcised in infancy (the rite had not been carried out when Paul wanted to take Timothy with him, Acts 16:1-3), but this does not mean that his spiritual education had been neglected. Both his grandmother and his mother were devout (2 Tim. 1:5), and he had been instructed in the Scriptures from his childhood (2 Tim. 3:14-15). He seems to have been somewhat timid in disposition, but Paul thought highly of him. Paul took him on missionary journeys, sent him on missions (Acts 19:22; 1 Cor. 4:17; Phil. 2:19), and included him in the salutations of letters (2 Corinthians, Philippians, Colossians, 1 and 2 Thessalonians, and even the little letter to Philemon). In the account of the preaching at Thessalonica given in Acts 17 Timothy is not mentioned, but since we hear of him earlier and later in the same journey, and since he is joined in the greeting here and in 2 Thessalonians, we may safely assume that he was one of those who brought the gospel to Thessalonica.

There is some difference of opinion as to how far Silvanus and Timothy were concerned in the actual composition of the letter. In a comparable case, Philippians, Paul associates Timothy with him in the greeting, but by verse 3 he is using the first person singular. Though he sometimes returns to "we," for the most part it is clear that the letter came from Paul, his mention of Timothy being largely a matter of courtesy. When we find that "we" is used almost throughout Thessalonians we may well feel that Silvanus and Timothy had a somewhat larger share in the letter than did Sosthenes in 1 Corinthians.[2] Yet Paul can use the plural (and even add "alone" in the plural; so the Greek) where clearly he is referring to himself (1 Thess. 3:1). This, taken with the practical difficulty of seeing how three people could combine to write such homogeneous letters as those before us and the fact that the style is that of Paul's other letters, leads to the conclusion that Paul's is the hand behind these writings also. We need not doubt that he consulted the others, nor that they endorsed what he wrote. The steady use of "we" may be meant to associate the others more closely than was usually the case with Paul's collaborators. But Paul was chiefly responsible for the form the letter took.

Paul usually calls himself an "apostle" in the opening of his letters (not in Philippians), but to the Thessalonians he is just "Paul." There is no need to protest his position to these good friends. This letter (like 2 Thessalonians) is addressed to "the church of the Thessalonians," a form of address not used elsewhere. It is difficult to understand why this one church should be addressed differently from all the others.[3] Perhaps in this early letter Paul has not yet settled into a regular style of addressing churches. Whatever the reason, this wording directs attention to the group of believers comprising the local church, whereas such a salutation as "to the church of God in Corinth" (1 Cor. 1:2) brings to our minds rather the great universal church as it is manifested in a particular place.[4] For "church" see further on 2:14.

The following words, "in God the Father and the Lord Jesus Christ," are almost certainly to be taken with "the church,"[5] and they bring us the

2. Bruce thinks that Silvanus and Timothy "may have participated responsibly in the composition of the letter."

3. G. D. Fee notes the change from the church *of* the Thessalonians *in* God to the church *of* God *in* Corinth and suggests that this disallows the tendency of the Corinthians to think too highly of themselves as well as saying something about Paul and his relationship to the church (*The First Epistle to the Corinthians* [Grand Rapids, 1987], p. 31).

4. A point that does not seem to have been satisfactorily accounted for is that Paul addresses the church in his five earliest epistles (Galatians, 1 and 2 Thessalonians, 1 and 2 Corinthians), and "the saints," "the brothers," or the like in the later letters.

5. The doubt arises because there is no τῇ before the phrase, as we would have anticipated. Lightfoot notices the possibility accordingly of taking it with an understood χαίρειν or γράφουσι. New Testament usage in such matters is, however, variable (such an article is lacking, e.g., in 2:14; 4:16), and the sense of the passage is strongly in favor of the meaning we have adopted. It is Paul's habit to add some description of those to whom he writes. There is also the point made by Chrysostom that this particular ἐκκλησία had to be distinguished from πολλαὶ ἐκκλησίαι καὶ Ἰουδαϊκαὶ καὶ

characteristic of a Christian church. Christians are not simply people who have heard about God and trust him. They live "in" him day by day. All their deeds are done in him. Notice the close link between God and Christ: they are mentioned together, one "in" links them, and the church is related to both. It is Paul's usual habit to speak of being "in Christ," though "in God" does occur (Col. 3:3; cf. Eph. 3:9).[6] But throughout these two epistles he constantly associates the Father and the Son in the closest of fashions (cf. v. 3; 3:11-13; 5:18; 2 Thess. 1:1, 2, 8, 12; 2:16-17; 3:5; and see the note on 1 Thess. 3:11). No higher view could possibly be taken of the Person of Christ. God is occasionally called "Father" in the Old Testament, but Jesus taught his followers to see God as Father and it is a characteristic designation among the Christians.

In line with this is Paul's application to Jesus of the title "Lord." This is the regular word for Yahweh in the Septuagint, the Greek translation of the Hebrew Old Testament. In all probability it is from this source that we should derive Paul's usage, rather than from Hellenistic sources, where the term is in use for the god in the cultus of more than one deity. Yet Paul was not unmindful of the associations the term held for Gentiles. He employs a term that conveys the idea that Jesus is divine, be the reader's background Jewish or pagan.[7]

"Jesus" is the human name. Wherever it is used by itself it draws attention to the humanity of our Lord. The word is derived from the Latin, which in turn is from the Greek transliteration of the Hebrew "Joshua," an abbreviation for "Jehoshua," meaning "Yahweh is salvation" (cf. Matt. 1:21). "Christ" is from the Greek equivalent of the Hebrew word "Messiah" or "anointed one," and though it had become something of a proper name it yet retained its messianic associations.

Ἑλληνικαί (p. 324). We, with our associations, are apt to overlook the fact that to those who spoke Greek ἐκκλησία was a secular rather than a religious word (though, of course, those familiar with LXX would recall that it was used of the assembly of Israel). See further on 2:14. In Frame's judgment the absence of τῇ emphasizes the closeness of the attachment.

6. E. Best has an exhaustive discussion of the expression "in Christ" in the first chapter of his book *One Body in Christ* (London, 1955). He also discusses "in God" (pp. 21-22), though his conclusion that this "may merely indicate Paul beginning to feel after a theology" is scarcely adequate. The Thessalonian correspondence gives no indication that its author was still feeling for his theology. Rather, he was quite sure of his position.

7. "Throughout the N.T. period, from the first sermon of Peter recorded in Acts 2:36 on, the designation of Jesus as Lord was constant in Christian thinking" (Bailey).

Jesus is the chosen One in whom God is pleased to fulfill his purposes planned from of old. The combination of the three terms into one impressive title[8] gives us compactly a view of a Person who alone can be ranked with God.

The greeting is "Grace and peace to you." This is apparently a new form originated by Paul. It is not found before him, and is found in all his letters. "Grace" is from the same root as the salutation commonly employed in Greek letters: it is possible that Paul is taking over and adapting the usual salutation. "Peace" is the usual Hebrew greeting, so that this opening appears to be a combination of the Hebrew and Greek forms. Some interpreters hold that it derives from a form some Jews used in beginning letters, "mercy and peace." This may be so, but it is not easy to derive "grace" from "mercy."

But the change in the Greek form, though slight in sound,[9] is great in sense; it is a big step from "greeting" to "grace." Grace fundamentally means "that which causes joy,"[10] a shade of meaning we may still discern when we speak of a "graceful" action or of "the social graces." It comes to mean "favor," "kindness," and then especially God's kindness in providing for the spiritual needs of sinners. It comes to signify what is due to grace, namely, God's good gifts to us, especially the power to live as Christians, and finally the attitude of thankfulness that all this should awaken within the Christian. When it is used in greetings the free gift of God is meant, but the word necessarily evokes memories of the free gift on Calvary.

Among the Greeks "peace" was a negative concept (as it often is with us): it meant the absence of war. But for the Hebrews the term was positive. When a Hebrew said, "Peace be to you," he did not mean, "I hope you won't get into a fight," but rather, "I pray that you may prosper." The Hebrew *shālôm* meant prosperity in the widest sense. The root is concerned with "wholeness." The person who enjoys peace is thus the one whose life is well rounded. Peace was seen as a gift of God; there is a definitely spiritual aspect to the completeness it denotes.[11] The word

---

8. Neil adds: "The whole name, therefore, *Lord Jesus Christ,* and the significance of each of its component parts and all of them in conjunction, was essentially pre-Pauline, the faith of the church from the beginning."

9. From χαίρειν to χάρις.

10. "Joy" is χαρά.

11. I have discussed the biblical idea of peace in my *The Apostolic Preaching of the Cross* (London and Grand Rapids, ³1965), pp. 237-44. Notice also the point made by G. Aulén: in the New Testament sense peace "is a peace 'in spite of all' and

order is significant. *NIV* reads "grace and peace to you," but Paul actually says "grace to you and peace" (as he almost always does in letters to churches). This is all the more striking in view of the common use of "Peace to you" as a greeting. But for Paul grace is primary; it is only because of grace that we have real peace.

Paul's greeting, then, reminds his friends that they owe everything to God. It is in the nature of a prayer that God's grace and his peace, with all the richness of the concepts denoted by these terms, may be granted to the Thessalonians.[12]

II. PRAYER OF THANKSGIVING (1:2-4)

2 *We always thank God for all of you, mentioning you in our prayers.* 3 *We continually remember before our God and Father your work produced by faith, your labor prompted by love, and your endurance inspired by hope in our Lord Jesus Christ.*
4 *Brothers loved by God, we know that he has chosen you.*

Paul usually begins his letter with a thanksgiving (Galatians is a conspicuous exception). This was a normal way to begin a letter, but Paul clearly is doing more than adopting a convention: thanks for what God is doing in the churches is important to him. There is disagreement as to how much of this letter the thanksgiving occupies, with many exegetes taking it down to verse 7 and some as far as 2:16. Not much hinges on this, but in most of this section Paul seems to be more concerned with reminiscences than with thanksgiving.

2 Paul's thanksgiving is removed from the merely conventional by his insertion of "God": he is giving genuine thanks to the one true God, not making a casual reference to whatever gods there be. Far from the conventional also is the warmth of feeling the writer displays. Paul's

---

in the midst of the struggle. Because the forgiveness which brings peace is an act of God received and held by faith, or, in other words, because peace depends on fellowship with God, it can exist in the midst of darkness and tumult" (*The Faith of the Christian Church* [London, 1954], p. 310). Best comments, "the entire Gospel is involved in this word."

12. All Paul's later letters add "from God the Father and the Lord Jesus Christ"; perhaps in this early letter Paul had not yet worked out the formula that was to become habitual to him. This may be another argument for the traditional order of the two letters to the Thessalonians.

regard for his converts is deep and sincere. He includes them all in the thanksgiving, which is a mark of his satisfaction at their spiritual progress (contrast Corinthians or Galatians). Paul rates thanksgiving very highly. He enjoins his readers to give thanks in everything (5:18; cf. 2 Cor. 4:15; 9:11-12).

Frame takes "mentioning"[13] with "always," and understands it to mean, "Each time that they are engaged in prayer, the writers mention the names of the converts." But this does not seem justified. Rather, "always" qualifies "thank" and indicates that the thanksgiving is constant, not sporadic. While Paul is clearly affirming that he and his companions prayed often for the Thessalonians, we need not think that he could never pray without bringing in a reference to them. It is not certain whether the word rendered "continually" is to be taken with "mentioning" or with "remember" (v. 3). On the whole it seems probable that it goes with the former (NIV takes it with the latter and puts the word in v. 3).

3 The matter of the thanksgiving is threefold,[14] and, as Paul often does, he gives thanks for matters that will be raised in the letter: faith is the topic in chapters 1-3, love is prayed for in 3:12 (cf. 4:9-12), while concern for their hope and their steadfastness is found throughout the letter. First, "your work produced by faith." There is no reason to doubt that the meaning of this phrase is "your work that springs from faith."[15] Grammatically other meanings are possible (as, for example, Hendriksen shows), but none suits the context as well as this. Paul is very emphatic that salvation is a matter of faith, not works, and he uses the very strongest of expressions to make clear that people are not saved by works of any kind. But when this truth is not in dispute he does not hesitate to speak of the good works that characterize the life of faith (cf. 5:13; 1 Cor. 3:11-15; 15:58; 16:10). Faith, for Paul, is a warm personal trust in a

---

13. μνείαν ποιοῦμαι is found in Paul also in Rom. 1:9; Eph. 1:16; and Phlm. 4, each time being used of prayer. μνεία means "remembrance," and the expression could mean "to remember," as does the very similar expression μνήμην ποιεῖσθαι (2 Pet. 1:15). However, examples of its use in secular authors in the sense "to mention" are not lacking, and this phrase gives better sense here. In addition, the idea appears to be different from that conveyed by μνημονεύοντες in the next line. ἐπί signifies "at," "in the time of."

14. For the conjunction of ἔργον, κόπος, and ὑπομονή, and in that order, cf. Rev. 2:2.

15. Cf. Wilson, "Theirs was no barren assent to a dogma [Jas 2:17], but the dynamic outworking of a life-transforming principle [Gal 5:6]."

living Savior,[16] and such faith cannot but transform the whole of life and issue in "work" of many kinds (cf. "faith working through love," Gal. 5:6, *RSV*). The word "work" is very general, and we should not try to delimit it too closely.

"Labor prompted by love" is apt to be misunderstood, for we use the expression "labor of love" to denote small services we render without hope of reward. But Paul's term is a strong one,[17] and he means that, out of love, the Thessalonians have labored to the point of weariness. The word expresses the cost of their love, not its result. With or without visible success, love gives itself unstintingly.

Since the Greeks had a number of words for love, it is of interest that the Christians passed over all those in common use. They took up *agapē*, a word rarely used before them, and made it their characteristic word for love.[18] It rings throughout the New Testament. Not only did they have a new word, but they had a new idea, for, as John says, we can never know what *agapē* is from any human activity, not even from love to God. It is known only from God's great love to us shown in the propitiation wrought out on the cross (1 John 4:10).[19] We have food for thought here, for it may be that in our day popular ideas of love are as misleading as they were in theirs. The Hollywood brand of love will never do if we wish to understand the New Testament.

Among the Greeks the usual word for love was *erōs*. Basically this word means romantic love, love between the sexes. Though it came to be

16. Moffatt renders "active faith," but this is to put the stress on πίστεως while the Greek puts it on ἔργου. The same criticism might be leveled at his "patient hope," though curiously he renders the intervening expression (exactly the same Greek construction) by "labor of love."

17. His word is κόπος, on which Milligan comments, "As distinguished from ἔργον, κόπος brings out not only the issue of work, but the cost associated with it. . . . It is thus here the laborious toil (Grot. *molesti labores*) from which love in its zeal for others does not shrink." Paul, of course, often uses the term for his "labor" in the gospel. See further on 5:12.

18. For its use in the Septuagint see my *Testaments of Love* (Grand Rapids, 1981), ch. 6. In that book I have examined the New Testament idea of love in some detail.

19. Bicknell's additional note on love overlooks this. He begins with self-love and works outward. When he comes to the love of God he finds it surprising that Scripture does not speak of the love of God in creation, but rather in the cross. The point is that his direction is wrong. ἀγάπη cannot be understood from any human activity. We begin to know what it is only when we contemplate Calvary. It may be sufficient to refer to the literature cited in my *Testaments of Love* (see n. 18).

40

used of other loves, this is its characteristic meaning, and all others are derived from it. Now there are two important points about a young man's love for a young woman. First, he thinks highly of his beloved. Whatever the opinion of others ("I can't imagine what he sees in her!"), he thinks she's wonderful. Second, his love includes the desire to possess. I have never yet met a young man who said: "I'm head over heels in love with so-and-so, and I don't care who marries her!" On the contrary, he is determined that she will be his. These two ideas, the love of the worthy and the desire for possession, are of the essence of *erōs*. The result may be a crude lust or it may be a high and pure emotion, for example, the love of the good. It is no small praise of anyone when we can say that that person loves (in the sense of *erōs*) the good. For that is to say that he regards it as the most worthy thing and is determined to make it his own day by day. This is a fine concept. But it is not the Christian idea of love.

God loves us, not because we are worthy, nor even, as some think, because he sees in us possibilities as yet unrealized. God loves us although he knows full well our complete unworthiness. He knows that, at best, our righteousnesses are as "filthy rags" (Isa. 64:6, *KJV*). And still he loves us. He loves, moreover, without thought of advantage, for there is nothing that we can bring to him who made all things. He loves because it is his nature to love. He loves because he *is* love. Continually he gives himself in a love that is for the blessing of others, not for the enrichment of himself. This love is more than a matter of words. God's love is a love that costs. It is an active love, a love revealed in what Christ did on the cross. Indeed, it is only in the cross that we can really know what the love of a pure and holy God for sinners is.

God's love does not leave us alone. As soon as we discover what *agapē* really is, we are forced to a decision. We either yield to that love, in which case we are transformed by it, or we reject it. The acceptance of *agapē* means that we are made anew. By the grace of God we begin to see people in a measure as God sees them, and to love them, not for any worthiness they may have, but despite their unworthiness. We love them, not for our own advantage, but for theirs. Either we do this or we turn away and in so doing condemn ourselves. *Agapē* compels us to a decision. Here Paul is giving thanks for the way the divine *agapē* is being realized in the self-giving labor of the Thessalonians (even if he recognizes that there is still room for it to grow, 3:12; 4:9-10).[20]

---

20. Denney makes the point that passion is a necessary prelude to effective work: "The passion of the New Testament startles us when we chance to feel it. For

The third item in the thanksgiving is "endurance inspired by hope." "Endurance" (or "stedfastness," *ARV* mg.) is not a quiet, passive resignation, but an active constancy in the face of difficulties. As Barclay puts it, "It is the spirit which can bear things, not simply with resignation, but with blazing hope."[21] This springs from hope,[22] that hope which is more than pious optimism. It is a solid certainty. In the New Testament hope is always something that is as yet future, but that is completely certain. It is a significant feature of the early church, and marked it off from contemporary paganism.[23] It is a hope that is firmly grounded and that is related to the resurrection of Jesus (cf. 4:13-14).

It is not absolutely clear whether we should take "in our Lord Jesus Christ" with "hope," or, as Neil, for example, does, with the whole of the preceding, including the work of faith and labor of love. In the latter case it would mean that the whole of the life of the believer is lived in Christ. While this is true, yet here Paul seems rather to be saying that the Christian hope is in Christ. The Thessalonian epistles have a good deal to do with the second coming and associated events, and hope is very prominent in them. Similarly, "before our God and Father" is probably to be taken with "hope" rather than with the preceding.[24] The hope of the believer is in Christ, but it is also a hope that has reference to his standing before the Father, and not merely before other people.

This verse brings before us that conjunction of faith, hope, and love which we find in a number of places in the New Testament (5:8;

---

one man among us who is using up the powers of his soul in barren ecstasies, there are thousands who have never been moved by Christ's love to a single tear or a single heart throb. They must learn to love before they can labour."

21. *A New Testament Word Book* (London, 1955), p. 60. A little later he says, "George Matheson, who was stricken in blindness and disappointed in love, wrote a prayer in which he pleads that he might accept God's will, 'not with dumb resignation, but with holy joy; not only with the absence of murmur, but with a song of praise'. Only *hupomonē* can enable a man to do that" (p. 61).

22. Turner sees here a subjective genitive, "the sustaining patience which hope brings" (M, III, p. 211).

23. "The early church was sharply distinguished from its pagan neighbours by its intense hope, for the world of ancient Greek and Roman times was, despite its achievement and glories, pathetically hopeless" (Moore).

24. It is unlikely that ἔμπροσθεν τοῦ θεοῦ καὶ πατρὸς ἡμῶν goes with μνημονεύοντες (as Findlay inclines to think, *CGT;* so *RSV, NIV,* etc.), because it is so far from it in the sentence. It is more likely that we should take it with all the words τοῦ ἔργου . . . Χριστοῦ (so Bruce). But if we confine the reference of τοῦ Κυρίου . . . Χριστοῦ to ἐλπίδος it is difficult to avoid doing the same with the concluding expression.

Rom. 5:1-5; 1 Cor. 13:13; Gal. 5:5-6; Col. 1:4-5; Heb. 6:10-12; 10:22-24; 1 Pet. 1:21-22). 1 Corinthians 13:13 is especially important, for that chapter is about love, not faith or hope, yet at the climax the other two appear quite naturally. It was apparently an accepted Christian practice to join the three. While the linkage is found in several places, the order varies. In this verse hope comes last as a climax, which is very fitting in a letter in which hope is given so much emphasis.

Here we notice a characteristic of Paul's writing. The sentence might well have finished at "hope," and it would have been well rounded and complete. But Paul is not satisfied. He goes on to add another thought and another, so that his sentence does not finish till the end of verse 5 (or even later, in the opinion of some expositors). As Findlay says, "His thought flows on in a single rapid stream, turning now hither, now thither, but always advancing towards its goal. His sentences are not built up in regular and distinct periods; but grow and extend themselves like living things under our eyes" *(CBSC)*.

4 Paul addresses his readers as "Brothers loved by God."[25] He is fond of the address "brothers," using it twenty-one times in these two epistles (he uses the word "brother" another seven times). Brotherhood was a very real thing in the early church, composed as it was of people from every race and social class, but with a preponderance of those from the depressed classes (1 Cor. 1:26ff.). The members of the church knew a real brotherhood, a brotherhood that depended on the fact that they had all experienced the love of God. In view of much modern talk about "the brotherhood of man," we should be clear on the New Testament teaching. The brothers are those "beloved by God," and they are elect. There is a sense in which all people may be thought of as brothers. But in the sense that matters, brothers are brothers in Christ. The Christian brotherhood is the fellowship of the redeemed. It refers to those who can call God "Father."

Election is one of the great concepts of the Bible, and it looms large in both Testaments. It is often misrepresented (as in Burns's dreadful caricature). God is pictured as an arbitrary tyrant, damning or saving people without rhyme or reason. Against all such views we must insist that election, as Paul's words imply, proceeds from the fact of God's great love (notice the connection between love and election also in 2 Thess. 2:13). It

---

25. Usually when referring to people as "loved by God" the word is ἀγαπητός (e.g., Rom. 1:7). ἠγαπημένοι ὑπὸ τοῦ θεοῦ is found here only in the New Testament (though 2 Thess. 2:13 and Jude 1 are similar), and the perfect passive stresses the continuing love God shows to people.

is not a device for sentencing people to eternal torment, but for rescuing them from it. Election protects us from thinking of salvation as dependent on human whims, and roots it squarely in the will of God. Left to ourselves, we do not wish to leave our state of untroubled sinfulness. It is only because God first convicts us and enables us that we can make even the motion of wanting to turn from our sins. This is no afterthought of God, no sudden change in his plans, but his eternal purpose. He has chosen his own from before the foundation of the world (Eph. 1:4). Nothing gives security to salvation like the concept of election. Salvation, from first to last, is the work of God. Well may the seventeenth of the Thirty-Nine Articles of the Church of England speak of our election in Christ as "full of sweet, pleasant, and unspeakable comfort."

The word for election is always used in the New Testament of the divine action, though sometimes it refers to other things than election to salvation, as when it is used of election to the office of preaching (Acts 9:15). Lightfoot says that it "is never used in the New Testament in the sense of election to final salvation," but this seems impossible to maintain (see Rom. 11:5, 7, 28, to name no other). Here it is clearly God's choice of the Thessalonians for salvation that gives Paul matter for thanksgiving. Anything less is inadequate. He undertakes no explanation of what election is, so that the Thessalonians must have been familiar with the concept; clearly it was part of the original preaching. Notice that Paul expresses himself as quite certain of the election of the Thessalonians.[26]

III. REMINISCENCES (1:5–2:16)

A. RESPONSE OF THE THESSALONIANS TO THE ORIGINAL PREACHING (1:5-10)

5 *because our gospel came to you not simply with words, but also with power, with the Holy Spirit and with deep conviction. You*

---

26. Rutherford is surely wrong when he renders "the circumstances of your election." εἰδότες is a causal participle depending on εὐχαριστοῦμεν (so Frame and others), and Paul is giving thanks because he knows their ἐκλογήν. It is not the circumstances of their election but the fact of it that evokes his thanksgiving. In modern discussions the doctrine of election has not always received the attention its biblical importance warrants, though H. H. Rowley's *The Biblical Doctrine of Election* (London, 1952) is a welcome reminder of its importance. Loraine Boettner discusses election in ch. XI of *The Reformed Doctrine of Predestination* (Grand Rapids, 1948).

know how we lived among you for your sake. 6 You became imitators of us and of the Lord; in spite of severe suffering, you welcomed the message with the joy given by the Holy Spirit. 7 And so you became a model to all the believers in Macedonia and Achaia. 8 The Lord's message rang out from you not only in Macedonia and Achaia—your faith in God has become known everywhere. Therefore we do not need to say anything about it, 9 for they themselves report what kind of reception you gave us. They tell how you turned to God from idols to serve the living and true God, 10 and to wait for his Son from heaven, whom he raised from the dead—Jesus, who rescues us from the coming wrath.

Before dealing with the matters in which he feels the Thessalonians had failed, Paul lays a solid foundation by pointing to the areas in which they had succeeded. In this section he reminds them of what had happened when he and his associates first preached in Thessalonica. They had met with a warm response, such a warm response, indeed, that the converts had become model believers. This will leave them in no doubt about his warm approval of their general position when he later comes to deal with their shortcomings.

5 Paul proceeds to give his reasons for knowing that the Thessalonians are elect.[27] In verse 5 these reasons are chiefly subjective, relating to the experience of the preachers. In verse 6 he turns to the effects in the lives of the Thessalonians, and for this he goes back to the time when he and his companions had first preached the gospel in Thessalonica. The "gospel" means the content of the preachers' message, the good news of what God has done in Christ to bring salvation.[28] On occasion Paul can refer to "the gospel of God" (2:8, 9, etc.), stressing the divine origin of the message, or "the gospel of Christ" (3:2; Rom. 15:19, etc.), pointing to the centrality of what Christ has done to bring about the gospel. "Our gospel" directs attention rather to the fact that it

27. ὅτι may mean "that" (as *NEB* and many commentators; *REB* changes to "because"), but as Frame says, "We infer your election from the fact that (ὅτι = 'because' . . .)," and he cites 2 Thess. 3:7; Rom. 8:27; 1 Cor. 2:14 in support. The other view is certainly tenable, but Paul seems to be showing how he knows the Thessalonians to be elect, not showing in what the election consisted.

28. εὐαγγέλιον directs attention to the content of the message as good news, whereas κήρυγμα would stress rather the message as something given to be proclaimed, like the tidings of a herald. When Paul says the gospel "came," he draws attention away from the messengers to the divine activity.

was what the preachers had preached and that they had made it their own. Only out of his own experience of salvation through the atoning work of the Savior can the preacher deliver a message that rings true and is really his own (cf. "my gospel," Rom. 2:16).

Sometimes Paul had had the experience of being forbidden by the Spirit to preach at all in a given area (Acts 16:6-7). Sometimes he had spoken rather fearfully and haltingly (1 Cor. 2:3; though we should note that even here there was the powerful presence of the Spirit). It is a reasonable conjecture that in some of his discussions with the Jews he had felt that it was hopeless. But his experience in preaching at Thessalonica was different. There the apostle had been conscious that the power of God was at work. The preaching had not been "simply with words." Words alone are empty rhetoric, and more than that is required if people's souls are to be saved. Paul knew that the preaching at Thessalonica had been effective, and he makes three points about it.

First, the gospel "came . . . with power." The verb points to some vital force in operation, and the noun completes the thought. In many places we see evidence that the gospel is power, for God is in it (cf. Rom. 1:16). It is not simply that the gospel tells of power, though this, too, is true. But when the gospel is preached, God is there and God is working. The gospel *is* power. Sinful people do not wish to be told how to be better. They do not even wish to be told that Christ has died for them (unless there is a work of grace in their hearts). But whenever the gospel is faithfully proclaimed, there is power. Not simply exhortation but power, and that power can break down resistance.

Now there are various kinds of power, and not all work for good. The second point, then, is that this power is associated with the Holy Spirit. This is no evil power deluding people with false promises. It is the Holy Spirit of God, leading them into the salvation that God has prepared for them. "Spirit" lacks the definite article, but "The absence of the article need not imply that the personal Holy Spirit is not in view here" (Bruce, who cites other such passages).

The third point is that the gospel came "with deep conviction" (cf. Ward, "Christian certainty"). There is no repetition of the "in" in the Greek,[29] and the effect is to link "with the Holy Spirit" very closely with "with deep conviction." Assurance is not some human device whereby people persuade themselves. Rather it is the result of the activity of the

29. It is lacking in ℵ B 33 lat and, though read by A C D etc., is probably not original.

Holy Spirit working in believers. Some scholars have felt that the assurance meant here is that which came to the converts when they put their trust in Christ, and this may not be out of the apostle's mind. But his primary meaning is the assurance that the Spirit gave to the preachers, for Paul is dealing with the way he and his companions came to know the election of the Thessalonians. They had the assurance in their own hearts that, as they were evangelizing, the power of God was at work. The Spirit was working a work of grace.[30]

Paul appeals to what the Thessalonians knew of the original mission.[31] Several times he recalls to their minds the manner of life of the preachers.[32] This must have made a profound impression on the mixed population of the city, and it was evidence of the power the apostle has just been talking about. While many preachers in modern times will be hesitant about directing attention to their own lives, it yet remains true that no preacher can expect a hearing for his gospel unless it is bearing fruit in his own life. A feature of this letter is the way Paul keeps recalling the times when he was with his correspondents, often with a reminder of the teaching he then gave (cf. 2:1-2, 9-12; 3:4; 4:1-2, 6, 11; 5:1-2).

6 "You" is emphatic. The certainty that the Thessalonians were among the elect did not rest solely on the experiences of the preachers. There had been dramatic changes in the lives of the converts, and attention is now turned to this. The word order, imitators "of us and of the Lord," is startling, but a moment's reflection shows that this must be the historical order. The missionary must show the new way in his life as well as in his words.[33] His converts will begin by imitating him and go on to imitate his Master. Paul has no hesitation in saying to the Corinthians, "Therefore I urge you to imitate me" (1 Cor. 4:16), and again, "Follow my example, as I follow the example of Christ" (1 Cor. 11:1; cf. "imitators of God," Eph. 5:1).[34] The great example for Christians is

---

30. πληροφορία means "full assurance." There were no lingering doubts. G. Delling sees a reference to "great 'fulness of divine working' " (*TDNT*, VI, p. 311), but it is better to understand it of an inward assurance of "the powerful operation of the Spirit" (G. Schrenk, *TDNT*, IV, p. 179).

31. καθώς introduces an explanation or amplification of the preceding; cf. 1 Cor. 1:6; 3 John 3.

32. ἐν is omitted before ὑμῖν in ℵ A C 33 etc., but is read by B D G etc. It may well have been omitted by haplography (as Best holds). If it is read, the meaning will be "among you"; if it is omitted, "toward you."

33. Cf. Bicknell, "In so far as they are truly Christian, they [i.e., missionaries] represent not simply Christ's teaching but Christ's life."

34. Paul uses μιμητής five times (elsewhere in the New Testament it occurs

that of Christ. If they imitate their teachers it is in order that they may be brought to imitate him more closely thereby. This is further explained:[35] "in spite of severe suffering, you welcomed the message with the joy given by the Holy Spirit." The word for "welcomed" is that used for the reception of a guest (as in Luke 10:8, 10; Heb. 11:31), and it includes the thought of a warm welcome. The imitation of the Lord must mean imitating his bearing of affliction with joy (cf. Heb. 12:2); it cannot be said that he "welcomed the word."

From the beginning there had been opposition to the word in Thessalonica (Acts 17:5-9). It is thus relevant that the converts had welcomed it "in spite of severe suffering." The word for "suffering"[36] outside the Bible usually denotes literal pressure, and that of a severe kind. The corresponding verb, for example, was used of pressing the grapes in wine-making till they burst, and thus metaphorically it came to mean very great trouble. In the New Testament the noun is generally used in the figurative sense found here. It denotes not mild discomfort, but great and sore difficulty. The Jews who stirred up a riot against Paul (Acts 17:5) and followed him to Berea (Acts 17:13) would not have left the new converts unmolested, and there was further opposition from the local pagans (1 Thess. 2:14). There is every reason for thinking that the Thessalonian Christians had been sorely tried.[37]

But their affliction was "with the joy given by the Holy Spirit." It is certain that the believer will experience tribulation (John 16:33), but it is equally certain that he will have an inner serenity, even a joy, that nothing in the world can give and nothing in the world can take away

---

only in Heb. 6:12). The concept is discussed by W. Michaelis, *TDNT*, IV, pp. 666-74; C. J. Hemer, *ISBE*, II, p. 806.

35. δεξάμενοι is probably to be taken "as a participle not of antecedent action, 'when you had welcomed,' but of identical action, 'in that you welcomed' " (Frame).

36. θλῖψις. It is used again in 3:3, 7; 2 Thess. 1:4, 6, and the cognate verb in 3:4; 2 Thess. 1:6, 7.

37. A. J. Malherbe sees a reference to "the distress and anguish of heart experienced by persons who broke with their past as they received the gospel. Like other converts, these new Christians in Thessalonica continued to be distressed" (*Paul and the Thessalonians* [Philadelphia, 1987], p. 48). He gives examples of converts to philosophical systems who suffered mental and spiritual distress. But this does not appear to be what Paul is saying. His word rarely if ever in the New Testament means "distress" (perhaps it does in 2 Cor. 2:4; Phil. 1:17); it means "oppression, affliction, tribulation" (BAGD) and is often joined with διωγμός (e.g., Matt. 13:21; Rom. 8:35; 2 Thess. 1:4). In view of the open hostility Paul and others encountered in Thessalonica (Acts 17:5-9) it seems that "suffering" is the meaning here.

(John 16:22). Suffering is always unpleasant, but for those who have been saved through the suffering of their Lord it has been transformed.[38] As Lightfoot says, "The degree in which the believer is allowed to participate in the sufferings of his Lord should be the measure of his joy" (he draws attention also to Phil. 1:29; 1 Pet. 4:13). Paul and Silas knew something of this joy (cf. Acts 16:25), and so did those who, in an earlier day, went out from the council "rejoicing because they had been counted worthy of suffering disgrace for the Name" (Acts 5:41; see also 2 Cor. 7:4; 8:2, etc.). This transformation of suffering does not come about by autosuggestion or any other human device. It is specifically said to be "by the Holy Spirit." We are reminded that joy is part of the fruit of the Spirit (Gal. 5:22). It is a striking illustration of the way in which all of our values are transformed by the power of God's Holy Spirit when we enter into the salvation bought at the price of the blood of his Son. And it is a reminder that the Holy Spirit is at work in the process whereby sinners appropriate salvation.

7 But the imitators in their turn were imitated,[39] and that widely. Paul speaks of this with satisfaction. His word for "model"[40] is that from which we get our word "type." Originally it denoted the mark left by a blow (as in John 20:25, where it is translated "marks"). Then it came to be used of a figure stamped by a blow, like the design stamped on a coin. From that it came to denote any image, whether stamped or not (as in Acts 7:43), and then a pattern (Acts 7:44; Heb. 8:5). It comes to have ethical significance when it is used of a pattern of conduct, occasionally of a pattern to be avoided (1 Cor. 10:6), but more usually, as here, of an example to be followed (Titus 2:7; 1 Pet. 5:3, etc.). In the present passage the word is used in the singular. Paul is speaking of the church as a pattern community rather than of the individuals comprising it as so many individual patterns.

---

38. Dewailly and Rigaux make the point that sufferings, for the Christian, stimulate rather than diminish hope: "Tribulations, those of Acts 17:1-9 and those which followed, associate Paul and the Christians (3:3f., 7) with the sufferings of Christ, and are the measure of their future rest (II Thess. 1:7); thus they stimulate hope rather than diminish it (Rom. 5:3-5, etc.)."

39. On ὥστε γενέσθαι Milligan comments: "The inf. introduced by ὥστε is here consecutive, and points to a result actually reached and not merely contemplated . . . this result being further viewed in its direct dependence upon the previously-mentioned clause." When ὥστε is followed by the indicative the actuality of the result is stressed, but not its connection with the preceding.

40. τύπος.

They are an example "to all the believers in Macedonia and Achaia," which was an area comprising all of the land we know as Greece, together with the province to the north of it, a considerable area. This is the one place where Paul speaks of one church as "a model" for others; he sometimes speaks of churches imitating other churches (as this church imitated the churches of Judea, 2:14), but here only does he use the precise term "model"[41] of any church. He specifically makes the point that these believers are a pattern to other believers; he is not simply contrasting them with pagans who do not know the power of God. It is easy to pass over the significance of "all the believers," for nowadays great stress is placed on good works of various kinds, especially social service, and often people regard this as the essence of Christianity. Apostolic Christianity was in no danger of confusing the root with the fruit in this way. Throughout the New Testament the characteristic mark of Christians is their faith—their dependence on Christ alone for all things. Naturally and unobtrusively Christians are called simply "believers." That is the heart of the matter, and Paul's usage makes it clear. Nothing more is needed to characterize Christians, and nothing less will do.

8 "For" (which *NIV* does not translate)[42] introduces evidence for what Paul has just said, and the measure of his satisfaction with the progress of the Thessalonian church is the praise he now bestows on it. "From you" comes first in the Greek with emphasis; the apostle stresses the evangelistic work this church has done. He begins by speaking of them as examples to Christians in Macedonia and Achaia, Greece, and the province to the north of it.[43] There is some uncertainty about the status of these regions after the Romans conquered the area in 146 B.C., but in 27 B.C. Augustus made Achaia a separate province. Tiberius combined them in A.D. 15, and Claudius separated them again in A.D.

41. τύπος. The word has several shades of meaning, but here it signifies "example, pattern" (BAGD 5.b).

42. In modern translations there is a strong tendency to omit any rendering of γάρ. Thus in 1 Thessalonians it occurs 23 times and is omitted 11 times by *NEB*, 16 times by *REB*, 16 times by *GNB*, 10 times by *NIV*, and 17 times by *JB*. *RSV* omits it only once, and *NASB* not at all. Now it is of course true that on occasion γάρ may legitimately be omitted (cf. BDF #452 [1]), but it can scarcely be disputed that modern translators take this too far and in doing so rob their readers of access to a Pauline distinctive. Paul uses γάρ 454 times, about 44 percent of the New Testament total (Matthew comes next with 124, a long way short of Paul). The apostle liked to bring out logical connections with this causal conjunction.

43. See the article on Achaia in *IDB*, I, p. 25.

44.[44] Paul goes on to speak of the way the word of God has gone out from the Thessalonians into every place. This reflects something of the strategic situation of Thessalonica, on the great highway, the Via Egnatia, and with a harbor giving ready access to many places by sea. Paul himself would know what was going on in Achaia, while Priscilla and Aquila had just come to Corinth from Rome (Acts 18:2), doubtless bringing news of what was reported there. There is thus solid basis for what Paul is saying.

Paul says that "the Lord's message[45] rang out"[46] from them. Throughout this letter he comes back several times to the thought that the gospel is in very deed the word of God to us. He does not hesitate to use the strongest of terms to indicate this, and it is of the utmost importance that this part of his thought be grasped. If people think of the gospel only as another philosophy, the result of the reflection of certain admittedly profound, first-century thinkers on religious topics, they will never understand the burning zeal that sent the first Christian preachers through the world to proclaim what God had done for sinners. It is because the gospel is indeed "the Lord's message" that it can and must be presented without apology or amendment.

The one item that Paul picks out to show the change in the converts is their faith: "your faith in God[47] has become known everywhere." What

---

44. ἐν τῇ is lacking before Ἀχαΐᾳ in B K 6 33 etc., and is read by ℵ C D F G etc.; it seems probable that some scribes repeated the words from v. 7 and that they should not be read here. The two articles in v. 7 refer to the provinces in their separateness, whereas the one article here points to the totality, all Greece in contrast to "everywhere."

45. ὁ λόγος τοῦ κυρίου, "the word of the Lord," is found only here and in 2 Thess. 3:1 in Paul, though it occurs in Acts, and similar expressions are frequent in Paul. It is of course common in the Old Testament. The genitive is subjective ("the word that comes from the Lord") rather than objective ("the word that tells of the Lord").

46. The verb ἐξήχηται is found only here in the New Testament. It is a vivid word, and expositors from Chrysostom on have often thought the imagery to have been derived from the sounding out of a trumpet, though some prefer to think of the rolling of thunder. Either way there is nothing apologetic about it! The perfect denotes the continuing activity, as does the use of ἐν rather than εἰς (though this cannot be pressed). The word is pictured as still sounding forth.

47. Milligan comments, "the definite τὸν Θεόν emphasizes 'the God' towards whom the Thessalonians' faith is directed in contrast with their previous attitude towards τὰ εἴδωλα." We need not doubt that there is such a contrast, but it is the general structure of the sentence that gives it and not simply the use of the article. The article is lacking in a similar passage (Gal. 4:8), and in any case Paul mostly

distinguished the early Christians from their pagan contemporaries was just this, their faith. They had come to put their trust in God, and this trust affected all that they did. Because of this Paul found it unnecessary to say anything about his mission to that city, but what he says must have been an encouragement to them in their "severe suffering" (v. 6).

9 Wherever Paul went, people kept telling (continuous present) him of their own accord what had happened there.[48] In particular, they kept rehearsing "what kind of reception"[49] he and his companions had had and the evidence of the conversion of the Thessalonians. It seems very probable that we have here an example of the common terminology among the early Christians for the success of a mission, for there is very little that is specifically Pauline in the expression. It is difficult, for example, to imagine that Paul would give an account in his own words of people entering into a genuine Christian experience with no mention of their being justified by faith and without any reference to the cross.[50] It may fairly be said that these things are implied, but the point is that they are not expressed, and it is likely that Paul would have expressed them. But if he is taking certain terms from the accepted missionary vocabulary, then the situation is explained.

Paul makes three points. The first is "you turned to God from idols,"[51] an expression that shows that most Thessalonian believers

---

uses the article with θεός; in this epistle it has the article 27 times and lacks it 9 times.

48. The αὐτοί of v. 9 is in contrast to the ἡμᾶς of v. 8. It is not Paul and his companions who are spreading abroad the news about the Thessalonians.

49. εἴσοδον, translated "reception," is an unusual word in this connection. It may mean "the act of entering" (as in Acts 13:24; see mg.), or "the place of entering" (2 Pet. 1:11). The former would seem to be the meaning here, and perhaps "visit" would give the sense of it. "Welcome" (*RSV,* Rutherford) is not quite right (*RSV* renders the same word "visit" in 2:1). Though the expression is unusual, Deissmann is able to cite a parallel from a Latin letter of the second century A.D. (*LAE,* p. 198).

50. But F. F. Bruce points out, with reference to the account of the words of Barnabas and Paul to the people of Lystra (Acts 14:15-17), that "the description given by Paul, Silvanus, and Timothy of the Thessalonians' conversion from paganism (1 Thess. 1:9) presupposes preaching very similar to that given here at Lystra" (*The Book of the Acts* [Grand Rapids, ²1988], p. 277).

51. Neil has a pertinent comment on idol worship: "When we are inclined to stress the beauty and symbolism of paganism, and shed a tear over the shattered statues of the Acropolis or the Forum, we should remember that Paul condemned the whole system, root and branch—and he was there, and we were not. . . . The idols that moulded life were not the austere images of Pallas Athene and Apollo, but the obscene figures that desecrated public and private altars."

were Gentiles. Becoming a Christian involves a very definite break
with non-Christian habits. Whatever the believers' previous background, there must always be a turning from idols of some sort. The
act of conversion involves a change of direction of the will. This is a
decisive happening, a reorientation of the whole of life. This is so in
every age, but especially was it true of Christians in the Greek world
of the first century A.D. There is a sense in which Greek as well as
Jew prepared the way for the coming of the gospel,[52] but the most
characteristic thing was not the continuity, but the decisive break. As
F. V. Filson reminds us: "In government, religion, business, amuse-
ment, labor, and social clubs the pagan world was built on the pattern
of polytheism," whereas "the attitude of Apostolic Christianity to the
polytheistic world was one of militant hostility."[53] There was no attempt to find a place for Christ in the polytheistic milieu. Such an idea
was preposterous. No matter how greatly their habitual practices had
to be changed, the Christians of the first century saw that there could
be no place for an idol alongside Christ.

But becoming a Christian is not a negative thing, as many carica-
tures of Christianity have supposed from apostolic times on. The second
point Paul makes is that the Thessalonians turned "to serve[54] the living
and true God." The absence of the article with "God" does not mean
that Paul left open the possibility of other gods. His adjectives give
emphatic expression to his monotheism. Rather, the form without the
article puts the stress on the nature rather than the person of God. The
converts had come to serve One whose nature it is to be God living and
true. "Living" means not only alive but active, as we see from Acts
14:15. It contrasts sharply with dead idols, "gods" who can do nothing
(Pss. 96:5; 115:4-7). The living God orders all things both in heaven and
on earth. God is also "true," and the word Paul uses[55] conveys the idea
of "genuine, real" (BAGD). Its opposite is not so much "false" as
"unreal." Moffatt says that it is " 'real' as opposed to false in the sense

52. Cf. the title of the book by G. H. C. Macgregor and A. C. Purdy, *Jew and
Greek: Tutors Unto Christ* (London, 1937).
53. F. V. Filson, *The New Testament against Its Environment* (London, 1950),
p. 30; cf. n. 51.
54. δουλεύω means "to serve as a slave" and indicates the completeness of the
Christian's surrender to God. Paul often uses the metaphor of slavery to describe the
Christian's service, though usually he speaks of being a slave to Christ (Rom. 1:1, etc.).
The word, according to Milligan, is not used in pagan literature in a religious sense.
55. ἀληθινός, which Paul uses only here.

of 'counterfeit' " *(EGT)*. Paul is affirming that the converts had begun to worship a real God in contrast to the shadowy and unreal objects that had previously claimed their allegiance.

10 The third point in their conversion is that they had come "to wait for his Son from heaven."[56] The word for "to wait"[57] is found only here in the New Testament. Grimm-Thayer suggest that, in addition to the thought of awaiting someone expected, it includes "the added notion of patience and trust." Findlay thinks that it implies *"sustained* expectation" *(CGT)*. The prominence given to the second coming is important. This subject is mentioned most frequently of all in the New Testament (there is said to be a reference to it on the average once in every thirteen verses from Matthew right through to Revelation). It appears to have been given some emphasis in the preaching to the Thessalonians. Since the stress in this verse is on the second coming, it is all the more interesting to find the Son ("his Son" here only in Thessalonians) referred to as him "whom he raised from the dead." Both before and after this phrase there are eschatological references. It is clear that the resurrection had caught the imagination of the preachers. It was natural for them to think of Jesus as the one whom the Father had raised. We might notice also that it is characteristic of the New Testament to attribute the raising of Jesus to the activity of the Father (though occasionally it is said that Jesus rose).

The chapter concludes with the reminder that the deliverance effected by Jesus is one with permanent significance. The participle translated "rescues" is a timeless present, much as though Jesus were being called "The Rescuer." Deliverance is from "the coming wrath." The idea of the wrath of God is uncongenial to many people in modern times, and there have been determined attempts to get rid of the whole idea. It is sometimes said that it has no foundation in the Old Testament, the prophets and psalmists being concerned only to point out that when people sin disaster inevitably follows. God's direct intervention is not stressed, so that a more or less impersonal process is being described. Such an attitude can be maintained only by neglecting a great number of important Old Testament passages. The prophets and the psalmists

---

56. Some expositors have seen in the plural οὐρανῶν a reference to the plurality of the heavens, as in the rabbis and in 2 Cor. 12:2. But the singular and plural of this noun are often used in the New Testament without perceptible difference of meaning, and it would be unwise to press the plural here.

57. ἀναμένειν.

know nothing of an impersonal process of retribution. They see the hand of God everywhere, in the punishment of the wicked as well as in the rewarding of the righteous.

The same is true of the New Testament. That we sometimes come across expressions like "the wrath" (without express mention of God) should not blind us to the fact that in the thought of the New Testament writers there is no place for an impersonal agency that can act in independence of God. "All things are of God" (2 Cor. 5:18; cf. Acts 17:28; 1 Cor. 8:6). In any case the wrath is explicitly linked with God (John 3:36; Rom. 1:18; 9:22; Eph. 5:6; Col. 3:6; Rev. 11:18; 14:10, 19; 19:15). There is also the singular difficulty of doing without the idea that the wrath is God's. Are we to think of God as not caring about sin? Or not caring enough to act? Or, if we are asked to think of an impersonal activity of retribution, what is the meaning of such an activity in a genuinely theistic universe? To say that God has made people and their environment in such a way that when they sin inevitable consequences follow, means that God is responsible when those consequences do follow. It is not really possible to get rid of the idea of the divine wrath without sacrificing a very great deal that is important in our understanding of the ways of God and the nature of God.

This is not to deny that wrath must be understood carefully. The wrath of God is no vindictive passion, and it does not imply lack of control, as human wrath does. But whenever we apply any term to God, even love, we must make the mental reservation: without the imperfections that characterize the human. Who can think that that puny thing which human love is at its best really gives us a picture of God's mighty love? But we do not hesitate to speak of God's love.

So with wrath. God's wrath lacks the imperfections that are bound up with the purest of human righteous indignation. But it gives strong expression to the active opposition of a holy God to all that is evil. We cannot do without this concept.[58]

When Paul speaks of "the coming wrath," he brings before us the eschatological wrath. The wrath of God is not only something that

---

58. See further the discussion in chs. V and VI of my *The Apostolic Preaching of the Cross*. The idea that wrath is not a fit description of anything in God's attitude has been vigorously argued by C. H. Dodd in, e.g., *The Bible and the Greeks* (London, 1935) and his Moffatt commentary on Rom. 1:18. See further R. V. G. Tasker, *The Biblical Doctrine of the Wrath of God* (London, 1951); the Addendum in P. T. Forsyth, *The Work of Christ* (London, 1948); the article ὀργή by G. Stählin, in *TDNT*, V, pp. 382-447; and Best, pp. 84-85.

is experienced here and now. It will endure to the end of all things. Indeed, it will be especially manifested in the end of all things. It is inevitable, a thought conveyed by the present participle: it is coming even now.[59]

59. Moffatt comments on this verse: "In preaching to pagans, the leaders of the primitive Christian mission put the wrath and judgment of God in the forefront . . . making a sharp appeal to the moral sense, and denouncing idolatry. . . . Hence the revival they set on foot. They sought to set pagans straight, and to keep them straight, by means of moral fear as well as of hope" *(EGT)*.

1 THESSALONIANS 2

B. THE PREACHING OF THE GOSPEL AT THESSALONICA (2:1-16)

1. The Preachers' Motives (2:1-6)

1 *You know, brothers, that our visit to you was not a failure.* 2 *We had previously suffered and been insulted in Philippi, as you know, but with the help of our God we dared to tell you his gospel in spite of strong opposition.* 3 *For the appeal we make does not spring from error or impure motives, nor are we trying to trick you.* 4 *On the contrary, we speak as men approved by God to be entrusted with the gospel. We are not trying to please men but God, who tests our hearts.* 5 *You know we never used flattery, nor did we put on a mask to cover up greed—God is our witness.* 6 *We were not looking for praise from men, not from you or anyone else.*

It seems clear that Paul had been the object of some sharp criticism, and this might well have predisposed some of the Thessalonians to disregard what he wrote. So he reminds them that he and his companions had been absolutely sincere when they first preached in the city. They had never sought human approval but only tried to serve God well.

1 "For"[1] (which *NIV* omits) usually links what follows with what immediately precedes, but on this occasion it goes back in thought to

---

1. For γάρ see the note on 1:8. γάρ is used here in an unusual way. Milligan thinks that it is almost equivalent to "however," though he cites no parallels. A better position is that of Lightfoot: "the explanation of γάρ is to be sought rather in the train of thought which was moving in the Apostle's mind, than in the actual expressions: 'I speak thus boldly and confidently as to my preaching, *for* I have such a witness at hand. You *yourselves* know, etc.'" Grimm-Thayer deny that such an ellipse is ever found, but Liddell and Scott give it as an established usage.

1:9. The unusual word there rendered "reception"[2] is repeated and is here rendered "visit," while "you" here corresponds to "they themselves" in 1:9. There Paul cited outsiders as witnesses; here he says that the Thessalonians needed no one else to bear witness, for they themselves knew what had happened. "You" is emphatic, as is brought out by Rutherford's translation, "You at any rate have no need to be told." The verb "know" is also important: others had heard about it, but the readers *know*.

This calling of the Thessalonians to witness was a masterly defense. It is clear that Paul had been accused of insincerity. His enemies said that he was more concerned to make money out of his converts than to present true teaching. The accusation would be made easier because itinerant preachers, concerned only to feather their own nests, were common in those days.[3] The apostle was being represented as nothing more than another of this class of vagrant preachers. Paul's emphatic calling of the Thessalonians to witness did two things. In the first place it showed his confidence in them. He had no fear that they would succumb to the propaganda being put before them. In the second place it demonstrated that all the facts required for his vindication were facts of common knowledge. Neither Paul nor the Thessalonians had any need to search for material to prove his *bona fides*. An accusation of insincerity could scarcely stand in the light of such public knowledge of the man and his work.

There is some difference of opinion as to what is meant by the word rendered "a failure."[4] Some understand it to mean "fruitless" (cf. Way, "barren of results"), but this meaning is rejected by Milligan and Lightfoot, who understand it to refer rather to the character of the preaching. Hendriksen thinks of it as having the same sort of meaning as in Mark 12:3, and as signifying that Paul did not come to them empty-

---

2. For "visit" see p. 52, n. 49.

3. "There has probably never been such a variety of religious cults and philosophic systems as in Paul's day. East and West had united and intermingled to produce an amalgam of real piety, high moral principles, crude superstition and gross license. Oriental mysteries, Greek philosophy, and local godlings competed for favour under the tolerant aegis of Roman indifference. 'Holy Men' of all creeds and countries, popular philosophers, magicians, astrologers, crack-pots, and cranks; the sincere and the spurious, the righteous and the rogue, swindlers and saints, jostled and clamoured for the attention of the credulous and the sceptical" (Neil on v. 3). Cf. also Dibelius, cited on p. 8, n. 12.

4. κενή; Paul has it in 12 of its 18 New Testament occurrences.

handed but with something to give them. Frame's view is similar. Against the first suggestion is the fact that the meaning of the word is "empty" rather than "ineffective." Against the last that it is the "visit" rather than the preachers that is thus described. Our best understanding, then, is something like "hollow, empty, wanting in purpose and earnestness" (Lightfoot; cf. 1 Cor. 15:10, 14; Gal. 2:2; Eph. 5:6). Paul is affirming as a well-known fact the purposeful manner of the visit.[5]

2 Paul's *but* is the strong adversative,[6] which makes what follows a strong contrast to the preceding. The visit to Thessalonica was certainly no failure. Despite[7] all the ill-treatment that had been meted out to them in Philippi, the preachers had not been discouraged but had preached boldly in Thessalonica. Paul had come from Philippi after being badly treated there. He had undergone physical hardship ("previously suffered"), and to that had been added verbal abuse ("been insulted"). Acts 16 tells us that the physical suffering had included flogging and the placing of his feet in the stocks. On that occasion, when it had been suggested that the jailor should simply free Paul and Silas, the great apostle had refused to leave until the praetors themselves had come to make amends for their treatment of Roman citizens. In his insistence on upholding the dignity of Roman citizenship we see something of the deep hurt Paul had experienced in the indignities heaped on him. So now, as he recalls those days, he uses a word that evokes memories of the insolence of those who had ill-treated him. The same verb is employed in Acts 14:5 ("mistreat them").[8] All this is something of which the Thessalonians have knowledge, as Paul reminds them ("as you know"). Throughout this section of the letter the apostle keeps appealing

5. The lasting results may also be indicated by the verb γέγονεν. Frame remarks that γέγονεν "denotes completed action; the facts of the visit are all in, and the readers may estimate it at its full value." Similarly, Findlay thinks that γέγονεν "implies *a settled result . . .* their work has proved thoroughly successful. Its fruit is permanent" *(CBSC)*.

6. ἀλλά. In the Greek this word comes first, but *NIV* puts it before "with the help. . . ."

7. The participles appear to be concessive here. "A concessive participle is used when attention is called to something having been done in spite of unfavorable circumstances" (W. D. Chamberlain, *An Exegetical Grammar of the Greek New Testament* [New York, 1941], p. 102).

8. "We are so used to reading about the physical and psychological sufferings of the N.T. Christians that we can easily fail to realize how shattering they must have been, and how remarkable it is that they were not overwhelmed by bitterness and despair" (Whiteley).

to the knowledge the Thessalonians had of what he had done (vv. 1, 5, 9, 10, and 11).

Time-servers would have been discouraged by such treatment. Not so the little band of preachers. They had come from this treatment at Philippi but had preached with boldness. The verb rendered "dared"[9] is full of interest. It comes from two words that mean literally "all speech." It denotes the state of mind when the words flow freely, the attitude of feeling quite at home with no sense of stress or strain, an attitude that includes both boldness and confidence (in fact, the corresponding noun is sometimes translated "boldness," sometimes "confidence"). When it is used in the New Testament the verb always has to do with the proclamation of the gospel.[10] The boldness and confidence it denotes here are not natural attributes, for Paul speaks of daring "with the help of our God" (more literally, "in our God"). Because he lived "in" his God he was always at home, no matter what the outward circumstances, and thus he always had that attitude of ready speech of which we have been thinking. It was because he lived and moved in God (cf. Acts 17:28) that no hardship and no opposition were able to take away his confidence and his courage (cf. 2 Cor. 4:7).

Paul proceeds to designate the message he and his associates had proclaimed as "the gospel of God" (*NIV*, "his gospel"). There are occasions when it is proper to speak of the gospel as the gospel of its preacher (cf. 1:5), for unless he has appropriated it and taken it within himself in such a way that it is completely his, he cannot proclaim it with conviction. But from another point of view the gospel is not his at all. It does not take its origin in anything human but in God. It originates in God, it tells about God, and it invites people to take God's way of salvation.[11] Accordingly, when Paul writes of "the gospel of God" he turns his readers' thoughts away from any human contrivance to God's perfect way. This thought is one that he develops with power in this chapter, and the phrase "the gospel of God" recurs (vv. 8, 9; cf. v. 13).

The opposition at Philippi of which Paul has spoken in the first part of this verse did not cease when he came to Thessalonica. There, too, as he preached, it was "in spite of strong opposition" (more literally,

---

9. ἐπαρρησιασάμεθα.

10. Bruce cites W. C. van Unnik, "it comprises both the full truth of the gospel and full freedom towards the judgement of men."

11. "It is the good news about God: it tells not only what he is like but what he has done; and not only what he has done but what he offers" (Ward).

"much conflict"). The word "conflict" is a vivid one, taken from the vocabulary of athletics, where it meant a contest or a race.[12] It is that from which we derive our word "agony." It denotes not a token opposition, a tepid struggle, but a very real battle. It is used of fighting the good fight of faith (1 Tim. 6:12; 2 Tim. 4:7), and that is no half-hearted fight. The use of the word here reminds the Thessalonians that the opposition that Paul had met had been intense, and his preaching had not been easy. How, in the face of this, could it be urged that he preached only for what he could get out of it?

3   In this defense Paul clearly faces the accusation that he was no better than the usual run of wandering preachers. The apostle starts with the truth of his message, and we should not miss the force of the *for* that links this verse to the preceding. As the Thessalonians well knew, when Paul first came to them he had been tested by sufferings and ill treatment. That he persisted with his message despite hardships shows that he was concerned for the truth, not private gain. The noun rendered "appeal"[13] has the original meaning of "a calling to one's side," that is, a call with a view to being helped. It acquires other meanings such as "entreaty," "exhortation," and "encouragement" (it is cognate with the word rendered "Comforter" in John 14:16, etc.). Here it means "exhortation," "appeal."[14] It is the outward approach (whereas "the gospel of God" of the previous verse stresses the content of the message). The preachers' appeal, says Paul, did not have its origin in "error." The word so translated sometimes means "deceit" (so *KJV*), but in the New Testament it always seems to have the passive meaning, "error." Paul had been accused of being completely mistaken in his preaching.

The second accusation was more serious: "impure motives" or

---

12. ἀγών (see *TDNT*, I, pp. 134-40). *RSV*, rather like *NIV*, renders "in the face of great opposition," but the word goes beyond opposition and denotes actual strife. Phillips has "whatever the opposition might be," but this obscures the fact that the conflict was actual, not potential. Moffatt, "in spite of all the strain," points us to an inward state, which Frame takes as highly possible. Knox renders, "with great earnestness," but this seems wide of the mark. The word ἀγών in later Greek did tend to mean a state of mind, but in this context the reference seems to be rather to actual outward opposition than to inward stress.

13. παράκλησις. The word occurs 20 times in Paul out of 29 times in the New Testament; it is a characteristically Pauline word. BAGD set forth three main meanings in the New Testament: "encouragement, exhortation," "appeal, request," and "comfort, consolation" (they put this passage in the first group).

14. O. Schmitz sees the meaning to be "the authoritative offer of salvation" (*TDNT*, V, p. 795). Cf. 2 Cor. 5:20.

"uncleanness" denotes moral impurity.[15] The charge is startling to modern ears, but it must always be borne in mind in interpreting early documents that sexual impurity was a regular feature of many of the cults of antiquity, especially those from the East. Ritual prostitution was carried on in connection with many temples, the idea apparently being that one effected union with the god by union with one of his "consecrated ones." The Jews, at least in later times and perhaps as early as this, frequently brought the accusation of immorality against the Christians.[16] It had apparently been suggested in Thessalonica that Paul and his companions had been associated with such practices, and the apostle repels the charge with decision.

The third accusation is that of using trickery.[17] The word rendered "to trick" originally had reference to catching fish by means of a bait. From this it came to mean any piece of cunning. The wandering sophists and jugglers resorted to all sorts of devices to attract people and so get their money. Not so the preachers. They had not tried to ensnare their hearers.

4 The strong adversative[18] is rendered "on the contrary." Over against each of the points listed in the last verse comes its refutation.

---

15. Hendriksen rejects this meaning in favor of avarice or the seeking of honor, as does Denney. Neither, however, cites examples of the word used in this sense, and only strong evidence would allow such a meaning to a word with the basic sense of "uncleanness." It can mean dishonoring the body (Rom. 1:24), and it may be linked with fornication and lasciviousness (2 Cor. 12:21; Gal. 5:19). It is joined with πλεονεξία (Eph. 4:19; 5:3), but in both places the context has to do with impurity, and it is this that the word seems to denote. It occurs in other passages where the context does not establish the meaning, but impurity fits them all. Frame says that ἀκαθαρσία "regularly appears directly with πορνεία or in contexts intimating sexual aberration." Findlay is impressed by the fact that Paul is not elsewhere charged with *fleshly* impurity. He argues for "uncleanness *of spirit,*" and says that in classical Greek the word denotes "moral *foulness, dirty ways* of any sort" *(CGT).* The word is not unlike the English "immorality"; this word may denote a lack of uprightness of many kinds, but has overtones of sexual looseness. Marshall thinks that here the word "will include sensual elements, but is not confined to them."

16. As the church grew, such accusations became part of the stock-in-trade of its enemies. See, e.g., H. B. Workman, *Persecution in the Early Church* (London, 1906), pp. 157ff. The Apologists regularly refuted such slanders.

17. The change in preposition from ἐκ with πλάνης and ἀκαθαρσίας to ἐν with δόλῳ switches the attention from origin to atmosphere. The appeal did not spring from error or from sexual depravity, but neither was it conducted in an atmosphere of trickery.

18. ἀλλά.

Paul's preaching could not have proceeded from error, for he was entrusted by God with the message. He was not impure, for he had been
approved by God. He was not a trickster, for he aimed at pleasing God,
not people.

The word translated "approved" basically means "to test." At the
end of this very verse it is used in that sense ("tests"). Moffatt translates
"attested . . . tests" and thus retains some of the wordplay of the original.
But "to test" readily passes over to the meaning "to approve by test."
Milligan points out that there is a technical use of the word "to describe
the passing as fit for election to a public office." In the New Testament
the verb is often used in this sense of approving.[19] Since the gospel is
of divine origin, no one may take it upon himself to proclaim it. God
chooses his messengers, and he tests them before committing the gospel
to their trust.[20] The verb is in the perfect tense, signifying not only a past
approval but one that continues into the present: "we stand approved"
is the sense of it. It is out of this context that Paul and his companions
habitually speak (continuous present).[21]

This meaning is further brought out by an emphatic disclaimer[22]
of any attempt to please people (cf. Gal. 1:10). The verb rendered
"please" broadened in late Greek into the idea of actual service: "For
the idea of *service* in the interests of others which underlies several of

19. In the New Testament the implication seems to be that when the test is
applied it will be surmounted successfully. By contrast πειράζω, which also means
"to test," often looks for failure, and the meaning passes over into "to tempt."

20. The verb πιστευθῆναι, rendered "to be entrusted," reminds Deissmann of
the Imperial Secretary for Greek correspondence, known as ὁ τὰς Ἑλληνικὰς ἐπιστολὰς
πράττειν πεπιστευμένος or τάξιν ἐπὶ τῶν Ἑλληνικῶν ἐπιστολῶν πεπιστευμένος (*LAE*,
p. 374). If Paul was glancing at such an exalted official, we have another indication
of the dignity of his office as preacher of the gospel. Clarke points out that this has
implications for our understanding of the nature of God. People today all too easily
think of "an easygoing God modeled in the shape of Mr. Pickwick — genial, expansive,
tractable, who can be trusted to deal leniently with both sin and the sinner; one who
can be easily wheedled from his purpose, whose moral judgment will swerve when
confronted by our dark idolatries, who has no more backbone than a jellyfish and the
persuadable disposition of a half-wit. . . ." It is not such a God who tests people
before entrusting them with the gospel.

21. οὕτως answers to the preceding καθώς and is not the antecedent of the
following ὡς.

22. Paul has the unusual construction of οὐ with the participle ἀρέσκοντες; this
puts some emphasis on the factuality of what he is saying. Elsewhere he can say "I
try to please everybody in every way" (1 Cor. 10:33), but that is in the sense that he
seeks to profit others, not himself.

the NT occurrences of this verb (1 Th. 2⁵ . . .), we may compare its use in monumental inscriptions to describe those who have proved themselves of use to the commonwealth" (MM). There is something of this meaning here. Paul in fact might serve people, but he never served with the aim simply of pleasing them. If he served them, it was in the spirit of "ourselves as your servants for Jesus' sake" (2 Cor. 4:5). So now he says that his aim had been to render service that would be well pleasing to God.

That pleasing God could not comprise merely outward deeds, but was concerned with inward motives, underlies the reminder that God tests (the tense is continuous, "keeps testing") people's hearts. We are apt to misunderstand references to the heart in the Scriptures, for we often use the term to denote the affections. But in antiquity the affections were thought of as located in the intestines (cf. "bowels of compassion"). The heart, even though it might sometimes be used in a sense not far removed from our own, stood for the whole of the inner life, thought and will as well as emotions.²³ Here the meaning is that God searches out the whole of our inner life. Nothing is hidden from him. In passing we might note that the plural, "our hearts," is unlikely to be an editorial plural. It associates Silas and Timothy closely with Paul in this great affirmation.

5 "For" at the beginning of this verse (which *NIV* omits) takes up the "for" of verse 3. There Paul had argued for the truth of the message; now he moves on to the integrity of the messengers (though with some overlap with the previous section). "Never" covers the whole period; no room is left for exceptions. Paul goes on to disclaim three specific defects. By inserting "you know" he calls on the Thessalonians themselves to bear witness to the truth of what he is saying. First he deals with "flattery"; a literal translation might run: "neither have we come to be in a word of flattery." The verb is one with a wide range of meaning. With the construction used here it seems to mean that the subject entered into whatever state is spoken of and stayed in it (as of coming to be "in Christ," Rom. 16:7, or of Eve entering "into transgression," 1 Tim. 2:14).²⁴ Paul denies, then, that he and his companions had

23. Cf. J. Behm, "That the heart is the centre of the inner life of man and the source or seat of all the forces and functions of soul and spirit is attested in many different ways in the NT" (*TDNT*, III, p. 611).
24. The construction is γίνομαι ἐν. It indicates that the state entered was continuous but not necessarily permanent. It is used of the incarnation (Phil. 2:7; cf. 1 Cor. 2:3; 2 Cor. 3:7).

made flattery their method. Perhaps "flattery" is not quite the meaning. We can use this English term of remarks that, though insincere, are directed to the pleasure of the person being flattered. The Greek term has rather the idea of using fair words as a means of gaining one's own ends. It is a matter of using insincerity as an instrument of policy, as a means of persuading another to do one's will.

The second charge refuted also contains the idea of insincerity. The term "mask" denotes a specious pretext that conceals the real motive. It is used of putting forward something that is plausible and that might well be true in itself, but that is not the real reason for doing whatever deed is referred to. So here Paul denies that evangelism had been simply a cover for an underlying "greed." This latter term denotes more than love of money.[25] It is derived from two words meaning "to have" and "more"; it signifies an eager desire for what one does not have. It is self-interest in the widest sense (cf. Moffatt, "self-seeking"), and is one of the evil things that proceed from the heart (Mark 7:21-23). It is sometimes associated with impurity (Eph. 4:19, where it is translated "greediness"; cf. Eph. 5:3), for in sexual relations there can be the gratification of one's own lusts with a complete disregard for the rights of others. The word often signifies the desire for material possessions (Luke 12:15). Basically it is idolatry (Col. 3:5), for it exalts self to the highest position; it regards self with a veneration that amounts to worship. A few verses further on Paul is to affirm that he and his companions had given themselves unstintingly for the Thessalonians. Here he puts the negative side of it. They had had no selfish motives in their mission. Covetousness, of course, almost invariably comes with a cloak; people never admit to being covetous, and some specious reason can always be found to hide their real motives. Paul's words are a warning to all his readers to be rigorous in their self-examination.

In the first part of this verse Paul denies using flattery and calls the Thessalonians to witness that what he says is true. In the second he avows the purity of his motives and invokes God as witness. There can be no mistaking the intense seriousness with which he writes, nor the depth of his conviction that the methods and motives of the preachers would bear the closest scrutiny. He repeats this appeal to a double witness in verse 10; it points to observable behavior (which the Thessalonians

---

25. Lightfoot defines πλεονεξία as "greediness" or "entire disregard for the rights of others" (on Col. 3:5). Milligan distinguishes the word from φιλαργυρία "as the wider and more active sin."

could see) and to purity of motive (which is not the less important because only God can see it).

6 The third point Paul makes is that he and his associates had not sought the esteem of people, whether of the Thessalonians or of any others[26] (which might mean other Christians or other people in general). He has already said something much like this (v. 4). There his point was that they did not pursue ends that would have the approval of people; here he claims that they did not seek praise for themselves, the emphasis being on the inner state of the preachers. The preachers did not look for commendation. They may well have received it, and they certainly deserved it, but Paul's point is that they did not seek it. Their motives were pure.[27]

7 There is some confusion as to where verse 6 ends. The clause about "apostles of Christ" is regarded by some as belonging to verse 7 (e.g., most Greek texts, *NIV, GNB, JB, REB*), by others as part of verse 6 *(RSV, LB, NEB)*. It is not only a problem of where to put the division; there is also the question of whether the words about apostles are to be taken with what precedes (as *ARV, RSV,* etc.) or with what follows (as *NIV*). Either makes good sense, but in this revision I shall follow *NIV*.

"We could have been a burden to you" is the translation of a Greek expression that is patient of more than one meaning.[28] The noun means "weight," "burden," and *KJV* renders it "we might have been burdensome." On this view the meaning is that they, being apostles of Christ, had every right to be maintained by those to whom they preached. Paul frequently uses words cognate with that used here to refer to this right to maintenance (e.g., v. 9; 2 Cor. 11:9; 12:16; 2 Thess. 3:8). He makes with some emphasis the point that preachers have this right, even though he himself frequently forbore to exercise it.

But, of course, "weight" readily passes over into the meaning of "importance." The word is used quite often in this sense (though not, apparently, in the New Testament; the nearest approach is in 2 Cor. 4:17). Nevertheless, many think this to be the meaning here. It would be quite

---

26. There is probably no significance in the change of the preposition from ἐξ with ἀνθρώπων to ἀπό with ὑμῶν and ἄλλων, for the two are often used interchangeably in Hellenistic Greek (cf. M, III, p. 259). But if there is a difference, ἐκ denotes the ultimate source and ἀπό rather the intermediate agent.

27. The change of connective from οὐδέ which links the members in v. 3 to οὔτε here may point to the qualities now mentioned as being more closely linked to each other than were those in the earlier verse (see Grimm-Thayer on οὐδέ).

28. The expression is ἐν βάρει εἶναι.

in the Pauline manner to use the word with a hint at both meanings. But
if he does this, the primary emphasis seems to be on "burden," and thus
the right to maintenance.[29] Chrysostom was in no doubt. He commented,
"But here he also says concerning money, 'when we might have been
burdensome . . .'" (p. 330).

Paul speaks of "apostles of Christ." We read of the appointment
of the apostles in Mark 3:14-15, where Jesus chose twelve men "that
they might be with him and that he might send them out to preach and
to have authority to drive out demons." This gives us the primary function
of the apostles. They were to preach in Christ's name and perform certain
miracles. After Judas fell, the early church took steps to see that his place
was filled. But they neither selected nor commissioned Matthias. They
recognized that God had already chosen a successor (Acts 1:24), and
when, in answer to their prayer, God showed who the new apostle was,
they simply numbered him with the eleven (Acts 1:26). In the same vein
Paul stressed that his apostolate was not of human origin (Gal. 1:1).

In the providence of God apostles were used to establish churches.
Inevitably they became the leaders in the Christian church, and their
prestige was great. In modern times many people have inferred that they
were the source of all authority to minister in the church, so that only
those ministries which can claim direct descent from the apostles (those
in the "Apostolic Succession") are to be thought of as validly ordained.
There is much that could be said about this,[30] but we content ourselves
with noticing that this is a function that the New Testament does not
ascribe to the apostles. In the words of Jesus, as we have seen, their
primary functions are preaching and healing, and throughout the New

---

29. Frame thinks that the meaning is likely to be "to be in honour," but he
quotes from a letter written to him by Dr. Milligan in which that scholar says that he
"is inclined to think the more literal idea of 'burden,' 'trouble,' was certainly upper-
most in the Apostle's thought and that the derived sense of *'gravitas,' 'honour'* was
not prominent, if it existed at all."

30. I have drawn attention to what seem to me to be the most important points
in *Ministers of God* (London, 1964), pp. 39-61, 114-28. The literature on the subject
is vast. For an advocacy of the view that the essence of ministry is to be found in the
Apostolic Succession see K. E. Kirk (ed.), *The Apostolic Ministry* (London, 1946),
and for the opposing view S. Neill (ed.), *The Ministry of the Church* (London, 1947),
and T. W. Manson, *The Church's Ministry* (London, 1948). There are some valuable
observations on the apostolate in A. Kuyper, *The Work of the Holy Spirit* (Grand
Rapids, 1946), pp. 139ff. For the view that the apostolate is of Gnostic origin see
W. Schmithals, *The Office of Apostle in the Early Church* (Nashville and New York,
1969).

Testament these are the important things. The apostles come before us as Christian leaders noteworthy for their proclamation of the authentic gospel and for their founding of churches.

2. The Preachers' Maintenance (2:7-9)

7 *As apostles of Christ we could have been a burden to you, but we were gentle among you, like a mother caring for her little children.* 8 *We loved you so much that we were delighted to share with you not only the gospel of God but our lives as well, because you had become so dear to us.* 9 *Surely you remember, brothers, our toil and hardship; we worked night and day in order not to be a burden to anyone while we preached the gospel of God to you.*

Paul insists that those who preach the gospel have the right to be maintained by the church as they preach (1 Cor. 9:14). But he was sensitive to the accusation that he made money out of his converts, so he did not insist on his rights (1 Cor. 9:15-18). In accord with this, he now reminds the Thessalonians that when he was with them he had refused to "be a burden" to them; he had worked hard and constantly, and had always been considerate of them.

7 There is a first-class textual problem in this verse, namely, whether we should read "gentle" or "babies,"[31] two words that in the Greek differ from one another by only one letter. Whichever word was original, it would have been easy for scribes to have misread the text, especially so in the early days when there were no spaces between words. Paul generally uses "baby" in a derogatory sense as he refers to people who had failed to develop as they should (cf. Gal. 4:3; 1 Cor. 13:11). The case for "gentle" proceeds by noting that this word is rather rare, being found only once elsewhere in the New Testament (2 Tim. 2:24). Scribes had a tendency to replace less usual forms by more usual ones,

---

31. νήπιοι is read by P⁶⁵ ℵ B C* D* OLᵐˢˢ vg saᵐˢˢ etc. and ἤπιοι by A C²? Dᶜ K P etc. Neither reading has a convincing argument from transcription, for νήπιοι could have arisen by a repetition of the ν that is the last letter of the preceding word, while ἤπιοι could be the result of an accidental omission of an ν by a scribe who had just written that letter. Paul uses νήπιος ten times elsewhere and ἤπιος only once, so that a scribe might alter the less usual to the more usual word. But against this Paul never elsewhere calls himself a νήπιος (always he applies the term to his converts). The difficulty of a decision is brought out by the fact that a majority of Metzger's committee went along with the attestation in the MSS and favored νήπιοι, while Metzger and Wikgren add a note arguing that "only ἤπιοι seems to suit the context."

so it is urged that "gentle" stood in the original text. Again it might be argued that "gentle" is required as a contrast to "a burden."

These arguments are not decisive. Taking the last point first, we have already noticed that the alteration need not have been intentional; since the two words are so similar it probably was not. There is confusion between the two words elsewhere; for example, in a passage where it is accepted that "gentle" is the right reading some MSS read "babies" (2 Tim. 2:24), and in another where "babies" seems correct some MSS read "gentle" (Eph. 4:14). We should probably agree that the mistake, whichever way it was made, was accidental. Again, the derogatory meaning often attaching to "babies" in Paul's letters proves little, for when it suited him he could use the word in a good sense (1 Cor. 14:20). The mixture of metaphors is not very significant either, for Paul does this quite often.[32] In this very chapter he compares himself to a father (v. 11) and to an orphan (v. 17, where "when we were torn away from you" is really "being orphaned"). Then there are some grammatical points, such as the fact that a noun would be more natural after "apostles" earlier in the verse. So, too, the phrase "among you" would in Greek be more natural after "babies" than after "gentle." These points do not prove much, for Paul could be impatient of grammatical niceties, but for what they are worth we should take notice of them. Finally, there is the point that Westcott and Hort make so forcefully: "the change from the bold image to the tame and facile adjective" that is "characteristic of the difference between St. Paul and the Syrian revisers."[33]

When the arguments are so nicely balanced it is not possible to be absolutely sure of the original text. In general the balance of probability seems to favor "babies." If we accept this reading, the meaning is that when they preached in Thessalonica the apostles spoke as simply as possible, as simply as babies. It is a strong expression for the extreme lengths to which they went to meet the needs of their hearers.[34]

32. Lightfoot cites a number of examples of this, but does not include a building growing (Eph. 2:21), and a body being built (Eph. 4:12).

33. "Notes on Select Readings," p. 128 (Appendix to *The New Testament in the Original Greek*, Introduction (London, 1907). S. Fowl has argued strongly for the reading νήπιοι (*NTS* 36 [1990], pp. 469-73).

34. Findlay cites Origen's comment: λαλοῦσα λόγους ὡς παιδίον διὰ τὸ παιδίον, and that of Augustine, *delectat . . . decurtata et mutilata verba inmurmurare* ("delights . . . to murmur shortened and mutilated words"). He adds, "But this is only a single trait of the picture: the nurse-*mother* (θάλπει τὰ ἑαυτῆς τέκνα) is child-like with her children—as far from selfish craft as they, and filled besides with a care for them

Paul speaks of being "in the midst of you" and not simply "among you"[35] (as *NIV*). There may be no significance in this, but the expression would more naturally indicate the taking of a place of equality than would the other. It is of interest that Jesus used the same expression when he said, "I am among you as one who serves" (Luke 22:27). There, too, the thought is of a condescension to the level of others. Paul then compares his behavior to that of a nurse (*NIV* reads "a mother," but the Greek means "a nurse") among children.[36] *ARV* renders "cherisheth her own children," and "own" is probably correct.[37] A nurse in such a position could be relied on to give the children the most tender care;[38] Ward draws attention to the mother of Moses, who "was both nurse and mother." Paul claims to have given care like this to the Thessalonians. So far from trying to make gain of them he had become one with them. He had lavished affectionate care[39] on them.

8 All this had followed naturally enough from the fact that Paul and his companions had cherished such a deep regard for the Thessalonians. Now he employs a most unusual word to express it, a verb found only here in the New Testament and very rarely elsewhere. It expresses a real depth of desire: "we loved you so much" brings out much of its significance, but Paul is not using any of the usual words for love.[40] He

---

(see v. 8) which they cannot feel nor reciprocate toward her" *(CGT)*. Bicknell says, "The idea is the condescension of the true Christian pastor who is willing to put himself on the level of others, which is the essence of sympathy. It is the application of the principle of the Incarnation itself."

35. ἐν μέσῳ ὑμῶν, and not ἐν ὑμῖν or παρ' ὑμῖν.

36. ὡς ἐάν with the subjunctive is a fairly rare construction. It seems to be a case of the late use of ἐάν for ἄν and to be distinguished from the ordinary use of the indicative as denoting contingency. Findlay speaks of it here as implying "*a standing contingency*—'as it may be (may be seen) at any time.'" Milligan cites examples of the construction from the papyri.

37. I.e., understanding ἑαυτῆς to mean "her own." Sometimes this is used in a sense equivalent to αὐτῆς and then it means simply "her." In that case it would denote somebody else's children entrusted to the nurse's care. But here there seems to be every reason for giving ἑαυτῆς its natural sense.

38. Cf. Calvin, "a mother in nursing her children manifests a certain rare and wonderful affection, inasmuch as she spares no labour and trouble, shuns no anxiety, is wearied out by no assiduity, and even with cheerfulness of spirit gives her own blood to be sucked."

39. His verb θάλπω means "keep warm" and thus "cherish, comfort." It is used of the mother bird with her young (Deut. 22:6).

40. The best-attested reading appears to be ὁμειρόμενοι (most MSS), the variant being ἱμειόμενοι (with 323, 629, 630, etc.), this latter verb meaning "to desire, to long

does not say "we would have been delighted to share with you," but simply "we were delighted to share with you." The turn of phrase points us to what was actually done rather than what was contemplated. It is part of the picture Paul is painting for us that this should be so definite. The verb is in the imperfect, a continuous tense, and the implication is that this was no passing whim of the apostles, but their habitual style. Throughout their stay in Thessalonica they had been happy continually to be giving to their hearers.

When Paul speaks of the gift they made, he puts "the gospel of God" first. Even when he is putting the emphasis elsewhere, he never loses sight of the fact that it was the gospel that gave the reason for the very existence of the preachers. They were "slaves of Christ." They lived to render service to God. The particular service to which they were called was the imparting of the blessed news of the salvation that God himself had made available to sinners through the atoning death of his Son. Nothing must ever obscure that great fact.

But true preaching of the gospel implies the total commitment of the preachers to the task. Paul has already made it clear that they gave a message (vv. 2, 3); now he goes on to make the point that they gave themselves. He makes this clear by the addition of "but our lives as well." By "lives" he means their whole personalities; his expression sums up their innermost being.[41] Thus he is saying that in their preaching the

---

for" (ἵμερος = "longing"). Two suggestions are made about the derivation of ὁμείρομαι, the one that it comes from ὁμοῦ and εἴρειν and thus means "to be attached to," the other that it is a strengthened form of μείρομαι (= ἱμείρομαι). Objections may be urged against both, and we cannot be sure of the derivation. But in either case the word denotes strong affection; H. W. Heidland says it denotes a "warm inward attachment" (*TDNT*, V, p. 176). Milligan notes the attractive conjecture of Wohlenberg that it is a term of endearment from the nursery. This would suit the context admirably. He also regards derivation from ὁμοῦ and εἴρειν as "philologically impossible," and proceeds to cite Moulton's idea of a root meaning "to remember." MM cite a sepulchral inscription (4th century A.D.) that speaks of the parents as "greatly desiring their son." Moulton and Howard suggest that "It may be a compound of μείρομαι *obtain,* which in the conative present could take the required meaning or we may compare directly the root *smer* 'remember'" (M, II, p. 251).

41. Findlay sees the difference from καρδία (v. 4) thus: "καρδία is the inner man *by contrast with* the outer, while ψυχή is the man himself as *feeling and acting through* the outer organs, the soul within the body" *(CGT)*. ψυχή is discussed in books on the nature of man, e.g., H. Wheeler Robinson, *The Christian Doctrine of Man* (Edinburgh, 1926), pp. 108-9; W. David Stacey, *The Pauline View of Man* (London, 1956), ch. VIII. See also E. Schweizer and others, *TDNT,* IX, pp. 608-66; he sets forth the meaning here as "the giving of that which constitutes life, e.g., time, energy

apostles gave themselves without stint (cf. also 2 Cor. 12:15; Phil. 2:17). It is clear that this meant much to Paul. He was entirely given over to living out the implications of the gospel and proclaiming it wherever he could. R. F. Hock argues that the apostle would have used the workshop as a place for his preaching; he sees the apostle as "busy at tentmaking and busy at preaching the gospel."[42] There is nothing improbable in the thought that Paul "gossiped the gospel" as he engaged in his trade.

The verse ends, as it began, with an expression of tender affection. We, the preachers, have done all this, says Paul, "because[43] you had become so dear to us." "So dear"[44] brings before us the specifically Christian quality of love; its use brings to mind that that love is essentially self-giving. It is not a desire to possess the beloved, but a desire to give, a desire inspired by the nature of the God whom Christians worship. Paul had come to see the Thessalonians as the objects of God's love, and therefore as the objects of the love of God's servants too.

9 He invites his readers to recall the incessant toil of the preachers, toil undertaken with a view to their imposing no burden on those to whom they preached. It was a Jewish custom, emphasized in the teaching of the rabbis, that every boy should learn a trade.[45] This custom does not seem to have arisen from any conviction that a well-rounded life with interests in many directions was highly desirable, as much as from sheer economic necessity. There were no paid teachers in Palestine.[46] It was necessary therefore for a rabbi to have some other means of income

---

and health" (p. 648). Robinson's view that in this passage the term means "life" seems preferable to that of Stacey that it signifies " 'energy' or 'vitality'."

42. *CBQ* 41 (1979), p. 450. He points to the activities of Socrates in the workshop of Simon the shoemaker (p. 444) and to the Cynics active in many workshops (p. 446) to show that such a setting is not improbable for Paul.

43. διότι. This is equivalent to διὰ τοῦτο ὅτι, "on this account," "for"; in the New Testament it always seems to mean "because." See further the note in my *The Epistle to the Romans* (Grand Rapids, 1988), p. 79, n. 206.

44. ἀγαπητοί.

45. "R. Judah said: He who does not teach his son a craft, teaches him brigandage." As the Soncino editor explains, "Having no occupation, he must take to theft" (*Kidd.* 29a).

46. Making money out of teaching the Law is expressly discouraged in the Mishnah. Thus Rabban Gamaliel said, "Excellent is the study of the Law together with worldly occupation, for toil in them both puts sin out of mind. But all study of the Law without (worldly) labour comes to naught at the last and brings sin in its train" (*Aboth* 2:2, Danby's translation). Similarly, R. Zadok, "Make them [i.e., the words of the Law] not a crown wherewith to magnify thyself or a spade wherewith to dig." "And thus used Hillel to say: He that makes worldly use of the crown shall

than the gifts that might now and then be made to him. It was natural accordingly for teachers to stress the importance of a trade. But whatever the motive, the fact is clear. Even boys from well-to-do homes were taught a trade as a matter of course. From Acts 18:3 we learn that Paul's trade was tentmaking; since tents were often made of leather, this may mean that he was a leatherworker. But since a kind of canvas was also used (Lightfoot says it was manufactured from the goats' hair of Paul's native Cilicia, which may account for the choice of this trade), we cannot be sure. What is plain is that Paul and his companions had worked, and had worked hard, to support themselves and to ensure that no burden was placed on their converts.

The two words rendered "toil and hardship" occur together elsewhere (2 Cor. 11:27; 2 Thess. 3:8). The former word is derived from a verb meaning "to strike." Thus properly it means "a blow." It came to denote the result of the blow, and thus work that produces such an effect. In other words, it denotes work that produces tiredness, wearisome toil. The other word comes from a root with the idea of difficulty. It brings before us the thought of that labor which is an overcoming of difficulties. The combination stresses that the work that the preachers had done had not been token work, something in the nature of a public show meant only to demonstrate their willingness. It had been laborious toil. They had had to work hard. They had also had to work constantly: "night and day." We do not know at what hours they had been able to engage in evangelism, but whatever those hours were they had had to fill up their other hours with toil, whether by night or by day, in order to effect their purpose.

This purpose was "in order not to be a burden to anyone." Paul had no doubt as to his right to be maintained as he preached (1 Cor. 9:6, 12). On occasion he received gifts (or "pay," 2 Cor. 11:8, Moffatt) from his converts. While he was in Thessalonica he was helped by his Philippian friends (Phil. 4:16). But he made a point of seeing that any such gift should be received only when it would help in the furtherance of the gospel. It was another example of the working out of his great principle: " 'Everything is permissible for me'—but not everything is beneficial" (1 Cor. 6:12). He would not accept anything from those to whom he was preaching if it imposed a burden on them.[47]

---

perish. Thus thou mayest learn that he that makes profit out of the words of the Law removes his life from the world" (*Aboth* 4:5, Danby). Hillel's saying is reported also in *Aboth* 1:13.

47. In the New Testament there does not appear to be a great difference between

This section concludes with a reiteration of the divine origin of the message. The verb rendered "preached" is that which signifies the action of a herald.[48] It is the function of a herald simply to pass on the words given to him. His is not to give a message of his own devising, nor even to elaborate what has been given to him. He simply passes on what he is told. So Paul thinks of the preacher as one who passes on "the gospel of God." This conviction that the message comes from God is fundamental to effective preaching. And the message must indeed be that which comes from God. Little moral essays will never take its place. It is easy to distort the message or to substitute something else for it. But what gives Christianity its power is that the gospel *is* "of God." Any trifling with it is bound to result in loss of power.

3. The Preachers' Behavior (2:10-12)

10 *You are witnesses, and so is God, of how holy, righteous and* *blameless we were among you who believed.* 11 *For you know that* *we dealt with each of you as a father deals with his own children,* 12 *encouraging, comforting and urging you to live lives worthy of* *God, who calls you into his kingdom and glory.*

The apostle continues his insistence that he and his preaching companions had acted rightly and compassionately when they brought the gospel to Thessalonica. It is important that the converts bear this in mind when Paul comes later to rebuke and give further instruction.

10 A striking feature of Paul's defense of his position is the confidence with which he appeals to the Thessalonians themselves to bear witness to the truth of what he says. It is abundantly clear that the true facts of his mission were known to them all. Earlier he called on them as people who knew the facts and invoked God as witness to the truth of what he said (v. 5). Now he does the same, though this time the two are joined more closely and Paul is more emphatic. His *you* is strongly emphatic.

Three adverbs[49] (literally "holily," "righteously," and "un-

---

ἐπιβαρέω, "to place a burden *upon*" (the word used here) and καταβαρέω, "to weigh *down.*" Frame cites Ellicott as saying that ἐπιβαρεῖν is "nearly but not quite equivalent in meaning to καταβαρεῖν."

48. κηρύσσω is used 19 times by Paul, but only here in the Thessalonian correspondence (the word for herald is κῆρυξ).

49. With the verb ἐγενήθημεν we would have expected adjectives (cf. v. 7). BDF note the construction as found in the classical language (#434).

blamably") are used to indicate the upright conduct of the preaching band during their stay in the city. All three are rare elsewhere in the New Testament, though the corresponding adjectives are more common. Attempts have been made to distinguish between "holily" and "righteously" along the lines that the former refers to conduct before God and the latter to that before people (so, for example, Lightfoot). But it is difficult to substantiate this in the New Testament, whatever may be true of the classics. In the Bible "righteous" fundamentally means "conforming to God's law."[50] This word may refer to one's duty to God or one's duty to other people. It is better to understand that all the conduct of the Christian, be it toward God or people, springs from the fact that he is born again. The significance, then, of our adverbs is a piling up of the necessity for right conduct somewhat in the manner of Titus 2:12. This is first put positively, "holily and righteously," and then negatively, "unblamably."[51]

In the New Testament "believers" is often a synonym for Christians, so fundamental is faith to Christianity (see on 1:7). Here Paul does not mean that he had behaved in one way toward believers and in another way toward people outside the faith. He is simply reminding the Thessalonians that there was nothing to complain about in the way he and his companions had conducted themselves, a truth that believers above all people would know. There is possibly also an emphasis on the difference between the reaction of the church and that of outsiders. Whatever other people might think of the apostles, the Thessalonian church had good reason for a high opinion of them. They had believed the message; therefore they must trust the messengers.

11 Paul has been concerned with his own conduct and that of those who worked with him; now he turns to the conduct appropriate to the Thessalonians. The construction of this sentence is difficult, for there does not seem to be a main verb. *NIV* supplies "dealt with," which makes very good sense, but some exegetes have thought that the verb of verse 10 should be repeated, others that the participles of this verse are used

50. For the essentially legal basis of righteousness in the Bible, see the chapters on Justification in my *The Apostolic Preaching of the Cross* (London and Grand Rapids, ³1965).

51. Cf. Frame, "A man is ὅσιος who is in general devoted to God's service; a man is δίκαιος who comes up to a specific standard of righteousness; and a man is ἄμεμπτος who in the light of a given norm is without reproach. All three designations are common in the LXX, and denote the attitude both to God and to men, the first two being positive, the third negative."

for the indicative. There are other suggestions of greater or less complexity. Fortunately the meaning is fairly clear, so that not much hinges on the particular construction we adopt. The suggestion of *NIV* seems as good as any, and we understand the verse accordingly.

Once again we have an appeal to the personal knowledge of the Thessalonians. On this occasion the knowledge is of the personal dealings the evangelists had had with their converts. "Each of you" implies attention to individuals.[52] It may signify house-to-house visiting as well as public preaching (cf. Acts 20:20), but it is more probable that it means giving attention to the individual needs of those converted through the public preaching. House-to-house visitation in a city the size of Thessalonica would have presented problems to a small group like the apostolic band, especially if the campaign were short.

12 The note of affection is combined with care that the right way should be chosen, both in the use of the metaphor of a father with his children[53] and in the participles that follow. Paul has compared himself to the Thessalonians as a mother to her children (v. 7), a figure that fitted the situation of caring for babies in the faith. But in the ancient world it was the father who was responsible for the education of the child, so the change in imagery is appropriate. The word rendered "encouraging"[54] is from the same root as the noun "appeal" in verse 3 (where see note). The meaning here is probably that Paul and his friends had directed the converts into suitable lines of conduct. "Comforting"[55] is from a verb that in the classics means much the same as does the preceding verb; it is used elsewhere in the New Testament only in 5:14 and John 11:19, 31. In the first of these passages it is used of comforting the fainthearted, and in John of comforting the bereaved; clearly it is well adapted to the thought of consolation. We shall not be far wrong in assuming that here it is used with special reference to those who found it difficult to live

---

52. ἕνα ἕκαστον is stronger than the simple ἕκαστον and puts an emphasis on the individual.

53. Elsewhere he pictures himself as a mother bringing forth children (Gal. 4:19)!

54. παρακαλοῦντες. It is perhaps worth noting that the nouns corresponding to these two verbs are linked in 1 Cor. 14:3; Phil. 2:1.

55. παραμυθούμενοι. BAGD favor the translation "encourage, cheer up." As here, the word is often linked with παρακαλέω. G. Stählin says, "In the NT, however, admonition becomes genuine comfort and *vice versa*, so that it is hard to separate or distinguish between the two. . . . The unity of admonition and consolation is rooted in the Gospel itself, which is both gift and task" (*TDNT*, V, p. 821).

the Christian life in the face of the opposition they encountered. To them the apostles spoke words of cheer and inspiration.

The third participle, "urging," is from a verb that properly means "to bring forward a witness" and hence "to declare solemnly" (perhaps with the idea of calling God to witness); it has this meaning of solemn affirmation in other passages (Acts 20:26; Gal. 5:3). It is thus a good word to use for the solemn declaration of the truth (Best renders it "insisting"). It may refer to serious words addressed to slackers or the like.

If Paul could be tender and considerate, he yet never lost sight of the high demands Christ makes on his followers. Thus all the encouraging and comforting and urging were directed toward the aim of seeing that the Thessalonians should "live lives worthy of God," or more literally, "walk worthily of God."[56] Walking is for Paul a favorite way of designating the whole of one's life (see on 4:1); the verb has this sense here. The expression to which it is joined sets before us the highest standard that could possibly be conceived. While it is well that we should appreciate the wonder of God's lovingkindness and the fact that his love does not grow less no matter how low we may fall, yet we should not waver in our grasp of the complementary truth that such a God must be served with all our powers. Nothing less should be offered to him who gave his Son for us than all that we have and all that we are.

Paul rapidly turns from contemplating what people should do for God to what God does for them. He says that God "calls" the Thessalonians, where the tense is a little unusual for the apostle; he more commonly uses the past tense (which gives an air of finality to the call). This leads some to hold that we should see here a meaning like "God the caller," but it is better to see this timeless present as bringing out the truth that God's call never ceases. Always he is calling people. Since the call is "into his kingdom and glory," there may well be the thought also that the call is effectual; those called will finally be with God in his kingdom.

The kingdom of God is not a very frequent concept in the Pauline correspondence (though in Acts 20:25 it sums up Paul's preaching at Ephesus). In the Synoptic Gospels the kingdom is, of course, the most

---

56. Some idea of purpose does seem to be expressed here by εἰς τό, though Moulton says, "Purpose is so remote here as to be practically evanescent" (M, I, p. 219). But this is to make the exhortation purposeless, which is not Paul's meaning. Nor is he simply giving the content of the exhortation, but exhorting with a view to a certain result in the lives of the Thessalonians.

frequent topic in Jesus' teaching. The kingdom is in some sense present and in some sense future. That is to say, people may enter the kingdom here and now, and experience some of its joys (cf. Rom. 14:17). But the full apprehension of what it involves cannot be attained until the end of the age (cf. 2 Thess. 1:5). Further, the kingdom is essentially dynamic; it is something that happens, not a static realm (Moffatt's translation "realm" is inadequate). It is God's righteous rule operating within and over people. Some readers have held that we should labor to establish the kingdom of God on earth. This is a noble ideal, but it is not the biblical idea of the kingdom. In the Scriptures it is clear that God and no other establishes the kingdom. The death of the Son is not linked with the kingdom in so many words, but throughout the New Testament the cross is viewed as integral to its being set up. It is in virtue of what Christ has accomplished for his people that their sin is put away and that God's rule becomes operative in them.[57]

In this passage the "kingdom" is closely linked with the "glory"; in the Greek they share a common preposition and a common article, while one "his" covers them both. Phillips's rendering, "the splendour of His Kingdom," may be going just a little too far,[58] but the two are certainly seen as closely related. For "glory" see on verse 20. It stands for the manifestation of God's glory to people, the revelation of God in his majesty. Paul holds out this glorious future as an incentive for the Thessalonians to live worthily here and now. They have been saved by a wonderful God. They have been brought into his kingdom. They face a glorious future. Let them so live here and now as to be worthy of such a God!

4. The Preachers' Message (2:13-16)

13 *And we also thank God continually because, when you received the word of God, which you heard from us, you accepted it*

---

57. There is an immense literature on the kingdom of God. G. E. Ladd has a useful survey in *Crucial Questions about the Kingdom of God* (Grand Rapids, 1954); see also his article in Walter A. Elwell (ed.), *Evangelical Dictionary of Theology* (Grand Rapids, 1984), pp. 607-11, and the literature cited there. See also the article by B. Klappert on "King, Kingdom," in *NIDNTT,* II, pp. 372-90 with its useful bibliography.

58. Cf. Milligan, "The two expressions must not however be united as if = 'His own kingdom of glory,' or even 'His own kingdom culminating in His glory,' but point rather to two manifestations of God's power, the first of His *rule,* the second of His *glory.*"

not as the word of men, but as it actually is, the word of God,
which is at work in you who believe. 14 *For you, brothers, became*
imitators of God's churches in Judea, which are in Christ Jesus:
You suffered from your own countrymen the same things those
churches suffered from the Jews, 15 *who killed the Lord Jesus and*
the prophets and also drove us out. They displease God and are
hostile to all men 16 *in their effort to keep us from speaking to the*
Gentiles so that they may be saved. In this way they always heap
up their sins to the limit. The wrath of God has come upon them
at last.[a]

[a]16 Or *them fully*

Paul goes on to the way the message of the preachers had been received.
The Thessalonians had recognized its divine origin, and, receiving it as
the very word of God, they had endured persecution, just as the Judean
believers had done. There is something of a parallel to the first chapter,
where Paul follows his reminder of the way the gospel came to the
Thessalonians (1:5) with the result in the lives of the believers (1:6). In
both passages Paul is pointing to the validity of the Thessalonians' faith.

13 Fundamental to Paul's preaching was the conviction that what
he spoke was not his own message but God's (see on v. 9). He rejected
human wisdom and thought little of mere eloquence (1 Cor. 2:1ff.). He
was content to pass on, in the manner of a herald, what God had given
him. There were learned philosophical systems that were at variance with
the stark simplicity of the preaching of the cross, and the pressure to
accommodate his message to the demands of the "modern thought-
world" of the day must have been great. But Paul rejected all this. His
drive and forcefulness came not from some thought that he was abreast
of contemporary trends in philosophy or religion or science, but from
the deep-seated conviction that he was God's mouthpiece, and that what
he spoke was the veritable word of God.[59]

So he thanks God, and says he never ceases to do so, where "for

---

59. Cf. Denney, Paul "was conscious that . . . [his theology] rested at bottom
on the truth of God; and when he preached it—for his theology was the sum of the
divine truth he held, and he *did* preach it—he did not submit it to men as a theme
for discussion. He put it above discussion. He pronounced a solemn and reiterated
anathema on either man or angel who should put anything else in its stead. He
published it, not for criticism, as though it had been his own device; but, as the word
of God, for the obedience of faith."

this cause" (which *NIV* omits) surely refers forward to what follows, but may also have a backward reference to the things of which Paul has just spoken (Whiteley). He gives thanks[60] that[61] the Thessalonians had recognized this feature of the gospel when it was first preached to them. The word preached was "of God." Paul finds matter for thanksgiving negatively, in that the Thessalonians had not received it as of human origin,[62] and positively, in that they had perceived it for what it really was, "the word of God." He underlines this with his contrast between "from us" and the very emphatic "of God."[63] The preachers were the immediate source of the message. But Paul and his companions were no more than intermediaries in proclaiming a gospel whose ultimate source and originator was none less than God himself.

There is an interesting and significant contrast between the ways in which the receiving of the message is spoken of in the two halves of the verse.[64] In the first half the word for receiving is one that denotes an objective, outward receiving. What is heard is likewise called "the word of hearing," a peculiar phrase[65] that also directs attention to the

60. καὶ ἡμεῖς is emphatic, "we, for our part." Lake thinks the proper force of the expression "can be given only if we assume that St. Paul means 'we give thanks just as you say that you do' " (*The Earlier Epistles of St. Paul* [London, 1919], p. 87), and finds in it evidence that Paul was replying to a letter. The case was put strongly by Rendel Harris (*Expositor,* 5th Series, VIII, pp. 168ff.). He found other evidence for such a letter in the repeated "you know" (1:5; 2:1, 5, 10; 3:3, 4), which he argued means "as you said." Others emphasize the way new steps in the argument are brought in in 4:9, 13; 5:1. This is very similar to the way correspondents in antiquity referred to points raised in letters to which they were replying, but we can scarcely say more.

61. Taking ὅτι not as causal, but as introducing the content of the thanksgiving (so Best).

62. That is, accepting the insertion of "as" by *NIV.* There is nothing corresponding to it in the Greek, and Bicknell says, "its insertion seriously alters the drift of the sentence. What causes St. Paul to thank God is not the attitude of the Thessalonians to the Gospel, or their appreciation of its divine origin, but the fact that the word that they accepted is divine and therefore charged with divine power." While there is no doubt that Paul is stressing the divine nature of the gospel, yet he does seem to be thankful that the Thessalonians had recognized it for what it was. The insertion of "as" seems to be necessary.

63. παρ' ἡμῶν is to be taken with παραλαβόντες (so Frame), and τοῦ θεοῦ is in emphatic contrast. It must be taken as a subjective genitive, "the word from God," "the word originating with God," and not as objective, "the word that tells of God," "the word about God."

64. παραλαβόντες and ἐδέξασθε.

65. λόγον ἀκοῆς. It occurs elsewhere only at Heb. 4:2 (where both nouns have the article). There is also a contrast between the merely outward reception that it

outward. Unless the variation is purely stylistic, the second word for receiving denotes rather a subjective reception, a reception that involves welcome and approval (the word is the usual one for the reception of a guest; cf. Ward, "a 'hospitality' word"). It is followed by an expression indicating the presence of faith in the recipients and the working of the power of God.

The verb rendered "is at work"[66] is almost always used in the New Testament to denote some form of supernatural activity. Mostly it is that of God (1 Cor. 12:6; Phil. 2:13, and elsewhere), but sometimes, by contrast, that of Satan (Eph. 2:2). It can be used of faith (Gal. 5:6), prayer (Jas. 5:16), and life or death (2 Cor. 4:12), in each case referring to a force not human. Here it draws attention to the fact that the power manifested in the lives of the converts is not of this world, but divine. Where the word of God is welcomed with obedient faith, there the power of God is at work. And it is a present reality: "it is still a living power among you who believe it" *(JB)*. When he speaks of believing[67] Paul uses the present tense, conveying the idea of a continuous process of belief (rather than the single act of decision that would more naturally be expressed by the aorist). It is the condition of the working of God in people that they continue to exercise faith. Or to put it another way, we cannot live today on the spiritual capital of yesterday.

14 The firm adherence of the Thessalonians to the word of God had resulted in persecution. Persecution in some form is the common lot of Christians and, in the nature of the case, always must be (cf. 2 Tim.

---

denotes and the hearing of faith. The outward reception, however, is a necessary step on the way to a genuine faith (Rom. 10:17), and Paul can even refer to an ἀκοὴ πίστεως (Gal. 3:2, 5).

66. ἐνεργεῖται. Lightfoot maintains that Paul always uses this verb in the active of God (and, by contrast, of Satan), and in the middle in all other cases. Here, then, he takes it as middle, with the subject, ὅς, referring back to λόγον, not θεοῦ. But J. Armitage Robinson contends that in the New Testament the passive is to be understood rather than the middle of this verb (*St Paul's Epistle to the Ephesians* [London, 1907], pp. 241-47). Milligan and Findlay accept this. Armitage Robinson's argument is difficult to accept in its entirety, but what is quite clear is that the New Testament makes a distinction between God's working and that of intermediaries. Where God is directly spoken of, the active is used; where it is his word, or such an activity as "faith working through love" (Gal. 5:6), a more oblique form is found. Milligan would bring this out by rendering, "which is also set in operation," thus emphasizing that it is God, and not some quasi-magical power in the word itself, that works.

67. The verb is used absolutely. Even at this early stage it was not necessary to add in whom they believed, so central is faith to Christianity. See further on 1:7.

3:12). Rolston remarks that the evangelists "preached an intolerant faith which branded the worship of the Greek and Roman gods as idolatry, as the worship of gods which had no real existence. When men received this faith, a line of division came between them and their unbelieving neighbours." Paul sees the way the Thessalonians had borne severe persecution as evidence of their real Christianity.[68] It showed that they had indeed received the gospel as divine in origin, that the gospel had produced results in them, and that it was still working in them. The persecution came from "your own countrymen," an expression that may be in part geographical and include Thessalonian Jews, but that certainly points to a large Gentile element in the opposition.[69] We are probably not far wrong in seeing the opposition as rooted in the hostility of the Jews, but as extending also to the Greeks who were so stirred up by the Jews that they took action on their own account. Incidentally, the expression reveals that the church was predominantly Gentile.

In their endurance of persecution the Thessalonians had become imitators of the Palestinian churches.[70] Paul is not speaking of conscious imitation but of the experience of the Thessalonians as repeating that of the Palestinians. The word rendered "churches"[71] is not a specifically religious word. It could be used of such assemblies as that of the rioting Ephesians (Acts 19:32, 39, 41). We find it in the Septuagint for the assembly of Israel, but that assembly, of course, was just as much political as religious. The word does not seem to have been used in a religious sense in Greek literature generally. Beside this we should set the fact that the Christians passed over the many Greek words for religious brotherhoods.[72] The force of this is that the early believers did not envision Christianity as just another religion. It is not to be named

---

68. Bengel comments on γάρ: "Divine *working* is most of all seen and felt in affliction." Thomas remarks, "Welcoming the Word and enduring sufferings because of it often go together (cf. 1:6)."

69. The basic meaning of συμφυλέτης indicates this, and so does the use of ἰδίων and the contrast with ὑπὸ τῶν Ἰουδαίων. But the word appears to have more of a national than a racial content. As Lightfoot points out, it "would include such Jews as were free citizens of Thessalonica."

70. Ἰουδαία could be used in a restricted sense to denote the province of Judea, but it could also bear a wider sense, meaning all Palestine. The latter seems to be the meaning here. Turner calls the genitive here "mystical": the churches are OF God and IN Christ (M, III, p. 212). Cf. Gal. 1:22.

71. ἐκκλησία.

72. K. L. Schmidt lists a number of titles used for religious groups and points out that the Christians adopted none of them (*TDNT,* III, p. 516).

with any of the words proper to religions in general. Its designation is unique for a religious community.[73] At the same time there were many "assemblies," both Jewish and Greek. The Christian assemblies are distinguished as being "God's," and further as "in Christ Jesus." The order "Christ Jesus" is almost peculiar to Paul (who has it 73 times as against 18 times for "Jesus Christ," while in 24 cases the manuscripts are divided). It indicates that "Christ" is already thought of as in the nature of a personal name (see further on 1:1). It is typical of Paul to think of the churches as being "in" Christ. In him they live and move and have their being.

We do not know the exact force of the reference to persecution by the Jews. It may point to an allegation by the Thessalonian Jews that in taking action against the Christians they were simply doing what their compatriots in Judea had earlier been compelled to do. Or it may be that the sufferings of the Palestinian churches were well known in Christian circles and could be used as the basis of instruction without further explanation anywhere among the believers.

15-16 This reference to persecution leads on to a denunciation of the Jews more severe than anything else in the Pauline writings, and some interpreters, finding a contradiction with the apostle's attitude, for example in Romans 9–11, hold that these verses were added by a later hand.[74] But Paul is not here writing about all Jews, but only those involved in the activities he names;[75] Marshall takes up W. Marxsen's suggestion that "Paul is writing here about particular Jews, those who have shown hostility to God's messengers, and not about the Jews in general." This is surely the way we should understand the passage. It is not an outburst of temper, but "the vehement condemnation, by a man in thorough sympathy with the mind and spirit of God, of the principles on which the Jews as a nation had acted at every period of their history" (Denney). Paul begins with the accusation that they had killed the Lord Jesus, this being apparently the one place where he says that "the Jews" were responsible for the death of

73. On the church see *TDNT*, III, pp. 501-36. There is a useful bibliography in *NIDNTT*, I, pp. 305-7.

74. W. G. Kümmel cites Eckart for this view and rejects it on account of "the incontestably Pauline language" of this and other disputed sections (*Introduction to the New Testament* [London, 1966], p. 185).

75. Cf. W. D. Davies, "Paul is not thinking of all Jews, or of Israel as a totality, from whom the election and the promise have been taken away. The term he uses is 'Jews' ('Ιουδαῖοι), not 'Israelites' ('Ισραηλεῖται), or 'Hebrews' ('Εβραῖοι). The general Jewish failure did not include all Israel" (*NTS* 24 [1977-78], p. 8).

Jesus. His use of "killed" rather than "crucified" may point to the fact that the Jews were responsible for the death, whereas it was the Romans, not the Jews, who did the crucifying. The unusual word order emphasizes both "Lord" and "Jesus." They had killed the heavenly Man, the Lord, and they had killed one who was of their flesh, the human Jesus. Paul emphasizes the heinousness of the crime, and proceeds to bring out that this was no isolated act. "Was there ever a prophet your fathers did not persecute?" asked Stephen (Acts 7:52). This is Paul's thought, too. The slaying of the Lord Jesus was the outworking of the same essential attitude as that displayed so often to the prophets.[76] Jesus, of course, had himself denounced with some emphasis what his nation had done to the prophets (Matt. 23:33-35).

And the persecution continued. They "drove us out." Paul's verb[77] is a compound found only here in the New Testament; it denotes the extreme in persecution. The manner of life of these persecutors is such that they "displease God," where the present tense marks the habitual attitude (for the meaning of the verb see on v. 4). Just as they displease God, so they are "hostile to all men." We are reminded of Tacitus's accusation that the Jews were "haters of the human race." The word "hostile" is usually referred to things, such as winds (Mark 6:48; Acts 27:4), or to deeds (Acts 26:9; 28:17). This is the only place in the New Testament where people are said to be hostile, and we may take this as a measure of the apostle's feeling. Ordinary expressions will not serve. His indignation mounts as he thinks of their trying to prevent the gospel from being preached to the Gentiles, quite in the spirit of the Pharisees who opposed Jesus (Matt. 23:13). Such preaching was in order that people might be saved. The Jews' attempt to prevent this underlines their guilt. Paul probably had in mind the opposition that provoked the riot when he was at Thessalonica (Acts 17:5ff.), which is an excellent example of the conduct he is condemning.

---

76. Grammatically the reference to the prophets could be taken with what follows to give the sense, "who killed the Lord Jesus, and drove out both the prophets and us." But it is more natural to link "the Lord Jesus" with "the prophets"; cf. Luke 11:47-48; 13:33; 20:9ff.; Acts 7:52; Rom. 11:3. Frame points out also that the argument would be weakened if προφήτας were attached to ἐκδιωξάντων. Some expositors have taken the prophets to mean the New Testament prophets, but no sufficient reason has been produced for this. It is the continuing opposition of the Jews to God's messengers through the centuries that forms so powerful an argument.

77. ἐκδιώκω, "persecute severely" (BAGD).

Paul brings out the inevitability of the divine punishment of the conduct he is deploring by using a construction expressing purpose.[78] The Jews have done their persecuting to "heap up their sins to the limit," which we might well understand in Frame's words: "The obstinacy of the Jews is viewed as an element in the divine plan." Moffatt brings out something of the determination of these sinners with "So they would fill up the measure of their sins to the last drop!" They are seeing to it that nothing is left out in the catalogue of their sins! The plural "sins" points to the aggregate of their separate evil acts, and not to the general abstract concept of "sin." The consequence is sure. Paul speaks of "the wrath" as coming on them ("retribution" is the translation of *JB* and *REB*, but this is not the meaning of the Greek; Paul's word expresses the strong, personal opposition of God to all evil). Indeed, so sure is their punishment that he uses the aorist tense, which might be rendered "came" upon them. The use of this tense does not refer to the imminence of the punishment but to its certainty;[79] Paul is speaking of wrath in an eschatological setting. It is at the last great day that the people of his nation will receive the due reward of their misdeeds. But though it is postponed, there is no doubt about what their fate will be. "The cup of the nation's sin is now full. They can do no more to provoke the divine wrath" (Bicknell).

At the same time we should notice that Paul's anger is the anger of a man with his own nation, his own people. He is very much part of them, and he sorrows at their fate. He is not gleefully invoking dire disasters on them, but grieving over the effects of their misdeeds. Phillips brings out something of this with "Alas, I fear they are completing the full tale of their sins and the wrath of God is over their heads." It is the anguish so poignantly expressed in Romans 9. And here the apostle's sorrow is not mitigated by any ray of hope. We could

78. εἰς τό with the infinitive may also indicate result (see Burton, *MT,* 411). This is possible, but purpose seems to be Paul's meaning. Cf. Turner: "the purpose of God (final)" (M, III, p. 143). Cf. *JB,* "They never stop trying *to finish off the sins they have begun.*" Best quotes Moule, "the Semitic mind was notoriously unwilling to draw a sharp dividing-line between purpose and consequence," and thinks that the clause "may be either final or consecutive or both."

79. Cf. R. H. Fuller, "he is using the familiar prophetic device of speaking of a future event as though it were already present. The certainty of the event is so overwhelming, the signs of its impendingness so sure, that it is said to have occurred, or to be occurring already" (*The Mission and Achievement of Jesus* [London, 1954], p. 26). Whiteley also refers to this aorist as "referring prophetically to the future."

understand the Greek to mean that the wrath is come on them "to the uttermost" ("in full," BDF #207 [3]).[80] Judah's sin had been so constant and so serious that Paul sees no other possible outcome.

IV. THE RELATIONSHIP OF PAUL TO THE THESSALONIANS (2:17—3:13)

A. PAUL'S DESIRE TO RETURN (2:17-18)

17 *But, brothers, when we were torn away from you for a short time (in person, not in thought), out of our intense longing we made every effort to see you.* 18 *For we wanted to come to you— certainly I, Paul, did, again and again—but Satan stopped us.*

Paul has been engaging in reminiscences about what had happened when he was in Thessalonica on the mission that had resulted in the foundation of the church there. Now he turns to his continuing warm relationship to that church, and begins with his deep longing to go back to them and see them again.

17 As Paul enters this new section of the letter, it is not without a backward glance at the last. His "But" is an adversative conjunction[81] contrasting him with the Jews, and there is another contrast in the emphatic "we." It seems probable that one of the accusations leveled against him had been that he had never intended to revisit Thessalonica and that his failure to return was evidence that he was a charlatan. His continued absence was urged as further proof that he had no real regard for his converts. So Paul addresses them affectionately as "brothers," and goes on to use a very strong term to express his sense of loss at their absence from him. "When we were torn away from you" is really "being orphaned"; while the word had developed the general sense of "being bereaved," it seems likely that Paul is not unmindful of its original significance. In this chapter he has already likened his attitude to them to that of a mother-nurse (v. 7) and to that of a father (v. 11). The present verb, while it may radically alter the imagery by making Paul the "orphan," continues the thought of the tender affection that

---

80. εἰς τέλος might also be rendered "at last" (as *NIV*) or "to the end" (cf. *REB*, "for good and all").

81. δέ.

bound the apostle to his converts.[82] This deep sense of bereavement had arisen even though their separation had been only for a very short time, "a season of an hour." He stresses that the separation is only physical: they are still joined in heart. "Out of sight, out of mind" runs our proverb, and Moffatt brings out some of the significance of Paul's words here with his "out of sight, not out of mind." For "heart" (*NIV*, "thought") see on verse 4.

Because of this deep feeling Paul had made a determined attempt to see them. We have no precise equivalent of the Greek word rendered "made every effort," a word that manages to combine the two ideas of haste and eagerness.[83] It means that Paul did not delay, nor did he put forth a token effort only. Rather, he had used all his might and used it speedily in his endeavor to come to them. He reinforces this strong verb with a comparative adverb, "the more eagerly"[84] (*RSV*), which should leave them in no doubt as to the strength of his endeavors.

But he is not finished yet. He tells his readers that he had endeavored to see them "with great desire" (*NIV*, "out of our intense longing"). The last word is rather surprising, for it nearly always means something like "lust" in its New Testament occurrences. It is generally mentioned only to be condemned. Here Paul uses it in its original sense of very strong desire, almost of fierce passion (cf. Rutherford, "absence has made us anxious out of measure to see you face to face with passionate desire"). He wants his friends to be in no doubt as to the strength of his feelings for them.

82. Cf. Chrysostom: "He says not χωρισθέντες ὑμῶν, not διασπασθέντες ὑμῶν, not διαστάντες, not ἀπολειφέντες, but ἀπορφανισθέντες ὑμῶν. He sought for a word that might fitly indicate his mental anguish. Though standing in the relation of a father to them all, he yet utters the language of orphan children that have prematurely lost their parent" (cited by Frame). The word might be used of a parent without children (so that Paul may be picturing himself as a bereaved parent), just as of a child without parents; common to both uses is the sense of bereavement.

83. σπουδάζω. BAGD gives its meaning as "1. *hasten, hurry* . . . 2. *be zealous* or *eager.*"

84. In late Greek the comparative tends to take over the functions of the superlative, and thus it is likely that περισσοτέρως here is to be understood as elative (so Frame). Some commentators, however, maintain that in Paul it always has a strictly comparative force (e.g., Lightfoot, Milligan). But they are not at all agreed as to what has to be supplied here as the other member of the comparison (see the reconstructions in Frame). It seems simpler to take the elative sense. It is very doubtful whether the strictly comparative sense will hold in 2 Cor. 7:13, and that may well serve as a parallel to the elative sense here.

18 Paul repeats that he had wished to come to them.[85] The verb "wanted" expresses something of the emotions as well as the will.[86] It strengthens the emotional element that is so marked a feature of this section of the letter. Whatever had kept Paul away from the Thessalonians, it had not been his personal desires. This again underlies his emphatic "I Paul."[87] Throughout these two letters, as we have noted, the plural is used much more than in most of Paul's letters, which makes the singular more significant when it does occur (again in 5:27; 2 Thess. 2:5; 3:17).[88] Here the intense personal feeling breaks through, and we have the emphatic singular reinforced by the personal name. Paul had not simply made one attempt. He had wished to come, according to *NIV,* "again and again." This represents an unusual Greek expression that seems to denote a plurality of occasions with no attempt at giving the exact number. "More than once" is probably our nearest equivalent.[89]

---

85. Moule points out that the plural may be epistolary, in which case it simply means "I wanted"; if it is a genuine plural, then others also had this desire (*IBNTG,* p. 119).

86. The verb is θέλω. The distinction between this verb and βούλομαι has been understood variously, with scholars sometimes reaching diametrically opposite conclusions. According to Grimm-Thayer, βούλομαι "seems to designate the will which follows deliberation" and θέλω "the will which proceeds from inclination." This does not, however, seem to be the New Testament usage. It must be borne in mind that the two verbs are close in meaning and on occasion seem to be used interchangeably. Also that θέλω was tending to encroach on the territory of βούλομαι; in the New Testament θέλω is used more than five times as often as βούλομαι (the figures are 207 and 37). Where the two words differ βούλομαι implies more strongly "the deliberate exercise of volition" (AS).

87. This is the only place in these epistles where the emphatic ἐγώ is found (κἀγώ in 3:5). μέν normally implies a contrast, but this seems not to be the case here. Cf. BAGD, μέν "serves to emphasize the subject in clauses which contain a report made by the speaker concerning his own state of being, esp. intellectual or emotional" (2.a). "I, Paul, indeed" is the thrust of it.

88. E. Stauffer discusses Paul's use of "we" and "I" (*TDNT,* II, pp. 356-62).

89. The Greek is καὶ ἅπαξ καὶ δίς. The first καί is usually taken as part of the expression, but this is probably incorrect. ἅπαξ καὶ δίς occurs four times in LXX (each time meaning "more than once," the number of times not being specified). Similar expressions occur without a preliminary καί, e.g., ἅπαξ καὶ ἅπαξ. If we can accept ἅπαξ καὶ δίς as the idiomatic expression, then the first καί here will be ascensive and the meaning "and that more than once." The expression occurs again in Phil. 4:16, where the meaning appears to be "both (when I was) in Thessalonica and (καί) more than once (ἅπαξ καὶ δίς) (when I was in other places) you sent. . . ." This is very near to Frame's understanding of the expression, the difference being that he prefers the slightly stronger "repeatedly." See further my note in *Novum Testamentum* I (1956), pp. 205-8.

Paul had been able to send Timothy (3:2), so whatever the hindrance was it was evidently personal to Paul.

However, Paul's endeavors had been frustrated by Satan (for Satan, see on 3:5). The verb here translated "stopped" means literally "to cut into";[90] Milligan agrees with Lightfoot that the idea is that of cutting up a road to make it impassable, and thence of hindering in general. A number of suggestions have been made as to the particular form Satan's activities took. But we are completely in the dark in this matter, and all attempts to understand it are no more than guesswork. There is no way of knowing exactly what Paul had in mind. Clearly the Thessalonians were expected to catch the allusion, but we lack their detailed knowledge of the circumstances. One thing of importance is clear to us, though, and that is that Satan makes his presence felt to Christian workers. He even prevents them from doing things they would dearly love to do. Scripture makes it clear that his power is derivative, and always subject to God's overruling. But within the limits allotted to him he does hinder God's servants.

B. PAUL'S JOY IN THE THESSALONIANS (2:19-20)

19 For what is our hope, our joy, or the crown in which we will glory in the presence of our Lord Jesus when he comes? Is it not you? 20 Indeed, you are our glory and joy.

It is important for the apostle that the Thessalonian Christians be aware of the high esteem in which he holds them. His later exhortations must be understood in the light of that esteem. So now he has a little section in which he makes it clear that he is proud of them.

19-20   Paul brings this section to a climax with an excited outburst of esteem for his converts. It is probable that the two questions in *NIV* should be regarded as one, with a shorter little question as a parenthesis: "For what is our hope, our joy, or the crown in which we will glory (are not you?) in the presence of our Lord Jesus. . . ?" It is possible that we should read "and" instead of "or," as Best does;[91] it is

---

90. ἐγκόπτω. Lightfoot says that it is "a metaphor derived from military operations. The word signifies 'to break up a road' (by destroying bridges, etc.) so as to render it impassable" (*Saint Paul's Epistle to the Galatians* [London, 1902], p. 205).

91. ἤ . . . ἤ . . . is commonly disjunctive, but Best points out that it can be copulative; that may well be the way we should take it here.

not easy to think that Paul is choosing between hope, joy, and crown as he thinks of his friends. There were two words in common use in Greek for "crown."[92] That used here commonly denoted something like a festive garland or a laurel wreath awarded to the victor at the games. It is likely that Paul has in mind thoughts of joyfulness and victory[93] as being symbolized by the crown (though we cannot be dogmatic on this point, for the word is sometimes found in the sense of a royal crown also). It is described as "the crown in which we will glory," the last word giving the thought of the outward expression of the feeling of joy. It denotes a rather exuberant activity, and is sometimes rendered "boasting." It is from a different root and expresses a different idea from that rendered "glory" in the next verse. Paul is not engaging in an outburst of pride, but saying forcefully that his joy is rooted in what God has done in these converts. Moore sees the Thessalonians as "Paul's emblem of work well done and of victory achieved." This high place assigned to the Thessalonians in Paul's esteem is further emphasized with the insistence that it is "in the presence of our Lord Jesus"[94] (which raises it to the highest level) and "when he comes" (which sounds the eschatological note and makes it permanent).

This is the first occurrence in Christian literature of the important word rendered "coming"[95] in *RSV* (*NIV* with "comes" makes a verb of it) and commonly transliterated *parousia*. Its basic meaning is simply "presence" (1 Cor. 16:17; 2 Cor. 10:10). This gives rise to the sense of "coming to be present," "arrival" (2 Cor. 7:6-7). In the ordinary language of the people the term was especially used for the arrival of a great personage, a king or an emperor, and it was the usual word for a royal visit.[96] In the New Testament it became a technical expression for *the* royal visit, the second coming of our Lord. From the New Testament it

---

92. στέφανος (used here; a festive garland) and διάδημα (the crown of royalty).

93. J. B. Lightfoot says that the idea conveyed by the word "is not dominion, but either (1) victory, or (2) merriment, and the wreath was worn equally by the conqueror and by the holiday-maker. Without excluding the latter notion, the former seems to be prominent in this and in the parallel passage; for there, as here, the Apostle refers in the context to the Lord's coming. His converts then will be his wreath of victory" (*Saint Paul's Epistle to the Philippians* [London, 1908], p. 157).

94. Paul has "Lord Jesus" or "Lord Jesus Christ" 24 times in the eight chapters of these two letters, and this is more often than anywhere else in the New Testament. The much longer Acts has it 17 times, and Romans 16.

95. παρουσία.

96. See Deissmann, *LAE,* pp. 368-73, for examples.

passed into Christian literature generally. Milligan maintains that, as distinct from other words for the second coming, it "lays stress on the 'presence' of the Lord with His people, which, while existing now, will only at that Return be completely realized."[97] So here Paul uses for the first time in Christian literature that term which was to be the characteristic designation of the Lord's triumphant return.[98] And even then, says Paul, the Thessalonians will be his hope and joy and crown of boasting. It may not be without significance that on the occasion of a royal *parousia* the people sometimes found themselves under the necessity of providing a crown. But at the coming of this King, the crown will be his people's.

Paul rounds off this section with a further statement that the Thessalonians are "our glory and joy." The word for "glory"[99] could be used of human splendor (Matt. 4:8), but came to have its characteristic use in connection with the "glory" of God (as in Rom. 1:23). It could similarly be used of the glory of Christ (2 Cor. 4:4), and even of the glory that is won for the believer (Rom. 8:18 and elsewhere). It is a word with many overtones. Paul uses it here to indicate that the Thessalonians are the cause of great rejoicing to the apostles: "Yes, you are indeed our pride and our joy!" (Phillips). His "you" is emphatic: Paul is giving a special place to no other than the Thessalonians. And while he looks forward to continuing to esteem them right up to the time of the Parousia, he yet insists that at the moment of writing, right now, they *are* his pride and joy.

97. Additional Note F, p. 151.

98. See also the note on this word in G. Vos, *The Pauline Eschatology* (Grand Rapids, 1953), pp. 74ff.

99. δόξα originally meant "opinion" or the like (a sense not found in the New Testament). It came to mean "good opinion" and thus "praise" or "honor" (Luke 14:10; Heb. 3:3). In LXX it was used to render the Hebrew כָּבוֹד and thus acquired the significance "splendor," "magnificence." G. Kittel points out that the word does not have the meaning "radiance," "glory" in secular Greek and that in the New Testament "the word is used for the most part in a sense for which there is no Greek analogy whatever" (*TDNT*, II, p. 237).

1 THESSALONIANS 3

C. TIMOTHY'S MISSION (3:1-5)

1 *So when we could stand it no longer, we thought it best to be left by ourselves in Athens.* 2 *We sent Timothy, who is our brother and God's fellow worker*ª *in spreading the gospel of Christ, to strengthen and encourage you in your faith,* 3 *so that no one would be unsettled by these trials. You know quite well that we were destined for them.* 4 *In fact, when we were with you, we kept telling you that we would be persecuted. And it turned out that way, as you well know.* 5 *For this reason, when I could stand it no longer, I sent to find out about your faith. I was afraid that in some way the tempter might have tempted you and our efforts might have been useless.*

ª2 Some manuscripts *brother and fellow worker;* other manuscripts *brother and God's servant*

Paul had made clear his deep concern for the Thessalonian converts. He had had to leave them, but he described that as being "torn away" from them (2:17). He had desperately wanted to see them again but could not. So he now recalls that in that situation he had sent his trusted Timothy to encourage them. That showed something of his interest in their spiritual welfare.

1 More than one problem makes its appearance here. First, there is the problem of the movements of the missionaries. In Acts 17:14 Paul went on to Athens alone, leaving Timothy and Silas at Berea. From Athens he sent for them (17:15). Then he preached to the Athenians, and proceeded to Corinth (18:1), where Silas and Timothy joined him from Macedonia (18:5). However, from this passage it is clear that Timothy at any rate was with Paul in Athens. This does not involve a contradiction with Acts, as some have supposed. The writer of Acts has omitted the journey of Timothy to Athens and back to Thessalonica, which is not surprising, for it was not important for his purpose. But it was important for Paul's purpose in writing this letter, and he writes about it accordingly.

Then there is the problem of "we."[1] As we saw on 1:1, the practice in this epistle differs somewhat from that in the Pauline letters generally. The plural is used almost throughout, whereas in most of his letters Paul prefers the singular (the singular occurs in 2:18; 3:5; 5:27; 2 Thess. 2:5; 3:17). Some commentators deny that Paul ever used the epistolary plural, maintaining that the plural is always meant to associate others with him. This, however, does not seem tenable. In the present passage even the emphatic use of the singular in verse 5 cannot outweigh the fact that one person is meant by the plural in verse 1. This seems clear from the plural form of the adjective "alone" (*NIV,* "by ourselves"), which yet can only refer to Paul. It is reinforced by the fact that the same subject is also to be understood of the verb "sent" in verse 2. We cannot think of Timothy as sending himself. It is hard to think of Silas as being included, for, in the first place, we do not know whether he was in Athens or not and, in the second, it is difficult to think of "we" as meaning two people out of three (though Ward and others accept this). So certain does it seem to Moffatt that one person only is meant that throughout these verses he translates "I" and not "we."

The emotional atmosphere of the preceding verses continues to be in evidence (the chapter division is unfortunate, for this section is very closely connected with the preceding). The separation Paul has been speaking of became unendurable,[2] and thus he took action. "We thought

1. Milligan discusses the problem of the epistolary plural in Note B in his commentary. See also O. T. Allis, *Revision or New Translation* (Philadelphia, 1948), pp. 61-62; A. T. Hanson, *The Pioneer Ministry* (London, 1961), pp. 46ff.; Moule, *IBNTG,* pp. 118-19. Moule holds that the plural here "must (by the very meaning of μόνος) surely be 'epistolary' " (*IBNTG,* p. 119; curiously Best says that Moule "argues μόνοι almost definitely implies more than one person," whereas Moule, after the words already quoted, says "and iii.5 [ἔπεμψα] appears to be identical in meaning with iii.2 [ἐπέμψαμεν]" and proceeds to cite another epistolary plural). Cf. Thomas, "For Paul to have used 'we' in v. 1 in any other than a singular sense would have defeated his apologetic desire to express his loneliness." Bruce, however, finds the epistolary plural "difficult."

2. στέγω ("forbear") means first "to cover," then "to ward off by covering," and thus "to see something through," "to bear up," "to endure." This last seems to be the meaning in each New Testament occurrence of the verb (v. 5; 1 Cor. 9:12; 13:7; though in 13:7 some exegetes see the meaning as "cover"). Another line of development from "to cover" leads to the idea of "to conceal," but although some adopt this meaning here, the sense appears to be "to endure."

it best" renders the same verb as that rendered "we were delighted" in 2:8; it points here to something in the nature of a resolve, but the word has a definite emotional content. This is continued with "to be left," which means strictly "to be abandoned." It is used of leaving one's loved ones at death (Mark 12:19), and in the papyri it is the technical term for leaving something in a will.[3] Linked with the emphatic "by ourselves," it gives us some idea of the depths of the apostle's feelings. We must not think that it was easy for him to stay and preach in Athens, the intellectual capital of the world. Many of its inhabitants were cultured people who would regard Paul's message as unacceptable in polite society, while not a few were cynical and ready to mock at the gospel Paul preached. Paul was not insensitive, and he did not relish the prospect of working alone in such a place. He realized that it was necessary for Timothy to go for the good of the work, but this verse gives us a glimpse of what it cost him.[4]

2 This cost is further emphasized in that when he was facing such a grim prospect Paul sent to them one whom he valued as highly as he did Timothy. According to the most probable reading he calls Timothy "God's minister in the gospel of Christ" (the alternative is "God's fellow worker," *NIV;* so *REB*).[5] "Minister" is the rendering of *diakonos,* from which we get our word "deacon." It is sometimes used in the New Testament to denote a member of one of the orders of the Christian

3. See MM *sub* καταλείπω.

4. Cf. Denney, "He seems to have been in many ways dependent on the sympathy and assistance of others; and, of all places he ever visited, Athens was the most trying to his ardent temperament. . . . Never had he been left alone in a place so unsympathetic; never had he felt so great a gulf fixed between others' minds and his own." Bicknell also remarks, "Athens was particularly uncongenial to St. Paul's temperament."

5. The textual questions are whether we should read διάκονον (with ℵ A P Ψ) or συνεργόν (with B D* 33 OL^mss) and whether to include τοῦ θεοῦ (ℵ A P Ψ 81 etc.) or omit it (B 1962). Not surprisingly, the Byzantine text combines the two. Metzger argues that "the reading that best accounts for the origin of the others is καὶ συνεργὸν τοῦ θεοῦ." Although this form of words occurs in 1 Cor. 3:9, it is a bold, even startling expression, and a scribe would perhaps be ready to alter it by substituting another noun or by dropping τοῦ θεοῦ. Yet this is not decisive, for διάκονον τοῦ θεοῦ is neither an easy expression in itself (though it does occur three times outside this passage), nor is it a usual way of referring to Timothy. Moreover, when διάκονος became a title for one of the orders of ministry, scribes may well have hesitated to apply it to one so important as Timothy. The problem is complicated and it is impossible to be sure of what Paul wrote, but our best course appears to be to accept what is perhaps the better-attested reading, διάκονον τοῦ θεοῦ.

ministry in the technical sense, but it is very unlikely to have that meaning here. Originally the word denoted the service of a table waiter, and from that it came to signify lowly service of any kind. It was often used by the early Christians for the service that they were to render habitually both to God and to people. Where a word like "slave," which is often used of Christians, puts the emphasis on the personal relation, this word draws attention to the act of service being performed. It is not Paul's habit to refer to Timothy in this way (he prefers to call him "our brother" or the like, but cf. 1 Tim. 4:6). The elaborate and high-sounding title may be meant to impress on the readers the importance he had attached to Timothy's mission.

When Timothy's service is defined as "in the gospel of Christ" (there is nothing in the Greek corresponding to *NIV*'s "spreading"), Paul is referring the gospel to him whose death is its basis. It is the news of what Christ has done for sinners. The gospel may also be called "the gospel of our Lord Jesus" (2 Thess. 1:8), "the gospel of God" (2:2, where see note), and "our gospel" (1:5, where see note). The purpose of Timothy's mission was twofold, but both verbs have the the notion of strengthening. That rendered "to strengthen" has the idea of putting in a buttress, a support, and in classical Greek it is mostly used in the literal sense. However, the metaphorical sense is found in late Greek and is usual in the New Testament. "To encourage" also renders a Greek verb that conveys the notion of strengthening (we have just seen it in 2:12). Basically it means "to call to the side of," and from this various ways of helping are derived. It is used in a legal sense ("Advocate" in 1 John 2:1 is a noun from this root) as well as in a more general sense. It is primarily help by way of exhortation, and thus means encouragement. Timothy's visit, then, had been for the purpose of encouraging the Thessalonians by buttressing their faith.[6]

3 This purpose is further explained.[7] The sense of the verb rendered

---

6. See further on 2:3. ὑπέρ is not well translated "concerning." The word means "on behalf of," and it often has the meaning "for the advantage of," though it is sometimes used in neutral fashion (as when Christ is said to have died ὑπέρ our sins). Here the meaning is that Timothy's visit was to benefit the faith of the Thessalonians. T. W. Manson has argued that ὑπὲρ τῆς πίστεως ὑμῶν "refers to the faithfulness of the Thessalonian Christians to their profession" (*BJRL* 35 [1952-53], p. 440, n. 2). But the word πίστις, when used in the New Testament of people, never seems to mean "faithfulness" (see further on 2 Thess. 3:2). I see no reason for abandoning the usual meaning of the word here.

7. τό introduces a statement in apposition to the foregoing, or, as Lightfoot

"be unsettled"[8] is not certain. Most translations agree with *KJV,* "be moved" (e.g., Moffatt, "being disturbed"; *RSV,* "be moved"; Phillips, "to lose heart"), as do most recent commentators. But the word does not often have this meaning. More usually it is closer to its original meaning of a dog's wagging its tail—"to fawn upon" or "to wheedle." Here Paul seems to have in mind the possibility that, while the Thessalonians were in the middle of their troubles, some of their enemies might by fair words wheedle them out of the right way.[9] Perhaps while the Gentiles were persecuting them some of the Jews spoke kindly to them (or Paul feared that they would) with a view to persuading them to accept Judaism, which, of course, would have as one of its effects the immediate cessation of persecution. It was their being Christian that aroused hostility so that to apostatize from Christianity would mean instant relief. We must not minimize the attractiveness of this prospect for people suffering persecution.

The trouble in which the Thessalonians found themselves arose not from the suffering that is the ordinary lot of people in general, but from what Rolston calls "the peculiar difficulties which they face as Christians in the midst of a secular society which acknowledges a different set of values." To compromise might appear to be an easy way out of their troubles, but Paul insists that they knew better. "You" is emphatic (really "you yourselves"), and the sense of this part of the verse is well given by Moffatt, "Troubles are our lot, you know that well" (i.e., so long as we understand "lot" not as the action of some blind fate, but as the portion God allots to his people). The verb translated "were destined"[10] conveys the impression of something stable, something that

---

thinks, it is more or less equivalent to ὥστε, giving the result of the preceding. Moule thinks that this is an exception to the rule that the articular infinitive is preceded by a preposition (πρός, εἰς, ἕνεκεν) expressing purpose (*IBNTG,* p. 140); Best also accepts purpose.

8. σαίνω. AS gives the meaning as "1. prop. . . . of dogs, *to wag the tail, fawn.* 2. Metaph., of persons, c. acc., *to fawn upon, flatter, beguile.*" So also MM, "the Apostle dreaded that the Thessalonians would be 'drawn aside,' 'allured,' in the midst of the afflictions which were falling upon them." BAGD prefer here "move, disturb, agitate" and point out that this meaning is that of the ancient versions and Greek interpreters. H. Chadwick argues for such a meaning (*JTS* n.s. 1 [1950], pp. 156-58), as does F. Lang (*TDNT,* VII, pp. 54-56).

9. This interpretation is supported by the fact that the process he speaks of takes place "in" their troubles (Bruce, "in the midst of these afflictions"). We would expect "by" if the verb meant "moved." Bruce understands the verb to mean "perturbed." For θλῖψις see on 1:6.

10. κεῖμαι.

cannot be altered. As Calvin puts it, it "is as though he had said, that we are Christians on this condition." Tribulation is not to be wondered at by Christian people as though some strange and unusual happening befell them. Under the conditions of the world, with so many opposed to the gospel and not taking the trouble to understand it, tribulation is inevitable (cf. Mark 8:34; John 16:33; Acts 14:22). More, it is the means of teaching us many lessons. Human nature being what it is, we will learn some things only the hard way. If we are in trouble and need help and advice we do not run over our list of friends and say: "Ah, there's so-and-so. Never had a day's trouble in his life: he'll be just the one to help!" Rather, we know that there are qualities of character that are brought out only by affliction. In our hour of need, someone who has these qualities is invaluable (cf. 2 Cor. 1:4). Suffering, then, is part of the very process of living out the Christian life, and Paul suggests that we should not regard it as something monstrous and alien. The God who is over all watches over his children, and the affliction that comes to them is only such as he permits. There is always some lesson to be learned from it. It is always part of our being shaped into what God would have us be. It is inevitable. We are appointed to it.[11]

4 Paul had asserted that the Thessalonians knew this basic truth. He now reminds them that he had foretold their sufferings when he was in their city, and foretold them repeatedly, for such is the force of the continuous tense he employs (cf. Rutherford, "the warning was often on our lips"). The certainty of persecution loomed large in the apostle's mind, as well it might, both from the nature of things and from his own experience. So he often spoke of it. He further said "that we would be persecuted." This assertion emphasizes the certainty of the affliction and hints at its divine appointment (Clarke heads his exposition of this paragraph "The Cup That Will Not Pass").[12] This same expression[13] is used in a number of places in the New Testament to give greater certainty than the use of the simple future and to hint at the fact that God is in the particular act being foretold (e.g., Rom. 8:13, 18; Gal. 3:23; cf. also

---

11. For the whole question of suffering see C. S. Lewis, *The Problem of Pain* (London, 1940).

12. Clarke asks why so many Western churches are unafflicted and goes on, "The only answer which we can give—a sad and solemn one—is that the Cross is no longer central; we have lost the vision of the kingdom of God, and have no intention of being the suffering servants of humanity. Ichabod!"

13. The use of μέλλω "denoting an action that necessarily follows a divine decree" (BAGD 1.c.δ).

Acts 14:22 for coincidences both of thought and language). So Paul reiterates what he had said in the previous verse, that trouble, for the Christian, is not to be dismissed as totally evil. The hand of God is in it. He has appointed his people thereto.

Once more Paul appeals to the knowledge of the Thessalonians. He is not telling them something strange and novel. He does not need to produce proof at every step. He had repeatedly foretold suffering. This was not just so much empty sound, for his predictions had been fulfilled.[14] The Thessalonians themselves had knowledge that this was so.

5 There is a good deal of repetition in these verses. Paul was very stirred as he wrote. He is anxious to leave his correspondents in no doubt as to his essential meaning, so he does not scruple to repeat his points. In this verse he says again what he has said in verses 1 and 2, that he sent Timothy when he could no longer endure the separation. He is very emphatic about his personal feeling and action, and adopts the unusual course in this letter of using the singular, and that with the emphatic pronoun.[15] In the earlier verses he has referred to Timothy's being sent to strengthen the faith of the Thessalonians. Now we have the other side of it, namely, that he has been sent also in order that[16] the apostle might be reassured. Paul was anxious to hear that the faith of his converts had not failed in the time of testing.

The concluding part of the verse employs a change of construction, from indicative to subjunctive, which it is impossible to reproduce in English. The effect of the indicative (*NIV*, "might have tempted") is to give the impression that the writer feels it probable that the tempter has indeed tempted them, but the subjunctive ("might have been useless")

14. Rather curiously, E. G. Selwyn sees in vv. 3 and 4 evidence of "the close connection between persecution and the approaching final judgment" (W. D. Davies and D. Daube [eds.], *The Background of the New Testament and Its Eschatology* [Cambridge, 1956], p. 399). While there is a good deal of eschatology in the Thessalonian letters, these verses do not seem to form part of it. Paul is talking about persecutions that have already come to pass, not those that will herald the End.

15. Also with καί, the form being κἀγώ. The force of this is "I also," "I for my part." Frame thinks that it means "I too as well as Silvanus," but this seems to be reading rather much into the expression. We do not know whether or not Silvanus was with Paul in those days. In any case, the Greek expression seems simply to emphasize the "I." Moule thinks that the force of καί here is "I actually sent," "that is in fact why I sent" (*IBNTG*, p. 167).

16. Turner sees purpose in εἰς τό with the infinitive, "in order to know" (M, III, p. 143).

throws doubt on the idea that the preachers' labor had been in vain.[17] In other words, Paul manages to convey his confidence that they had resisted the temptation that he knew they would have encountered.[18] The evil one is called "the tempter" again in the New Testament only in Matthew 4:3, though he is elsewhere said to tempt people. The same evil spirit is called Satan in 2:18. Consistently he opposes the divine purposes (cf. 1 Cor. 7:5).

The reference to the activity of the tempter should not be overlooked. Satan is referred to in every major division of the New Testament. He is supreme in the realm of evil spirits (Eph. 2:2; 2 Thess. 2:9). His activities are always opposed to God and to the best interests of people.[19] Afflictions like sickness are often attributed to the activity of his minions, and Paul describes his "thorn in the flesh" as "a messenger of Satan to torment me" (2 Cor. 12:7). Satan's activities in the realm of the spirit are seen in the taking away of the good seed from people's hearts (Mark 4:15), and "sowing" evil people in the world (Matt. 13:39). As "the god of this age" he blinds the minds of the unbelieving (2 Cor. 4:4). He tempted Jesus (Matt. 4; Luke 4), and he tempts his followers (Luke 22:3; 1 Cor. 7:5). He hindered Paul's missionary work (1 Thess. 2:18). He sought to gain advantage over the faithful (2 Cor. 2:11). Had he been successful in what he was doing among the Thessalonians Paul's hard work (the apostle's word means toil to the point of weariness; it is that rendered "toil" in 2:9) would have been rendered futile. Yet he is not conceived of dualistically, as commensurate with God. He is surely the chief among the enemies to be subjugated at the end (1 Cor. 15:25). Indeed, he has been defeated already (Col. 2:15). Christians here and now may defeat his purposes (Eph. 6:16).[20]

17. According to W. D. Chamberlain, this is one of only two places in the New Testament where μή πως is used with the aorist indicative, "referring to a past event where the purpose is conceived as unfulfilled" (*An Exegetical Grammar of the Greek New Testament* [New York, 1941], p. 188); it signifies "feared result" (BDF #370 [2]).

18. It is possible also that the subjunctive clause looks to the future. Paul is sure of the temptation of Satan and nothing can be done about it. But it was possible to do something to prevent his toil being in vain, so he sent Timothy.

19. It is often said that Satan is not invariably opposed to people in the Old Testament, but this is difficult to establish. He is opposed to Job (Job 1–2), and similar opposition seems to be present in all the other places where he is referred to by name in the Old Testament (1 Chron. 21:1; Ps. 109:6; he is discredited in Zech. 3:1, 2). Cf. also the serpent (Gen. 3).

20. H. P. Liddon has a forceful passage on the existence of Satan that is still relevant after the passage of many years: "We are told that men no longer believe in

D. TIMOTHY'S REPORT (3:6-8)

6 *But Timothy has just now come to us from you and has brought good news about your faith and love. He has told us that you always have pleasant memories of us and that you long to see us, just as we also long to see you.* 7 *Therefore, brothers, in all our distress and persecution we were encouraged about you because of your faith.* 8 *For now we really live, since you are standing firm in the Lord.*

Timothy's return marked a change. Where the previous section was pervaded by the note of uncertainty and stress, Paul makes it clear that with the news Timothy brought there is now reassurance and hope.

6 A new section begins at this point, and there is a real break in the sense. Paul has been speaking of what took place in the past, but here he comes virtually to the present moment. It is evident that he was writing very soon after Timothy's arrival, which he speaks of as having taken place "just now." We have seen how all the indications are that Paul had been rather depressed at the turn of events. But the coming of Timothy with news of the way in which the Thessalonian converts had not only stood firm, but had made progress in the faith, had acted on him like a tonic. He wrote immediately with a full heart. Which makes passages like 2:17–3:5 all the more poignant, for they were in fact written after Timothy's return.

Something of his joy comes out in his description of Timothy's news with the term "brought good news." The verb he employs is the one usually translated "preach the gospel."[21] Indeed, this is the only place

---

Satan; that for our generation the invisible house of bondage, with its fallen monarch, no longer exists! If this be so, a great deal more is or will be presently disbelieved in as well; but a Christian who submits to and accepts the teaching of the New Testament cannot but be struck with this fresh proof of the finished ingenuity of our great spiritual enemy. Like those masters of the art of earthly war who conquer less frequently by an ostentatious display of force on the battle field than by carefully concealed surprises which turn the position of an antagonist, so Satan, it seems, has persuaded a frivolous and shallow generation that he no longer exists but as a discredited phantom of the past, as an extinct terror, as a popular joke! Ah! he has not been at work upon the human heart for nothing during these many thousands of years; he knows how to lull us to sleep to the best advantage, that he may take our thoughts and affections, and, above all, our passions, well into his keeping" (*Sermons on Old Testament Subjects* [London, 1904], pp. 29-30).

21. εὐαγγελίζομαι. It is used of the "good news" Gabriel brought to Zechariah (Luke 1:19). But such a usage is rare in the New Testament.

in the whole of Paul's writings where it is used in any other sense than that. Some scholars have felt that the news that the Thessalonians were making progress in the Christian life was itself part of the gospel, but this seems farfetched. It is more likely that the term is used because it is the most expressive one open to Paul. For Christians generally there is no good news that can compare with the tidings that God has given us life through the death of his Son. One word became the technical term to denote this best of good news. That Paul uses it just this once for other good news is an indication of the joy that that news had brought him.

Paul enumerates three points. The first is the news about the faith of the Thessalonians. His deep concern for their faith has been noted already (vv. 2, 5). He expresses his relief now that they have not wavered in maintaining a right attitude to God.

The second point is that they had continued in love. Just as faith is the characteristic attitude of Christians toward God, so love is their characteristic attitude toward people. It stands for their complete readiness to give themselves in wholehearted service to others (see on 1:3). Timothy had gladdened Paul with the news that the Thessalonians were exercising this virtue. The combination of faith and love is no mean summary of the whole duty of Christians. As Paul says elsewhere, "neither circumcision nor uncircumcision has any value. The only thing that counts is faith expressing itself through love" (Gal. 5:6). Calvin comments: "in these two words he comprehends briefly the entire sum of true piety. Hence all that aim at this twofold mark during their whole life are beyond all risk of erring: all others, however much they may torture themselves, wander miserably."

The third point is their attitude to Paul. He had evidently wondered how far the propaganda of his enemies had been effective. He had feared that his converts might now hold him in low esteem. But he was delighted to find that not only did they remember him, but that "you cherish happy memories of us" (Phillips). The Thessalonians had not allowed hostile propaganda to distort their recollections of the visit of the great apostle. They still looked back on it with joy. They did more. They looked forward with eager longing[22] to a reunion, and were just as anxious to see Paul again as he was to see them.

---

22. The verb is ἐπιποθέω, which looks like a stronger expression than the simple ποθέω, though this cannot be pressed in view of the well-known fondness of later Greek writers for compound forms. More decisive is the fact that the verb does seem to have a marked emotional content in passages like 2 Cor. 5:2; Phil. 1:8; 2:26, and, we conclude, here also.

101

7 Paul says that he was comforted "for this cause" (*NIV,* "therefore"). He uses the singular, so that he is gathering up the faith and the love and the good remembrance and the eager desire to see him into one whole. All these were aspects of one great fact. It was the total impression left by these various facets of the attitude of the Thessalonians that meant so much. The verb "encouraged" is that used in verse 2 (where see note). It does not mean that he was soothed, but that he was given new strength. The news Timothy brought had reinvigorated him. He uses the warm address "brothers," very apt in a context in which he expresses his thankfulness for what the Thessalonians had come to mean to him. "About you" is really "upon you," where "upon" is an unusual preposition in such a connection; its significance is that Paul's new strength was securely based "on" the Thessalonians. The same preposition is used in the expression "in all our distress . . ." (*NIV,* "in"), and while it is very difficult to find one English word that will do justice to the Greek, it is not hard to grasp the force of the word. The idea is still something like "over" or "upon," and the impression it leaves is that the new strength given Paul enabled him to rise above the difficulties in which he found himself.[23]

That Paul was in no easy situation when Timothy reached him is brought out by his reference to "distress and persecution" (*LB,* "our own crushing troubles and suffering"). The former of these words basically denotes "necessity." It is that which constrains one into a certain position. From this it gets the derived notion of compulsion, and so straits, distress (cf. Luke 21:23). "Persecution" is the word used in 1:6 (where see note). We should probably not make too sharp a distinction between the two terms in this context, but the combination shows that the apostle was carrying on his work under grave difficulties and in the face of strong opposition. Rutherford renders, "We were altogether miserable and crushed; but your faith has recovered us." This is the fourth time in this chapter that Paul has mentioned the faith of the Thessalonians.[24] It was this faith that strengthened him. He comes back to it again and again. There is more to Christianity than faith, but faith is the primary thing.

8 This truth is brought out in another way in the reference to

23. "The first ἐπί denotes the basis of the encouragement; the second ἐπί the purpose for which it was welcome; and the διά the means by which it was conveyed, 'through this faith of yours' (ὑμῶν being emphatic . . .)" (Frame). Turner also points out that ὑμῶν is emphatic (M, III, p. 190); we might have expected that Paul's own faith sustained him, but he says "*your* faith."

24. He will mention it again in v. 10. He also uses the verb πιστεύω of their faith twice in this chapter.

standing fast in the Lord.[25] Elsewhere Paul speaks of standing by faith (Rom. 11:20; 1 Cor. 16:13; 2 Cor. 1:24). We need not think that this was out of his mind here. The thing that really made him rejoice, the thing that really strengthened him, the thing that gave him life, was the fact so clearly demonstrated by Timothy's mission, that the Thessalonians did indeed believe. They had a strong tie to the Lord. Their lives were characterized by faith. This meant that they had a place in God's kingdom, and this in turn indicated that Paul's work among them had not been in vain.

Elsewhere Paul writes, "to me, to live is Christ" (Phil. 1:21). The present passage gives another facet of the same truth. The service of Christ was for Paul no halfhearted thing, but that which mattered most in life. This service did not mean an idle contemplation of the excellencies of the Savior. It was the active, fruitful work of preaching Christ and his atonement among the Gentiles. Thus Paul could equally say that Christ was his life, and that it meant life to him to know that his converts were standing.[26] It was his service to Christ to win people for him ("so that by all possible means I might save some," 1 Cor. 9:22). Thus it was life indeed to know that this had happened. "You" is emphatic, which indicates some of the importance Paul attached to the conduct of the Thessalonians. At the time of which he was writing it was they and no other who were the vindication of the gospel that he preached. Similarly, the verb he uses for "stand firm" is important. It is not the ordinary word for standing. By the use of the less usual term Paul manages to convey the idea of a firmness, a steadfastness in the stand they had taken.[27]

E. PAUL'S SATISFACTION (3:9-10)

9 *How can we thank God enough for you in return for all the joy we have in the presence of our God because of you?* 10 *Night*

---

25. Commentators differ about whether νῦν should be taken as temporal or logical. The truth appears to be, as Lightfoot says, that "in a case like this it is almost impossible to distinguish the temporal sense of νῦν ('now') from the ethical ('under these circumstances'). The one meaning shades off imperceptibly into the other."

26. On this unusual use of ἐάν BDF remarks, "Sporadically ἐάν appears for εἰ (= ἐπεί)" (#372[1]). Elsewhere in the New Testament only 1 John 5:15 appears to be cited for the construction. The use of the indicative rather than the subjunctive shows something of Paul's certainty that the converts stood firm. Bruce regards the indicative as "a colloquialism."

27. The verb στήκω is a late form deriving from ἔστηκα; it means *"to stand . . . with an emphasis, to stand firm"* (GT).

*and day we pray most earnestly that we may see you again and
supply what is lacking in your faith.*

Paul's love for his Thessalonian converts and his concern for them in
the trials he knew they were undergoing and had been undergoing from
the beginning (cf. 1:6) are manifest throughout the letter. Now he asks
rhetorically how he can offer adequate thanks to God for them and speaks
once more of his constant prayers for them.

9 The turn of events could be interpreted as providing an opportunity for the founders of the church at Thessalonica to indulge in some
self-congratulation. They had built well, and their handiwork had survived a severe test. But Paul's satisfaction is not in any way self-
satisfaction; it is satisfaction at what God has wrought. He knew—
none better—that it is not of human beings to do a spiritual work. That
is done only by the grace of God. Now that he has had such a signal
manifestation of this grace he asks what thanksgiving (not "thanks" but
the expression of thanks is meant) can be rendered[28] to God for all that
he has done (cf. 2 Cor. 4:15). That he asks his question with this verb
shows that any thanksgiving he may offer is bound to be inadequate.

At the end of the verse Paul rejoices mightily at what has happened.
We should not overlook the fact that he has just referred to the troubles
in which he found himself (v. 7), but even in the middle of severe trouble
he knows that God brings joy (cf. 1:6). So Paul refers not merely to
happiness, but to joy before God; his joy is a spiritual state, a joy of
divine origin, and not a fleshly satisfaction. But if it is true that his
thoughts are God-centered, it is also true that he finds a large place for
the Thessalonians. "Our God" links Paul and the Thessalonians in the
divine presence. Findlay points out that in verses 6-10 he has used the
Greek pronoun for "you" in one of its cases no less than ten times *(CGT)*.
He dwells on the Thessalonians with frank delight.

10 In harmony with this he is always praying for them. P. T.
O'Brien points out that up to this point "issues of the past and present
have been at the centre of Paul's thanksgiving." But this petitionary
prayer looks to the future and thus "marks a major turning-point in the
whole letter."[29] The move from the concerns of the past and the present
to those of the future is significant. "Night and day" does not denote

---

28. ἀνταποδοῦναι conveys the idea of a recompense that is both due and
adequate. Lightfoot translates, "What sufficient thanks can we repay?"

29. *Introductory Thanksgivings in the Letters of Paul* (Leiden, 1977), p. 157.

prayer at two set times, but rather continued prayer. And if his prayer is continual it is also fervent, an unusual adverb being employed to bring this out.[30] Paul uses it elsewhere only in 5:13 and Ephesians 3:20, and nobody else in the New Testament employs it at all. There are various ways of expressing the thought of abundance, and this double compound is probably the most emphatic of all. There is nothing perfunctory or merely formal about Paul's prayers. They come from his heart and his passionate yearning to see his friends again. In line with this he uses here a word for "pray" that basically signifies "a want" or "a lack" rather than the more common word expressive of devotion. His prayer springs from a sense of deprivation. He feels that he needs them and he prays accordingly.

His prayer is first of all that[31] he might see them. This follows on much that he has said earlier, and that has left no doubt of his deep desire for reunion with his friends. But when he joins them again he does not want simply to talk about the weather. So he goes on to say that he prays that he may "supply what is lacking in your faith" (cf. Rom. 1:11). Notice this further reference to the faith of his converts. Throughout this chapter he has come back to their faith again and again. Yet in his joy at the faith that they undoubtedly possessed he was not oblivious of the sterner realities of the situation. His desire to be with them was accompanied[32] by the desire to be useful by remedying the defects there were in that faith.

This comes out both in the verb he employs for "supply"[33] and the noun rendered "what is lacking." The former means basically "to render complete" and of itself indicates that its object is not complete. It is used in the material sphere of such an activity as mending nets (Matt. 4:21), while in the spiritual realm the cognate noun is employed of the process of bringing the saints to perfection (Eph. 4:12). It is such a sense as this last that is in mind here. "What is lacking"[34] is our rendering of a plural noun from a root meaning "to come behind." It may be used of material

30. ὑπερεκπερισσοῦ means "*quite beyond all measure* (highest form of comparison imaginable)" (BAGD).

31. Turner says that εἰς τὸ ἰδεῖν here = ἵνα ἰδῶμεν (M, III, p. 143).

32. The closeness of the connection between the two ideas is shown by the fact that the two infinitives are linked under a single article.

33. καταρτίζω "really means 'to put into unified and good working condition'" (Bailey).

34. ὑστέρημα signifies "*lack, shortcoming* as a defect which must be removed so that perfection can be attained" (BAGD 2).

lack (2 Cor. 8:14; 9:12, etc.) but also, as here, of deficiencies in spiritual matters. The plural points us to the fact that more than one thing needed rectification. The time that the preachers had been able to spend with the Thessalonians when the church was established had been limited. It had been quite impossible to give them all the teaching that they needed, and defects were now showing up accordingly. Paul has dwelt with obvious delight on the state of the Thessalonians, but that did not mean that he was blind to their failings. As a true pastor he knew that there was much that had yet to be done for them. Timothy's report doubtless brought Paul up to date on what was still lacking in this church. It was his aim to play some part in seeing that they were set forward on the right road. He cannot be there in person to do this, so he is writing instead, and perhaps we should see chapters 4 and 5 as directed to that end.

F. PAUL'S PRAYER (3:11-13)

11 *Now may our God and Father himself and our Lord Jesus clear the way for us to come to you.* 12 *May the Lord make your love increase and overflow for each other and for everyone else, just as ours does for you.* 13 *May he strengthen your hearts so that you will be blameless and holy in the presence of our God and Father when our Lord Jesus comes with all his holy ones.*

Out of all that has happened Paul utters a prayer that we might have expected to be one of thanksgiving, but that is concerned rather with his constant hope to return to Thessalonica and with what he wants God to do in his friends there. He still looks for the greatest possible achievement in their Christian lives, and the rest of the letter may be regarded as setting forth the things for which Paul here prays.

11 It is characteristic of Paul's letters that he frequently slips into some short prayer. Thus at this point, where he is so concerned with his friends at Thessalonica and has given such evidence of his desire to be with them, he breaks out in a prayer that God will bring them together. It is typical that he should speak of God as directing him to them, and not simply of his paying a visit or the like. Paul does not forget that God rules in the affairs of this world; even his incidental expressions reveal how much the sovereignty of God means to him. He speaks of God as "our God and Father," a manner of address that brings out the characteristic Christian insight into the nature of God. The possessive "our" directs attention to the personal relationship that has been established. It is God's nature to be Father. But it is not the teaching of Scripture that he is indiscriminately a Father to all people. Rather, he makes provision for people to become sons by adoption (cf. Rom. 8:15; Gal. 4:5, etc.). But both Paul and his friends had entered the heavenly family by faith. Thus he can make use of "our" when he speaks of the Father.[35]

It is significant for Paul's understanding of the nature of the Godhead that he joins so closely his references to the Father and to the Son. Here he links the two by making them the joint subject of a verb that is in the singular (cf. 2 Thess. 2:16-17).[36] This is not a formal trinitarian definition, but it is the kind of understanding of the nature of the Godhead that led inevitably to the formulation of the dogma of the Trinity. This is all the more impressive in that it is done incidentally. Paul is not giving a theoretical discourse on the nature of deity, but engaging in prayer. Out of his understanding of God there proceeds naturally this form of expression in which the highest place is given to Jesus. In the first edition I said "Full deity is ascribed to Him," which has not unnaturally been held to mean "ascribed to him in this passage." It would give a clearer statement of my position if I were to say that what Paul says about Christ throughout his letters ascribes full deity to the Lord and that what he says here arises naturally from that basic position. These words do not

35. Some commentators have felt that αὐτός is emphatic and that, taken in conjunction with the adversative δέ, there is a strong contrast between God and either people praying (v. 10) or Satan. This seems unlikely. δέ introduces a new section of the letter and does not seem to be strongly adversative (so Best). The emphatic αὐτός is sufficiently accounted for by Paul's stress on God's active rule in the affairs of people (cf. 5:23; 2 Thess. 2:16, etc.).

36. When two or more words constitute the subject, a verb that precedes the subjects or stands between them normally agrees with the first subject (see M, III, pp. 313-14). But here the double subject precedes the verb. The best explanation seems to be that Paul sees the two subjects as essentially a unity. This construction is found in Matt. 5:18; Jas. 5:3, and some other places, so that it cannot be said that the singular verb proves the oneness of Father and Son. But it can be said that in such cases it is "the totality that is emphasized" (Robertson, p. 405). J. A. Hewett objects to my saying "Full deity is ascribed to Him" (i.e., Christ), but he goes on to say that Paul used this construction "in order to avoid either a *complete separation* or a *complete merging* of the two to whom he prayed" (*ET* LXXXVII [1975-76], p. 54). I am not trying to say more. Paul did hold to the deity of Christ, and this construction arises naturally from that conviction. See further my *New Testament Theology* (Grand Rapids, 1986), pp. 42-43. Bruce does not consider the construction in itself "theologically significant," but Best finds it "surprising" and points out that "the singular may be used in Greek where two subjects are regularly thought of together."

prove the full deity of Christ, but they arise naturally out of this doctrine.[37] In that Paul feels no necessity to produce arguments to demonstrate this we must feel that the point was accepted just as fully by the Thessalonians as by the apostle. And in view of the early date of this writing it is important for the development of Christian doctrine. The deity of Christ was apparently accepted without question rather less than twenty years after the resurrection. It is not to be regarded as the culmination of a lengthy process of growth and reflection.

Paul prays that his God will "clear" his way to the Thessalonians.[38] The verb has the idea of "making straight," perhaps even of "making level." The imagery appears to be that of preparing a road so that all unevenness is removed and travel facilitated. Paul looks to God to remove the obstacles that until this time had prevented him from paying the longed-for visit to the Thessalonians.

12 Paul begins this verse with "But" (which *NIV* omits). The Greek conjunction is adversative, and the sense of it is "whatever be the case with me and my companions, as for you, may the Lord. . . ." Paul says something like "May the Lord make you to increase and abound in love" (rather than *NIV*'s "make your love increase . . ."), where "you" is emphatic, setting the Thessalonians over against Paul and his companions. Paul could desire earnestly to be with his friends and impart to them some spiritual gift. But he recognizes that their spiritual growth was in the Lord's hands, not his. So his prayer moves on from his own desire to see them again to the more important matter of their growth in the faith. Theoretically "the Lord" could refer to either of the Persons just mentioned, the Father or the Son, but it is Paul's habit to refer to Jesus by this title. The probability, then, is that it is the Lord Jesus that he has in mind here. There are several passages in these epistles where the Father and the Son are linked very closely (see the passages listed in the note on 1:1). It is evident that Paul did not separate them very decisively in his thought.[39]

---

37. Cf. Marshall, "Paul *assumes* the divinity of Jesus—to call him 'Son of God' in the way in which Paul uses the phrase cannot mean anything else."

38. In this verse and the next we have three of Paul's 15 uses of what Chamberlain calls the "volitive optative" (i.e., exclusive of μὴ γένοιτο, which occurs another 15 times in Paul): κατευθῦναι, πλεονάσαι and περισσεύσαι (see the list in Chamberlain, *Exegetical Grammar,* pp. 83-84). Moule remarks that the optative may express "a *wish*, one might say, as distinct from the more resolute *resolve* of the hortatory Subjunctive" (*IBNTG*, p. 23). Here he finds the optative "of prayerful expectation," as also in 5:23; 2 Thess. 3:16 (*ibid.*, p. 136).

39. "The importance here is that Paul does not distinguish the two" (Whiteley).

Paul goes on to pray that his friends will increase in love. Some exegetes make a distinction between the two verbs he uses, but they seem to be more or less synonymous. The apostle's use of both rather than one of them is a device for giving emphasis to what he is saying.[40] The latter verb is the more emphatic, and it is used by Paul much more frequently than the former, which in this transitive sense is found only here in the New Testament. The latter is often used of the divine grace abounding. Paul looked for Christians to abound in love just as the grace of God abounds in them.

Christians should have a special regard for one another within the family of God.[41] They should also look on those outside the family as God does, with love (cf. *JB*, "love . . . the whole human race"). Paul brings both these thoughts into his prayer, and he makes petition that they may increase in love (for the specifically Christian idea of love see the note on 1:3). It is love for people quite apart from their worthiness or otherwise, a love that proceeds in the first place from the loving heart of God. When the miracle takes place and someone passes from death to life, when someone becomes a new creature in Christ Jesus, then that person comes to see people in a measure as God sees them. He comes to love them selflessly.[42] Paul has already recognized that the Thessalonians exercise this quality, and his prayer at this point is that they may increase in this divine activity. Characteristically he appeals to the example he had set them (see on 1:6). Paul knew full well that no preacher can call on people to do what he himself is not prepared to do. He did not hesitate on more than one occasion to point out that he practiced what he preached. It may be that under modern conditions the preacher is not wise to direct attention to himself. But it is still as true as ever that if a preacher's message is to carry conviction it must first be found true in his own life.

13 While Paul was interested in the here and now he was not preoccupied with this present life. His prayer looks forward to the second

40. Cf. Chrysostom, "Do you see the unchecked madness of love which is indicated by the words? He says πλεονάσαι and περισσεύσαι instead of αὐξήσει" (cited by Frame).

41. I have drawn attention to the fact and the importance of brotherly love among New Testament Christians in *Testaments of Love* (Grand Rapids, 1981), pp. 203-11. It is doubtful whether the infant church could have survived without it.

42. Moffatt comments, "no form of ἁγιωσύνη which sits loose to the endless obligations of this ἀγάπη will stand the strain of this life or the scrutiny of God's tribunal at the end" *(EGT)*.

coming of the Lord. The abounding for which he prays is in order that the Thessalonians may be unshaken even at the second coming. We have met the verb "strengthen" in verse 2 (where see note). The prayer here is that God will so supply the needed buttress that the Thessalonians will remain firm and unmoved whatever the future may hold. The heart, as in 2:4 (where see note), stands for the whole of the inner life and not simply for the seat of the emotions, as with us. It is easy enough for people to become prey to fears and alarms, to take up every new doctrine, to accept the unreasoning hope that leads inevitably to irresolution, disillusionment, and disaster. Paul longs to see his converts delivered from all such instability. He prays that they may have such a sure basis in love that they will be delivered from all this sort of thing. If God gives them this good gift he will establish their whole personality.

Yet we must not think of this as nothing more than a prayer for personal calm and confidence. There is in Paul's complex thought for them a pronounced ethical and spiritual element. This comes out in the succeeding expressions. He prays that they may be "blameless." Nothing less than the very highest standard will do for the Christian. Even before he became a Christian Paul felt that this word could be applied to his conduct (Phil. 3:6). The Christian certainly can have no lower standard. Indeed, the word has a fuller meaning here. In Philippians Paul had claimed blamelessness only as regards "a righteousness . . . that comes from the law," but there is no such limitation here. Rather, the thought is of blamelessness before God. We should be in no doubt as to the high standard that is set before us.

But the thought is not exclusively ethical. The apostle goes on to bring in the notion of holiness, in which the basic idea is that of being set apart for God. Paul's word is one that signifies the state rather than the process. In the Greek Old Testament it is used only of God himself, and in the New Testament it is applied to people in only one other passage (2 Cor. 7:1). Paul leaves no doubt as to the wholeheartedness with which the Christian is given over to his Lord. The most usual designation of Christians in the New Testament is simply "the holy ones," or, as we usually translate it, "the saints," the word being from this same root. Believers do not simply live uprightly; they belong to God and thus are set apart entirely for God's service. Paul's prayer is that this may be fully realized among the Thessalonians.

The apostle takes this notion as far as it will go by bringing in the thought of the second coming (see on 2:19). He prays that right through, until this event that will usher in the end of this age, the Thessalonians will realize the glorious destiny of which he has been speaking. It is that aspect of the Parousia which means the end of this present form of existence that is in mind.

There is something of a difficulty with the final expression, rendered "with all his holy ones." As we have just seen, this is the way Christians are most commonly referred to in the New Testament, but the word can scarcely have that meaning here. These "holy ones" will be coming with Jesus, and Paul is praying that believers *on earth* will have their hearts established at that coming. He is distinguishing between believers on earth and the "holy ones" who will come with the Lord.

But "holy ones" is an expression that lends itself to other meanings. In particular, angels may be meant,[43] or the saints who have departed this life. Good but not decisive arguments can be ranged in support of either view. Thus angels are designated "holy ones" in the Greek Old Testament, the Bible of the early church (Ps. 89:5; Dan. 4:13 [Th.]; 8:13; Zech. 14:5). Angels are also associated with the second coming in the New Testament (Matt. 13:41; 25:31; Mark 8:38; Luke 9:26; 2 Thess. 1:7). In view of the fact that the Qumran scrolls bring us examples of Jewish literature of the immediate pre-Christian era it may not be without significance that they use the term "holy ones" of angels. Millar Burrows tells us that the *Manual of Discipline* mostly uses "angel" for evil spirits. For good spirits it prefers "holy ones" or "sons of heaven." Similarly, the *Thanksgiving Psalms* refer to "the army of the holy ones" and "the assembly of thy holy ones."[44] It is clear that in the Judaism of the post-Old Testament period "holy ones" was an accepted designation of angels. Against this identification is the fact that angels never seem to be called simply "holy ones" in the New Testament. As used by the early Christians this expression seems always elsewhere to refer to people; it is the term for the "saints," those who have been made holy by the saving work of Jesus and the indwelling of the Holy Spirit.

In this particular case there seems to be no reason for holding that Paul's thought is limited to one class or the other. Those who do this do not usually give attention to the facts (a) that in Scripture "holy ones" clearly sometimes means angels and sometimes means believers, and (b) that here Paul speaks of "all" God's holy ones. After all, "all" is a

43. Best inclines to this view, though allowing that "saints" is "a real alternative"; he rejects the view that both are in mind. Marshall and Whiteley also see a reference to angels.

44. Millar Burrows, *The Dead Sea Scrolls* (London, 1956), pp. 261-62.

very inclusive term. It is clear from the New Testament that both angels and the departed saints will be associated with the Lord when he returns. There seems to be no reason at all why Paul should be intending to eliminate one of these classes at this point. It is best to understand the "holy ones" as all those beings who will make up his train, be they angels or the saints who have gone before.[45]

45. This interpretation is accepted by such commentators as Bengel, Neil, Lightfoot, and Milligan, and by O. Allis, *Prophecy in the Church* (Philadelphia, 1945), pp. 185ff. Thomas, however, says that this possibility "can be eliminated in that Paul would hardly include two such diverse groups in the same category." It is, however, precarious to argue as to what Paul would or would not do, and Thomas does not face the critical fact that the apostle prays here that his correspondents will be strengthened at the coming of the Lord, which seems to mean that they will be here on earth, while "the holy ones" will be with Jesus at his coming. It is intelligible to say that there are certain "holy ones" who come with Jesus and to link those on earth with them, but it is scarcely so to limit the "holy ones" who are expressly said to come with him to those awaiting him on earth.

1 THESSALONIANS 4

V. EXHORTATION TO CHRISTIAN LIVING (4:1-12)

A. GENERAL EXHORTATIONS (4:1-2)

1 *Finally, brothers, we instructed you how to live in order to please God, as in fact you are living. Now we ask you and urge you in the Lord Jesus to do this more and more.* 2 *You know what instructions we gave you by the authority of the Lord Jesus.*

It is Paul's habit to treat doctrinal matters, answers to correspondents, and the like in the earlier part of his epistles. Then at the end he deals with the practical implications for living the Christian life. Throughout this letter his concern for spiritual advance in the Thessalonian church has surfaced a number of times, but now he gives it more concentrated attention. Until now he has had a good deal to say about what had happened in the Thessalonian church, but now he launches into a section telling them what they should do and there is a sharp rise in the use of imperatives.

1 "Finally therefore" (*NIV* omits Paul's "therefore") is an expression that marks the transition to the way the Christian life is to be lived. It does not mean, as the English might suggest, that Paul is in process of ending the letter (Whiteley speaks of "Finally" as a "mistranslation"). It does signify that the main section of the letter is concluded, though the subsidiary section that it introduces may be rather lengthy and very important.[1] "Therefore" may refer to the whole of the preceding

---

1. The expression is λοιπὸν οὖν, a combination found nowhere else in the New Testament, though Milligan says that it occurs in the papyri. λοιπόν or τὸ λοιπόν however, is reasonably common (λοιπόν is read here by some MSS). It means "for the rest" and may introduce an additional item (as in 1 Cor. 1:16) as well as a section of an epistle. Milligan thinks that in late Greek "it is practically equivalent to an

113

argument rather than to the immediately preceding words (so Thomas; Bailey, however, refers it to the preceding sentence).

Paul's exhortation to the Thessalonians is meant very seriously. He underlines it with the double injunction, "we ask you and urge you." The two verbs have their own proper meanings, but in this context the difference is not important; they simply reinforce one another, and the combination gives emphasis to the apostle's request.[2] The affectionate "brothers" fits into this pattern, for Paul is putting the right way before people who were dear friends of his. Indeed, it is this which makes his exhortation so very important to him. He exhorts them "in the Lord Jesus." That is to say, he is not taking up any position of superiority, nor, on the other hand, is his attitude one of hesitant timidity. He speaks as one who has authority committed to him by the Lord. He speaks as one who has "the mind of Christ" (1 Cor. 2:16). He speaks to people who themselves are in Christ.[3] He speaks of the conduct that befits people in Christ. *NIV* has paraphrased this verse, which more literally reads, "Finally therefore, brothers, we ask you and exhort in the Lord Jesus that, as you received from us how you must walk and please God, just as you are also walking, that you may abound more." "Received" translates a verb that had something of the technical sense of accepting the tradition handed on in Christian circles.[4]

---

emphatic οὖν." Bailey says, "It indicates only that they are making a definite transition in the discussion." Cf. *REB,* "and now."

2. The two verbs occur in 5:12, 14 and, of course, in Phil. 4:2-3 (where there does seem to be a difference in meaning). On the use of ἐρωτάω Findlay remarks, "Ἐρωτάω conceives the request in a question form ('Will you do so and so?') . . . thus gives a personal urgency to it, challenging the answer as αἰτέω does not" (*CGT*).

3. The position of ἐν κυρίῳ Ἰησοῦ at the end of the clause, with ὑμᾶς between the two verbs, probably means that "in the Lord Jesus" is to be taken with the verbs or with "we," the subject, rather than with ὑμᾶς. However, the connection is not so strong that a side glance at ὑμᾶς may not be included, especially since Paul elsewhere insists that the Thessalonians, too, were in Christ. It is, of course, possible to take the Greek in the sense, "we ask you and urge. . . ." The main point, though, is the authority with which Paul speaks, an authority proceeding from the fact that he is "in the Lord Jesus."

4. παραλαμβάνω was used outside Christianity as well as inside it: G. Delling speaks of great figures like Plato and Aristotle as employing it to express their link to earlier generations (*TDNT*, IV, p. 11). He shows that Paul used it for his inheriting "the formulated laws of Christian morality," but also that the apostle "emphasises very strongly that the life which he passes on is not in any sense inherited by him from human bearers of revelation . . . but that he has received it directly from the Author of this revelation on the Damascus road" (*ibid.,* pp. 13, 14). Paul can appeal to the tradition that had been received in churches not of his foundation (cf. Rom.

In these first two verses Paul is not concerned with specific problems of behavior (though he is using them to introduce his treatment of some specific problems), but with the whole of the Christian life. His expression is stronger than *NIV,* for he says "how you must[5] walk and please God" and goes on to speak of "abounding." "Walk" is commonly employed, especially by Paul and John, as a way of referring to the whole of a believer's manner of living (cf. 2:12). So common is this use of the verb that Grimm-Thayer can give as one of the meanings of the word, "Hebraistically, *to live*" (cf. the rabbinic concept of *halakhah*). This may connect with the fact that a favorite designation of Christianity in the earliest days was "the Way" (Acts 9:2; 19:23; 24:22). Or it may be that the metaphor suggested itself from the idea of continual, if unspectacular, advance, which should of course characterize the Christian. Walking is connected with pleasing God (for "please" see on 2:4). The whole Christian life is God-centered. Christians do not "walk" with a view to obtaining the maximum amount of satisfaction for themselves but in order to please their Lord (elsewhere Paul warns against walking in evil paths, 2 Cor. 4:2; 10:2). Paul does not specify any particular way in which they should "please" God; he is concerned with the whole bent of the life.

There is nothing new in all this, as Paul is at pains to make clear. He had told the Thessalonians to live in this way at the time of his mission among them ("as you received from us"), and he is not now introducing some novelty. He had told them then that they "must" behave in the fashion outlined, and thus had brought before them the compelling necessity under which Christians live. When anyone is saved by the work of Christ it does not lie open before him as a matter for his completely free decision whether he will serve God or not. He has been bought with a price (1 Cor. 6:20). He has become the slave of Christ. Christian service is not an optional extra for those who like that sort of thing. It is a compelling obligation that lies on each one of the redeemed.

It is Paul's habit to blend his exhortations and reproofs with a judicious mixture of praise where that can in good conscience be done. It does not surprise us accordingly to find him interjecting, "just as ye

---

6:17); the tradition was not a Pauline idiosyncrasy but teaching handed down throughout the church. παραλαμβάνω is also the verb usually employed to denote the receiving of the message by converts (e.g., 1 Cor. 15:3). It has reference rather to the formal external act of reception than to the subjective act of welcoming (δέχομαι); cf. 2:13 (where see note).

5. δεῖ.

are also walking." He is not complaining that the Thessalonians had not been living out the Christian life. They had heeded the exhortation when it was originally given (cf. 1:3, 6-10, etc.), and Timothy's report showed that they were still putting it into practice. Paul lets them know that he is not unmindful of their achievement. But the Christian can never rest satisfied. So Paul urges them to further endeavor. The substance of his exhortation is that[6] they should "abound more and more." This is an unusual way to employ this verb, for it is much more common to specify the quality that is to abound. This is the case, for example, in 3:12, where the apostle speaks of abounding in love (cf. Phil. 1:9). The absence of any such specific virtue in this place is in keeping with the fact that this is the general introduction, and Paul is dealing with the whole of life. Specific instructions are to follow, but here he is concerned with the thought that Christians are to grow continually. Their lives are to be far from static. Paradoxically it can be said of them that they are the slaves of Christ and at the same time that they are the freest of people (John 8:36).[7] The Thessalonians were under the necessity of living to please God, but far from leading them into a narrow and cramped existence, this opened for them the door to the abundant life (cf. John 10:10).

2 Again Paul looks back to the days of his visit to assure his readers that he is doing no more than to lead them along the way he had showed them then. "You know," he says, calling them to witness to the truth of what he is saying. The word "instructions" is plural: Paul and his companions had given instructions on several matters, possibly in the form of rules. The word is an unusual one in a Christian context; it is found elsewhere in the New Testament of commands to believers only twice (1 Tim. 1:5, 18). It is more at home in a military environment, being a usual word for the commands given by an officer to his men (cf. its use in Acts 5:28; 16:24).[8] It is thus a word with a ring of authority. It is this which makes it suitable for this context where Paul is stressing the authoritative nature of the injunctions in question.

---

6. ἵνα here resumes the ἵνα earlier in the verse; so much has been included between "beseech and exhort you . . . that" and the content of the exhortation that Paul puts in another ἵνα to make it clear.

7. Cf. the remark of Martin Luther, "A Christian man is a perfectly free lord of all, subject to none. A Christian is a perfectly dutiful servant of all, subject to all" (*The Works of Martin Luther* [Philadelphia, 1915-32], II, p. 312).

8. παραγγελία is probably a command passed along (παρά) a line of soldiers. From this it comes to signify any authoritative order. Though this noun is rare in the New Testament, the cognate verb is used quite often.

These, though given by Paul, did not originate with him. He makes the point that they were given "through the Lord Jesus" (*NIV* has "by the authority of the Lord Jesus"). "Through" is not the preposition that we might have expected. It may be a shorthand way of saying that the commandments referred to came from the Father, and that therefore they came with all the authority that was possible. Or it may mean that Paul spoke only on the authority of the Lord Jesus.[9] Either way he is disclaiming personal responsibility and ascribing the highest authority to the injunctions to which he refers.[10]

B. SEXUAL PURITY (4:3-8)

3 *It is God's will that you should be holy; that you should avoid sexual immorality;* 4 *that each of you should learn to control his own body*[a] *in a way that is holy and honorable,* 5 *not in passionate lust like the heathen, who do not know God;* 6 *and that in this matter no one should wrong his brother or take advantage of him. The Lord will punish men for all such sins, as we have already told you and warned you.* 7 *For God did not call us to be impure, but to live a holy life.* 8 *Therefore, he who rejects this instruction does not reject man but God, who gives you his Holy Spirit.*

[a]4 Or *learn to live with his own wife* or *learn to acquire a wife*

It comes as something of a surprise to modern people to find an exhortation to sexual purity in the forefront of practical directions to a Christian church. This, however, was very much in place in writing to the inhabitants of a first-century Greek city, for among the Greeks sexual sin was but lightly condemned.[11] Continence was regarded as an unreasonable demand on a

9. Moule gives the meaning as "in the name of the Lord Jesus," though he proceeds to ask whether it may not signify "as those who are in contact with the Lord Jesus" (*IBNTG*, pp. 57-58). Plainly the expression indicates that the words to which it refers are authoritative.

10. Either way also he is connecting the Father and the Son in the closest possible fashion. Denney cites this as one of the passages in which we see "this co-ordination of Christ with the Father, this elevation into the sphere of the divine in which Christ and the Father work harmoniously the salvation of men." Denney proceeds, "Every function of the Christian life is determined by it" (*Jesus and the Gospel* [London, 1908], pp. 31-32). See also the comment on 3:11.

11. This is not surprising considering the questionable morality of their gods and goddesses. As Rolston remarks, "It was difficult to feel a sense of guilt in the

man. In society at large it was taken for granted that men would naturally seek the satisfaction of their sexual desires outside the marriage bond. The pressure to conform to the easy standards accepted throughout society must have been strong on the early church[12]—especially so since so large a proportion of its membership consisted of men and women of limited ability and circumscribed outlook, men and women, moreover, who of necessity were imperfectly instructed in the Christian faith. Yet the leaders of the church did not compromise for one moment. They knew that God required of them the highest standard, and they had no authority to lower that standard. Thus they refused to allow the practice of the Christian church to be determined by the ideas of contemporary society.

What Paul is saying is not to be understood as no more than a useful regulation applicable to first-century Christians only. It is of continuing relevance. Just as much in the twentieth century as in the first it must be insisted that Christian standards are to be taken from God and not from the low ideals of contemporary society. This is true of all of life, but we must not overlook its relevance in the sphere of sexual morality. Paul does not mention any specific sin of this kind as having taken place among the Thessalonians (contrast 1 Cor. 5:1ff.), and there is no reason for thinking that the Thessalonians had actually given way to the temptation. The strong warning is probably to be understood in the light of the prevalence of low standards. It is meant to prevent rather than to rebuke sin. Had a definite case occurred we must think that Paul would have been much more direct. But he takes no risks with his beloved Thessalonians and so he warns them.

3 The apostle puts chastity before his readers as "God's will."

---

presence of the gods of Greece and Rome." This was not the case among the Jews. SBk, e.g., cite rabbinic statements that regard unchastity as incompatible with holiness.

12. This pressure would be even stronger at Thessalonica if, as Lightfoot thought, the cult of the Kabeiroi there promoted "gross immorality . . . under the name of religion," and gave rise to "foul orgies" (*Biblical Essays* [London, 1893], p. 258). Such practices were common in many forms of worship, and there is nothing improbable in Lightfoot's suggestion (though Bruce regards it as doubtful). R. Jewett regards "the Cabiric cult" as an important part of the life of Thessalonica. Cabirus, he says, was "a martyred hero, murdered by his brothers, buried with symbols of royal power, and expected to return to help lowly individuals and the city of Thessalonica in particular" (*The Thessalonian Correspondence,* p. 128). Jewett holds that what had been a popular and significant part of the life of the Thessalonian community had been incorporated into the civic cult of Thessalonica, one result of which was that many humble Thessalonians felt that they had lost their cult figure. He thinks that this may have been a factor in their decision to turn to Christ.

"Will" is without the article in the Greek, the force of which is that this is not the whole of God's will for them. God's will includes many things,[13] but of great importance for them is the one of which Paul speaks. Paul's direction, then, is on the very highest plane. He does not speak on the level of ethics or prudence or ecclesiastical regulations. This is what God wants his people to do and there could be no higher sanction.

This is Paul's point also in referring to sanctification ("that you should be holy"), which is "at once a gift and a demand" (Wilson). We have already noticed the consistent New Testament doctrine that everyone who believes is holy, that is, set apart for God (see on 3:13). We come to Christ in all our sin, and we receive cleansing by his atoning death. Then day by day we become more and more what God would have us to be. We increasingly experience the reality of being set apart for him. Sanctification is the name given to this process, as holiness is to the final state. When Paul speaks here of sanctification as God's will for the Thessalonian converts, he is reminding them of the implications of their having been purchased by the blood of Christ. Henceforth they belong to God and their lives must reflect this. But Paul is not here concerned with a general dissertation on the dedicated Christian life. He is dealing with the particular aspect of sexual purity. So he proceeds to the point "that you should avoid[14] sexual immorality." His verb is a strong one, and it is reinforced by a preposition that emphasizes the separation. The Christian must have no truck with this evil thing. The noun strictly means fornication, but it is used of all forms of illicit sexual intercourse.[15] These are incompatible with the sanctification required of a Christian. The whole question of sex relationships has to be viewed in the light of the fact that the body of the Christian belongs to God (cf. 1 Cor. 6:19-20).

4 Having said negatively that one should abstain from certain forms of conduct, Paul now puts the positive side of the same truth,

---

13. Lightfoot and Frame cite Bengel: *multae sunt voluntates*. Bruce maintains that "the will of God for his people is not wider than their sanctification," but Best says, "Paul is not giving the total extent of that will but its relevance to one sphere of conduct." See 5:18 for a repetition of the clause about the will of God.

14. For the complex construction with its succession of infinitives in this and the next verse see the note in Frame.

15. The word is πορνεία, strictly the use of the harlot (πόρνη), but applied to all forms of sexual sin. A. J. Mason writes, "The word is often used in late Greek for any kind of impurity . . . but here it must be understood in its strict sense. To the Gentile mind, while the wickedness of adultery or incest was fully recognized, it was a novelty to be told that fornication was a 'deadly sin'" *(ad loc.)*.

namely, that people should live continently. He says, "that each of you should learn . . ." (the verb means "know"), as though it would be impossible for any believer who knows what this sin really is to engage in it. The big problem in this verse is to know exactly what he had in mind in the expression *NIV* translates "to control his own body" (so *REB*), but there are some ancient and many more recent commentators (e.g., Best, Moore) who maintain that in this passage it signifies "wife" (so *RSV*). In favor of the former are the facts that the early Greek commentators usually understand it this way. The word literally means "vessel," and this word without qualification does not often mean "body," though it certainly has this meaning on some occasions.[16] This, for example, is the way it is to be understood in the incident in which David asked Ahimelech for bread and was told that there was holy bread "if only the young men have kept themselves from women" and included in his reply the words "when I came out, the vessels of the young men were holy . . . how much more then today shall their vessels be holy?" (1 Sam. 21:4-5; Bruce draws attention to this passage and sees it as referring to the body).[17] There are also partial parallels, such as the reference to treasure "in earthen vessels" (2 Cor. 4:7). Moreover, in Greek writers generally, the body is often thought of as the instrument or vessel of the soul. The big difficulty in the way of accepting "body" as the meaning is the verb, which really means "to acquire," and it is not easy to see how a man can "acquire" his own body. There is, however, evidence from the papyri that it could be used in the sense "possess,"[18] so this difficulty is not insuperable.[19]

16. In *The Epistle of Barnabas* 7:3; 11:9 we have the expression "the vessel of His Spirit" (τὸ σκεῦος τοῦ πνεύματος αὐτοῦ), which refers to the body of our Lord. Again in Hermas, *Mandate* 5:2, σκεῦος is the vessel in which the Holy Spirit dwells. LSJ note "the *body,* as the *vessel* of the soul" as one meaning of the word and class this passage under that head.

17. Bruce thinks that the expression refers specifically to "the *genitalia,*" and J. Whitton, in an article entitled "A Neglected Meaning for *SKEUOS* in 1 Thessalonians 4.4" (*NTS* 28 [1982], pp. 142-43) notes the use of the Hebrew equivalent as "a euphemism for the male organ" and argues that the meaning here is "controlling one's sexual urge."

18. MM cite a papyrus dated A.D. 23 where κτάομαι is used with the meaning "have": "I swear that I have thirty days in which to restore to you the man whom I bailed out of the public prison." A meaning like "acquire" is impossible here. It should, however, be added that their own opinion of the verb in this verse is that it means "gradually obtain the complete mastery of the body." The perfect of the verb is, of course, used regularly in the sense "to have acquired," "to possess." The importance of the papyrus cited is that it shows that the present took on this meaning also. LSJ cite Luke 18:12 as another example of this use. ·

19. Some exegetes see a difficulty also in the use of ἑαυτοῦ, feeling that it is

A few early commentators like Theodore of Mopsuestia and Augustine held that the word means "wife," and a good number of modern writers follow them. The strongest argument for this view appears to be that there are a few passages where this verb, in combination with "woman," means "to marry."[20] This is said to be supported by the reference to the wife as "the weaker vessel" (1 Pet. 3:7). This latter argument must, however, be discounted, for the wife is not spoken of as the husband's "vessel" at all. Both are "vessels" of the Holy Spirit, the wife being the weaker. Thus the passage does not really bear on our problem. Among the rabbis the Hebrew equivalent of the Greek word here is used of the wife,[21] and this may have influenced Paul.

It is not easy to decide the point, but it does seem that it would not be very natural for a Greek writer to speak of a wife as a "vessel." And in this case it would be the less likely since Paul is inculcating a high view of marriage, whereas it is a very low view that sees the wife as no more than a vessel for gratifying the husband's sexual desires. We should also bear in mind that this comes in a letter addressed to the whole church, women as well as men, and it is impossible for a woman (married or single) to acquire a wife. This, taken in conjunction with the positive evidence above, inclines me to the view that "body" is meant. Paul then is exhorting his Thessalonian friends to keep their bodies pure. He does not use the term "pure," but prefers to use the idea of sanctification again, and with it he joins honor. There is a right use for a body that is set apart for the service of God. Sanctification excludes impurity. Again, impurity dishonors the body, so that Paul's linking of honor with sanctification is much in point.[22] Lightfoot well remarks: "The honour due to the body as such is one of the great contrasts which Christianity offers to the loftiest systems of heathen philosophy (e.g., Platonism and Stoicism)."[23]

---

inapplicable to the body. However, the word is often used in a nonemphatic way in late Greek, and this is to be taken as an example of such. Mason thinks that it means "the vessel or instrument which consists of himself" *(ad loc.)*.

20. GT cite two passages in LXX and one in Xenophon for this usage.

21. See the passages in SBk, III, pp. 632-33. C. Maurer, however, shows that in Judaism "purely formally" the word "is used of the woman only in a figurative sense. But the underlying phrases 'to use as a vessel,' 'to make one's vessel,' etc. are to be regarded as established euphemisms for sexual intercourse" *(TDNT,* VII, p. 362).

22. ἁγιασμῷ and τιμῇ are linked by one preposition, ἐν, and Findlay comments, "the 'honour' of the human person has a religious basis in the devotion of the body and its functions to God" *(CGT)*.

23. Cf. the comment of C. Wordsworth: "The deadly sin here reprobated . . . was excused by parents *(Terent.* Adelph. I.ii.21), *commended* by moralists *(Horat.* I Sat. ii.32; cp. *Cicero pro Coelio* 48), and consecrated by the Religion of Heathenism,

5 The positive state of sanctification and honor is further defined, the absence of a connecting particle showing that the same idea carries on. The God-empowered person rules his body and is not caught in the grip of uncontrollable sexual desires, what Paul here calls "the passion of lust"[24] (for the combination cf. Gal. 5:24; Col. 3:5). The word "passion" is always used by Paul in a bad sense. It denotes not so much a violent desire, which the English "passion" suggests, as an overmastering desire. The root connects with the thought of suffering, and the noun expresses the feeling that anyone suffers. It expresses the passive side of the vice. "Lust," on the other hand, is the active, aggressive word.[25] It is used of strong desire of any kind. Occasionally it is used of some good desire, as in 2:17 (where see note), but more characteristically it denotes an evil desire, and that a very strong one. Paul is picturing people who give themselves over to their lusts.

This conduct, Paul says, is typical of "the heathen" (perhaps better "the Gentiles"). The word is a very general one, and means "the nations." As used by the Jews in its normal sense it denotes the entire non-Jewish world, and we become accustomed to it as signifying non-Jews. It is not usual to find it in the sense "non-Christians," but that is quite plainly the meaning here. This does not mean that Paul is including the Jews among

---

especially in Greece, and particularly at *Corinth* where St. Paul now was" *(ad loc.)*. Similarly, W. E. H. Lecky says, "In Greece monogamy, though not without exceptions, had been enforced, but a concurrence of influences very unfavourable to chastity prevented any high standard being attained among the men, and almost every form of sensual indulgence beyond the limits of marriage was permitted" *(History of European Morals* [London, 1869], pp. 106-7).

24. It has been remarked that "to take a wife in the passion of lust" (which would be required if we took σκεῦος as meaning "wife" in v. 4) is "an extraordinarily strange idea."

25. GT give the difference between the two words πάθος and ἐπιθυμία thus: "π. presents the passive, ἐπ. the active side of a vice; ἐπ. is more comprehensive in meaning than π.; ἐπ. is (evil) desire, π. ungovernable desire" *(sub* πάθος). Similarly, J. B. Lightfoot says, "While πάθος includes all ungovernable affections, ἐπιθυμία κακή reaches to all evil longings" *(St Paul's Epistles to the Colossians and to Philemon* [London, 1876], p. 212). Trench affirms that ἐπιθυμία "in Scripture is the larger word, including the whole world of active lusts and desires, all to which the σάρξ, as the seat of desire and of the natural appetites, impels; while the πάθος is rather the 'morosa delectatio,' not so much the soul's disease in its more active operations, as the diseased condition out of which these spring . . . the 'lustfulness' ('Leidenschaft') as distinguished from the 'lust' " (Trench, p. 324). AS says that πάθος "represents the passive, ungoverned aspect of evil desire, as opp. to ἐπιθυμία, which is the active and also the more comprehensive term" *(sub* πάθος).

those who succumbed to impurity, for their high moral standards were well known. Rather, he is thinking of Christians (who at Thessalonica were predominantly non-Jewish in origin, as we see from 1:9) as non-Gentiles. He is dividing the world into Christians and Gentiles. It is an eloquent commentary on the lax standards of sexual morality that were prevalent that Paul speaks of sexual vice as so entirely characteristic of the world of his day.

He puts it all down to people's ignorance of God. They are "Gentiles who do not know God." His thought on this matter is more fully developed in the first chapter of Romans, where he points out that they rejected the knowledge of God that was afforded them: "they did not think it worthwhile to retain the knowledge of God" (Rom. 1:28). Because of this, God delivered them up to unnatural lusts (Rom. 1:24, 26, 28). It is a solemn thought that those who reject the knowledge of God that has been afforded them thereby make it inevitable that they will be given over to evil passions. Though his thought here is condensed, there is no doubt that Paul has in mind the sort of thing he has expressed more fully in Romans 1.

6 There are many ways of viewing sexual license. The way Paul chooses here is one that sees it as involving defrauding another of his rights.[26] "You cannot break this rule without in some way cheating your fellow-men" (Phillips). The verb rendered "wrong"[27] means "to go beyond," that is, "beyond what is right," and thus "transgress." But where it has an object it means something like "to overreach." If we are to understand it here as being closely joined with the following verb and governing "brother,"[28] the meaning will be something like "defraud" (so Moffatt).[29] Joined with "take advantage of him," it reminds us that all sexual looseness represents an act of injustice to someone other than the two parties concerned. Adultery is an obvious violation of the rights of

26. Cf. Moffatt, "The metaphors are drawn from trade, perhaps as appropriate to a trading community" *(EGT)*.

27. The construction τὸ μὴ + infinitive seems to indicate something different from the appositions of vv. 3-4; it perhaps indicates purpose.

28. While "brother" in the New Testament commonly denotes another member of the Christian community, the meaning here may well be wider, "brother man." If, however, we understand it as "fellow-Christian," the meaning of the passage will be, in Bicknell's words: "This does not imply that it is allowable to wrong a non-Christian, but that it is doubly wicked to wrong a brother in Christ."

29. It is, of course, quite possible to take ὑπερβαίνω here as intransitive (as *ARV*), in which case the thought of defrauding another is to be discerned in πλεονεκτέω only.

another. But promiscuity before marriage represents the robbing of the other of that virginity which ought to be brought to a marriage. The future partner of such a one has been defrauded. And, of course, if a child is born as the result of this sin, the little one bears the stigma of illegitimacy. Some interpreters have thought that this verse does not refer to sexual morality at all, taking "this matter" (literally, "the matter") to refer to conduct generally (e.g., *KJV,* "that no man go beyond and defraud his brother in any matter"), or to business affairs (Denney and Bicknell note this view but reject it). However, the article with "matter" points to the issue under discussion,[30] and the fact that impurity is mentioned again in the next verse indicates that the thought is being continued throughout the whole passage.

Paul now gives reasons why this sort of conduct should be eschewed. His first point is that God will take action against people who sin like this, as he had already warned them. It is noteworthy how often he comes back to the point that he had told them of this matter or that. It is clear that his instruction of the converts had been thorough, and had embraced the important matters that he felt called on to emphasize in his letter.

The form in which this particular warning is cast is that of a reminder that the Lord is "an avenger" (*NIV,* "will punish"). It is possible to take "the Lord" here to signify the Lord Jesus (as it usually does in the New Testament). But that God is the avenger is a frequent thought in the Old Testament (e.g., Deut. 32:35), and, with somewhat different terminology, in the New also. This is probably the way we should take it here. We must not understand vengeance in the sense of settling private scores, but rather of the administration of an evenhanded justice. People are required to live in accordance with moral law. If they do not, unpleasant consequences follow. These consequences are inevitable, for the hand of God is in them. Since he is the avenger, no one can reckon on escaping the consequences of evil deeds. "All such sins" is more exactly "all these things," but *NIV* probably gives the sense of it; Paul is referring primarily to the sins of which he has just been speaking and says people who commit them will render account to God in due course. There is a sense in which this happens here and now, for the sinner is less a person because of his sin (cf. also the process described so solemnly in Rom. 1:18-31). In another sense the full

---

30. ἐν τῷ πράγματι has sometimes been held to signify "in business." But while the plural τὰ πράγματα may have this meaning, it does not seem to be attested for the singular.

requital for wrong will not be exacted until the last day. It is likely that Paul is glancing at the great Assize.

7 A second reason[31] for purity is the whole character of the Christian life. In verse 4 Paul has spoken of "sanctification and honor," and it is this sort of thing that he has in mind now. Indeed, he uses the same term "sanctification," and adds to it the thought of the divine call, a call that involves the rejection of "uncleanness" (*NIV*, "to be impure"). This last word can theoretically be used in various senses. In one passage it refers to the uncleanness inside a tomb (Matt. 23:27), but everywhere else in the New Testament (and especially in Paul) it seems to refer to moral impurity, as is the case here.

Paul looks for his converts to live wholesome and pure lives. He bases his demand for the renunciation of all uncleanness on the priority of the divine in the Christian way of life. God has called believers, and called them "in sanctification." The priority of God's call is a major point in Pauline theology. Everywhere the apostle insists that our salvation is brought about not because we have taken action, but because God has. He goes further. When the natural man learns that he cannot remove the burden of his sins but must rely on Christ's atoning work for it all, he may try to save some shreds of self-respect by claiming at least the credit for turning from sin to God. But that, too, is ruled out. People come to God only because of God's effectual call. In this place it is not so much the fact that God called the Thessalonians initially that is in mind as the kind of living to which he has called them. He has called them to be set apart for him, that is, to live in sanctification (see on v. 3). The change of preposition from "for" with uncleanness to "in" with sanctification is interesting.[32] The former expresses purpose (cf. its use in Gal. 5:13; Eph. 2:10). When God called the Thessalonians it was not an aimless procedure. He had a very definite purpose, and that purpose was not uncleanness. "In" gives us rather the thought of atmosphere, of the settled condition in which he required them to live out their lives. This atmosphere for the believer is sanctification. This is the very air he breathes.

---

31. γάρ seems to refer back to the whole argument from v. 3 on, not simply to that at the end of v. 6.

32. οὐ . . . ἐπὶ ἀκαθαρσίᾳ ἀλλ' ἐν ἁγιασμῷ. Turner comments, "Paul carefully distinguishes ἐπί from ἐν in 1 Th 4⁷ and has a reason for the change from one preposition to the other"; he goes on to say that the construction with ἐν means "in the sphere of" (M, III, p. 263). Turner also says, "No one, having examined 1 Thess. 4⁷, would charge St. Paul with anything short of precision in his use of prepositions where the finer points of theology are at stake" (*Grammatical Insights*, p. 121).

8 We come to a third reason for chastity, namely, that impurity represents a sin against the Holy Spirit. This thought arises out of what has just been said, and the "therefore" that introduces the verse should not be overlooked. Impurity must be seen in the light of the fact that God has called us to live in sanctification. A failure to obey this call is thus more than simply a failure to keep some human rule. It is a sin against the living presence of God. The heinousness of this sin is brought out by the contrast between rejecting people and rejecting God[33] in the first part of the verse. The verb is not an easy one to translate,[34] and it is rendered in various ways in its various occurrences in the New Testament. Basically it means something like "to hold as null and void" (cf. its use for annulling a will, Gal. 3:15). From this various meanings arise. Here the significance is that anyone who holds sexual sin as a thing indifferent thereby treats God (not simply another person, Paul himself?) as of no account. Such a sinner thinks of God as One who can be neglected with impunity, this God who has just been spoken of as "an Avenger" (v. 6), and is about to be described as the continual Giver of his Holy Spirit.

The seriousness of this sin is further emphasized by an unusual word order ("his Spirit, the holy"), which has the effect of emphasizing "holy" (and also that the Spirit is none less than God's). The conduct in question outrages the Spirit, who is not only mighty but holy. This sin is understood in its true light only when it is seen as a preference for impurity rather than the Spirit who is holy. This is brought out by referring to God as him "who gives[35] you his Holy Spirit."[36] The verb is in the present,[37] which is unusual for Paul; he generally thinks of the

---

33. The use of the article with θεόν and its absence from ἄνθρωπον are noteworthy: "rejects not a man, but the one God."

34. ἀθετέω. Cf. R. MacPherson, "The primary significance of the word is to *render* or *consider invalid* (ἄθετον), *to set aside something laid down* (θετόν τι), *to bear oneself toward a thing as if it were not, to ignore*"; here he renders it "to *ignore, to treat with contempt as deserving no recognition*" (James Hastings [ed.], *A Dictionary of Christ and the Gospels,* I [London, 1906], pp. 453-54).

35. καί is found before the verb in ℵ D F G etc., but is lacking in A B D and other MSS. It should probably be read and be understood in the sense "indeed."

36. The Spirit is spoken of as given εἰς ὑμᾶς, "into you," and not simply ὑμῖν, "to you." The Spirit is given to be within the believer, strengthening his innermost being. Cf. Rutherford, "God, who offers his Holy Spirit to dwell in you."

37. Some MSS have the aorist δόντα (ℵ² A Ψ etc.), but the present is better supported (ℵ* B D F etc.), and since Paul mostly uses the aorist, scribes would tend to alter the reading to that tense. The present should surely be read.

Spirit as given once for all (though cf. Gal. 3:5). But in this passage there is a profound truth in the use of the present. Anyone who carries on an act of impurity is not simply breaking a human code, nor even sinning against the God who at some time in the past gave him the gift of the Spirit. He is sinning against the God who is present at that moment, against the One who continually gives the Spirit. The impure act is an act of despite against God's good gift at the very moment it is being proffered.[38]

C. BROTHERLY LOVE (4:9-10)

9 *Now about brotherly love we do not need to write to you, for you yourselves have been taught by God to love each other.* 10 *And in fact, you do love all the brothers throughout Macedonia. Yet we urge you, brothers, to do so more and more.*

It is perhaps artificial to separate these verses from those that follow (and they certainly are closely connected). I have marked them as a special section in order to emphasize the importance of love for this apostle. It is not always realized that Paul uses the words for love more often than anyone else in the New Testament. For him it is a major part of the life of the believer (cf. 1 Cor. 13). It is thus not surprising that he devotes a section of this letter to the way the Thessalonians had responded to his teaching about love and the importance of their making still more progress. He is here mostly concerned about love within the fellowship, brotherly love.

9 Something that should give modern Christians much food for thought is the way in which the early church was characterized by love. "Behold how these Christians love one another"[39] is hardly the comment that springs spontaneously to the lips of the detached observer nowadays. But if our manner of life was based on the New Testament picture, something like it would be inevitable. The characteristic Christian attitude, as we see there, is one of profound faith in God, a faith that spills out into all of life in the form of self-denying, self-giving love.

Paul has had occasion to remark on the way the Thessalonians displayed this virtue (1:3; 3:6). They showed that steadfast love to others

38. It is of course possible to take the present as nontemporal and as simply referring to God as the Giver.
39. Tertullian, *Apology* 39.

which can come about in someone only when that person has been transformed by the power of the divine *agapē*, and has come to see people in a measure as God sees them. But there is something more than this. When the miracle occurs in people, they find themselves in company with others of like mind and will be naturally drawn to them. Their soul will be knit to those others. Thus, in addition to *agapē*, self-denying love toward all people, they come to practice *philadelphia*, love of the brothers.[40] This is often insisted upon, and it has always been a hallmark of vital Christianity that love of those within the brotherhood has abounded. John, indeed, gives this as the criterion whereby one may know that one really has "passed from death to life" (1 John 3:14; cf. 3:10).

It is this that is in mind when Paul praises his friends.[41] He gladly acknowledges that there is no real need for him to write on such a subject to people so well taught as they. Yet, in the spirit of verse 1, he does write. He is never satisfied. While he is mindful of their very real achievement, he yet knows that the Christian must look ever onward. So he urges them to "do so more and more" (v. 10). He makes their well-known love for one another the basis of an appeal that they would go on to ever new heights of love. When he later wrote 2 Corinthians he praised the practical expression of their love in making a substantial gift for the poor saints in Jerusalem (2 Cor. 8:1ff.). It is this kind of thing that he has in mind here also. The passage in 2 Corinthians may indicate how well his remarks were heeded.

Paul gives as his reason that he need not write to them the fact that they were "taught by God." He uses a very uncommon word,[42] one that occurs here only in the New Testament (though a very similar expression is found in John 6:45). We also read of being taught of the

---

40. φιλαδελφία outside the New Testament almost invariably denotes affection for the brother by birth. In the New Testament, however, it always denotes love within the Christian brotherhood. It is not that Christianity sits loose to natural ties. On the contrary, it insists that they should be conceded their due and great importance, and it castigates those without natural affection (Rom. 1:31; 2 Tim. 3:3). But it catches up natural ties into the wider circle. The really significant thing is membership in the heavenly family (Luke 8:21). φιλαδελφία is distinguished from ἀγάπη in 2 Pet. 1:7.

41. "But concerning" (περὶ δέ), which introduces this section, is often used when a writer turns to new topics in answering a letter (1 Cor. 7:1, 25, etc.); as a result some expositors have thought that Paul is here answering a letter from the Thessalonians. This is not impossible, but we have no knowledge of such a letter and the expression reads well without that hypothesis.

42. θεοδίδακτοι. In John 6:45 we have διδακτοὶ θεοῦ.

Spirit (1 Cor. 2:13). This is relevant to our present passage because Paul has just been speaking of the Holy Spirit given "into" the Thessalonians. So his thought is that God within them shows them the right way.

10 Not only does God show them, but they act on what he shows them. Paul rejoices that they practice this God-taught love toward all the Christians in Macedonia.[43] Some have felt that this is something in the nature of an extravagant statement, for there were Macedonian churches only in Philippi and Berea besides that at Thessalonica. But to this we must add the qualification, "of which we know." There may well have been many churches of which we have no record. Our knowledge of the details of church life in New Testament times is very meager. We know that missionaries like Silvanus, Timothy, and Luke had worked in Macedonia, and we know that the early Christian communities were evangelistically minded. Consequently there is nothing improbable in the idea that a number of groups of Christians had sprung up (cf. 1:7-8, and the notes there). However, be the number large or small, Paul's point is that his friends in Thessalonica had acted with a commendable Christian love toward them all. His use of the continuous present tense indicates their habitual attitude. That they practice such love toward the wider circle is proof of the reality of their brotherly love. As Calvin says, it is "an argument from the greater to the less; for as their love diffuses itself through the whole of Macedonia, he infers that it is not to be doubted that they *love one another.*"

But tenderly (note the affectionate "brothers") Paul urges them to "do so more and more." Christians must never be weary in well-doing. To sit back satisfied with what one has done is to sound the death knell of effective Christian service. For the verb "urge" see on 3:2 (where it is rendered "encourage"). It fits the note of tenderness, while yet leaving no doubt as to the urgency of the course of action being recommended. "Do" is the verb we have already met in 3:12 of overflowing in love, and in 4:1 of the Christian life in general. While it here it has no object, yet it is implied that the Thessalonians should abound in love of the brothers. Since Paul goes on to speak of the importance of working with one's hands (v. 11) it is tempting to think that perhaps the undoubted love for one another that marked the Thessalonians did not always

---

43. The καί in καὶ γάρ, as Lightfoot says, "marks this statement as an advance upon the preceding one. 'You are not only taught the lesson, but you also practise it, and that, to every one of the brethren throughout Macedonia, i.e., all the brethren with whom you can possibly come in contact.'"

include a willingness to get one's hands dirty. But the love of which Paul writes is intensely practical. That is the quality for which he looks. He wants his friends to excel in its practice. It is interesting that three times within such a short space Paul should have thought of the Christian life in terms of abounding. It illustrates something of the exuberant quality of a right Christian faith. Far from acting as a brake on our enjoyment of life, as so many wrongly think, it opens the door to real living (cf. John 10:10).

D. EARNING ONE'S LIVING (4:11-12)

11 *Make it your ambition to lead a quiet life, to mind your own business and to work with your hands, just as we told you,* 12 *so that your daily life may win the respect of outsiders and so that you will not be dependent on anybody.*

We could take this section as part of the preceding one (as many commentators in fact do). But it deals with the practical outworking of Christian love rather than with that love itself, so I have made it a separate section. This is the first indication we have had in this epistle that some of the Thessalonians were so excited by all the wonderful things in the Christian faith that they were not bothering to earn their living. But there are a number of indications in the Thessalonian correspondence that this was so (cf. especially 2 Thess. 3:11). A number of possible reasons for this have been suggested, but it is most likely that it arose out of second advent speculations.[44] The Thessalonian believers had learned very well that the Lord would be returning in mighty power, and evidently some of them felt that it would be very soon. Accordingly there was no point in continuing in some steady job. It was much more realistic, they evidently reasoned, to be about the business of proclaiming the near end of the world. If they had need of this world's goods in the meantime, why, there were others, Christian brothers, who could be relied on to come to their rescue (it may be no accident that verses 11-12 follow a section in which Paul stresses brotherly love). This kind of thing can be done from a sense of serious purpose, but, human nature being what it is, it can easily degenerate into downright laziness and idleness. People can be so taken up with the spectacular, with excitement over the near

44. It may not be without significance that in the very next section of this epistle Paul deals with problems arising out of the second advent.

approach of the Lord, that they pass over the important things of everyday life. So Paul gives attention to such matters, and counsels these brothers to mend their ways.[45]

11 "Make it your ambition to lead a quiet life" is a striking paradox. The verb rendered "make it your ambition" is a compound with the basic meaning "to love honor," hence "to be ambitious." It may well be that this is the significance of the verb in this verse, when Paul's remark would be something like "be ambitious to be unambitious." But the verb develops another meaning "to fix one's aim on," "to strive earnestly for." If this is the meaning here (as it is in Rom. 15:20; 2 Cor. 5:9, the only other New Testament passages where the verb is found), then the paradox will be "seek strenuously to be still." Whichever way we take it, Paul is urging his converts to lead a quiet life. The verb rendered "to lead a quiet life" is used of silence after speech (Luke 14:4), cessation of argument (Acts 21:14), and rest from labor (Luke 23:56). It denotes tranquility of life, which of course does not mean inactivity (Ward sees quietness as opposed to "being busybodies"). It is possible to be very active in the Lord's service and still be at peace. It is clear that some of the converts were far from living the simple life, and Paul is very anxious to recall them to calmness and simplicity. If the Lord were coming soon, then the best way for him to find them would be doing their ordinary work, but this they had not learned.[46]

Paul joins to the general injunction to be quiet the specific one to "mind your own business" (Moffatt). The expression is found only here in the New Testament, though it is not uncommon in nonbiblical Greek.

45. Cf. Luke 12:35-38 for a very different way of preparing for the coming of the Lord. On this Lukan passage J. M. Creed comments, "The expectation of the Lord's return does not paralyse energy. The imperatives call up a fine picture of preparedness" (*The Gospel according to St. Luke* [London, 1950], p. 175). I have noted in the Introduction the view of S. Russell that it is the refusal of "the urban poor" to work for their living, even when converted to Christianity, that is in mind here (p. 9, n. 16), but that view does not seem to have been substantiated. Best finds a reference to "eschatological expectation" the "most satisfactory solution," and Bruce considers this view "quite probable."

46. Neil quotes from Paterson Smyth a story from New England "of a day during one of those times of excited expectancy of the end of the world when a sudden darkness at noon interrupted the session of the Assembly. Some cried fearfully: 'It is the coming of Christ: it is the end of the world.' But the old President ordered lights to be produced: 'Bring in candles,' he said, 'and get on with your work. If the Lord is coming, how better can He find us than quietly doing our duty?' "

It perhaps points to a tendency to interfere in the running of the church on the part of those who were not church officers. It does not seem extravagant to suggest that, meeting trouble in their endeavor to be kept by the earnings of their brothers, some members had attempted to have the church officially support their demands. Or it may be that Paul is condemning taking undue interest in the concerns of one's neighbors. It is not impossible that these are the people accused of being busybodies in the second letter (3:11), though there again there is uncertainty about the precise meaning. At any rate, it is clear that Paul wants each to put his attention where it belongs.

Closely joined to this is the command to work with their hands.[47] This unashamed advocacy of manual labor in a letter to a community in a Greek city must be remarked. The typical Greek attitude was that slaves did this sort of work, but that freemen would not stoop to it. It was degrading. Here, as in so many other ways, the Christians refused to take their standards from the community in the midst of which they lived. Rather, they held that all things they did should be done as service to Christ (Col. 3:17), and they specifically held that manual labor was good (Eph. 4:28). Doubtless they remembered that Jesus himself had been a carpenter (Mark 6:3). How could the followers of the Carpenter do other than welcome manual work?[48]

This reference probably points us to the status of the Thessalonians. While, of course, manual work may be skilled as well as unskilled, we are probably right in thinking that the majority of the believers came from the lower social classes and were poor rather than rich.[49] Once again Paul insists that he is not bringing some new teaching. He is simply repeating what he had said when he was among them. It is remarkable that he had been able to provide so well for the future needs

47. Some MSS read ἰδίαις, which would put some emphasis on their "own" hands. But the attestation is far from certain (ℵ* A D etc.), and *NIV* appears to be right.

48. Denney draws another inference from this section of Thessalonians. With reference to the earning of our daily bread he says: "The bulk of most men's strength, by an ordinance of God that we cannot interfere with, is given to that humble but inevitable task. If we cannot be holy at our work, it is not worth taking any trouble to be holy at other times."

49. Malherbe holds that at Corinth it is likely "that Paul's converts came from the artisans, tradespeople, and manual laborers" and that it is likely that a similar situation obtained in Thessalonica (Malherbe, p. 15). So also Barrett, who notes that the expression "implies that the great majority of the Thessalonian Christians were manual workers, whether skilled or unskilled; this is in line with all we learn elsewhere about the early Christian community."

of his band of converts. The pity of it is that they had not learned as well as he had taught.[50]

12   Paul gives two reasons for earning their living in this way. The first is the effect of their behavior on those who are not Christians. What *NIV* renders "so that your daily life may win the respect of outsiders" is more literally to "walk[51] becomingly toward those outside." Believers must always bear in mind the impact of their conduct on those who are without faith.[52] What they do may be done from a good motive but yet appear to the outsider in quite a different light. Under these circumstances it is impossible for faithful followers of the Lord to go ahead without regard to appearances. They must reflect that they are their Lord's ambassadors, and their conduct must commend the Lord to others. If that is so in the case of things that are indifferent in themselves, much more is it so in matters like the one before Paul at this moment. When some of the believers did no work at all, but lived on the charity of others, with the result that they spent their time in what must have looked like idle gossip, what could outsiders think? It would be a sure way of bringing the church into disrepute. Paul urges the Thessalonians to consider the implications of all this. He suggests that they should walk (see on 4:1) "becomingly," his adverb directing their attention to the fitness of things (cf. Col. 4:5). See further on 2:9.

There is a slight doubt about the exact meaning of Paul's second reason for working. The words rendered "not be dependent on anybody" could equally be translated "have need of nothing" (cf. *REB,* "never be in want"); the gender is indeterminate. In actual practice, though, it comes to much the same whichever interpretation we adopt. The situation clearly was that those who were not working were depending on their more industrious brothers for their means of livelihood, and Paul is counseling them to work so that this undesirable state of affairs may be ended. He may mean, "Work, and then all your needs will be supplied. You will be in need of nothing." Or he may mean, "Work, and then you will have need of no one to help you. You will be quite

---

50. The verb rendered "told" is παραγγέλλω, which indicates authoritative commands. For example, it is used of commands given by military officers. Although not as exclusively military as the corresponding noun (see on 4:2), it yet gives the idea of a command with authority.

51. Turner thinks that the present signifies "go on walking" (M, III, p. 75).

52. On πρὸς τοὺς ἔξω cf. Frame, "πρός = 'with an eye to,' as in Col. 4:5; not *coram,* 'in the eyes of.'"

independent." Either way he is making the point that the Christian cannot be a parasite.[53]

This whole section on earning one's living is closely connected with the previous one on brotherly love, and that not only in syntax. Those who imposed on the generosity of their fellows were not living in love. Or, to put the same thing the other way around, the exhortation to brotherly love carries with it the necessity for providing for one's own needs, so that undue strain may not be placed on the brother (though Paul does not specifically mention this point).

VI. PROBLEMS ASSOCIATED WITH THE PAROUSIA (4:13–5:11)

A. BELIEVERS WHO DIED BEFORE THE PAROUSIA (4:13-18)

13 *Brothers, we do not want you to be ignorant about those who fall asleep, or to grieve like the rest of men, who have no hope.* 14 *We believe that Jesus died and rose again and so we believe that God will bring with Jesus those who have fallen asleep in him.* 15 *According to the Lord's own word, we tell you that we who are still alive, who are left till the coming of the Lord, will certainly not precede those who have fallen asleep.* 16 *For the Lord himself will come down from heaven, with a loud command, with the voice of the archangel and with the trumpet call of God, and the dead in Christ will rise first.* 17 *After that, we who are still alive and are left will be caught up with them in the clouds to meet the Lord in the air. And so we will be with the Lord forever.* 18 *Therefore encourage each other with these words.*

The Parousia (see on 2:19) is a difficult topic. Within the short space of the mission it would have been impossible for the apostolic band to have given anything like complete teaching about it. Clearly they had given it a good deal of attention, for the Thessalonian correspondence gives evidence of a lively interest in the whole subject.[54] It is worth asking

53. The issue may be decided in favor of "nothing" by the grammatical point that χρείαν ἔχω is more usually followed by a thing than a person. But this cannot be absolutely conclusive because in the nature of things one is more likely to speak of needing things than people.

54. D. Wenham has argued that there are significant connections between what

ourselves whether the comparative neglect of the doctrine in much modern Christianity has not resulted in great loss.

The Thessalonians had welcomed the teaching they had received. But with the passage of time and the march of events questions arose in their minds. The one that occupies our attention at this point is, "What becomes of believers who die before the second coming?" This question must have arisen quite early in the history of the church (which, incidentally, is evidence for the early date of this epistle). We get the impression that the Thessalonians had understood Paul to mean that the Parousia would take place within their lifetime. They had become perplexed when some (or even one) of their number died. Did this mean that they had lost their share in the events associated with that great day? What a calamity to be robbed of taking part in the ultimate triumph by failing to live out the few years intervening, and this after having passed out of the darkness of heathendom into the light of the gospel! It is possible that some of them thought of the deaths as indicating that the deceased were under the wrath of God (Ananias and Sapphira died as a punishment for sin, Acts 5:1-11, as did some Corinthians for their unworthiness in eating the Lord's Supper, 1 Cor. 11:30; cf. Rom. 1:32). If they were being punished for some sin, it would be natural enough that they should miss the Parousia. The converse, that missing the Parousia meant that they were being punished for some sin, may well have seemed true also.[55]

13 Paul introduces what he has to say on the topic with the formula "we do not want you to be ignorant," a formula that he employs elsewhere[56] and that usually seems to introduce something that is new to his readers. This is all the more noteworthy here in that so often in this letter Paul has written "as you know" or the like. The formula here is also generally used to indicate that Paul wants his readers to fasten their attention on what follows; it is important. It is invariably accompanied with the address "brothers," an affectionate touch that should not be overlooked.

He does not refer to the dead, but to "those who fall asleep."[57] In

---

Paul says in these letters and the eschatological traditions in the Synoptic Gospels (R. T. France and D. Wenham [eds.], *Gospel Perspectives,* II [Sheffield, 1981], pp. 345-75; IV [1984], pp. 110-14).

55. Marshall holds that if this were the case we might well expect that Paul would have been more explicit about the relationship of judgment to the Parousia. Perhaps. But it certainly remains a possibility.

56. The passages are Rom. 1:13; 11:25; 1 Cor. 10:1; 12:1; 2 Cor. 1:8. Milligan says that the corresponding formula γινώσκειν σε θέλω is very common in the papyri (it occurs also in 1 Cor. 11:3; Col. 2:1, though with the verb εἰδέναι).

57. The present participle κοιμωμένων is used, though the perfect is more usual

many religions death is spoken of in this way (cf. the frequent Old Testament statement that such-and-such a person "slept with his fathers"), but it is a metaphor that is much more at home in a Christian context than elsewhere. For Christians death is no longer that adversary whom no person can resist, that tyrant who brings all worthwhile existence to a horribly final end. Death has been overcome by the risen Lord, and that has transformed the whole situation for those who are in him.

So Paul goes on to the thought that they should not sorrow[58] like "the rest[59] of men, who have no hope." Paul is not saying that Christians never grieve; they have their sorrows like other people (cf. Phil. 2:27). But they sorrow as those who have an abiding hope. The apostle is not contrasting a lesser grief with a greater one; he is contrasting those with hope and those without it. When the non-Christian world is characterized as lacking hope it is probably not the absence of the hope of an afterlife that is primarily in mind, but the absence of the knowledge of God, much like those whom Paul describes as "without hope and without God in the world" (Eph. 2:12). But this shows itself strikingly in their attitude toward death. Few things are more impressive in the contrast between early Christianity and the surrounding pagan systems than their attitudes in the face of death. Nowhere outside Christianity do we find at this period any widespread view of a worthwhile life beyond the grave. There are some statements on immortality in pagan literature. Undoubtedly some of the philosophers had an idea of a life beyond the grave. But they did not glory in it, and, in any case, theirs was the lofty view of the few. Nowhere did it penetrate to the beliefs of ordinary people. The same might be said about the mystery religions. Sometimes they speak of a life beyond the grave for the initiates. But they do not have the ringing

---

(and is read here by D [F G] etc.). The use of the present points us to a continuing activity. Also, and perhaps more significant in the present connection, its use points forward to the future awakening more definitely than would the perfect. Frame notes the possibility that the present denotes a class, "the sleepers." It is perhaps worth noting that our word "cemetery" is derived from this term.

58. The verb is in the present subjunctive (λυπῆσθε), and the tense points to a continuing sorrow. The verb denotes primarily an inward grief, whereas words like πενθέω, κλαίω, etc., indicate the outward expression of grief.

59. οἱ λοιποί, "the rest," means much the same as τοὺς ἔξω, "them that are without," of v. 12. The difference is, as Findlay puts it, that "that expression implies *exclusion,* this implies *deprivation*" *(CGT).* Best points out that pagans are those "who know not God" (v. 5), but these concepts are related: "in so far as the pagan has gods they are unable to give him the hope that is given to the Christian by his God through the resurrection of Jesus."

certainty of the Christians, nor do such views influence very many. The typical attitude of the ancient world to death was one of utter hopelessness. Deissmann cites a letter of the second century, written to a friend who had been bereaved, that we may quote as typical.

> Irene to Taonnophris and Philo, good comfort. I am as sorry and weep over the departed one as I wept for Didymas. And all things, whatsoever were fitting, I have done, and all mine, Epaphroditus and Thermuthion and Philion and Apollonius and Plantas. But, nevertheless, against such things one can do nothing. Therefore comfort ye one another.[60]

It is clear that Irene feels for her friends, but her "comfort ye one another" is a pathetic little conclusion to a letter that reveals all too clearly that she has no comfort to give. "Against such things one can do nothing."

Over against that we might set Paul's triumphant words: "Where, O death, is your victory? Where, O death, is your sting?" (1 Cor. 15:55). Or his calm contemplation of his own decease, "For to me, to live is Christ and to die is gain. . . . I desire to depart and be with Christ, which is better by far" (Phil. 1:21-23).[61] When the apostle counsels the Thessalonians not to sorrow as the pagans do, he is not urging them to endure with a deep Stoic calm the buffetings of fortune that they cannot avoid. Nor is he counseling a callous indifference. Rather, he is rejoicing in the complete victory that Christ has won. Those who have died have simply fallen asleep in Christ, and they will wake with him. Clearly, in the face of this prospect there is no reason for despair.[62]

---

60. *LAE,* p. 176. Deissmann comments, "Irene, who knows how to write a business letter quickly and surely, experiences the difficulty of those whose business it is to console and who have no consolation to offer. . . . Who could help feeling for the helplessness of this woman. . . ?" Milligan remarks, "The general hopelessness of the pagan world in the presence of death is almost too well known to require illustration," but he cites a few passages such as Theocritus, *Idyllia* 4.42, ἐλπίδες ἐν ζωῖσιν, ἀνέλπιστοι δὲ θανόντες, "hopes are for the living, but the dead are without hope."

61. Lightfoot is of the opinion that even more striking is the difference between the inscriptions on the magnificent tombs of the heathen and those on the poor graves in the catacombs. "On the one hand there is the dreary wail of despair, the effect of which is only heightened by the pomp of outward splendour from which it issues. On the other the exulting psalm of hope, shining the more brightly in all ill-written, ill-spelt records amidst the darkness of subterranean caverns."

62. This, of course, does not exclude the natural feeling of sadness at parting. Paul is not giving a full account here, but simply drawing the attention of his friends to what was important for them to know.

14 The Christian confidence is not the result of some philosophical speculation, nor the elaboration of a religious myth. Rather, it rests on a sure historical foundation. Paul proceeds to draw his readers' attention to this fact and to the deductions that are to be drawn from it. "If we believe" is not to be taken as indicating any uncertainty (which is probably why *NIV* drops the "if"). The implication of this type of conditional clause is that the condition has been fulfilled (cf. *RSV,* "since we believe"). Paul thinks his statement is so far beyond dispute that he can safely throw it into the form of a conditional. Again, the reference to believing is not in order to introduce doubts, but to indicate the certainty of faith. Certainty comes out again in the next words. After "if we believe . . ." it would be natural to find "we should also believe. . . ." By avoiding this conditional form Paul conveys the certainty of the event he describes.[63]

Paul speaks of Christ not as sleeping, but as dying. In the New Testament there are two distinct strands of teaching about death. On the one hand it is the most natural of all things and is an inevitable part of the conditions of our earthly existence. On the other hand it is completely unnatural, a horror, the result of sin.[64] Christ in his death bore the wages of sin. He endured the worst that death can possibly be. Thereby he transformed the whole position of those who are in him. It is because there was no mitigation of the horror of death for him that there is no horror in death for his people. For them it is but sleep.

Jesus not only died, but also "rose again."[65] The resurrection was the great event that demonstrated that death really was conquered. Elsewhere Paul could say, "If Christ has not been raised, your faith is futile; you are still in your sins. Then those also who have fallen asleep in Christ are lost" (1 Cor. 15:17-18). The resurrection is the great triumphant act wherein the divine quality of the Christian gospel is conclusively demonstrated. In the light of the resurrection there can be no doubt that God

63. *NIV* omits the "If" before "we believe" and inserts a second "we believe" that is not in the Greek. Paul says something like "For if we believe that Jesus died and rose again, so also God will bring with him those who sleep through Jesus."

64. On the subject of death see further my *The Wages of Sin* (London, 1955), and the literature there cited.

65. Moore comments, " 'that Jesus died and rose again' . . . expresses the foundation for every aspect of Christian faith and hope." Perhaps we should notice that Paul uses the verb ἀνίστημι for rising rather than his more usual ἐγείρω and that he refers to "Jesus" where he usually says "Christ"; he may be using traditional language.

was in Christ, and if God was in Christ, then, just as he raised his Son, so in due time he will raise those who "have fallen asleep in" Jesus.[66] The resurrection is the guarantee of the Christian hope.

Paul draws this conclusion, though the form in which he puts it leaves us in some doubt as to his exact meaning. The difficulty is that "in Jesus" (*NIV* has "in him") is literally "through Jesus," and it is not certain whether it should be taken with "fallen asleep" (as *ARV*) or with "will bring" (so *NIV, RSV,* Moffatt). Those who take this second view probably do so because of the difficulty they have in understanding what "falling asleep through Jesus" can mean. But it raises difficulties of its own. For example, the balance of the sentence is against it, and so is the fact that if we adopt it we are left with the thought that *all* the dead (and not simply the Christian dead) will be brought through Jesus (the Greek will then mean, "God will bring through Jesus with Jesus those who sleep"). Moreover, it is not easy to think that Paul means "God will bring through Jesus with Jesus. . . ." This is tautology, and such a tame ending is not what we associate with Paul's vigorous mind. It is likely, then, that we should understand the passage as *ARV,* "them also that are fallen asleep in Jesus will God bring with him."[67] The meaning is probably that it is through what Jesus has done,[68] through Jesus, that Christians "sleep" only, and do not undergo the horrors of death.[69] "Death 'through Jesus' is but the prelude to resurrection 'with Jesus'" (Bruce).

Outside this verse the designation of our Lord simply as "Jesus" is found in these epistles once only (1:10). It is the name that brings before us the Man of Nazareth, the human Jesus. In this context we are

---

66. W. F. Moulton "suggested the possibility that ἐκοιμήθη in 1 Th 4¹⁴ might be a true passive, 'was put to sleep,' which gives a strikingly beautiful sense" (M, I, p. 162).

67. On the grammatical reasons for favoring this interpretation Frame quotes Ellicott, "The two contrasted subjects Ἰησοῦς and κοιμηθέντας διὰ τοῦ Ἰησοῦ thus stand in clear and illustrative antithesis, and the fundamental declaration of the sentence ἄξει σὺν αὐτῷ remains distinct and prominent, undiluted by any addititious clause."

68. Milligan speaks of διά as "pointing to Jesus as the mediating link between His people's sleep and their resurrection at the hands of God," so that the argument runs: "those who fell asleep through Jesus, and in consequence were raised by God through Him, will God bring with Him." Moule understands the expression to mean, "*those who have fallen asleep* (i.e. *died*) *as Christians* (perhaps *in contact with Jesus*)" (*IBNTG*, p. 57). But this seems inadequate.

69. Some interpreters have felt that the expression points to martyrdom, but it does not seem definite enough for that.

reminded of the historical facts of the death and resurrection. These things really happened, and they happened to Jesus. Moreover, the term reminds us that Jesus is "the firstfruits of those who have fallen asleep" (1 Cor. 15:20). The firstfruits imply later fruits.[70] As Jesus has risen, we are sure that one day we, too, will rise (cf. 1 Cor. 15:22-23; Col. 1:18).

One more point remains to be determined in this verse, and that is the meaning of "bring with Jesus." Some understand it to signify that Jesus will take these people with him into glory, but this does not seem to be justified. Paul is talking about the Parousia. It is their share in the events of that great day that is in view. It is best to understand the words to mean that Jesus will bring the faithful departed with him when he comes back. Their death does not mean that they will miss their share in the Parousia. Notice the definiteness of Paul's statement.

15 Paul does not speak of the resurrection of the faithful departed, and we are probably right in assuming that that was taken for granted. What worried the Thessalonians was not whether their friends would rise, but whether they would have any share in the great events associated with the Parousia. Now comes another expression indicating certainty, namely, a statement given on the authority of the Lord himself. "According to the Lord's own word" is literally "in the word of the Lord,"[71] and it would be very natural to understand this of a saying of Jesus. The difficulty urged against this is that there is no saying anywhere in the Gospels that closely resembles this one, or from which we might think this saying to have been adapted (Matt. 24:31 seems to be the closest parallel). This makes it likely that Paul is referring to a saying of Jesus that is not mentioned by any of the four Evangelists. There must have been many such sayings;[72] for example, one is recorded for us in Acts 20:35 (cf. John 20:30; 21:25). Moffatt's translation runs, "as the Lord has told us," which seems to point to a revelation made to Paul himself.[73]

---

70. Cf. the chapter "The Resurrection of the Church," in L. S. Thornton, *The Common Life in the Body of Christ* (London, 1942).

71. ἐν here probably has the force of "by means of."

72. Many commentators reject the view that this is a genuine saying of Jesus, alleging, e.g., that the Evangelists would not have omitted it. But is there any reason for saying that any or all of the Evangelists knew all the things Jesus said? And have we really such insight into their thinking that we can say what they would have included and what they would have omitted among the sayings they did have? If this does refer to a saying of the Lord it will, of course, have been adapted by the use of "we," "the Lord," etc.

73. Or, if the plural be pressed, it may point to a common Christian tradition. But this raises the question, Where did such a tradition originate?

This is not impossible, but there is no other evidence, and the Greek does not seem to mean so much. Some commentators have felt that we should understand the words to represent the apostle's thinking the problem through under the guidance of the Spirit (cf. 1 Cor. 2:16).[74] Or that the Lord spoke the words through a prophet of the early church. Others hold that it represents some saying of Christ's that has been expanded with traditional Jewish imagery. But all such explanations seem needless when we have the simple one, that it is a saying of Jesus unrecorded in the Gospels. If we had reason for thinking that all he said is recorded, matters would be different. But as it is, we are expressly told that many things are not included in the Gospel record (John 21:25). We feel that this is one of them.[75]

The saying raises the question of whether, when he said "we who are still alive," Paul expected that he himself would still be alive when the Lord returned. Many exegetes think that he did, but the Greek here does not affirm this.[76] The expression he uses may mean no more than "those Christians who will be alive at that day,"[77] and since Paul in this very context speaks of the time as unknown (5:2, 3) and keeps open the possibilities of "waking" or "sleeping" for both his correspondents and himself (5:10), it would be unwise to read more into his words. While there is nothing improbable in the idea that Paul or any other first-century Christian thought that the Parousia would take place in his own lifetime (some people seem to have thought this in every age of the Christian

---

74. In support of this might be urged Old Testament references to prophets speaking by the word of the Lord, בִּדְבַר יהוה (1 Kings 13:2, etc.).

75. O. Cullmann includes this among "the relatively small number of words of Jesus quoted by Paul" (*The Early Church* [London, 1956], p. 65), and J. Jeremias regards it as "an independent dominical saying" (*Unknown Sayings of Jesus* [London, 1958], p. 5; see also pp. 64-67).

76. E. M. B. Green thinks that Paul is quoting from some Thessalonians, in which case the words would not state Paul's position (*ET* LXIX [1957-58], pp. 285-86). I am not persuaded that this is the way the words should be taken, but at least it shows another possible way of understanding them.

77. Lightfoot gives as his paraphrase of οἱ ζῶντες, οἱ περιλειπόμενοι, "When I say 'we,' I mean those who are living, those who survive to that day." Denney thinks that the natural impression is that Paul expected to be alive, but adds a note, "It is easy to state the inference too strongly. Paul tells us expressly that he did not know when Christ would come; he could not therefore know that he himself would have died long before the Advent; and it was inevitable, therefore, that he should include himself here in the category of such as might live to see it." Cf. Marshall, "We may well ask how Paul could have said 'those of us who are living then' shortly and succinctly without using the actual wording employed here."

church, and some think so now), yet it must be borne in mind that he does not say so. It must also be remembered that he can class himself with those who will be raised (1 Cor. 6:14; 2 Cor. 4:14). Those who survive to that day will have no advantage over the faithful departed, and Paul uses an emphatic expression, "will certainly not,"[78] to underline his point. His concern is that there should be no doubt at all that believers who die will be at no disadvantage when the Parousia comes.

16 This verse makes us reflect on the very little that the New Testament has to say about the manner of the Parousia. Nowhere else do we have as full a description of what is to happen as here, but the details are few and do not paint a very full picture for us. The point of it all is that Scripture is intensely practical in this matter, as in others. There are many things that we would like to know, but the Bible was not written to gratify our curiosity. Rather, it is intended to help us in our Christian lives, and for that the important thing is that we should be ready when the Lord comes. Thus we are often warned to prepare, and told that the coming will be unexpected.

Paul makes three points here. The first is that the One who will come at the end of this age is no less than "the Lord himself." It will be no angel or other created being to whom will be committed the task of bringing this age to an end. The Thessalonians are assured that they look forward to nothing less than a divine intervention.

This is underlined by Paul's second point. The Lord's second coming will be one of majesty and honor. Paul lists various accompaniments that demonstrate this. It is not certain whether the "shout" (*NIV* has "loud command"), the "voice of the archangel," and the "trumpet call of God" are three ways of speaking about the same triumphant noise, or whether they are three different sounds.[79] We read of "a loud voice

---

78. οὐ μή is often used in the Gospels where there seems to be no particular emphasis. Close examination, however, reveals that it is used without emphasis only in quotations from LXX or in the words of our Lord. When these last were translated from the Aramaic it would seem that the emphatic οὐ μή was commonly used as congruous with the style of deity. Moulton speaks of "a feeling that inspired language was fitly rendered by words of a decisive tone not needed generally elsewhere" (M, I, p. 192, and see pp. 39, 187-92). The important point is that this gives a natural explanation of the frequent use of the expression in the Gospels, and disposes of the idea that in the New Testament it has lost its force. Paul uses it four times only (outside quotations from LXX), and each time it has its proper emphasis.

79. Frame thinks that the fact that the second and third clauses are joined by καί indicates that they are "in some sense an epexegesis of the first." He gives the

like a trumpet" (Rev. 1:10; cf. 4:1; 5:2, etc.), and some commentators hold that something of that sort is meant here. This may be so, but the impression left is that there are three distinct sounds. The "shout" often denotes an authoritative utterance. The word is found often. It is the cry made by the ship's master to his rowers,[80] or by a military officer to his soldiers, or by a hunter to his hounds, or by a charioteer to his horses. When used of military or naval personnel it was a battle cry. In most places, then, it denotes a loud, authoritative cry, often uttered in the thick of great excitement. All these associations make it an apt word for the great day to which Paul looked forward. It is not said by whom the shout will be uttered, but the probability is that it is the Lord (cf. John 5:28-29, "a time is coming when all who are in their graves will hear his voice and come out"). It will not mean, as some interpreters suggest, a command of God to Christ. The whole situation demands a command of God or Christ to the dead. We should avoid understanding the passage in the sense of *JB*, "At the trumpet of God, the voice of the archangel will call out the command and the Lord himself will come down." If anything is certain, it is that the Lord will not be responding to the command of an archangel.

The alternative is that the shout is to be identified with "the voice of the archangel." Neither of these nouns has the article (the Greek reads "a voice of an archangel"), which makes it unlikely that Paul is thinking of any particular archangel.[81] It is even possible that he does not mean that an archangel will actually say anything, but simply that the voice

---

meaning as "At a command, namely, at an archangel's voice and at a trumpet of God." This view would be supported by the consideration that κελεύσματι has no qualifying genitive, so that the following expressions might be naturally held to explain it. Hendriksen thinks of two different sounds, the "shout" being the voice of the Lord and the other sound being that of the archangel blowing the trumpet of God.

80. The cognate word κελευστής denotes the "boatswain, who gives the time to the rowers" (LSJ). O. Cullmann thinks of the κέλευσμα as pointing to God's sovereignty. He speaks of the time "when God, as in the first creation, will decide in his sovereign act (κέλευσμα, 1 Thess. 4:16) to constitute the *new creation* by means of the spirit of life" (*The Early Church*, p. 143).

81. Those who try to identify the archangel usually think of Michael, the only archangel named in the New Testament (Jude 9). Gabriel is mentioned, but he is called simply an angel (Luke 1:19, 26). Michael, Gabriel, and Raphael are mentioned in "The War of the Sons of Light with the Sons of Darkness"; see Millar Burrows, *The Dead Sea Scrolls* (London, 1956), p. 261. Jewish writings mention seven archangels and name them Uriel, Raphael, Raguel, Michael, Saraqa'el, Gabriel, and Remiel.

that will be uttered will be a very great voice, an archangel type of voice. But more probably the meaning is that some archangel will add his voice to the call that wakes the dead.

Then there will be "the trumpet call of God." Trumpets are often mentioned in the Old Testament in connection with times of festivity and triumph. They were a frequent accompaniment of great religious occasions. Paul speaks of the trumpet elsewhere in connection with the Parousia (1 Cor. 15:52). It fits in as part of the pageantry, stressing the majesty of the Lord and the greatness of the day.[82]

The third point that Paul makes in this verse is that the faithful departed will rise first. The Thessalonians had been agitated by the possibility that their deceased loved ones would not have a place in the events of the great day. Far from that, Paul assures them, they will be very prominent. Indeed, they will rise before those who are alive on earth when that great day arrives.[83]

17 It is only after the faithful departed have been raised that the saints on earth will "be caught up with them" to meet the Lord. There is a minor problem in that the faithful departed will be coming with Jesus (v. 14), but the point made here is not so much the order of events as the truth that the Lord's people will be united at the Parousia. The reunion with those who have died is sometimes overlooked in the exposition of this passage, but to Paul it was clearly important. He stresses that they will be together,[84] and mentions it before saying that they will be caught up. It is a very precious thought, especially to those who have been bereaved, as apparently had some of the Thessalonians.

---

82. Jesus likewise spoke of the trumpet in connection with the gathering of the elect (Matt. 24:31). The sounding of the trumpet is associated with the activity of the Lord in Old Testament passages (e.g., Exod. 19:16; Isa. 27:13; Joel 2:1; Zech. 9:14). J. Klausner attests the idea for first-century Judaism (*From Jesus to Paul* [London, 1946], pp. 538-39). The trumpet is frequently mentioned in the descriptions of battles in the War scroll (Millar Burrows, *The Dead Sea Scrolls*, pp. 390ff.).

83. "First" must be taken here as first in relation to the events mentioned, i.e., before the rapture spoken of in the next verse. It cannot be pressed to mean first in relation to nonbelievers, as though the first and second resurrections (Rev. 20), however these are understood, were being described. That is not the thought of this passage.

84. He does not say simply σὺν αὐτοῖς but ἅμα σὺν αὐτοῖς, and he places the expression early, before the verb. ἅμα is usually taken as an adverb giving a separate idea, "simultaneously, together with them." This may be so, but Lightfoot maintains that the combination ἅμα σύν is too common to allow the words to be separated. Moule, however, denies that it forms a "compound preposition," and says further,

The verb Paul uses for "caught up" is one that means "to seize, carry off by force" (GT). There is often the notion of a sudden swoop, and usually that of a force that cannot be resisted. The applicability of such a verb to the snatching away (the "rapture") of the saints is obvious. Some scholars have seen in this a secret action that will suddenly remove the saints from the world preparatory to the great tribulation (Rev. 7:14). To this two things must be said. One is that this is the only place in the New Testament that speaks unambiguously of the rapture (there are other places that may justly be held to refer to it when it is established by this passage, but none that is sufficient to establish it). Therefore we must not be unduly dogmatic about it. Had we an abundance of detail recorded we could say a great deal, but as it is we have no more than a few simple facts. We must not read our pet theories into them.

The other is that it is very hard to fit this passage into a secret rapture. Paul has said that the Lord will descend "with a loud command, with the voice of the archangel and with the trumpet call of God." It may be that from this he intends us to understand that the rapture will take place secretly, and that no one except the saints themselves will know what is going on. But one would scarcely gather this from his words; it is difficult to understand how he could more plainly describe something that is open and public.[85] I do not doubt that, if he so chose, God could make the voice of the archangel, the shout, and the trumpet audible only to believers. But I very greatly doubt whether that is what Paul is saying.

It should be understood that the precise words Paul uses here do not take us far in our understanding of the details of that day. It is legitimate for students to ponder what he says and to draw their inferences therefrom. But that does not give them license to condemn others who do not draw the same inferences. There must be room for legitimate differences of opinion among those who respect the revelation given in the Bible.[86]

"there is nothing to prove that ἅμα is there doing any of the duty of a preposition, any more than *simultaneously* in the phrase *simultaneously with"* (*IBNTG*, p. 82). It is found twice only in the New Testament (again in 5:10); in our writings it stresses the "togetherness."

85. Cf. Calvin, "As a commander summons his army to battle with the notes of a trumpet, so Christ will call the dead to Him, by His resounding proclamation, which will be heard distinctly all over the world" (*The First Epistle of Paul the Apostle to the Corinthians,* trans. J. W. Fraser [Grand Rapids, 1960], p. 343).

86. This point is very well made by G. E. Ladd, *The Blessed Hope* (Grand Rapids, 1956), *passim.*

There may be significance in the meeting place being "in the air." In the first century the air was often thought of as the abode of demons (Satan is described as "the ruler of the the kingdom of the air," Eph. 2:2).[87] That the Lord chooses to meet his saints there, on the demons' home ground so to speak, shows his complete mastery over them. The expression rendered "to meet"[88] may be used of commonplace meetings, but it has also a more formal use, and, for example, Milligan cites examples of its use for "the formal reception of a newly arriving magistrate." It implies the "welcome of a great person on his arrival" (Moffatt, *EGT*). It may well be that there is a touch of the formal here, with the thought of a royal reception. The saints are to be presented to the King.

Do the saints go on to heaven with the Lord? Or do they all proceed to earth? To a renewed earth? Paul does not satisfy our curiosity. He brings his account of these glorious happenings to a close with the assurance, "so we will be with the Lord forever." Everything leads up to this, and after this has been said there is nothing to add.[89] Nothing could more adequately indicate the Christian's bliss.

18 In the light of this glorious prospect Paul calls on his readers to encourage one another (for "encourage" see on 3:2). It is interesting that he does not urge them simply not to faint. This information, he thinks, should impel them to be active in seeking one another out and strengthening one another. And well they might, for it is an inspiring thought that death makes no difference for our relationship to the Lord. All things and all people are in his hands. When it is his will to bring in the end of this age, those who have died in him and those who still survive will be united in his presence. The thought gives meaning to existence and suggests the certainty of ultimate triumph.

Neil asks whether Paul's words are any encouragement to us, and proceeds, "If we seek information as to the actual procedure to be gone through by believers after death, or the events that will accompany the end of time and history, our own guess is as good as Paul's or the

---

87. See SBk, IV/1, p. 516 for the idea in Judaism.

88. εἰς ἀπάντησιν. When used of meeting dignitaries there is often the thought that the great one is escorted to the city of his destination. But it would be perilous to push the expression here to mean that the saints will escort the Lord as he returns to the earth.

89. It is possible that nothing more is added because the sequel is so well known. The teaching of "eternal judgment" is among "the elementary teachings about Christ" (Heb. 6:2). Paul may have it in mind that the Thessalonians were in no doubt on that score.

apocalyptists.' " He then argues that we can look beneath "the traditional superstructure of eschatological imagery" and reach the conviction that "those who die in Christ live in Christ." We can perhaps reach a more satisfactory position by another route. Phillips translates, "God has given me this message on the matter, so by all means use it to encourage one another." While we may feel that this is more of a paraphrase than a translation, yet it faithfully reproduces the thought of the apostle. He is not suggesting that he has made a guess, which he believes to be a good one, and of which they may care to make some use. He speaks "according to the Lord's own word" (v. 15; cf. Phillips, "Here we have a definite message from the Lord"). It is because God has been pleased to reveal this part of his purpose that the Thessalonians (and we) may comfort one another. It is not on Paul's guesses or our own that our strength rests. It is on what God has revealed.

1 THESSALONIANS 5

B. THE TIME OF THE PAROUSIA (5:1-3)

1 Now, brothers, about times and dates we do not need to write to you, 2 for you know very well that the day of the Lord will come like a thief in the night. 3 While people are saying, "Peace and safety," destruction will come on them suddenly, as labor pains on a pregnant woman, and they will not escape.

Having begun to speak about the Parousia, Paul uses the certainty of the Lord's coming as a means of urging the Thessalonians to greater efforts in Christian living. He has so far been concerned with the way the Parousia will affect the dead, but he now turns to the way the living relate to it. But before he actually gets into this exhortation he has a few words to say on the subject of the time of the Parousia.

1 "Now, brothers, about times and dates" introduces a new section of the letter.[1] The distinction between the two words "times" and "dates"[2] is not very easy to reproduce in English, for we habitually regard time simply as a matter of duration. Our idea of time is very nearly identical with that conveyed by the former of the two words. Indeed, we derive our word "chronology" from it. It denotes time simply as sequence. The word rendered "dates" can be more difficult. Sometimes the two words have much the same meaning, and the difference between them can easily be exaggerated, but when it is used distinctively this second word means time in its qualitative rather than its quantitative aspect. It can indicate the suitable time for the purpose in mind, and thus can mean something like "opportunity." It is the kind of time we have

---

1. Paul often uses περὶ δέ to introduce a new section (cf. 4:9). It marks the transition from relating the Parousia to the dead to pointing to its importance for the living.

2. χρόνος and καιρός. They are joined again in Acts 1:7.

in mind when we think of "one crowded hour of glorious life." This second word, then, can have a reference to the kinds of events that are taking place rather than simply to the duration that is being measured.[3] The combination of the two is perhaps a way of bringing before the mind both the duration of time that must elapse before the coming of the Lord and the nature of the events that will characterize the end time. But it should be added that most scholars see little difference between the words here (Ward and Moore, however, distinguish them).

Paul maintains that there is no real need[4] for anyone to write to the Thessalonians about the times. This is not to be taken as the language of complimentary exaggeration. Paul did not hesitate to castigate his converts when they fell down on the job, nor to put them right when they were in error. There is abundant evidence from the two letters that he had spoken a good deal about the Parousia during his initial preaching.[5] An expression such as the one we are considering means that Paul was quite happy with the way the converts had learned this part of their lesson. It is not beyond the bounds of possibility that a number of the Thessalonians had been disturbed when some of the believers died. They may have wondered not only about the fate of these people when the Lord would come again, but also about whether they themselves would

3. The two words have been the subject of a good deal of discussion, as in J. A. T. Robinson, *In the End God* (London, 1950); John Marsh, *The Fulness of Time* (London, 1952); O. Cullmann, *Christ and Time* (London, 1951), and the chapter "Time and Times," in E. Stauffer, *New Testament Theology* (London, 1955). J. Barr has made some strong criticisms of the view that the two words can be sharply distinguished in *The Semantics of Biblical Language* (Oxford, 1961) and *Biblical Words for Time* (London, 1962). It appears that too much has been made of the difference between the two words, but by the same token Barr seems to have made too much of their similarity. In a context like the present one, καιρός is the right word. Marsh cites S. H. Butcher as saying that the Greeks tried to depict καιρός in sculpture as a "youth pressing forward with wings in his feet and back, holding a pair of scales, which he inclines with a slight touch of the right hand to one side. His hair is long in front and bald behind; he must be grasped, if at all, by the fore-lock." Marsh adds, "Thus while *kairos* presents an opportunity, it does not do so indefinitely" (*The Fulness of Time,* pp. 117-18).

4. As in 4:9 there is no need for him to do this, but he does it anyhow. He does not confine himself to doing the minimum for his friends.

5. It is widely accepted in modern theology that early Christian teaching was thoroughly eschatological. An important work is the volume of essays presented to C. H. Dodd, *The Background of the New Testament and Its Eschatology* (London, 1956), in which the contributors make it clear that eschatology is to be seen throughout the New Testament. Subsequent writing has underlined this.

live through to see the great day. Yet this did not mean that they were unsound on the matter of "times and dates." They knew quite well that there was no way of predicting when the great event would take place, but they had been reminded of their own mortality. They feared lest they should lose their place in the Parousia. Paul's answer to the previous difficulty should have cleared up the position for such people. But he leaves nothing to chance. He reminds them of what they already knew on this subject, and helps them to relate this knowledge to their current problem.

2 What Paul has said negatively in verse 1 he repeats positively when he says that the Thessalonians "know very well." He puts the emphasis on "you yourselves";[6] they have no need of an instructor in the matter. So also "very well" means that their knowledge in this matter is complete and needs no supplement. There is a touch of irony about this way of putting it: you know very well that no one can know when this will be! Some have held that the term implies that this knowledge rested ultimately on a saying of Jesus. That would mean that it was solidly based and that no addition or modification need be looked for. Such a saying might be Matthew 24:43 (= Luke 12:39), or that reported in Acts 1:7, which is noteworthy in that it makes use of the same expression "times or dates" as here.[7] But we cannot be sure that this is really implied.

The coming day is spoken of as "the day of the Lord."[8] This is a very ancient expression, for it was already well known in the time of Amos, who mentioned it for the express purpose of refuting erroneous ideas about it then current (Amos 5:18-20). The idea was thus older than his day, and perhaps considerably older. The point that Amos made was that the day would be one of judgment on all people. The Israelites could expect to be punished then for their sins, just as they expected that other people would be punished. This is one of a number of places where concepts used of Yahweh in the Old Testament are applied to Christ in

6. He uses the pronoun αὐτοί and puts it first in the sentence.

7. Except that in Acts 1:7 neither word has the article.

8. Neither noun has the article, which indicates that the expression was a stereotyped one, almost a proper noun. Milligan thinks that in addition "emphasis [is] laid on the character of the day, a day *of the Lord*." He cites Davidson: it "belongs to Him, is His time for working, for manifesting Himself, for displaying His character, for performing His work—His strange work upon the earth." For the concept of "the day of the Lord" in the Old Testament see H. H. Rowley, *The Faith of Israel* (London, 1956), pp. 177-201. Rowley gives full references to the literature on the subject.

the New, a revealing insight into the ways the first Christians viewed their Savior. The thought of final judgment carries over into the New Testament understanding of the Day, and one way of referring to it is to call it "the day of judgment" (2 Pet. 2:9). In line with this is its designation as "the day of God's wrath, when his righteous judgment will be revealed" (Rom. 2:5). By contrast it may be thought of as "the day of redemption" (Eph. 4:30). Again, its connection with the Deity may be stressed, for on that day God's action will be manifested as never before. Thus we find "the day of God" (2 Pet. 3:12), "the day of Christ Jesus" (Phil. 1:6), "the day of the Lord" (1 Cor. 5:5), and "the day of our Lord Jesus Christ" (1 Cor. 1:8). It may be simply "that day" (2 Thess. 1:10; see *RSV*), or "the last day" (John 6:39-40), or "the great Day" (Jude 6). It is clear that the early church found a large place for the events of that Day, and that it was a major concept for them. Here the emphasis is on the Parousia, the great event of that great day. In view of the many-faceted character of that Day it is not surprising that it presented problems to the Thessalonians; later on this was to be in part the cause of the second letter (2 Thess. 2:2).

The event is vividly before Paul's mind, and he makes use of the present tense rather than the future (which *NIV* for some reason substitutes; the tense "suggests certainty rather than immediacy," Whiteley). Yet despite the fact that it is so vivid to his mental vision, he knows full well that its coming will be totally unexpected. In this we see the combination of two strands of teaching that are common throughout the New Testament. On the one hand that Day is certain, and believers must continually be expecting it. The Lord comes "soon" (Rev. 22:20). Yet no one can know when it will be (Mark 13:32).[9] It will come on the world unexpectedly. It will come like "a thief in the night." The comparison to the coming of a thief is found elsewhere, but this is the only place where "in the night" is added[10] (Paul will pick up the "night" motif in the following section). The addition completes the picture of a totally unheralded approach, devastating in its unexpectedness. This does away with all date fixing.

What he says bears on another matter that is a source of dispute

9. This is one of the many points in which Paul's understanding of the End is derived from that of Jesus. G. R. Beasley-Murray has convincingly demonstrated that Paul's eschatology, as shown in these epistles, is dependent on that of Jesus (*Jesus and the Future* [London, 1954], pp. 232-34).

10. The addition is found in some MSS of 2 Pet. 3:10, and it occurs, e.g., in *KJV*. But it is absent from P⁷² ℵ B P Ψ etc. and should not be read.

among evangelicals, namely, as to whether believers will be left on earth to pass through the great tribulation of the last days. The language of this section could be understood either way. It seems to me that the probability is that it should be taken as signifying that believers will pass through the day spoken of. Paul speaks of them as being ready (v. 4), not as being taken out of the trouble in question.[11] But I fully recognize that other interpretations are possible, and suggest that it is not wise for any of us to condemn those who understand such passages differently.

3 The unexpectedness of the coming of that Day is illustrated by the behavior of unbelievers when it comes.[12] The verb ("are saying") has no expressed subject, but there is no real doubt as to who are in mind.[13] Unlike the Christians, the unredeemed world will have no thought of a cataclysmic end to the universe, and it will be rejoicing in a fancied security right up to the very moment of the disaster.[14] Moffatt brings this out by rendering, "when 'all's well' and 'all is safe' are on the lips of men." "Peace," as we saw in our comments on 1:1, usually in the New Testament denotes the prosperity of the whole person, but in this context the emphasis is rather on the absence of alarms. Paul is speaking of a complete failure to reckon with the realities of the situation. So also with the word "safety." It is an unusual word with a basic meaning like "that cannot be shaken."[15] Under the circumstances this is the height of folly and misapprehension.

11. For the question of whether Paul expected believers to undergo the events of that Day or escape them, may I refer once more to the very sane and able discussion in G. E. Ladd, *The Blessed Hope* (Grand Rapids, 1956). Ladd argues for a premillenarian, posttribulationist coming of the Lord. Although his subject is so very controversial, his discussion is in a thoroughly irenic spirit and is on a high plane throughout.

12. The thought of the previous verse is continued without a connecting particle (though some scribes felt the need of one and inserted δέ or γάϱ).

13. When believers are mentioned in v. 4 it is with the words ὑμεῖς δέ, ἀδελφοί. This expression indicates a marked contrast with the preceding, who must accordingly be unbelievers. But we scarcely need the grammatical point; the sense is clear enough.

14. The present, λέγωσιν, indicates that they will still be saying these words at the very moment when the "destruction" comes "suddenly." On the construction see E. A. Abbott, *Johannine Grammar* (London, 1906), p. 385.

15. ἀσφάλεια = ἀ privative + σφάλλω, "to make to totter." MM inform us that in the papyri the noun occurs innumerable times in the commercial sense, 'a security'." Frame considers the two words (rendered "peace" and "safety") to be "virtually synonymous," but he notes Ellicott's distinction: "εἰϱήνη betokens an inward repose and security; ἀσφάλεια a sureness and safety that is not interfered with or compromised by outward obstacles."

The startling nature of the disaster is further emphasized by the use of the unusual adjective rendered "sudden"[16] (*NIV* changes to the adverb). This word is placed in an emphatic position, right in the forefront of the clause. Again, the verb is in the present tense for greater vividness, and it is a verb that is often used of sudden appearances (though the verb itself does not necessarily include the idea of suddenness).

The disaster itself is described as "destruction." It is not completely clear what this means, but we are probably right in refusing to see in it anything approaching annihilation. Rather, the term is to be understood to mean loss of fellowship with God, the loss of that life which is really life. Like the term "death" when applied to ultimate reality, it is the opposite of life and not simply the cessation of existence. The word is used again in 2 Thessalonians 1:9, and there it clearly means banishment from the living presence of the Lord. This is its meaning here also.

If the destruction in question is to be sudden, it is also inevitable. This is the point of the last words of the verse. Sometimes the figure of childbirth is used to bring out the thought of the pain of birth (Isa. 13:8; Jer. 4:31; Matt. 24:8; Gal. 4:19). But here the thought is different. When the time has come for the pregnant woman, what is in the womb must come forth; the travail cannot be avoided. So will it be with the destruction of which the apostle writes. It is written into the nature of things and must inevitably come to pass.[17]

It will be completely impossible for people to escape, and Paul does not leave this to be inferred but states it categorically. He employs the emphatic form of the negative (which, outside quotations, he uses four times only in all his epistles; see the note on 4:15) and the compound form of the verb. It still needs emphasis that there are no other alternatives than life with the Lord or eternal loss. One or the other is inevitable.

C. CHILDREN OF THE DAY (5:4-11)

4 *But you, brothers, are not in darkness so that this day should surprise you like a thief.* 5 *You are all sons of the light and sons of the day. We do not belong to the night or to the darkness.* 6 *So*

---

16. αἰφνίδιος, elsewhere in the New Testament only in Luke 21:34.

17. Some expositors hold that the figure of childbirth is another way of indicating unexpectedness. But from early days in her pregnancy the mother-to-be is aware of the approximate time of the birth. The idea of inevitability is much more clearly indicated than unexpectedness.

then, let us not be like others, who are asleep, but let us be alert and self-controlled. 7 For those who sleep, sleep at night, and those who get drunk, get drunk at night. 8 But since we belong to the day, let us be self-controlled, putting on faith and love as a breast-plate, and the hope of salvation as a helmet. 9 For God did not appoint us to suffer wrath but to receive salvation through our Lord Jesus Christ. 10 He died for us so that, whether we are awake or asleep, we may live together with him. 11 Therefore encourage one another and build each other up, just as in fact you are doing.

Paul is led from a consideration of the day of the Lord to the thought that the Thessalonians have nothing to fear from the coming of that Day. This leads to the further thought that their lives should be in harmony with all that that Day stands for. It is not a difficult step from the idea of the day of the Lord to that of walking in the light, from that of the coming of Christ to that of the character of Christian people as "sons of the light." The coming of that Day must inspire God's people to live lives appropriate to their calling.

4 The Thessalonians are put in strong contrast with the unbeliev-ers of whom Paul has been speaking: "But" is adversative and "you" is emphatic. Paul sets believers over against the others as people who decidedly will not come into the condemnation he has been describing. "Darkness" is a common metaphor for the unsaved, just as light is a natural designation of the sphere of the saved. "In" darkness points us to darkness as the atmosphere in which such people live and move. Those immersed in such an atmosphere may well be surprised by the coming of that Day,[18] but not the Thessalonians.

That Day will come with all the suddenness and unexpectedness of a thief. The mention of "darkness" leads Paul to repeat his metaphor of verse 2. Perhaps, though, we should notice that there is a variant reading, "thieves," which yields a somewhat different sense. The mean-ing then would be, not that that Day will come as unheralded as a thief, but that it will surprise people, just as thieves are surprised by the coming of dawn. Those who are not ready will be surprised by daybreak on "the

---

18. The construction ἵνα . . . καταλάβῃ is an example of what Burton classes as "Clauses of Conceived Result." In such clauses "the action of the principal clause is regarded as the necessary condition of that of the subordinate clause, the action of the subordinate clause as the result which is to be expected to follow from that of the principal clause" (*MT*, 218, 219). BDF think that ἵνα is "substituted for the infinitive of result" (#391[5]).

day of the Lord." But both the attestation and the sense of "like a thief" are better, and we accept this reading accordingly.[19]

5 Having given the reason why they will not be overtaken in the calamity that will befall the unbelievers, Paul proceeds to consider more attentively what is involved in their character as believers. We should notice his "all"; among believers there are no exceptions. "You are all sons of the light," he says, which means that "light" is their distinguishing feature. In Semitic languages generally to be a "son" of something means to be characterized by that thing.[20] It is this manner of thinking which underlies the apostle's expression at this point. He does not say only that they walk in the light or live in the light, but that they are "sons of the light," that is, they are characterized by light. It points us to the complete transformation that takes place when anyone believes.

To this Paul adds the further expression "sons of the day" (an expression found only here in the New Testament). In this context we must understand "day" to refer to the day of the Lord.[21] While no doubt the term is suggested by the reference to light, it goes further. Believers find in the day of the Lord a situation in which they are perfectly at home. Just as light is their characteristic, so also is participation in all the glorious events of the day of the Lord. It should not be overlooked that Paul says this of them "all." There were some members of the church whom he must castigate, but even those he includes in this great description. He proceeds to change the subject from "you" to "we,"[22] making

19. Nevertheless it should be noted that many scholars accept the plural. The principal reason is that scribes would not be likely to alter κλέπτης to κλέπτας, whereas the reverse procedure is readily intelligible. This is of course true, but deliberate alteration is not the only explanation of the variant. If κλέπτης were original, κλέπτας could easily arise by a process of mechanical corruption, the ending being assimilated to that of the nearby ὑμᾶς. The reading κλέπτης is favored also by the possibility that there is a reminiscence of the words of our Lord reported in Matt. 24:43; Luke 12:39. Furthermore, in this context the sons of darkness who are surprised are not awake and watchful, like thieves, but asleep or drunken. Marshall further argues against thieves overtaken by day that "this extension and allegorisation of the metaphor is unlikely to be original."

20. For this idiom in Semitic or Greek see the note in A. Deissmann, *Bible Studies* (Edinburgh, 1901), pp. 161-66. It is not without interest that one of the Qumran scrolls is called "The War of the Sons of Light with the Sons of Darkness." Turner speaks of the construction as "the Hebrew genitive of quality" (M, IV, p. 90).

21. Cf. Bruce, "The day had not yet arrived, but believers in Christ were children of day already, by a form of 'realized eschatology.' The day, in fact, had cast its radiance ahead with the life and ministry of the historical Jesus and the accomplishment of his saving work."

22. The Western text reads "you" (D* F G etc.), but "we" is much more probable.

his expression more comprehensive still. It indicates that Paul is not laying down some hard regulations for the Thessalonians only, but setting forth the plain duty of all Christian people. And it aligns the apostle with his converts; he shares with them in Christian privilege and Christian duty. "We do not belong to the night or to the darkness," he says, setting "night" over against "day" and "darkness" over against "light." Those who "belong to the night" have no share in the day of the Lord, while "darkness" properly describes their spiritual condition.

6 Since Christians are not bound in the darkness of unbelief, certain consequences follow.[23] They must not be characterized by the kind of conduct that is proper to the night. Paul calls on them not to sleep as do "others." When he used this expression in 4:13 (there translated "the rest of men") he spoke of such people as being without hope. This is very much in point here, too, where he is thinking of the glorious hope of the Christian at the coming of the Lord. Unbelievers may well "sleep";[24] they are spiritually insensitive. But the believer should not take his standards from them. They are of the world and therefore they behave as they do. Those who are not of the world should not conform their conduct to that of those who are. "Sleep" is natural enough for the sons of night, but it is entirely out of place in the sons of light.

So Paul urges the Thessalonians to wakefulness and sobriety. His word "watch" (*NIV*, "be alert") is a natural antithesis to "sleep," but we should not overlook the fact that this very verb is used a number of times for watching for the second coming (e.g., Matt. 24:42-43; 25:13; Mark 13:34-37). It denotes watchfulness with some effort.[25] Joined to it is an injunction to be sober (*NIV*, "self-controlled"), which should probably not be thought of as a warning against drunkenness[26] (there is no indica-

23. ἄρα οὖν is a strong expression indicating that what follows is a necessary conclusion. In the New Testament it is found only in the Pauline writings.

24. The verb for "sleep" here (*NIV*, "are asleep") is καθεύδω, and not κοιμάω as in 4:13-15. It is probably not without significance that καθεύδω is sometimes used of carelessness in moral issues (e.g., Eph. 5:14). Nor is it insignificant that it was used of the disciples in Gethsemane, after which Jesus said to them: "Watch and pray, so that you will not fall into temptation" (Mark 14:38).

25. γρηγορέω is a verb formed from the perfect ἐγρήγορα (from ἐγείρω), "to have been roused." Whereas ἀγρυπνέω indicates simply the absence of sleep (AS relates it to ἄγρυπνος, "seeking sleep"), γρηγορέω has also the idea of a determination to keep awake.

26. Nevertheless it should be noted that a warning against drunkenness is joined with an appeal to be watchful for the coming in two other passages, Luke 21:34 and Rom. 13:12-13.

tion anywhere in either epistle that such a warning was necessary at Thessalonica) but as an exhortation to temperateness and balance (cf. Best, "let us be alert and clear-headed").[27] The word has its affinities with the preceding one, and indeed Grimm-Thayer treat them as near synonyms. They give the particular meaning of this present verb as "a state untouched by any slumberous or beclouding influences . . . it becomes a term for wariness against spiritual dangers."[28]

7 The thought that certain kinds of conduct are appropriate enough in the sons of night but quite unbefitting to Christians underlies this whole section, as we have already seen. This thought now comes to the surface. Paul lists sleep and drunkenness in particular as activities of the night. The verb for "sleep" is that employed in the previous verse. While it may well be that there is a side glance at the fact that moral indifference well suits those who belong to the night, yet the main force of the verb simply seems to be that some activities are appropriate to the night, and sleep is preeminently one of them. Similarly, drunkenness is not usually carried on by the light of day (cf. Acts 2:15).[29] Those who are drunken revel at night.[30]

8 Once more Paul sets believers over against worldly people with his emphatic "But we."[31] Conduct of the sort he has been outlining has no place in believers, for they "belong to the day." This expression

27. Since drunkenness "may suggest either stupid unconsciousness or abnormal exultation," Frame suggests that the exhortation may be "either to perfect control of the senses without which vigilance is impossible or to quietness of mind (4:11) without which the peaceable fruits of righteousness essential to future salvation are unattainable." H. Preisker remarks, "he demands sobriety, and issues a special warning against the tension which might easily be caused by eschatological speculation" (*TDNT,* IV, p. 547).

28. Cf. O. Bauernfeind, who notes that in the New Testament νήφειν "consists in acknowledgment of the reality given with God's revelation and in discharge of the resultant ministry by worship, hope, love and warfare" (*TDNT,* IV, p. 939; he interprets the word as "hope" in the present passage).

29. It is counted as especially blameworthy when people "carouse in broad daylight" (2 Pet. 2:13).

30. The two occurrences of "get drunk" in this verse represent two different Greek verbs. The first is μεθύσκω, which in the active means "to make drunk" and in the passive "to get drunk," "to become intoxicated." The second, μεθύω, denotes "to be drunk." But in this passage it does not seem as though the difference is to be pressed; the two words are being used as synonyms. *RSV,* however, renders "those who get drunk are drunk at night."

31. ἡμεῖς δέ. The participle ὄντες is causal; *RSV* renders "since we belong to the day" (cf. *IBNTG,* p. 103).

probably has a double reference, pointing us both to the light and to the day of the Lord. Christians are characterized by light. Therefore they can have nothing to do with the deeds of darkness. They look for the day of the Lord. Therefore they must not be caught up in this world's night. "Be self-controlled" is the same verb as that used in verse 6, and it has a similar meaning of general temperateness, with the avoidance of all kinds of excess. It is given point here by the reference to drunkenness in the intervening verse.

All this reminds Paul that the Christian is a soldier,[32] and he changes his imagery to that of the armor with which the warrior is clad. This is a favorite device of the apostle. He employs it in a number of passages (Eph. 6:13-17 is perhaps the most notable, but see also Rom. 13:12; 2 Cor. 6:7; 10:4).[33] A comparison of these various passages will show that Paul is not consistent in the significance he attaches to the various pieces of armor. It is the general idea that attracts him, not the particular details. Thus in Romans he thinks of "the armor of light" without going into details. In 2 Corinthians 6 it is "weapons of righteousness in the right hand and in the left," while in 2 Corinthians 10 the reference is a general one to "the weapons we fight with." In Ephesians 6 the armor is different from that mentioned here, notably in the absence in that list of hope and love. Clearly Paul found the analogy helpful, but just as clearly he regarded the details as unimportant. They could be omitted altogether, or varied to suit the occasion.

Paul refers again to the great triad of faith, hope, and love, as in 1:3 (where see note). These three virtues are of paramount importance to the Christian and may well be insisted on again and again. Something of the centrality of these virtues to the Christian life may be indicated by the particular pieces of armor that symbolize them. The breastplate and the helmet are probably the most important items in a suit of armor, and Paul may intend us to infer that nothing in the Christian's equipment surpasses faith, love, and hope.[34] He mentions only defensive armor, for his interest here is in defense, namely, defense against surprise. It may

---

32. Just what the connection is between the day and the armor of the soldier is not easy to grasp (perhaps the soberness expected of soldiers?), but Paul makes the same transition in Rom. 13:12-13.

33. Cf. Isa. 59:17 with its description of Yahweh as a warrior armed. See also Wisd. 5:17-22.

34. Calvin comments, "He omits nothing of what belongs to spiritual armour, for the man that is provided with *faith, love,* and *hope* will be found in no department unarmed."

also be relevant to notice that here, as in 1:3, hope comes last, following the logical order of Christian experience but also as a sort of climax. This is especially appropriate in this place where so much attention is being given to the second coming with all that that means to the Christian in terms of hope's fulfillment. We should not overlook the fact that the verb "putting on" is an aorist participle. It may well be that it is meant to convey the idea of a decisive act.[35]

The last phrase in the verse brings salvation before us, the inclusive concept that sums up Christ's great work for sinners. The term reminds us of the peril in which we are placed by our sin, for otherwise we would be in no need of being saved. It reminds us, too, that the fundamental question to be faced is that of the Philippian jailor, "What must I do to be saved?" (Acts 16:30). It reminds us, further, of the adequate provision for our salvation that has been made in Christ, and of which the great New Testament concepts like redemption, justification, and the rest are aspects. In one sense this salvation is a very present reality, but in another it is yet to be brought to its consummation, and it is this forward-looking aspect that is before us when we read of "the hope" of salvation. At the same time we should be clear that the use of the term "hope" does not imply any uncertainty. The New Testament idea of hope includes the notion of certainty, for it is grounded in the divine action. But it is not realized as yet, and thus it is still hope, not sight.

9 Being launched on the subject of salvation, Paul follows it up. Salvation is both "now" and "not yet," and Paul neglects neither. His first point is that salvation proceeds from God's appointment. This is a point of considerable importance for him, as we see from the prominence it has throughout his writings. We have already noticed his emphasis on the divine call (2:12; 4:7), and the way he speaks of Jesus as delivering us from the wrath (1:10). In one way or another this great truth is always coming out, for it is central to the gospel. All other religions in the last analysis present people with something that they must do if they would be saved. Christianity alone tells us that all has been done. This is true of the manner of our salvation, for our sins were taken away through the blood of the cross. It is also true of the fact that we are saved at all. That is a matter of the divine appointment, of the fact that God calls us into this state. It is not to be understood as though we simply decided to

---

35. Though Frame identifies it as the participle "of identical action," Findlay thinks that it forms "a part of the exhortation: νήφωμεν enjoins a state; ἐνδυσάμενοι an act belonging to the state, and that goes to determine and characterize it" *(CGT)*.

belong to God. The word "appoint"[36] is not as specific as words like "called" or "predestinated," but here it amounts to much the same. It rests our salvation on the divine initiative.

Paul proceeds to speak of salvation negatively and positively. God's purpose for us is not wrath (see the note on 1:10). Modern translations (e.g., *JB,* "the Retribution"; *NEB,* "the terrors of judgment") often misrepresent what Paul is saying, but we should be clear that Paul writes of "wrath." Although the modern world likes neither the term nor the idea it connotes, we can scarcely do without either. There is an implacable divine hostility to everything that is evil, and it is sheer folly to overlook this or try to explain it away. Salvation includes the fact that God did not destine his own to experience his wrath.

On the contrary, he purposed that they should obtain salvation (with all that that means) through the Lord Jesus Christ. There is a little difficulty about the word rendered "to receive," which is often understood in some such way as "to obtain" *(KJV).* Such a translation makes it sound too much as though we ourselves are doing what is necessary to acquire our heavenly possessions. Against this it is suggested that the word has a rather negative meaning, and that it signifies something like "adoption" (i.e., being adopted). It can have a passive sense (e.g., Eph. 1:14; 1 Pet. 2:9) and may then be translated "possession." But while such a meaning is undoubted in some passages, it is hard to see how this fits into the present passage. Moreover, "acquiring" seems nearer the intrinsic meaning of the word (cf. its use in 2 Thess. 2:14, "share"; and Heb. 10:39, faith for the "acquiring" of salvation). To adopt this understanding of it is not to maintain that we are saved by our works, but simply that we are to make salvation our own by entering fully into the possession of it. Salvation, after all, is not an abstract theological concept, but an experienced reality, appropriated in the present life of faith. That nothing in the way of human merit or initiative is meant is made very clear by the following "through our Lord Jesus Christ." The full title is impressive, and the expression shows that the salvation spoken of is one that comes through Christ's work for us and not through anything that we do.

36. ἔθετο, used in John 15:16; 1 Tim. 2:7; 2 Tim. 1:11; 1 Pet. 2:8. F. J. A. Hort, discussing the use of this verb in the last-mentioned passage, says that it is "a somewhat vague word in itself," but adds that it "expresses simply the ordinance of God, perhaps with the idea of place added, that is, place in a far-reaching order of things" (*The First Epistle of Peter* [London, 1898], p. 123).

10 This is underlined by drawing attention to the basis of all salvation, the atoning death of the Lord. This is the one place in the two letters to the Thessalonians where Paul positively says that Christ died for[37] us; this may fairly be held to be implicit in a number of other places, but this is the only place where it becomes explicit. It is impossible to argue that the failure to mention the cross more often means that Paul had as yet no theology of the atonement. In the first place we must bear in mind that the Thessalonian letters are not doctrinal treatises, but occasional letters to meet specific needs. It is all the more significant that the cross should be mentioned at all in such letters. Then there is the fact that at the very time he was writing these letters Paul was preaching in Corinth, where his gospel gave full space for the cross (cf. 1 Cor. 2:1-5; 15:3-8). Moreover, where in the Thessalonian correspondence he does refer to the work of Christ for sinners, the full Pauline doctrine seems to be implied (see 1:10, for example, and the passage on the transformation of death through what Jesus has done, 4:14). There is also the point that the very casual manner of the reference here argues that the significance of the death was well known to the Thessalonians. Otherwise it would have had to be demonstrated for them.[38] The references to the *kerygma* throughout the New Testament show that the cross was the central element in the proclamation of the gospel to those outside. There is not the slightest reason for thinking that things were at all different in Thessalonica, and indeed Acts 17:3 shows that the cross *was* preached in that city.

The purpose of Christ's death is that believers should live[39] with him whether[40] they live or die. The verb "are awake" is the one we

---

37. Moule sees περί here (read by א* B 33) as synonymous with ὑπέρ (*IBNTG*, p. 63), so that it does not matter greatly which we read (but ὑπέρ should probably be accepted).

38. Moore points out that "Paul offers no explanation in these epistles as to *how* Christ's death was vicarious, nor why. This is because there was, in the matters under discussion in these letters, no occasion or necessity to do so." Cf. Wilson, "The simplicity of the reference points to the Thessalonians' familiarity with the doctrine of Christ crucified."

39. Milligan thinks that the use of the aorist ζήσωμεν points us "to this 'life' as a definite fact secured to us by the equally definite death (τ. ἀποθανόντος) of our Lord."

40. It is difficult to see any real difference in meaning between εἴτε with the subjunctive, and ἐάν with that mood (used, e.g., in Rom. 14:8). Burton regards the construction here as due to a preference for εἴτε . . . εἴτε "in spite of the fact that the meaning called for a Subjunctive" (*MT*, 253).

161

have seen in verse 6, where it is translated "be alert" (see note). In that
verse it has reference to an attitude of general watchfulness in the light
of the coming of the Lord. Here, however, it simply means "live."
Moffatt renders "waking in life" to make this meaning clear. A similar
comment must be passed on the verb "are asleep." It is that used with
reference to the conduct of the sons of night in verses 6 and 7, but here
it means death (Moffatt, "sleeping in death"). From 4:14 on, Paul has
been insisting that death is not victorious over the believer, and this is
his thought here, too. The believer is in Christ, and death cannot affect
that relationship.

It should be stressed that all this implies a very full theology. Paul
is maintaining that the death of Jesus has brought about a new relationship between God and sinners. Those who are Christ's live with him.[41]
There is the thought of that close union which elsewhere is expressed in
the pregnant phrase "in Christ." This relationship is not disturbed by
even such a final and decisive happening as death. Death is final and
decisive only when we speak in worldly terms. For believers the whole
concept has been transformed. For them it holds no terrors. In life or in
death they are in Christ.

11 Paul rounds off this section, as he had a previous one (4:18),
with an exhortation to "encourage one another." Phillips renders, "So go
on cheering and strengthening each other with thoughts like these." The
tense of the imperatives is the present continuous, and it conveys the
thought that this is something that they should do habitually. The verb
translated "encourage" has the idea of strengthening by one's words and
thus means a little more than "exhort" (see further on 3:2).

The second imperative brings before us the thought that these great
truths about the Parousia are not simply to enable us to hold our ground.
The Christian faith is never static, and the New Testament envisages the
Christian way as a continual growth. Those who are in Christ are people
who are growing in spiritual stature and in the knowledge and love of
God. Paul envisages the use of the great truths about the second coming,
the day of the Lord, the character of Christians as sons of that Day and
sons of the light, the necessity for watching, for understanding that God
has called us not unto wrath but unto salvation, and this at the cost of
the death of his Son, and the other matters to which he has been referring
—all as a means of promoting growth. The Thessalonians are to build
each other up. It should perhaps be added that Paul is very fond of this

---

41. "With" is ἅμα σύν, for which see the note on 4:17.

idea of the building up of Christians. The word he uses is properly applicable to such matters as building houses, but Paul habitually uses it metaphorically, of the building up of Christians in the faith.

He looks to the Thessalonians to accomplish this themselves, under the guidance of the Spirit. He uses two different expressions, "one another" and "each other,"[42] but they do not differ greatly in meaning. Together they emphasize the mutual responsibility of believers for one another and the kind of service they can render one another. His concluding expression, "just as in fact you are doing," shows us that what he enjoins is no airy idealism. He knows the way in which the Thessalonians were assisting one another, and he commends them for it. But he urges them to go forward on this way. Christians may never relax on the grounds that they have made sufficient progress.

VII. LIFE IN THE CHRISTIAN COMMUNITY (5:12-22)

12 *Now we ask you, brothers, to respect those who work hard among you, who are over you in the Lord and who admonish you.* 13 *Hold them in the highest regard in love because of their work. Live in peace with each other.* 14 *And we urge you, brothers, warn those who are idle, encourage the timid, help the weak, be patient with everyone.* 15 *Make sure that nobody pays back wrong for wrong, but always try to be kind to each other and to everyone else.*

16 *Be joyful always;* 17 *pray continually;* 18 *give thanks in all circumstances, for this is God's will for you in Christ Jesus.*

19 *Do not put out the Spirit's fire;* 20 *do not treat prophecies with contempt.* 21 *Test everything. Hold on to the good.* 22 *Avoid every kind of evil.*

There were evidently some problems in personal relationships among the Thessalonians, and in the concluding moments of his epistle Paul

---

42. The latter expression, εἰς τὸν ἕνα, is very unusual, but it does not seem to differ greatly in meaning from the preceding ἀλλήλους. Lightfoot thinks that it is "somewhat stronger" than ἀλλήλους. Malherbe denies that the two expressions are equivalent; he holds that εἰς τὸν ἕνα signifies "person to person" (*NTS* 36 [1990], p. 388).

gives attention to them. There is some difference of opinion as to whether officebearers in particular are being addressed, and some have settled the point by reasoning that there were probably no officebearers at this early period in the church's history. Perhaps "officebearers" is the wrong term; for some of us it arouses associations of clearly defined official positions and a rigid division between those who hold office and those who do not. But it is hard to think of a better term, and it is very difficult to accept the view that there was nothing corresponding to "officebearers." Can any society function without some form of official leadership?

The first groups of Christians seem to have been organized on the model of the synagogue (an assembly of Christians is even called a synagogue in Jas. 2:2), and thus would have had a group of elders exercising oversight. This seems implied in the numerous references to elders from the earliest times. Thus Paul, as early as his first missionary journey, is pictured as appointing elders "in each church" (Acts 14:23). We have no reason for thinking that any local church continued for long without its elders. The functions of the leaders may not have been closely defined and perhaps were not the same in every place, but every group produces leaders of some sort. Granted that there were elders in the Thessalonian church, the likelihood is that they were not men of experience in any position of authority, for all our information seems to show that the church in this city was drawn predominantly from the lower strata of society. There is nothing improbable in the idea that inexperienced leaders exercised their authority in a rather tactless fashion. Some of the believers were misbehaving, refraining from working for their living and perhaps in other ways. The leaders of the church attempted to put things right, and their manner of doing so may well have aroused opposition. This was not serious, as in the case of the church at Corinth, which was rent by the disputes that took place. But Paul felt it wise to say a few words that might clear the matter up. These words have reference primarily, but not exclusively, to the leaders of the church. But since they have relevance to all, they are addressed to the church at large.

Some of the injunctions in this section of the letter are such as to be applicable to many churches, and it has been argued accordingly that Paul is giving the kind of teaching that would be used in most places. For this reason it is argued that we should not apply the words too closely to Thessalonica. There may be something to this, but at least we can say that Paul felt that what he was writing was needed at Thessalonica.

12 The occasion is one for appeal rather than authoritative commands, and Paul's address is gentle. There is nothing peremptory about his verb "ask"; it is often used of making request.[43] In keeping is the affectionate "brothers," so common in these epistles. The apostle asks them to "know" (*NIV*, "respect"; so BAGD; cf. 1 Cor. 16:15) their leaders, where the verb has the idea of knowing fully, appreciating their true worth. It indicates that the brothers had not realized as they should have the rightful position and worth of the people in question, and they are called on to know them better.

Those who have not been receiving due respect are described as "those who work hard among you, who are over you in the Lord and who admonish you." The Greek construction here has three participles following a single article, which means that it is one group of people who discharge all three functions, and not three different groups. It is this as much as anything that inclines us to think that the elders of the church are being addressed. Who else would discharge this triple function? But it is perhaps significant that they are given no title here; their work was more important than a title. It may well be that the duties performed by the leaders were not the same in every place; we are in the early period when the new church was feeling its way. But there is every reason for thinking that it is the people who were in due course (if not yet) called "elders" who are in mind. The verb for "work hard" is cognate with the noun "labor" in 1:3 (where see note). It indicates that these people had toiled till they were weary in the service of the church.[44] Though the term itself is not an ecclesiastical word,[45] and could be used of wearisome labor in general, it is noteworthy how often it is used of the labor of Christian preachers. If not a technical term, at least it was well adapted to expressing what is involved in Christian ministry.

It is possible that the two following participles represent two different and coordinate activities, but it is perhaps more likely that they

43. For the verb ἐρωτάω see the comment of Findlay quoted in the note on 4:1.

44. Calvin pungently deduces from the phrase "work hard" "that all idle bellies are excluded from the number of pastors."

45. Deissmann argues that the word springs from the life of the *manual* laborer. "With regard to all that Paul the tentmaker has to say about *labour*, we ought to place ourselves as it were within St. Paul's own class, the artisan class of the Imperial age, and then feel the force of his words" (*LAE*, p. 313). Paul uses the verb in 14 of its 22 New Testament occurrences; it may be used of the work of women (Rom. 16:12) as well as of that of men.

are to be understood as explanatory of the preceding one. The labor in question is that of exercising leadership and admonition, though this should not be understood as defining it exhaustively. The labor is of various kinds, but especially is it oversight and admonition.[46] Those who "are over you in the Lord," coming as it does between "work hard among you" and "admonish you," is not an official description of a technical order of ministry. But it is difficult to understand who could be meant other than officebearers in the church. It is sometimes urged that we should see the meaning as "them that care for you." Now all the members should be caring for one another, but if a particular group of "carers" is picked out, who would they be other than the officebearers? The verb may be used of informal leadership, but it is also an official word, describing the function of those who are officers.[47] The addition of "in the Lord" also seems to point us to officebearing in the church, while at the same time it adds the idea of the spiritual fitness of things. This is not a cold, external authority, but one exercised in the warmth of Christian bonds. Being "in the Lord," it is an authority to be exercised for the spiritual good of believers (2 Cor. 10:8), and not to give the officebearers opportunity for lording it over them (Luke 22:25-27).

The third function of these people is that of admonishing. The verb is Pauline,[48] and while its tone is brotherly, it is big-brotherly. There is

46. Cf. Frame, "the correlative καὶ . . . καί suggests that of the various activities involved in τοὺς κοπιῶντας ἐν ὑμῖν, two are purposely emphasized, leadership in practical affairs, and the function of spiritual admonition." Best holds that the word here signifies "caring for you," and he cites the relation of a father to his children (1 Tim. 3:4-5, 12). But in those passages, too, there is the thought of oversight.

47. MM say that προΐστημι means " 'put before,' 'set over,' and intrans. 'preside,' 'rule,' 'govern.' " They cite a number of examples to show that the term is used in the papyri of the activities of many kinds of officials. A. J. Malherbe firmly rejects the idea that we have a reference to officebearers and says of the translation "who are over you in the Lord" that it "is incorrect. . . . The verb *proistēmi* here describes caring for someone. . . ." He goes on, however, to admit that "the moral philosophers do not describe their pastoral care with these two terms" (Malherbe, p. 90; he puts a good deal of emphasis on the relationship of the moral philosophers to their students). We must not, however, interpret Paul by what the philosophers did. He was not a philosopher but an apostle; he was writing not about a philosophical school but a church.

48. νουθετέω is found in the New Testament only in the Pauline epistles and in Paul's speech to the elders of Ephesus (Acts 20:31). J. Behm says that strictly the verb means "to impart understanding (a mind for something)" and further, "It denotes the word of admonition which is designed to correct while not provoking or embittering" (*TDNT*, IV, pp. 1019, 1021).

often the notion of some tie between the admonisher and the admonished, and there is the thought of blame attaching to some wrongdoing that is being rebuked. "I am not writing this to shame you, but to warn you as my dear children" (1 Cor. 4:14) is a passage that brings out both thoughts: the tenderness that is unwilling to shame, and the blame for failure to do the right.

13 Paul adds the further request that the Thessalonians should hold their leaders in high regard.[49] There is some discussion as to whether what he says should be understood with the primary emphasis on high esteem (with love added loosely), or on esteem in love (with "exceedingly highly" inserted to show that this should be done without stint). In general, it seems most probable that the former is to be preferred. What is beyond dispute is that Paul is urging his readers to both attitudes (cf. Moffatt, "hold them in special esteem and affection"). He wants the officials to be highly regarded, and not dismissed as of no account. His adverb "exceedingly highly" (*NIV* paraphrases) is a very expressive and emphatic compound, found in this precise form here only in the New Testament.[50] Paul wants them to be loved (*REB* and *JB* have "affection," but Paul is speaking of more than this; he says *love*); they are not to be regarded simply as the cold voice of authority. Love is the characteristic Christian attitude to people, and this should be shown in the church. Especially is this so in relationships like those between the rulers and the ruled, which in other groups are apt to be formal and distant. Christian love, *agapē*, is not a matter of personal liking (see on 1:3), and it is in keeping with this that Paul expressly says that they are to esteem their rulers in love "because of their work." It is not a matter of personalities. It is the good of the church that is the important thing. The church cannot be expected to do its work effectively if the leaders are not being loyally supported by their fellows. It is a matter of fact that to this day we are often slow to realize that effective leadership in the church of Christ demands effective following. If we are continually critical of those who are set over us in the Lord, small wonder that they are unable to perform the miracles that we demand of them. If we bear in mind "because of their work," we may be more inclined to esteem them very highly in love.

49. ἡγέομαι usually means "to deem." The meaning "to esteem" is found very rarely, if at all, outside this passage. This has led to other suggestions (see Frame's note). These, however, are unconvincing, and the context makes it clear that "esteem" is right.

50. I.e., if we read ὑπερεκπερισσῶς (with B D* F G). The related ὑπερεκπερισσοῦ is found in Eph. 3:20; 1 Thess. 3:10 (and in ℵ A D² Ψ in the present passage).

Some exegetes have felt that the exhortation to be at peace brings us to a different subject. It is true that the verb is quite general in its meaning and that injunctions to be at peace are to be found elsewhere where there is no disciplinary problem. Yet in this place it seems that Paul is continuing to deal with the situation in mind in the earlier part of the verse. Any failure of the rank and file to be on proper terms with their leaders is serious, so the apostle includes an injunction to set these things right (notice the change from "we ask you, brothers" to the imperative, "Live in peace"). The form of the imperative indicates that Paul himself is trying to keep the peace by not taking sides. He does not say "be at peace with them," which would savor of calling on the church members to subject themselves to their leaders, but "Live in peace with each other," which makes the injunction equally binding on leaders and followers. Both are to keep the peace (cf. Mark 9:50; Rom. 12:18; 2 Cor. 13:11).

14 The address "brothers" shows that these words are addressed to the whole of the membership and not simply to the leaders (as Chrysostom held: "Here he addresses those who have rule"). In verse 12 the "brothers" seem to be distinguished from "those . . . who are over you in the Lord"; now we have a further exhortation to the "brothers," which surely is to be understood in the same way. Just as verse 12 was addressed to the whole church (not simply to the leaders), so is this verse. The content of this charge is to look to the needs of certain people in the church. While this would be in a special measure the responsibility of those holding office, it was also something that lay on the shoulders of all (perhaps it was something the leaders should lead others to do). It was (and is) characteristic of the Christian understanding of life that the entire brotherhood is charged with responsibility for all. For Christians care for others is not to be left to any special class of believers.

For "warn" see the note on verse 12 (where it is translated "admonish"). The word translated by "idle" is really a military word, and originally referred to the soldier who is out of step or out of rank, or to the army moving in disarray. Milligan's long note[51] shows that the term was used in Hellenistic Greek for idleness. Frame adds that it is not idleness in the sense of legitimate leisure[52] that is meant, but loafing. The use of this word makes it quite clear that some Thessalonians had ceased to work and were

---

51. Additional Note G.
52. Which is σχολάζω (1 Cor. 7:5); cf. the use of σχολή, "a school." Yet it should be borne in mind that σχολάζω can have the idea of culpable idleness, as we see from Exod. 5:8, 17 (LXX).

imposing on the generosity of others. Paul counsels them all to take steps to end this state of affairs; as Bruce reminds us, this was the concern of all. It brought discredit on the whole church, and it was church members who had to support the slackers who brought the discredit.

If the first point has to do with pulling up the slackers, the second is concerned rather with exercising tenderness toward the discouraged. For "encourage" see on 2:12 (where *NIV* translates "comforting"). The word is well adapted to expressing a tender concern, quite in the spirit of "a bruised reed he will not break" (Isa. 42:3). There are those who are not naturally bold, or who are temporarily overwhelmed by the stress of life. Such should not be condemned by their more robust colleagues, but consoled and encouraged, so that they may be fitted for the battle once more. A similar sympathetic attitude is inculcated by the next words, "help the weak,"[53] where the verb is one that is often used of holding on to someone (e.g., Luke 16:13). The thought is that it is good for weak souls to know that there are others who are with them, who will cleave to them in the difficult moment, who will not forsake them. In various places Paul has a good deal to say about the weak (notably in Rom. 14 and 1 Cor. 8). He leaves us in no doubt that there is a place for such in the church, and further that the strong have a particular duty toward them. So here the weak are not to be simply abandoned, but made to feel that they belong, and that they have strong comrades in Christ.

Paul rounds off the exhortation with "be patient with everyone."[54] This should be taken as putting in general terms and with some amplification what he has just been saying in particular cases. Christians should not be putting their own interests first and taking a strong line with those who do not agree with them. Rather, they must be patient with all people, bearing their manners, and patiently seeking to lead them in the way of the Lord. It is more important for them to render service

---

53. τῶν ἀσθενῶν here refers to the weak spiritually, as most commentators agree. The word can mean weak physically, but the sense of this passage is not "look after those who are unable to work," but rather "look after those who are weak in the faith." It is sometimes suggested that this means people like those troubled with problems associated with meat offered to idols (1 Cor. 8:7), or those with moral weakness. But we have no reason to see such a definite reference here, and it is better to take the term as a general one.

54. Wilson cites Lenski, "Longsuffering toward all means not only toward all in the three groups mentioned but toward all, including even outsiders, who may be very trying at times because of their hostile actions. The verb means to hold out long before taking action; God himself is longsuffering toward us."

than that their ego should be satisfied. To this end they must bide their time, refusing to be affronted, walking in the steps of the Lord.

15 This leads naturally to the thought that Christians are not to be provoked into acts of retaliation (cf. Matt. 5:44-45; Rom. 12:17).[55] Rather, their ruling attitude must be one of benevolence toward all, even those who act toward them in hostile fashion. Indeed, especially toward those who are hostile to them.[56] It is easy enough to be well disposed toward those who treat us well, but it is of the essence of the Christian attitude that *agapē,* self-giving love, be practiced toward all, even the unkind and vindictive. Our Master, for our salvation, endured patiently the insults and the injuries of wicked men. He, the Just, died for the unjust. In both these ways his example is important for his people. As the servant is not greater than his Lord, we must expect the same kind of treatment, and therefore we must expect to be called on to show the same kind of patience under provocation. And since he came to die for sinful people, we must expect that our meekness is to be by way of ministering to the needs of the sinful also.

Thus it is that the New Testament often calls on believers to forgive injuries. This is expressed in the Lord's Prayer, and Jesus insisted on the point more than once (Matt. 5:38-42; 18:21-35; Luke 6:35, and elsewhere). There are very close parallels to the present passage (Rom. 12:17; 1 Pet. 3:9), which indicates that it was something in the nature of a standard injunction in the early church. It may even go back to some saying of Jesus. That such a precept was so widely accepted in a body subject to such constant ill-treatment as the early church is remarkable enough. That it was put into practice to such a large extent is even more so. It may be that this was responsible in some measure for the impact the early Christians made on the people of their day. At any rate, it is worth reflecting when we are tempted to think of the clash of hostile forces today, and of how difficult it is for us to put such precepts

55. The combination of second and third persons, ὁρᾶτε μή τις, perhaps conveys the idea that the whole group is being held responsible for the conduct of each individual. They are not only to abstain from retaliation, but to be sure that none of their number retaliates. "Blessed are the peacemakers" (Matt. 5:9). Bengel comments, "A person who has received an injury, and is in a passion, sees too much; his neighbours therefore ought to see (for him)."

56. Cf. Calvin, "For particular excuses are wont to be brought forward in some cases. 'What! why should it be unlawful for me to avenge myself on one that is so worthless, so wicked, and so cruel?' But as vengeance is forbidden us in every case, without exception, however wicked the man that has injured us may be, we must refrain from inflicting injury." Denney brings out the difficulty we experience in restraining ourselves by reminding us that "revenge is the most natural and instinctive of vices."

into practice, that the Thessalonians to whom these words were addressed were themselves in no easy situation. Subject to constant harassment from both Jew and Gentile, they could easily have become embittered. But it was just in this situation that they were called on to render to no one evil for evil. The great precepts of the Christian faith have always been addressed not only to those who find them easy to keep but to all. And they can be kept, because with the command God provides the power.

The positive exhortation, "always pursue what is good toward one another" (which *NIV* renders "always try to be kind to each other") must, in this context, refer to acts of love in the face of hostility rather than to ethical goodness in general. At the same time it should be noted that the term is a broad one. Paul is not simply saying, "Do little deeds of love when you might be expected to retaliate." He is laying down goodness in the face of provocation to evil as a great general principle that must underlie the conduct of Christians at all times. It is one of their springs of action. The verb is in the continuous present, so that a habitual attitude is inculcated, and this is reinforced by the adverb "always." The verb is "pursue," which means follow with some eagerness.[57] The line of conduct in question is to be exercised toward members of the brotherhood and outsiders alike. As we saw on 4:9, there is a brotherly love that Christians should practice among themselves, but this pursuit of goodness in the face of provocation is something that they should not restrict. No matter where nor how they are provoked, the obligation lies on them to follow the good unswervingly (cf. 3:12; 4:12).

16 Paul proceeds to three activities that should characterize the Christian (and which he links elsewhere, Phil. 1:3-4). Perhaps the first of these, "Be joyful always," is especially suitable after what he has been saying. The refusal to nurse grudges and to retaliate when provoked is not something that is to be attempted in a spirit of suffering resignation. It is possible ostensibly to forgive, but to make quite clear that the forgiver is deserving of great credit for his restraint, and that he is very conscious of the magnitude of the wrong that has been done to him. Jesus did not give that impression, and Paul is saying that his followers should not do so either. Forgiveness ought to be a joyous affair, with genuine Christian zest for life bubbling through. Christians are people who have been born all over again (John 3:3, 7); they have been created anew (2 Cor. 5:17). They do not see

---

57. διώκω also means "persecute"; "It is striking that Paul the former persecutor could use a verb meaning 'pursue' or 'persecute'. . . . Did he want his readers to put the same intensity into altruism as he had put into his persecution?" (Ward). It is used of the pursuit of love (1 Cor. 14:1); peace (Heb. 12:14); righteousness (1 Tim. 6:11).

171

things as the earthling sees them, but, as children of the heavenly Father, they go rejoicing through their Father's world. The New Testament does not give us a picture of believers as people who are always screwing themselves up to the point of doing unpleasant things in the service of their God but rather of those who are glad to live out the implications of their faith. There is a serious purpose to life, and that is not overlooked. Sometimes it will lead to stern and serious action. But the emphasis is on the truth that by and large the way of Christians is a happy way. Their spiritual resources are so great that earthly things cannot disturb their composure, and they go on their way with a song in their hearts (Col. 3:16). Joy is part of the fruit of the Spirit (Gal. 5:22; cf. Rom. 14:17), and Paul has made it clear that the Thessalonians knew this joy (1:6). He is not writing about a joy that Christians produce by their own efforts. It is natural for people to be happy when things go well with them. But it is not this natural joy, dependent on circumstances, that is the special characteristic of Christians. It is the joy that comes from being "in Christ." Thus it is that the New Testament contains so many exhortations to joyful living—startlingly many, if we fix our attention on the outward circumstances of the early Christian communities. Persecution was always threatening and often actual. Believers were usually in straitened circumstances and compelled to work hard for their living. Their lot can rarely have been other than hard. But if we fasten our attention on these things, we put our emphasis in the wrong place. They thought more of their Lord than of their difficulties, more of their spiritual riches in Christ than of their poverty on earth, more of the glorious future when their Lord should come again than of their unhappy past. So the note of joy rings through the New Testament, and so Paul, who himself knew what it was to rejoice in difficult circumstances (Acts 16:25; Rom. 5:3; Col. 1:24), can say, "Be joyful always" (cf. Phil. 4:4),[58] and speak of the Christian as "sorrowful, yet always rejoicing" (2 Cor. 6:10).

---

58. Lightfoot points out that "on the other hand, it may be said no less truly that sorrow is especially the Christian's heritage. For with a fuller sense of the exceeding sinfulness of sin, of the fearful significance of death, he has more abundant matter for sorrow in the scenes amidst which he moves, than those whose convictions are less deep. Yet the two attitudes are not antagonistic. They may, and do, coexist." Cf. also W. A. Visser 't Hooft, "It is one of the impressive aspects of the life of the Church in history that the churches under pressure or under persecution know so much more about the secret of Christian joy than the churches which live in circumstances of tranquillity" (The Renewal of the Church [London, 1956], p. 73). He goes on to point to New Testament passages where "suffering is understood as the merciful act of God by which he tests the faith of his people" (ibid.).

17 The injunction to continual prayer (cf. Luke 18:1; Rom. 12:12; Eph. 6:18) springs out of the same great idea as that to continual rejoicing. Christianity is a religion that turns people's thoughts away from themselves and their puny deeds to the great God who has wrought a stupendous salvation for them in Christ. It is of the very essence of the faith that it insists on the inability of sinners to bring about their salvation, either in the sense of the initial act whereby they enter a state of salvation, or in the sense of the day-by-day living out of the Christian life. For the putting away of their sins the atonement wrought by the Son of God is necessary. For the living of the dedicated life the power of the indwelling Spirit alone suffices. All along the way they experience their own insufficiency. Paul's exhortation to continual prayer fits into this picture. The Thessalonian believers (like all others) were dependent on God for everything. Continuing prayer is the continuing expression of this dependence.

Christians, then, are always conscious that they depend on God, and that they are always surrounded by God's love. Therefore, although they are not able to achieve anything worthwhile in their own strength, they have all that they need. This knowledge will keep them always rejoicing. Why should they be otherwise? And it will keep them always in the spirit of prayer. Prayer and rejoicing are closely related, for often believers find in prayer the means of removing that which was the barrier to their joy. Prayer is not to be thought of only as offering petitions in set words. Prayer is fellowship with God. Prayer is the realization of the presence of our Father. Though it is quite impossible for us always to be uttering the words of prayer, it is possible and necessary that we should always be living in the spirit of prayer.[59]

But believers who live in this way, conscious continually of their dependence on God, conscious of his presence with them always, find that their general spirit of prayerfulness in the most natural way overflows into uttered prayer. Again and again in Paul's letters (and especially in these two letters to the Thessalonians) the apostle interjects little prayers into his argument. Prayer was as natural to Paul as breathing. At any time he was likely to break off his argument or to sum it up by a prayer. In the same way he looks for the Thessalonians to live lives with such an attitude of dependence on God that they will easily and naturally

---

59. Paul's verb is προσεύχεσθε, which expresses devotion, the Godward look, rather than δέομαι, which would fasten attention rather on our need (see on 3:10). προσεύχομαι is the more comprehensive term, and can include the other words for prayer.

move into the words of prayer on all sorts of occasions, great and small, grave and festive. Prayer is to be constant. This does not, of course, mean that they are to spend all their time in uttering words of prayer; throughout these letters there are too many exhortations to be active in daily affairs for that to be accepted. Paul is arguing for lives lived constantly in a prayerful spirit.

18 The trio of injunctions is completed with the command "give thanks in all circumstances." Like the preceding two, this one springs from the great central truth of the gospel. As worldly people go on their way they meet with some things that make them happy, and some about which they complain bitterly. They conceive of life as a matter more or less of chance. Accordingly they welcome those workings of chance which favor their purposes and object to those which do not. But when anyone comes to see that God in Christ has saved him, everything is altered. Now it is apparent that God's purpose is being worked out, and the evidence of this becomes clear in the believer's own life and in the lives of those about him. This leads to the thought that the same loving purpose is being worked out even in those events which the believer is inclined not to welcome at all. When we come to realize that God's hand is in all things, we learn to give thanks for all things. Tribulation is unpleasant. Yet in the midst of tribulation who would not give thanks, knowing that the Father who loves us so greatly has permitted that tribulation only in order that his wise and merciful purpose might be worked out? So out of this great central truth of Christianity Paul calls on his friends to practice the continual giving of thanks.[60]

As he has already done in another connection (see 4:3), the apostle proceeds to give what he has said the highest possible authority by rooting it in the will of God. "This" is singular, but it is very probable that it applies to all three of the preceding injunctions. As we have seen, they all proceed from one root and may fittingly be regarded as a unity. They do not represent three different attitudes to life, but three aspects of one attitude.

As he has already done in 4:3 (where see note), Paul uses the word "will" without the article. The significance of this is that he is making no attempt to deal with the whole will of God. That will includes many

---

60. The expression here, ἐν παντί, does not mean "at every time," and, indeed, it seems to be differentiated from πάντοτε in 2 Cor. 9:8. Rather, it means "in every thing," i.e., "under all circumstances" (cf. Phillips, "whatever the circumstances may be"). But in practice praying "at every time" means much the same.

things, and many things of importance to the Thessalonians. But among them is this of which he now speaks. On this occasion there is the interesting addition "in Christ Jesus." The centrality of Christ to Christianity cannot be emphasized too strongly. We do not know God of our own selves, but only as he has pleased to reveal himself to us. Preeminently he has revealed himself in Christ, and preeminently he has revealed his will in Christ. The use of the compound name "Christ Jesus" reminds us of both the deity and the humanity of our Lord, and in this way heightens the solemnity of the injunction. Not only is it in Christ that the will of God is revealed, but it is in him that the power is given to us to enable us to live according to that will[61] (see on 3:11 for the close connection between the Father and the Son).

19 Another unit, this time with five exhortations, begins with a reference to the Spirit. It is unusual to find such an exhortation as "Do not put out the Spirit's fire" (though we do read, "do not grieve the Holy Spirit of God," Eph. 4:30). "Put out" properly applies to the extinguishing of a flame of some sort, such as that of a fire (Mark 9:48) or a lamp (Matt. 25:8). This is the only place in the New Testament where it is used in a metaphorical sense, though we do find such a sense in the Septuagint. It is used there of quenching love (Song 8:7), anger (Jer. 4:4; 21:12),[62] a hot mind (Sir. 23:16), and passions (4 Macc. 16:4). It has particular relevance when used of the Spirit, for his presence is aptly symbolized by fire (Acts 2:3). The positive injunction, "fan into flame the gift of God" (2 Tim. 1:6), is another way of expressing the truth Paul is concerned with here.

Exactly how the Thessalonians were trying to put out the Spirit's fire is not clear. But many passages in the New Testament indicate that the manifestations of the Spirit occupied a large place in the life of the early church. Where we may think of the Spirit in terms of that power within the believer which enables him to overcome evil and to produce the "fruit of the Spirit," many early Christians just as naturally thought of him as the producer of ecstatic manifestations of various kinds, speaking with tongues, prophesying, and the like. Both the ethical and the ecstatic are attested in the New Testament, and it is a question which of the two is meant

---

61. This is probably to be understood as *RSV*, "this is the will of God in Christ Jesus for you," but some understand it as *GNB*, "This is what God wants from you in your life in union with Christ Jesus." Both of course are true, but perhaps the former is more likely to be Paul's meaning.

62. Both θυμός and ὀργή are used.

here. The majority of commentators favor a reference to the ecstatic. They feel that the situation in Thessalonica was the opposite of that at Corinth. There Paul had to restrain those who were going to excess. Here, it is said, those who delighted in the ecstatic manifestations had come under the censure of the more stolid, and there was a very real danger of their being discouraged.[63] This may be so, but it seems to be reading a lot into the words of this verse. There is no other evidence that can be cited. In view of the very general character of the expression it may be well to understand the term more generally. In the second century Hermas maintained that both "the doubtful mind and the angry temper" grieve the Spirit, for he was given as a "cheerful" Spirit.[64] The same kind of thing may well be said here. Loafing, immorality, and other sins about which Paul has had occasion to warn his friends will quench the Spirit in anyone's life and result in the loss of spiritual power and joy.[65]

20 Those who see in the injunction not to quench the Spirit a reference to ecstatic manifestations usually understand the words about prophecy in a similar fashion. Some of the Thessalonians, they tell us, were like the Corinthians. They had been so carried away by the ecstatic gifts like speaking in tongues that they were despising more important things like prophecy. Paul would then be trying to restore a proper sense of values by insisting on the place of prophecy. This may be so, but, like the previous conjecture, this one seems to be reading a good deal into a rather simple expression. All that we can say for certain is that apparently some members of the church at Thessalonica had come to think of

63. Jewett finds here "the presence of conflicts over ecstatic manifestations in the congregation" and "tendencies to stamp out such ecstatic manifestations entirely." He holds that the position of these injunctions (the final topic in the final section) is important; the discussion "assumes a position of emphasis and particular congregational relevance for the letter as a whole" (Jewett, pp. 101, 102). But it is difficult to regard this as a balanced view. There is no reason to see ecstatic manifestations in 1:5-6, so that these two short verses (seven words only in the Greek) form the only place where such manifestations are to be found in the letter. These seven words do not give us the clue to the whole even though they do come near the end. And it is far from certain that Jewett's interpretation of those words is the right one.

64. *Mandate* 10:2, 3 (cited from Lightfoot's edition). The word for "cheerful" is ἱλαρόν.

65. The use of μή with the present imperative and not the aorist subjunctive probably represents a command to cease quenching (though Bruce regards this as doubtful; Best, however, says of the five imperatives in vv. 19-22, "μή with the present imperative implying that the practices rejected are already in existence"). If the construction is used strictly, it implies that some, at least, of the Thessalonians were quenching the Spirit. Paul calls on them to stop.

prophecy more poorly than they ought. Paul accordingly urges that prophecy be not despised.[66] If we are to conjecture, it seems more in accordance with what we know of conditions in this church to associate the despising of prophecy with second advent speculations. We know that there was much interest in the Parousia among the Thessalonians, and we know that throughout the history of the church such interest has commonly gone hand in hand with prophetic outbursts. One result that has usually followed has been that the more staid have rejected with decision both the advent speculations and the prophecy that has gone with them. It may be that something of the sort had happened at Thessalonica, and that Paul was reminding the church of the very real value of prophecy (cf. 1 Cor. 14:1).

It is often thought today that prophecy in the early church was more or less like preaching today. There is something to be said for this, but the essence of prophecy as the early church understood it appears to have been that the Spirit of the Lord spoke to and through people. Prophecy was one of the gifts of the Spirit (1 Cor. 12:10); a prophet spoke because "a revelation" (1 Cor. 14:30) had been made to him. From the human standpoint this was completely unpredictable, so that the revelation might be made to some other person "sitting down" (1 Cor. 14:30) and apparently not expected to prophesy. Since God spoke through people in this way, no limits could be placed on what might be said. Modern discussions generally insist that a prophet's function was rather to "forthtell" than to "foretell." While there is truth in this, it should not be forgotten that on occasion the prophet would foretell the future (cf. Acts 11:27-28; 21:10-11). While this does not seem to have been his characteristic function, it should not be overlooked. Prophets were held in high honor, and we find them mentioned along with apostles several times (e.g., 1 Cor. 12:28; Eph. 2:20; 3:5). It does not seem likely that the Thessalonians would be despising such exalted personages. But prophesying might be carried out occasionally by people who were not regular prophets (e.g., Acts 19:6), and the term here is broad enough to cover such phenomena. Wherever the Spirit might convey the revelation, the apostle counsels his friends to be receptive.

---

66. The verb ἐξουθενέω is a strong one, with the meaning "to make absolutely nothing of." Findlay says that it "denotes contempt *objectively,* as it bears on the person or thing despised; while καταφρονέω (1 Cor. xi.22) describes contempt *subjectively,* as it is in the mind of the despiser" *(CGT).* μή with the present imperative here signifies "Stop treating prophecies with contempt."

21-22 Although in this last section of the epistle Paul introduces very varied topics and treats them but briefly, it is interesting to observe how they link up with one another. So as he turns from the thought of prophecy, it is to that of testing all things;[67] the sequence is the same as that in which prophecy is followed by "the ability to distinguish between spirits" (1 Cor. 12:10). Paul may mean that, although prophets should be held in high regard, everything they say is not necessarily to be accepted; those who hear them must apply tests to see whether a given saying comes from God. It is not only prophecy that is to be tested, but "everything." And testing in turn leads naturally enough to the retention of the good and the rejection of the evil. What Paul has said in the previous verse might be misconstrued as an injunction to accept without further ado any utterance by a person who claimed to be a prophet and speaking by the Spirit. This would open the door to boundless credulity and all kinds of evil, and it was far from the apostle's mind. So he makes it clear that he expects his readers to use their common sense in such matters and to apply the necessary tests. At the same time the words he uses are quite general, and they must be held to apply to all kinds of things and not simply to claimants to spiritual gifts. It is part of the process of living out the Christian life that constantly the servant of the Lord is called on to discriminate between the base and the true, and fashion his or her conduct accordingly.

From the earliest times there has been a tendency to interpret this passage in the light of a saying attributed to Jesus: "Be approved bankers" (or "money changers," i.e., people who test coins).[68] There is more indication of a connection in the Greek than in our English translations, though the absence of the word "money changers" makes it doubtful whether Paul has the saying in mind. The verb "test" is often connected with the testing of metals, and it is not unlikely that this is the basic meaning of the verb. It may be applied to gold ("gold, which perishes

67. "But" (*NIV* omits) should probably be read before "test," for it has excellent manuscript attestation (it is read by א^c B D G K P etc.). It should be understood as adversative; prophecy is not to be despised but neither is it to be accepted without proper testing.

68. γίνεσθε τραπεζῖται δόκιμοι. J. Jeremias cites and discusses the saying (*Unknown Sayings of Jesus* [London, 1958], pp. 89-93). He notes that this saying is quoted more than any other noncanonical saying of Jesus and comments, "The indefatigable Resch has assembled no less than thirty-seven quotations and twenty allusions, in which the consensus with regard to the wording and interpretation is remarkable" (p. 89). We should probably regard this as a genuine saying of Jesus.

even though refined by fire," 1 Pet. 1:7), and this usage is common outside the Scriptures. The verb is used both of applying the test and of approving as a result of the test. Though the word "good" is not as closely connected with metals as is the verb, yet it is the right term to designate the true coin over against the spurious.[69] It means that which is good or beautiful in itself. It is very close in meaning to the other word rendered "good" in verse 15.[70] But where the two have their distinctive meanings, our present word seems to denote, as we have said, that which is inherently good, that which is good by nature, whereas the other concentrates rather on that which is good in its results. A little thought will show how appropriate the two are in their respective places in the present passage.

The point of this injunction, then, is that the Thessalonians are asked to apply tests. There are things that appear on the surface to be good. There are manifestations that are claimed to come from God. Such are not simply to be accepted at their face value, for it is not part of Christian simplicity to be credulous. All things must be tested. And not simply tested, but accepted wholeheartedly or rejected decisively as a result of the test. "Hold on to" denotes the firm acceptance of the good.[71] There must be no half measures.

The verb "avoid" is likewise a strong one. It is the verb Paul has used in 4:3 of keeping clear of fornication (see note), and here, as there, it is reinforced by a preposition that emphasizes the separation. If a thing is evil, then the believer must have no truck with it whatever.

There is some difference of opinion as to the meaning of the word rendered "kind." It signifies basically "that which meets the eye," "the external appearance." But from this it develops the secondary meaning of "kind" or "species." Thus it is possible to understand the present verse either as "avoid every visible form of evil," or "avoid every kind of evil." On the whole it seems likely that the latter meaning is to be preferred.[72]

---

69. Rutherford brings out some of this in his translation: "Rather, assay all things thereby. Stick to the true metal; have nothing to do with the base."

70. Frame says, "It is questionable whether in Paul's usage τὸ ἀγαθόν and τὸ καλόν (v. 21) can be sharply differentiated" (on v. 15).

71. κατέχω is a word of many meanings, as the notes of Frame and Milligan, as well as the lexicons, show. Most of its usages, however, stem from the two main ideas, "hold fast" and "hold back." The former is the meaning here.

72. Notice that while the good is viewed as a unity, evil is of many kinds. There is some dispute as to whether πονηροῦ should be taken as a noun (as NIV) or as an adjective ("abstain from every evil sort"). It is probable that NIV is correct, but there is no real difference of meaning.

Yet if the former be accepted, it must be borne in mind that where this word is used of outward form (as it generally is in the New Testament, e.g., Luke 3:22; 9:29; John 5:37) there is no suspicion that the outward form does not correspond to something real. The meaning will be "evil which can be seen," and not "that which appears to be evil."

VIII. CONCLUSION (5:23-28)

23 *May God himself, the God of peace, sanctify you through and through. May your whole spirit, soul and body be kept blameless at the coming of our Lord Jesus Christ.* 24 *The one who calls you is faithful and he will do it.*

25 *Brothers, pray for us.*

26 *Greet all the brothers with a holy kiss.* 27 *I charge you before the Lord to have this letter read to all the brothers.*

28 *The grace of our Lord Jesus Christ be with you.*

Paul has completed what he wanted to say to the Thessalonians. It remains only to conclude the letter in his usual style. He asks for prayers for himself and his coworkers, greets the church members to whom he has been writing, gives such a charge that he is sure the letter will be read to all, and ends with "the grace."

23 Now that the exhortations are concluded Paul passes over to prayer for his readers. The way in which he effects the transition (with the use of an adversative conjunction,[73] left untranslated in *NIV*) indicates that it is only in the power of the God on whom he calls that his exhortation can be brought to fruition. "I have been urging you to do certain things, *but* it is only in God's strength that you will be able to do them" (cf. Moore, who says that the words "suggest a contrast between what is now asked of God and what was before exhorted of the converts").

The prayer is directed to "God himself, the God of peace." "Himself" reinforces what we have said above. It is only in God that the Thessalonians will be able to do what they have been asked. To describe him as "the God of peace" is peculiarly fitting in the light of the exhor-

---

73. The conjunction δέ. This could, of course, be simply a connective with the sense "now," but it is perhaps more likely to be adversative here. The opening to this prayer is the same as that at 3:11.

tations of verses 12-13, but we cannot feel that it was elicited solely by the situation presupposed there. Paul often uses the designation, especially toward the end of his letters.[74] Peace brings before us the prosperity of the whole person, prosperity in the widest sense, especially including spiritual prosperity (see on 1:1). That it should be associated with God in this way is a reminder that true peace can come only from him, and that he is such a God that peace may be said to be characteristic of him.

This epistle has had important things to say about sanctification (3:13; 4:3-8), and it is not surprising that in the concluding prayer Paul returns to the thought. The essential idea in sanctification is that of being set apart for God, but there is also the thought of the character involved in such separation. In this place Paul has both aspects in mind.[75] Moreover, while there is a human element, in that one must yield oneself up to God (cf. 4:4), yet the primary thing is the power of God that enables this to be done. Thus Paul's prayer is that God will bring about this sanctification. Some translations render the next word "wholly" (e.g., *RSV*; Milligan, Frame, and others accept some such meaning). The word is an adjective and a compound[76] of which the first part has the meaning "wholly." If the second part is to have its proper significance, we need something to bring out the thought of reaching one's proper end, the end for which one was made. The meaning is qualitative and not quantitative only. We need something like "so that you may be complete" (*NIV* has "sanctify you through and through").

So important is this sanctification that Paul repeats the prayer in another form, this time praying that the whole person may be preserved entire and without blame. Some interpreters see in the reference to spirit, soul, and body an indication that humans are threefold, and not twofold as a division into body and soul would imply (e.g., Marshall, Thomas).[77] But this is probably to press the language beyond what is warranted.

---

74. It is found in Rom. 15:33; 16:20; 2 Cor. 13:11; Phil. 4:9 (also Heb. 13:20), while "the Lord of peace" occurs in 2 Thess. 3:16.

75. Cf. Frame, "consecration includes not only religion, devotion to God, but conduct, ethical soundness."

76. ὁλοτελεῖς (here only in the New Testament). Lightfoot says that this word "not only implies entirety (which exhausts the meaning of ὅλους), but involves the further idea of completion"; cf. Bailey, it "suggests finality as well as completeness."

77. Frame thinks that "spirit" probably denotes the divine Spirit who dwells in believers and marks them off as different from unbelievers. Bicknell, however, maintains that this idea is "surely absurd. To speak of a 'portion' of the divine Spirit introduces an idea of spatial division which contradicts the essential nature of Spirit. Nor is it easy to see how the Holy Spirit can in any sense need to be kept entire."

Paul is not at this point giving a theoretical description of the nature of the human constitution, but engaging in prayer. We can no more take his words here to mean that our nature is threefold than we can take some of his words elsewhere to indicate that we are twofold (body and spirit, 1 Cor. 7:34), or those of Jesus in Mark 12:30 to show that we are fourfold (heart, soul, mind, and strength). Paul simply uses this graphic form by way of insisting that the whole person, and not some part only, is involved.[78] All our powers of whatever sort are to be sanctified, entirely set apart for God. This totality is brought out in another fashion in that the verb "kept" and the adjective "entire" are both singular, though they clearly are intended to apply to all three.[79] In different ways Paul emphasizes that sanctification applies to the whole of our person, and is not to be restricted to any segment. The word "entire" does not differ very greatly from the earlier word rendered "through and through," though there is probably some difference of emphasis. Whereas the former word brought us the thought of "that which has attained its end," this one signifies "that which is complete in all its parts."[80] It has interesting associations with sacrifice in the Greek Old Testament and elsewhere. It describes the "whole" stones that were used in making the altar, and

78. Cf. H. Wheeler Robinson, "this is not a systematic dissection of the distinct elements of personality; its true analogy is such an Old Testament sentence as Deut. vi.5, where a somewhat similar enumeration emphasizes the totality of the personality" (*The Christian Doctrine of Man* [Edinburgh, 1926], p. 101). Paul's inclusion of the body is significant, as Best points out, "To the Greek for whom the body was the tomb or prison of the immortal soul its ultimate fate was unimportant; for Paul there is no existence without the body (cf. 1 Cor. 15)."

79. Hendriksen has a long note on this verse during the course of which he maintains that there are two clauses here. He thinks that ὁλόκληρον applies only to πνεῦμα, something along the lines of the Berkeley Version, "May your spirit be without flaw and your soul and body maintained blameless." I cannot see any real reason for breaking up τὸ πνεῦμα καὶ ἡ ψυχὴ καὶ τὸ σῶμα. The unemphatic possessive ὑμῶν applies to all three, and so, it seems, does ὁλόκληρον. It is not uncommon for an adjective to agree in this way in number and gender with the nearest noun in a list, the whole of which it qualifies. There is, moreover, the point that it is difficult to take the adverb ἀμέμπτως simply with τηρηθείη (how could God keep people other than blamelessly?). It must surely, as Findlay points out, define ὁλόκληρον, so that the sentence will mean, "In full integrity may your spirit and your soul and your body be preserved,—found blamelessly so . . ." *(CGT)*. It is possible to agree with Hendriksen's main point, that the verse does not give us a trichotomist view of the nature of man, without accepting this piece of linguistics.

80. It is found, e.g., in Jas. 1:4, where its meaning is brought out by the following ἐν μηδενὶ λειπόμενοι, "lacking in nothing."

it is used also of the victims that were offered.[81] If Paul has this sacrificial usage in mind, it would fit in very well with the entire surrender of the person to God that is involved in sanctification. If the completeness of the surrender is in view in this word, it is rather the result that is in mind in the adverb rendered "blameless" (found in this epistle only in the New Testament[82]). The character involved in being a Christian is one that admits of only the very highest standards. Paul prays, not simply that they may live good lives, but that they may be blameless.

It is characteristic of this epistle that these words should be followed by "at the coming of our Lord Jesus Christ." It is clear from earlier passages that the thought of the Parousia loomed large in the thinking both of the preachers and their converts. They were looking for the coming of the day of the Lord, and it is entirely natural accordingly that Paul should refer to it. But his reference has added point, for it makes the sanctification spoken of very far-reaching. Paul is not thinking of a sanctification that may last but a little time here on earth, but of one that will continue at the Parousia. Primarily his thought is not "which will last until the Parousia" (although that is implied), but "which will exist at the Parousia."[83] As we have seen, the thought of judgment is associated with the second coming. It is a fitting climax to his thought on the sanctification of believers that he looks for them to be preserved blameless not only through the changes and trials of this earthly life, but also on that dread day when they stand before the eternal Judge.

24 Paul's prayer is no despairing wail, but a cry of faith. He is supremely confident that what he has asked will be done, and this verse reveals that the ground of his trust is the nature of God. As we saw on the preceding verse, Paul was sure that the Thessalonians would be able to obey his injunctions because their resources were in God. Now we see that he is sure that God will indeed supply their need in this matter, because he is "faithful."[84] Centuries before, Abraham had asked, "Shall

---

81. It is used of the stones of the altar in Deut. 27:6 (LXX), while Philo and Josephus use it of sacrificial victims.

82. Milligan draws attention to the fact that it is found in sepulchral inscriptions at Thessalonica, and he quotes one of them.

83. His expression is ἐν τῇ παρουσίᾳ.

84. "This is the central theme of the Bible: the faithfulness of God in spite of the faithlessness of his people" (Rolston). It is a theme to which Paul recurs. That God is faithful is the basis of the call of the Corinthians and is mentioned in the thanksgiving that opens the first epistle (1 Cor. 1:9). It is the same faithfulness that assures them that they will not be tempted beyond their capacity (1 Cor. 10:13). It is

not the Judge of all the earth do right?" (Gen. 18:25). Through all the intervening years the conviction that God can be depended on had sustained men and women of faith, as, indeed, it does to this day. It is not in the unstable qualities of people that trust must be placed, but in the eternal faithfulness of God. Paul does not mention the name of God, but proceeds to characterize him as "the one who calls you" (see on 2:12; 4:7-8). There may be something of a hint that God's call is always sounding in the ears of his people, so that the present call that they hear is their guarantee that God will see them through. Or it may be that God is being spoken of as "the Caller," the God who habitually calls to himself those whom he will have.

But God, besides being a Caller, is a Doer (cf. Phil. 1:6). The end of the verse fastens attention on this aspect of his being. The verbal idea is emphasized in the Greek in two ways, by the addition of "also" (God not only calls, he also acts; *NIV* leaves the word untranslated) and by the omission of the object (there is no "it" in the Greek). There is no real doubt as to what the object is, and its omission has the effect of fastening attention on the verb "do." The God to whom Paul prays is not a God who is inactive or ineffective. Paul thinks of him as one who will certainly bring to completion that which he has begun. "Does he speak and then not act?" (Num. 23:19). Because he is the faithful One, and because he is the One who has called them, the Thessalonians may know that he will do perfectly all that is involved in their call. It is profoundly satisfying to the believer that in the last resort what matters is not his feeble hold on God, but God's strong grip on him (cf. John 10:28-29).

25 It is easy to picture for ourselves Paul as a very great apostle ceaselessly occupied with his work of issuing directives to other people on how they should live out their faith, while he himself sits above the storm or calmly proceeds along on his undisturbed way. Such, of course, is far from being a true picture. Paul was very much caught up in the hurly-burly. He found himself in situations where he did not know how to act. Sometimes when he did act he was not at all sure that he had done the right thing (in 2 Cor. 7:8, for example, he says that he wrote a letter that he came to regret, but later did not regret; he changed his mind twice!). He was very conscious of his own limitations and knew that his

---

the same quality in God that assures them of the certainty of the message brought by Paul and his companions (2 Cor. 1:18). It is God's faithfulness again that assures believers that God will protect them from the evil one (2 Thess. 3:3) and that faithfulness abides, even if they are not faithful (2 Tim. 2:13).

only hope was in God. So quite often we find him seeking the prayers of his converts, as he does here.[85] He knew that he needed their prayers just as much as they needed his. So, as now for the last time in this epistle he uses the affectionate address, "Brothers," it is to request them to pray continually (continuous tense) for him.[86]

26 "Greet" is the normal word in a context like this, and Paul usually ends his letters by sending greetings. As a rule, when he writes to a church he knows he does not greet friends by name, which might have been invidious. As here, he sends his greetings to all. The "all" ensures that no one is to be left out. He has spoken of some people who were loafers, and some who were weak. There were possibly others with whom he was not well pleased. But in his closing greetings he includes them all. Some have seen in the word an indication that the church was seriously divided, and, indeed, it was split into two groups (see Introduction, pp. 23-25). But this is to read far too much into the word. It is not in an especially emphatic position, and is adequately rendered by *NIV*.

The reference to the kiss means "Give everyone a kiss from me" (cf. 1 Cor. 16:24). Paul could not be present in person to bestow this greeting, so he wrote it. In some other places Paul urged his readers to greet one another with a holy kiss, but that is not the thought here. Paul is not telling the Thessalonians how to greet one another but sending his own affectionate greetings to all. It is clear enough that this is not meant as anything more than a customary mode of greeting, much as we today shake hands. Not a great deal is known about kissing among the early Christians, but the "holy kiss" is mentioned several times (Rom. 16:16; 1 Cor. 16:20; 2 Cor. 13:12), and a "kiss of love" is also found (1 Pet. 5:14). Evidently the custom was widely practiced in New Testament times. The practice, first taken over from the ordinary usage of secular society as a mode of greeting,[87] in time came to have liturgical significance. Probably this arose

---

85. See Rom. 15:30; Eph. 6:19; Col. 4:3-4; 2 Thess. 3:1-2; cf. Phil. 1:19.

86. If "also" in some MSS is genuine, the meaning will be "pray for us as well as for yourselves and other people," or "pray for us as we have been praying for you"; perhaps the latter is more likely.

87. "In the ancient world one kissed the hand, breast, knee, or foot of a superior, and the cheek of a friend. Herodotus mentions kissing the lips as a custom of the Persians. Possibly from them it came to the Jews" (C. H. Toy, *A Critical and Exegetical Commentary on the Book of Proverbs* [Edinburgh, 1899], p. 453, n.). In New Testament times a host was expected to kiss his guest (Luke 7:45), and it was the goodwill it symbolized that made Judas's betrayal of Jesus with the use of a kiss so dreadful (Luke 22:48).

from the fact that the kiss would naturally be exchanged when the believers came together for worship.[88] It is usually held that the kiss was exchanged at first only between members of the same sex.[89] But in the course of time men and women exchanged kisses, and Tertullian, for example, speaks of a wife kissing "any one of the brothers" (*To His Wife* II.4). Understandably this led to undesirable scenes, and Clement of Alexandria speaks of people "who make the churches resound" with their kissing, and says further, "the shameless use of a kiss . . . occasions foul suspicions and evil reports" (*Instructor* III.11). Not surprisingly the early church councils passed a number of regulations governing the circumstances under which the kiss should be exchanged.

27 The use of the first person singular may indicate that Paul is following his practice of taking the pen to end the letter (cf. Gal. 6:11; 2 Thess. 3:17). It is not surprising that he should ask for his letter to be read to all. The word "read" will here mean "read aloud."[90] We do not know how far the early church was literate, but it is not likely that all the artisan members of the church at Thessalonica could read for themselves, so that reading aloud was the way in which the contents of the letter would be made known to all. Whether this means that Paul intends the letter to be read during public worship is not clear. In time such reading came to be accepted as a mark of canonicity, a sign that the writing was accepted as sacred Scripture. But it is uncertain either how old the custom of reading such letters during the service was, or how early this signified canonicity. On the whole the likelihood is that Paul did mean the letter to be read, if

88. The first explicit mention of the kiss used in the liturgy is found in Justin's description of a communion service: "Having ended the prayers, we salute one another with a kiss" (*1 Apol.* 65). Despite the confident assertions of some New Testament scholars, there is no evidence for the practice as a liturgical observance before this.

89. This is explicit in *The Apostolic Constitutions* (4th century). The deacon calls on the congregation: "Salute ye one another with a holy kiss," whereupon "the clergy salute the bishop, and the laymen the laymen, and the women the women" (*The Liturgy of the Eighth Book of 'The Apostolic Constitutions'*, ed. R. H. Creswell [London, 1900], p. 51). There is a useful account of the practice in J. G. Davies [ed.], *A Dictionary of Liturgy and Worship* [London, 1972], pp. 187-88).

90. It is often said that ἀναγινώσκω always means to read aloud, but the examples cited by Milligan show that it sometimes means simply "to read." The same examples make it difficult to hold, as some do, that reading was always aloud in antiquity. While there is no reason to doubt that reading was often aloud (cf. Acts 8:30), it is very difficult to believe that educated people had not learned to read silently. K. Lake and H. J. Cadbury consider this "surely incredible" (*The Beginnings of Christianity*, IV [Grand Rapids, 1965], p. 97).

not at worship, at least on the occasion when people assembled for worship (perhaps before or after the service). The point is that opportunities for those who were not leisured folk to meet were not many, and the gathering for worship would be the logical time for such a communication to be read to them all.[91] This probably established a precedent. In time the kind of letters that might be read at a service was sharply delimited, and so only letters held to be canonical were read.

But if it is not surprising that Paul should ask that the letter be read, it is surprising that he does so in language of such vehemence. "I charge you before the Lord" means "I put you on your oath as Christians."[92] This is something that comes from Paul himself, for he says "I" and not "we." Why should Paul be so very urgent about the letter being read to all? Harnack thought that it fitted into his picture of a church in two sections, and was a way of ensuring that it was read to both. But as we have seen in the Introduction, this solution to the problems of the Thessalonian correspondence is an unlikely one. Other scholars, while rejecting Harnack's view, think that the strength of the language must point to the possibility that some of the Thessalonians would withhold the letter from others and thus instigate a deep division. Others again hold that some of the obdurate members were likely to absent themselves when the letter was read. The charge, then, is laid on the elders to ensure that all come to know the contents. The objection to all such views is the cordial tone of the letter. Paul felt deeply on the subject of division, as we see from 1 Corinthians. It is difficult to imagine him writing in the strain he has done if there were such deep and serious divisions within the Thessalonian church.[93]

---

91. Some MSS read "holy" before "brothers," and this reading has good MSS support (including P[46 vid] ℵ[c] A K etc.), it is urged that it is the more difficult reading, it could have been dropped (but not added) by homoioteleuton, and it fits the context. But despite all this it is unlikely to be the true reading. The adjective is unnecessary; all the brethren, as Paul's insistence on sanctification shows, were holy. Again, the expression "holy brothers" is found in no other place in Paul's letters. The better MSS omit "holy" here. Its presence is explicable in that it may well have crept in from the previous verse. It is not surprising, accordingly, that almost all commentators omit it.

92. The verb he uses is the rare ἐνορκίζω (only here in the New Testament, and not often elsewhere). This seems to be a strengthened form of ὁρκίζω (Mark 5:7; Acts 19:13). It is an extraordinarily strong form to employ in such a connection.

93. Lightfoot thinks that Paul had a presentiment of a misuse of his name, a presentiment that, in the light of 2 Thess. 2:2, we see to have been amply justified. In the nature of the case we cannot verify or disprove such a conjecture, but it seems better to look for another explanation.

The best explanation available to us may well arise from a consideration of such passages as 2:17-18 (where see notes). Paul has several times used strong expressions in protesting his tender regard for these converts, and his desire to be with them. Apparently some of the Thessalonians had said that he had no real love for them, and that if he had wished to do so, he would have been able to return. That he had not done so showed him to have his affections set elsewhere. In this situation the ideal thing would have been for Paul to have returned. But his circumstances made this impossible; he had to use this letter as a substitute. Accordingly it was important not only that it should come before the notice of all, but also that it be seen plainly to be intended to come before the notice of all. In this way his care for them all would be manifest.[94]

28 It is characteristic of Paul that he brings his letters to an end, not with the customary "Farewell," but with a prayer for grace for those to whom he has written (see on 1:1 for the significance of "grace" in Christian greetings). Occasionally the prayer is shorter than this one,[95] and sometimes it is longer, the longest being 2 Corinthians 13:14 with its mention of each of the Persons of the Trinity. But characteristic in each case is the prayer for grace. It is the grace of the Lord that lingers in the apostle's thoughts, just as it is the grace of the Lord with which he begins his letters.[96] His own hand would seem to have penned these words in each epistle (see 2 Thess. 3:17 and note), for he took the pen from his amanuensis somewhere before the conclusion. Just where he did so in this letter is not apparent, though the use of the first person singular in verse 27 makes it appear that he wrote that verse himself.

94. It has been suggested also that Paul had a tender concern for the bereaved. He feared that some of them might be absent when his words of consolation were read, and in this way he ensured that everyone would come to hear what he had written.

95. The shortest of all is in Colossians, ἡ χάρις μεθ' ὑμῶν (the endings of the Pastorals are similar).

96. Cf. Denney, "Whatever God has to say to us—and in all the New Testament letters there are things that search the heart and make it quake—begins and ends with grace. . . . All that God has been to man in Jesus Christ is summed up in it: all His gentleness and beauty, all His tenderness and patience, all the holy passion of His love, is gathered up in grace. What more could one soul wish for another than that the grace of the Lord Jesus Christ should be with it?"

Commentary on
2 THESSALONIANS

2 THESSALONIANS 1

I. GREETING (1:1-2)

1 *Paul, Silas*[a] *and Timothy,*
To the church of the Thessalonians in God our Father and the
Lord Jesus Christ:
2 *Grace and peace to you from God the Father and the Lord*
Jesus Christ.

[a]1 Greek *Silvanus,* a variant of *Silas*

1-2 The greeting at the head of this second epistle follows that in the first letter fairly closely (see the notes on 1 Thess. 1:1); the same three names appear, and perhaps we should notice that after this Silvanus disappears from Paul's company. The only differences from the greeting in 1 Thessalonians are the inclusion of "our" before "Father" and the addition of the words that follow "peace" in verse 2. When the New Testament speaks of God as Father it sometimes refers to God as the Father of our Lord Jesus Christ, and sometimes to God as the Father of believers. The inclusion of "our" shows that it is this latter which is the thought here. Paul is thinking of what God has come to be to the believers in Thessalonica and of the bond that unites them with the apostles. The words added bring the shorter form given in 1 Thessalonians up to that which became Paul's standard mode of greeting. It is found in all the other epistles with the exception of Colossians (from which the words "and the Lord Jesus Christ" are missing). The effect is to remind his readers of the divine origin[1] of that grace and peace which had come to

1. Similarly Bicknell comments: "The Greek makes plain that the Father and Christ are one source. It is remarkable that even at this early date the Son is placed side by side with the Father as the fount of divine grace, without any need of comment."

mean so much, and also of the fact that the apostle prayed for them that they might enjoy this grace and peace to the full.[2] Wilson comments on the joining of the Father and the Lord Jesus as the source of grace and peace: "That such a construction could be used without comment not only implies the writer's belief in the deity of Christ, but also takes the readers' acknowledgment of it for granted."

II. PRAYER (1:3-12)

A. THANKSGIVING (1:3-5)

3 *We ought always to thank God for you, brothers, and rightly so, because your faith is growing more and more, and the love every one of you has for each other is increasing. 4 Therefore, among God's churches we boast about your perseverance and faith in all the persecutions and trials you are enduring.*

5 *All this is evidence that God's judgment is right, and as a result you will be counted worthy of the kingdom of God, for which you are suffering.*

We come now to one of Paul's long and complicated sentences, for in the Greek verses 3-10 form one sentence. It is too long and involved to fit comfortably into English, and translations break it into smaller sentences for easier understanding. But we should not miss the point that it is all one complicated piece of Paul's argument. In this section he moves from thanksgiving for the growing faith of the Thessalonians to the way they have stood up to persecution and the truth that this shows that God is with them.

3 A thanksgiving was the common epistolary convention at this point of a letter, but, as we saw in the first epistle, Paul adapts the conventional form to his own particular needs. Now he utters a thanksgiving, but it is far from being a perfunctory compliance with convention. Some

---

2. Findlay speaks of the Father as "the ultimate spring" and the Lord Jesus Christ as "the mediating channel" of grace and peace *(CGT)*. While we may feel that this is the true position, yet it does not arise out of the expression used here. The Father and the Son are closely linked, and no distinction is made between them. It is pertinent to notice in this connection that, whereas Paul seems usually to link peace with the Father and grace with the Son, he does not differentiate between them in his salutations.

expositors have seen in "we ought" (repeated in 2:13) and "rightly so" indications that this epistle is colder and more formal than the former one, all the more so in that Paul uses these expressions nowhere else. Besides overlooking the warmth of the expressions that follow, this view fails to take into consideration the whole context in which the words are set.[3] Paul has already written a very warm letter, containing some passages of high praise for the Thessalonian church. It is probable that in the subsequent communication that they had had with him (whether by letter, or by word of mouth) they had said that they were not worthy of such praise. Paul strongly maintains that his words had not been too strong. There is an obligation[4] resting on him, he says. The implication is that it would be wrong not to give thanks to God in such a situation. There is a certain emphasis on "we ought," and this is reinforced by the adverb "always." The quality of the Christian life of the Thessalonians imposed a lasting obligation on the apostles to render thanks to God. Paul passes from personal obligation to the fitness of things in the expression, "and rightly so."[5] In praising the advance of the Thessalonians in the faith he was doing no more than giving due recognition to the existing state of affairs.[6]

In the first epistle Paul had given thanks for their faith, love, and hope. The absence of "endurance inspired by hope" here is probably not significant, for as the letter proceeds it does not appear that he thinks the Thessalonians to be deficient in hope. Moreover, in verse 4 he says that he boasts of their "perseverance." It is significant that the two matters for which he now gives thanks are both mentioned in the former letter as subjects for improvement. In 3:10 he had spoken of his desire to perfect what was lacking in their faith, and in 3:12 he had prayed that their love might abound. Now he is able to thank God for the growth of

3. Roger D. Aus has argued that the words are derived from a liturgical setting (*JBL* 92 [1973], pp. 432-38). Now it is true that some ancient liturgies have expressions like "bounden duty," so that this must be seen as a possibility. But the fact is that we have no knowledge of liturgies used in the church as early as this or even of whether the early church used liturgies at all (were they entirely charismatic in their worship?). Until some evidence is found this must remain conjectural.

4. The verb he uses, ὀφείλομεν, is unusual in thanksgivings (though it occurs also in 2:13). It carries the idea of personal obligation, whereas δεῖ would denote something more in the nature of external compulsion.

5. καθώς, as Frame points out, "in Paul is slightly causal." Thus it must be taken with ὀφείλομεν, and not as indicating the degree or the manner of the thanksgiving.

6. Phillips exactly reverses the meanings of the two expressions in rendering, "I thank God for you not only in common fairness but as a moral obligation!"

their faith and the abundance of their love. His verb for "is growing more and more" is an unusual one (here only in the Greek Bible), and gives the thought of a very vigorous growth. The verb "is increasing" is the one he used in the prayer of 1 Thessalonians 3:12, so that he is recording the exact answer to his prayer.[7]

In several places in both epistles Paul uses expressions that indicate that all the Thessalonians are being included in some word of praise or greeting. He seems to be at pains to include them all, making no distinctions. It is as though he insists that, while he must rebuke some of them for their failings, yet there are no such grievous offenses as put people beyond the pale. Here we have a typical example. Paul points out that the love of which he speaks is to be found throughout the whole community. It is "the love every one of you has for each other." The expression is a strong one. Clearly Paul is making no exceptions. Love was a bond uniting the whole church.

4 All this has a most unexpected result.[8] "We" is strongly emphatic, "we ourselves," and is much more emphatic than we would have expected in such a connection. It implies a strong contrast. The difficulty is that no one is mentioned with whom "we" is being contrasted. Some exegetes have thought that the apostles are being contrasted with the fainthearted among the Thessalonians, or with the whole church. This may be so, but here there seems to be no real grammatical reason. Nor can we hold that Paul expected the Thessalonians to boast of their achievements. Our best understanding seems to be that it was very unusual for the founders of a church to boast of that church. Other people might do so (cf. 1 Thess. 1:9), but not the founders. Yet in the case of the church at Thessalonica the qualities of which Paul speaks had been displayed in such outstanding measure that even those whose preaching had brought that church into being could not forebear to utter its praises. They did not do this apologetically, for the word "boast" is not the usual one, but a strong compound (by the use of which, Frame says, Paul "intensifies the point"; cf. *JB*, "we can take special pride"). In line with this is the fact that his boasting is carried out "among[9] God's churches."

7. Of these two verbs Lightfoot says, "The words ὑπεραυξάνει and πλεονάζει are carefully chosen; the former implying an internal, organic growth, as of a tree; the other a diffusive, or expansive character, as of a flood irrigating the land." Paul has a special fondness for compounds with ὑπέρ.

8. ὥστε indicates the consequence of the preceding.

9. The dative might be understood as "within the churches," but there is not much difference in meaning.

There is no limit to any one region. We are not, of course, to understand that Paul had systematically told every church in existence about the Thessalonians, but his choice of such an inclusive expression indicates that his praise of them had been completely uninhibited.

In the previous verse Paul found two things in particular for which he thanked God, and now he mentions two for which he boasted about the converts. "Perseverance" is an active, courageous quality, rather than a passive resignation (see on 1 Thess. 1:3). It is closely linked with faith, there being a single article that unites them. We are probably to understand the former as the fruit of the latter. Calvin explains the passage in this way: "We glory in the patience which springs from faith, and we bear witness that it eminently shines forth in you." He goes on to say, "the more proficiency any one makes in faith, he will be so much the more endued with patience for enduring all things with fortitude, as on the other hand, softness and impatience under adversity betoken unbelief on our part." Some commentators understand "faith" here in the sense of "faithfulness" (e.g., Thomas), but this does not seem warranted. The word has this meaning when it refers to God (e.g., Rom. 3:3), but there are good reasons for doubting the contention that in the New Testament it sometimes means "faithfulness" when it is used of people.[10] In such contexts it almost always, perhaps always, has the meaning "faith," "trust." It has this meaning in the preceding verse, and there is no good reason for seeing a change here. It is the human response to the faithfulness of God. It is the believer's reliance on God's faithfulness for all things. It is a continuing on in one's life of faith. It is not any human virtue, be it constancy or any other. This concept is central to Christianity, and occurs many times. The frequency with which the word must denote "faith" is impressive. In this passage the apostle appears to mean that the faith of the Thessalonians had not failed under the stress of persecution, and for that he gloried on their behalf. See further on 3:2 (see also 1 Thess. 3:2, 5, 7, 10).

The way of the Thessalonian church had been far from easy (cf. 1 Thess. 1:6; 2:14, etc.). The use of "all" shows that their troubles had been many, while the present tense of the verb "are enduring" makes it plain that their difficulties were not yet over. Of the two words Paul uses to describe

10. But see an article by T. F. Torrance, "One Aspect of the Biblical Conception of Faith" (*ET* 68 [1956-57], pp. 111-14), the short reply by C. F. D. Moule (*ibid.,* p. 157), and the further notes by both writers (*ibid.,* pp. 221-22). Torrance speaks freely of the faithfulness of people, as well as that of God. But if I understand him aright, his "faithfulness" is a constant trust in God. He strongly emphasizes the priority of the faithfulness of God. BAGD begin their treatment of the word with, "that which causes trust and faith—a. *faithfulness, reliability.*"

their troubles "persecutions" is the more specific. It points to suffering endured on account of the faith.[11] "Trials" might mean troubles of any kind (see on 1 Thess. 1:6). In this passage there is not much difference between them. Both refer to the sufferings that the converts had had to endure as Jews and Gentiles alike tried to turn them from the faith. Paul boasted of their continuing endurance. We learn more about the trials this church had endured from Paul's treatment of the theme in 1 Thessalonians 3. It is clear that he had been deeply interested in both the troubles that church had endured and the way it had endured them.

5 But God is over all, and neither their sufferings nor their bearing under their sufferings should be interpreted other than in the light of this great fact.[12] It is at first sight somewhat difficult to follow the apostle's train of thought. To us the fact of suffering seems to deny, rather than to prove, that God is working out his righteous purpose.[13] But two things must be said here. One is that the New Testament does not look on suffering in quite the same way as do most modern people. To us suffering is an evil in itself, something to be avoided at all costs. Now while the New Testament does not gloss over this aspect of suffering it does not lose sight either of the fact that in the good providence of God suffering is often the means of working out God's eternal purpose.[14] It develops in the sufferer qualities of character. It teaches valuable lessons. Suffering is not thought of as something that may possibly be avoided by the Christian. For believers it is inevitable. They are appointed to it

---

11. This is the usual meaning in the Greek Bible. In nonbiblical writings it has other meanings, such as "pursuit."

12. There is a problem regarding the grammatical connection between vv. 4 and 5. Most translations supply "this is," but Bruce points out that it is also possible to take ἔνδειγμα as in apposition with αἷς ἀνέχεσθε. There is not a great deal of difference in sense. The main problem is seeing how "persecutions and trials" demonstrate "that God's judgment is right."

13. The New Testament often links present suffering and future glory, as in Jesus' own teaching (e.g., Matt. 5:11-12).

14. Jouette M. Bassler takes this very seriously. She argues from 2 Baruch where we read things like "His judgments which He has decreed against you that ye should be carried away captive . . . in order that, at the last times, ye may be found worthy of your fathers." She argues that similarly Paul is saying that God sends suffering (righteous judgment) on his people now, and the fact of their suffering is an indication that God is making them worthy of their future inheritance. See the article "The Enigmatic Sign: 2 Thessalonians 1:5" (*CBQ* 46 [1984], pp. 496-510). It may legitimately be objected that this is unlike anything we know to be Pauline, and that the date of the Jewish writings Bassler cites is rather late to be a convincing parallel to New Testament teaching.

(1 Thess. 3:3). They must live out their lives and develop their Christian character in a world dominated by non-Christian ideas. Their faith is accordingly not some fragile thing, to be kept in a kind of spiritual cotton wool, insulated from all shocks. It is robust. It is to be manifested in the fires of trouble and in the furnace of affliction. Furthermore, not only is it to be manifested there, but, in part at any rate, it is to be fashioned in such places. The very troubles and afflictions that the world heaps on believers become, under God, the means of making those believers what they ought to be. When we have come to regard suffering in this light, it is not to be thought of as evidence that God has forsaken his people, but as evidence that God is with them. Paul can rejoice that in his flesh he fills up "what is still lacking in regard to Christ's afflictions, for the sake of his body, which is the church" (Col. 1:24). Such suffering is a vivid token of the presence of God.

The second point we must bear in mind is that in this verse the "evidence that God's judgment is right"[15] is probably not suffering itself, but the whole of the previous clause. That is to say, it includes also the bearing of the Thessalonians under suffering.[16] God had used the persecutions and afflictions as the means of accomplishing that which he had pleased, namely, that the believers should be counted worthy (or perhaps "be shown to be worthy")[17] of the kingdom.[18] Translations like

15. ἔνδειγμα occurs here only in the New Testament. It means "evidence, plain indication" (BAGD). The judgment is usually held to be the judgment at the last day (so, e.g., Best, Bruce); if this is the way to take it, then the bearing of believers under their present sufferings shows what will be the case at the end of the age. "God sustains their faith now and will own it at the judgment. Their experience is therefore a pointer to God's righteous judgment" (Ward). Marshall holds that Paul is referring to present judgment.

16. Cf. Frame, "Since the object of boasting specified in v. 4 is not suffering, but the constancy of their endurance and faith in the midst of persecution, ἔνδειγμα is not to be taken with the idea of suffering alone . . . but with the idea of endurance and faith in spite of persecutions." Best interprets ἔνδειγμα in this way: "The Thessalonians are not sure of their position on the day of judgement; Paul says: 'I have boasted about you; this is a sign that God will count you worthy then.'" But Paul's boasting is surely an inadequate reason for the Thessalonians to be confident on judgment day. It is much more likely to be the way God has enabled them to bear their sufferings.

17. The construction is εἰς τό with the infinitive. The weakening of the telic force of this construction in late Greek leads a few interpreters to think that it may denote here either the content of the righteous judgment or its result. But in Paul the construction usually denotes purpose, and there is no real reason to think that the telic force is lacking here. Way renders, "a token . . . of His purpose that you may be adjudged worthy."

18. For "the kingdom of God" see the note on 1 Thess. 2:12. Here the thought is that of the kingdom in its future rather than its present aspect.

"that you may be made worthy" (*RSV*) or "you will become worthy" (*GNB*) miss the point. There is no idea that their endurance of suffering constituted a merit that gained them membership in the kingdom. The thought is that all is of God. He called them, and then proceeded to lead them in the right way. This means that the suffering they endure is to be seen as his Fatherly discipline. It helped to shape them into what he would have them be. He gave them all the grace needed to endure. Then at the end it is not said that they are worthy but that they are counted worthy. It is still all of God. God gives the verdict in accordance with his eternal purpose. The concluding "for which you are suffering" brings their suffering into intimate relation with the kingdom. It does not modify the previous statement in the direction of attributing merit to suffering. The Greek preposition rendered "for"[19] has the meaning "on behalf of," perhaps "in the interest of," and not "with a view to," "in order to gain which." The addition of "also" (which NIV omits) raises a small problem. It may link Paul with the Thessalonians. He was suffering for the faith, and they were suffering also. Or it may link present suffering and future glory. "You are both suffering and also being counted worthy" would then be the thought. Grammatically either is possible, but perhaps the former is slightly more probable (cf. Phil. 1:28).

B. DIVINE JUDGMENT (1:6-10)

6 *God is just: He will pay back trouble to those who trouble you* 7 *and give relief to you who are troubled, and to us as well. This will happen when the Lord Jesus is revealed from heaven in blazing fire with his powerful angels.* 8 *He will punish those who do not know God and do not obey the gospel of our Lord Jesus.* 9 *They will be punished with everlasting destruction and shut out from the presence of the Lord and from the majesty of his power* 10 *on the day he comes to be glorified in his holy people and to be marveled at among all those who have believed. This includes you, because you believed our testimony to you.*

Paul moves from the present situation with its problems and its distress to the coming of the Lord in triumphant majesty at the end of the age. He makes it clear that evil people will then be punished, and the people of God will be given relief. The Thessalonian believers will have their share in that

19. ὑπέρ.

great day. In their times of distress and persecution this picture of the majesty of their Savior would have brought comfort and inspiration.

6 That God's righteous purpose is being worked out is reiterated in the enunciation of a great principle. That Paul puts it into a hypothetical form ("if so be," which *NIV* omits) does not signify that the matter is open to dispute. It is rather his way of indicating that it is so sure that it can with safety be cast into this hypothetical mold. "If (as all agree) . . ." is the sense of it (cf. *RSV,* "since indeed . . .").

This verse resumes what has been said in the previous verse and, so to speak, gives the other side of it. The use of the term "just" shows that we are in the same circle of ideas as when Paul spoke of "God's judgment" as "right" (it is the same Greek adjective that *NIV* renders "just" and "right"). But now we have the negative aspect. Just as it is true that it is a righteous thing with God to bring believers to salvation and blessing in his kingdom, so it is a righteous thing with him to bring punishment to those who persist in courses of evil.[20] This is sometimes thought to be so un-Christian that the hypothesis of interpolation has been resorted to. This, however, does not seem warranted. If it is true that the New Testament speaks much of the love and mercy of God, it is also true that it does not gloss over the serious nature of moral issues. Our Lord spoke plainly of the fate of those who persist in ways of sin and impenitence (Mark 9:47-48; Luke 13:3, 5, etc.).[21] Those who followed after did not slur over this truth. They said plainly that the evildoer can look for nothing but the continuing wrath of God (Rom. 1:18ff.). Often retribution is pictured as overtaking people in the world to come, but not a few passages indicate that it may operate here and now (e.g., Rom. 1:24, 26, 28). This verse ought not then to be dismissed as un-Christian, but recognized as giving expression to a well-defined strand of New Testament teaching (even if it is unpalatable to many modern people).[22] We should not miss the point that there are

20. The verb ἀνταποδίδωμι, "to recompense," is a compound that conveys the thought of a full and due requital. It is used in a similar way of God's judicial recompense in Rom. 12:19. For "trouble," see on 1 Thess. 1:6, where *NIV* translates the same word as "suffering."

21. Cf. the reactions assigned by Jesus to one and the same king, with regard to one and the same servant, "The servant's master took pity on him, canceled the debt and let him go," "in anger his master turned him over to the jailers" (Matt. 18:27, 34).

22. Similar teaching may be found in the Qumran scrolls, e.g., "with God is the judgment of every living man; and he will repay to a man his recompense" (from the closing psalm in "The Manual of Discipline," cited from Millar Burrows, *The Dead Sea Scrolls* [London, 1956], p. 386).

differing aspects of the Lord's coming. In 1 Thessalonians 4:13-18 he will come to gather his people; here his coming is also a coming for judgment.

7 God's recompensing activity is not confined to the repayment of the wicked. It has its application to the relief of the righteous as well. Paul looks to God to grant rest to the afflicted. This word "relief" is frequently used by the apostle, and nearly always in contrast to affliction, as here. It denotes a freedom from restraints and tension.[23] The prospect of such relief given by God himself is held out before the suffering Thessalonians as something that will strengthen their spirits in the trying times through which they are passing. There is a tendency in modern times to look askance on heavenly rewards and the like. It is true that the Christian must serve God for what he is and not from selfish motives. It is true, too, that anyone who serves in order to obtain a reward has not caught the spirit of Christianity at all. Such a person has simply exchanged one form of selfishness for another, and the result is not pleasing. Yet when full allowance has been made for that, it remains that the New Testament does speak of a rest for the people of God (Heb. 4:9). We are not being true to its teaching if we overlook this. While it may well be true to say that if we are still serving God with a view to getting something for ourselves we do not know much about the Christian faith, it is also true that the contemplation of the rest that God has reserved for them is a normal and legitimate activity of the saints who are passing through trials (those who are in comfortable circumstances may despise the thought of final rest, but the troubled do not).

Paul speaks of rest "with us"[24] (*NIV*, "to us"), a little touch that reminds his readers that he is not delivering an academic disquisition on the nature of suffering and recompense. He is speaking out of his own difficult situation. Throughout his missionary career he was encompassed with trials, not least during his stay at Corinth during which this letter was written.

There is a sense in which retribution takes place in the here and now. There is a fuller sense in which it is reserved for the last great day, when it will form part of the revelation. It is this that Paul has especially in mind in the present passage, as he proceeds to make clear. The section that begins "when the Lord Jesus is revealed" and goes on to the end of

---

23. As in the slackening of a taut bowstring.

24. Frame quotes E. von Dobschütz, "these two little words belong to the genuine Pauline touches for the sake of which no one, with any feeling for the way in which the mind of Paul works, can give up the authenticity of this brief epistle."

verse 10 is of such a rhythmical character that a number of commentators have felt that it is a psalm of some sort. A necessary corollary seems to some to be that Paul is quoting from some other writer. While acknowledging that the section is poetic, we may feel that it does not follow that Paul is not the author. No valid reason has been adduced for doubting that Paul wrote it. He can employ a very elevated style, as 1 Corinthians 13 (to name no other) amply shows.

Various words are used of Christ's appearing on that day. The typical word (see on 1 Thess. 2:19) stresses the idea of coming. The word used here[25] directs attention rather to the thought of uncovering what is hidden. Now the Lord is hid from the view of the world, and it is even possible for people to deny his existence. But on that day he will be revealed in all his glory. He will be shown to be what he is.

Paul proceeds to describe this revelation[26] in a series of prepositional phrases. It will be (a) from heaven, (b) with the angels, and (c) in flaming fire. The first of these conveys the thought that the highest place of all is Christ's and is his now. He is enjoying the glory of the Father. When he comes it will be with the very highest authority, and his task will be the divine task of judgment. This thought of his glory is continued in the reference to "the angels of his power." In modern times it is usually held that "of his power" should be taken as equivalent to an adjective, and accordingly *NIV* renders "his powerful angels."[27] While this is a possible way of reading the Greek, the probability is that Paul's use of the noun should be respected. The point is that the passage is dealing with the Lord, and it is his power rather than that of the angels that is likely to be spoken of.[28] It is also the case that "angels of power" appear

---

25. ἀποκάλυψις (cf. 1 Cor. 1:7). The preposition is ἐν (ἐν τῇ ἀποκαλύψει), which signifies rather more than "at." It is not simply that the retribution will take place "at" the revelation; it will itself form part of that revelation. G. Vos has a useful note on ἀποκάλυψις in *The Pauline Eschatology* (Grand Rapids, 1953), pp. 77-79.

26. On this whole description Neil comments, "The most notable feature is the reticence of the description. What in normal apocalyptic literature would have included a lurid picture of the tortures of the damned and the bliss of the righteous, in Paul's hands becomes a restrained background of Judgment with the light focussed on the Person of Christ as Judge."

27. In the expression ἀγγέλων δυνάμεως αὐτοῦ Frame takes αὐτοῦ with the whole of the preceding and renders, "his angels of power." However, as a number of commentators point out, the position of αὐτοῦ (after δυνάμεως) is a principal reason for rejecting this translation. In this position it is very difficult to take αὐτοῦ as applying principally to "angels." It seems better to read it with the noun it follows, "the angels of his power."

28. Another view is that of Moore, who notes that δύναμις is a circumlocution

to be a definite class in apocalyptic literature. Frame is able to cite a passage from the Ethiopic Enoch in which these angels are expressly distinguished from "the angels of principalities." Possibly the expression implies that they are to be the agents of the divine will. But the main idea is that they are angels that belong to his power.

Some commentators prefer to take "in blazing fire"[29] with what follows as indicating the manner in which the vengeance spoken of will be visited on the wicked.[30] It seems preferable to take it with the preceding, and as being the third in the series of prepositional phrases describing the Lord's revelation. In that case the majesty of the appearance of the Lord who is revealed is brought out by comparing it to that of flaming fire. This comparison is to be found in other places (Exod. 3:2; Isa. 66:15; Rev. 1:13-14). On outstanding occasions, like the giving of the law on Mt. Sinai or the coming of the Holy Spirit at Pentecost, fire is the symbol of the divine presence.

8 Having spoken of flaming fire as the robe of the returning Lord, Paul moves on to his function, namely, that of administering justice. The

---

for the divine name in Mark 14:62 and holds that here " 'his power', with reference to Jesus, could be Paul's way of referring to Jesus' divinity, that which is to be openly manifested at the Parousia; Jesus is to be revealed with angels appropriate to and underlining his divine nature."

29. ἐν πυρὶ φλογός, "in fire of flame." We might have expected the simpler ἐν φλογὶ πυρός, "in flame of fire" (which is actually read by some MSS). However, ἐν πυρὶ φλογός is well attested, and the expression is found in a few other places, e.g., Sir. 8:10; 45:19. It is a genitive of quality (BDF #165; they see the construction in LXX and draw attention to the inversion of the construct state in Hebrew and many translations).

30. T. F. Glasson says, "The source of this doctrine is not the teaching of Jesus. We cannot conceive Him talking of Himself as coming with flaming fire rendering vengeance upon them that know not God. Nor is the conception due to Paul; there is nothing distinctively Pauline about it as there is in the case of Justification by Faith, 'in Christ', and 'the fruit of the Spirit'. This Parousia teaching was evidently part of the Christian tradition at that time and the language betrays its origin in the O.T." (*The Second Advent* [London, 1947], p. 168). He thinks that the connecting link between the eschatology of the Old Testament and that of the church was "the conviction that Jesus was Lord" (*ibid.*, p. 171). It is true that the early church made good use of the Old Testament, but Glasson has to resort to a good deal of critical surgery to empty the teaching of Jesus of all idea of the second coming. T. W. Manson shows conclusively from the standpoint of modern criticism that Jesus looked for his second coming in judgment (*The Teaching of Jesus* [Cambridge, 1943], pp. 260ff.). See also G. R. Beasley-Murray, *Jesus and the Future* (London, 1954). Dr. Beasley-Murray shows clearly that Paul's eschatology depends on that of Jesus, and that Jesus did teach that he would come again.

word rendered "punish" has no associations of vindictiveness.[31] It is a compound based on the same root as that of the word rendered "right" in verse 5 and "just" in verse 6, and it conveys the idea of a firm administration of unwavering justice. As Findlay says, "it is the inflicting of *full justice* on the criminal . . . nothing more, nothing less." He draws attention to the use of the term elsewhere (Luke 18:3, 7; Rom. 12:19; 2 Cor. 7:11). The passage in Romans is a quotation from Deuteronomy 32:35, where this process is ascribed to Yahweh. Yet here it belongs to the Lord Jesus. It is yet another example of the ease with which the church, from the very first, assigned to Christ the functions that the Old Testament reserved for Yahweh.[32]

The rest of the verse concerns the identity of those who will be the objects of this retributory justice. The use of separate articles in the Greek before "those who do not know God" and "do not obey the gospel" is most naturally taken as pointing to two groups of people (*NIV* ignores the second article). Some commentators accordingly understand the first expression to signify the Gentiles, and the second to refer to the Jews.[33] The objection to this is that the distinction is not made clearly enough, for the verse can be readily understood as an example of synonymous parallelism.[34] If Paul meant Jews and Gentiles, there seems to be no reason why he should not have inserted another word or two to make the meaning clear. While it is true that the Gentiles are sometimes described as people who do not know God, the Jews could also be spoken of in this way (John 8:54-55). Again, the Gentiles can be said to be disobedient to God (Rom. 11:30). Bearing in mind the Hebraistic coloring of this passage and the fondness for parallelism in elevated Hebrew style, we apparently have here two designations of more or less the same group of people. There is nothing in the context to prepare us for an allusion to Jew or Gentile. "Those who do not know God" refers, of course, not to people who have never heard of the true God, but to those who are culpably ignorant. It is the sort of thing that Paul speaks of in

31. See the note on the cognate word translated "punish" in 1 Thess. 4:6.

32. For the close connection between the Father and the Son see the note on 1 Thess. 3:11.

33. If this distinction can be sustained (as Marshall, e.g., argues) it will readily apply to the two groups of persecutors at Thessalonica.

34. There is also the point made by Lightfoot, "But if by τοῖς μὴ εἰδόσιν Θεόν are meant the heathen who rejected the Gospel when offered to them, they are not distinct from τοῖς μὴ ὑπακούουσιν; and if on the other hand the heathen world generally is signified, this is opposed to the doctrine which St. Paul teaches in Romans ii."

Romans 1:28, where he refers to people who "did not think it worthwhile to retain the knowledge of God." The second clause is then a specific example of this, and the most heinous of all, for it involves the rejection of the revelation that God has given in his Son. The gospel is a message of good news, but it is also an invitation from the King of kings. Rejection of the gospel accordingly is disobedience to a royal invitation. This is emphasized in the reference to Jesus as "Lord," a word that, in addition, has point in a second advent setting.

9 The thought of merited punishment continues. Paul does not use the simple relative but the relative of quality, which has the force of "who are of such a kind as to."[35] His verb has a legal background. The word "punishment" (the Greek means "suffer punishment," as *RSV*) is another word from the same root as "righteous" and "vengeance" in the earlier verses. It brings us the idea of a just penalty, of a punishment meted out as the result of an evenhanded assessment of the rights of the case.[36] Paul leaves us in no doubt either as to the fact of the punishment of the wicked or of the justice of this proceeding.

The nature of the punishment is "everlasting destruction."[37] The noun is used of the destruction of the flesh with a view to the saving of the spirit (1 Cor. 5:5). In that passage Paul clearly does not view destruction as annihilation, for there is no likelihood that he thought of such a one as being saved in a disembodied state. This has its relevance to the present passage, for it indicates that the word does not signify so much annihilation as the loss of all that is worthwhile, utter ruin. The adjective "everlasting" means literally "age-long," and everything depends on the length of the age. In the New Testament there is never a hint that the coming age has an end—it is the continuing life of the world to come.[38] When the life of believers beyond the grave is spoken of, it is with the

---

35. Cf. Lightfoot, "While the simple οἵ would define the persons themselves, οἵτινες regards them as members of a class, and points to their class characteristics."

36. The word is δίχη, on which Findlay says, "It connotes *justice* in the penalty, punishment determined by a lawful process." He distinguishes it from other words for punishment thus: "Punishment is δίχη from the point of view of the dispassionate judge; χόλασις from that of the criminal; τιμωρία from that of the injured party" (*CGT*).

37. The expression is found in the Qumran scrolls, namely, in "The War of the Sons of Light with the Sons of Darkness" (Millar Burrows, *The Dead Sea Scrolls,* p. 390).

38. Cf. the discussion by G. Dalman, *The Words of Jesus* (Edinburgh, 1902), pp. 147-62.

use of this same adjective. "Eternal life" is the life that belongs to the age to come; therefore it has no end. At the same time "eternal" is a quality of life. It is not only that life in the age to come will be longer than life here: it will also be of a different quality. All of this has to be borne in mind when we consider the other expression "everlasting destruction." It is the opposite of eternal life. It is the end of all that is worthwhile in life. As eternal life can be defined in terms of the knowledge of God and of the Lord Jesus Christ (John 17:3), so the eternal destruction that is here in mind is "from the presence of the Lord"; "from" appears to have the meaning "away from"[39] (contrast 1 Thess. 4:17). It indicates that separation from the Lord which is the final disaster.[40] The solemnity of this thought should not be minimized. Those who oppose the things of God here and now are not engaged in some minor error that can easily be put right in the hereafter. They are engaging in that defiance of the will of God which has eternal consequences. Life here and now has a high and serious dignity. In particular, facing up to the gospel invitation is a choice fraught with the most solemn and lasting consequences.[41]

The Semitic expressions toward the end of the verse serve a twofold purpose. They stress the certainty of the destruction spoken of, and in their insistence on the might of the Lord they bring a message of hope and cheer to the Thessalonians. It is as though Paul is turning their eyes away from the troubles through which they are passing to remind them that the power of their oppressors is as nothing compared to the might of the glorious Lord who is to be revealed. "The majesty of his power" is a very expressive phrase, and the choice of the word "power" in this context is suggestive.

10 This very long and complex sentence now concludes, and we

39. This is certainly the meaning of ἀπό in Isa. 2:10, LXX (of which this may be a reminiscence), and I take it as the most likely meaning here. Others have suggested, however, that it may be temporal, "from the time of the Lord's appearance," that it may indicate the source, "proceeding from the face . . . ," or that it may be causal, "by reason of the face."

40. Way renders, "Irrevocable destruction that bans them from the presence of the Lord."

41. Cf. Denney, "If the gospel, as conceived in the New Testament, has any character at all, it has the character of finality. It is God's *last word* to man. And the consequences of accepting or rejecting it are final; it opens no prospect beyond the life on the one hand, and the death on the other, which are the result of obedience and disobedience. . . . What God says to us all in Scripture, from beginning to end, is not, Sooner or later? but, Life or death?"

are back at the thought of the coming of the Lord. When this takes place,[42] it will be in order that (the construction expresses purpose[43]) he may be glorified in his saints (or "holy people," as *NIV* puts it). This, of course, refers to all believers, those set apart for the service of the Lord. The idea here is not a common one, namely, that the glory of the Lord will be seen in his saints, but it is strongly expressed. The verb "glorified" is an unusual compound (only here and in v. 12 in the New Testament), the preposition "in" being prefixed to the usual word for "glorify." Then "in" is repeated before "saints." The meaning probably is that the Lord will not only be glorified "among" the saints (as *REB*), but "in" them. There may be a recollection of Psalm 89:7, which in LXX speaks of God as being glorified "in the council of his holy ones" (which seems to refer to the angels), but here there is no reference to the council; it is the saints themselves in whom the Lord will be glorified. "In" may mean "among" or "by means of" or "because of." But we should perhaps bear in mind that Paul frequently speaks of believers as being "in Christ," and less frequently of Christ's being "in" his people. It seems that he is saying that those who are in Christ and in whom Christ dwells will by virtue of that fact share in his glory. On the great day it is not only the Lord himself who will be glorious, but his glory will also be seen in the saints.[44] The thought may be that they have been redeemed and indwelt by the Lord, and that this will cause the angels to ascribe glory to the Lord (so, for example, Frame). But it seems more likely that the idea is that of the Lord's glory being shared with or mirrored in his people. They are one with him and they will share his glory.

This clause and that which follows are a necessary corrective to any idea that the Lord at his coming will be preoccupied with the necessity for dealing with the wicked, which has been the center of attention in the preceding verses. That of course is important, especially for those undergoing persecution, but it is not all-important. The Lord comes primarily for other purposes, and dealing with the wicked is incidental to the establishing of the new order of things. This new order will far surpass anything that we can dream of, as will the Lord who

42. "When" is ὅταν, the indefinite conjunction. The fact of the Lord's coming is known; the time is not. Thus Paul says "whenever."

43. The simple infinitive, which is common in this sense after verbs of coming and the like.

44. Cf. Calvin, "Paul declares that our Lord Jesus in no sense reserves His glory to Himself but possesses it only in order to radiate it to all the members of His body" (cited in H. Quistorp, *Calvin's Doctrine of the Last Things* [London, 1955], p. 172).

establishes it.[45] Thus Paul can speak of him as being marveled at. The wonders of that day are not to be taken for granted. We might have expected him to use the present tense and say, "in all those who believe," both from the general sense of the passage and from the fact that it is Paul's habit to use the present tense of this participle. But in this verse he is drawing attention to the decisive act of faith rather than to the continuing belief, so he employs the aorist. He describes those who will marvel as "all those who will have put their trust in him."

"In that day," which comes last in the Greek, goes with the coming and its associated events. It makes clear to what they apply. Its detachment from the remainder of the expression gives it a certain emphasis. The intervening words are a parenthesis. They are not particularly easy to fit into the structure of the sentence, and it is not surprising, accordingly, that some exegetes have suggested excision, and others emendation. Even Hort, who was very conservative in these matters, resorted to a conjectural emendation of the text.[46] There seems to be no point in working through all the suggestions that have been put forward. The simplest explanation is that we need some such words as "you will be among them" to bring out the sense. Paul has been speaking of the glorious saints. He knows that there are some fainthearted souls among the Thessalonians, and on the spur of the moment and with scant regard for the niceties of grammar, he makes his interjection that will assure them that they will be of the number of the glorified ones in that day. The "testimony" reminds us that the essential task carried out by Paul and his companions had been bearing witness to the saving truths of the gospel. They had not expounded some philosophical or religious theory, but had testified to what God had done in Christ. "Was believed" (*NIV*, "you believed") is another aorist. It brings before us the thought of the decisive act of belief with which the Thessalonians had welcomed the gospel.[47] This picks up the thought of Paul's relationship to

45. Cf. the chapter "The Glory of His Coming," in L. Berkhof, *The Second Coming of Christ* (Grand Rapids, 1953).

46. He suggested emending ἐπιστεύθη, "was believed," to ἐπιστώθη, "was confirmed."

47. ἐφ' ὑμᾶς is not a usual construction after μαρτύριον, with which most commentators connect it here (in Luke 9:5 μαρτύριον ἐπ' αὐτούς is "a testimony *against* them"). Indeed, no instance parallel to this one appears to be cited. Milligan thinks that we must be content "either to regard this as a unique construction, intended to emphasize the direction the testimony took, or (with Lft.) connect ἐφ' ὑμᾶς with ἐπιστεύθη in the sense 'belief in our testimony directed itself to reach you.'" Bruce finds Lightfoot's rendering "too awkward to be acceptable" and prefers the simpler "to you."

the converts and his responsibility for bringing about their conversion that surfaces from time to time (e.g., 1 Thess. 2:15, 19).

C. THE CONTENT OF PAUL'S PRAYER (1:11-12)

11 *With this in mind, we constantly pray for you, that our God may count you worthy of his calling, and that by his power he may fulfill every good purpose of yours and every act prompted by your faith.* 12 *We pray this so that the name of our Lord Jesus may be glorified in you, and you in him, according to the grace of our God and the Lord Jesus Christ.*[a]

[a]12 Or *God and Lord, Jesus Christ*

Paul has been holding before his friends the prospect of deliverance and glory at the coming of the Lord. But he is mindful that they still have to live out their faith in the hard world of people who oppose themselves to the things of God. This they can never do in their own strength, but only in the strength that God supplies. Easily and naturally, then, the apostle passes over into prayer that God will see his friends through to the very end.

11 "With this in mind" is rather loosely attached to the whole of the preceding section, and is probably not to be taken closely with any particular word or words. It refers to the whole of the salvation that Paul has been holding out before them. The expression conveys the idea of purpose. Paul is saying that in order that this may happen he prays for his friends. In his previous letter he had counseled them to be unceasing in their prayers (5:17), and he puts his precept into practice. The "also" (which *NIV* omits) may indicate that the Thessalonians were praying about this matter, and Paul joins them in this. But more probably it arises from the fact that the apostle has been thanking God for them (v. 3), boasting about them (v. 4), and assuring them of their place in the scheme of things at the last day (vv. 7, 10). Not only does he do this sort of thing, but he also prays for them.

The first point in his prayer is that[48] "our God may count you worthy of his calling." The calling of God is a leading thought with Paul. Usually it denotes the decisive moment when God calls people out of darkness into his glorious light, and we might cite Romans 8:30 as the typical example

48. ἵνα is probably to be taken not simply as giving the content of the prayer, but with a telic force, "in order that."

of its use: "And those he predestined, he also called; those he called, he also justified. . . ." The call is an effective call, and implies that the one who is called obeys that call. The prayer here that God would count the Thessalonians worthy[49] of the call does not carry with it the thought that they might fall away from the status of called people. We must bear in mind that when people are called they are completely unworthy of this call (Gal. 1:13-15 is perhaps the classic instance of this). But God does not intend that they continue in such a state. They are to walk worthily of the calling wherewith he calls them (Eph. 4:1). It is this that Paul has in mind here. It is inspiring that God has called them, but they must not so exult in this thought that they grow slack in their Christian service. They must seek to be worthy. Since this is not something that can be accomplished in any human strength, Paul prays that God will count them worthy. That is to say, his prayer is that they may so live between this moment and the judgment that God will then be able to pronounce them worthy of the calling wherewith he called them. "You" is emphatic; it indicates Paul's special concern for the Thessalonians.

The next point is that God will "fulfill every good purpose." Some interpreters take this to mean that God is being asked to work out his good pleasure. While there is nothing unlikely in such a sentiment, the Greek here does not seem to mean this. The "act prompted by faith" that is parallel to this expression is something that people perform, and the natural understanding is that they are to work what is laid down in the first part also. Again, the word for "goodness" (the Greek means "purpose of goodness") in the New Testament is always used of human goodness. All in all, it seems clear enough that it is a work of God in the Thessalonians that is in mind. Paul is praying that God will produce a goodness of will in his friends. The parallelism with "work of faith" indicates that the meaning is "resolve proceeding from goodness," rather than "a resolve after goodness" or "a resolve to do good."

Parallel is "act prompted by your faith." "Every," which precedes "desire of goodness," is rightly taken with this phrase also (and *NIV* repeats the word). The expression reminds us that faith is not simply an intellectual attitude that does nothing. Faith is always busy. A true faith will clothe itself in works. So Paul prays that his friends will produce in their lives the works

---

49. ἀξιόω means "to deem worthy," "to reckon as worthy." Cf. the note on the compound καταξιόω in v. 5. *RSV* renders "make you worthy," but Bailey comments, "In no other passage known is the meaning 'to make worthy,' but always 'to deem worthy.' "

that spring from faith (see on 1 Thess. 1:3). When he asks that God will "fulfill" these things he implies that no human power is adequate. The divine is necessary. He reinforces this by adding "in power" with which the verse ends. Paul is not seeking some merely human reformation, nor some pious thinking. He wants to see that fruit of goodness which can come about only when the power of God is operative in human lives.[50]

12 The purpose of all this is now given: "so that the name of our Lord Jesus may be glorified in you." The name in biblical times was much more than a means of distinguishing one person from another. It summed up the person's whole character.[51] An instructive verse for an understanding of the name reads, "To him who overcomes, I will give some of the hidden manna. I will also give him a white stone with a new name written on it, known only to him who receives it" (Rev. 2:17). To our way of thinking a name that nobody knows is useless. The whole purpose of a name is to designate a person. But in the Revelation the name nobody knows is very much in point. It signifies a new character that is given to the person in question, something that is a secret between his Lord and himself.

Thus when prayer is made that the Thessalonians may so live that glory may be brought to the name of the Lord, the meaning is not that the angels may name his name "with loud acclaims" (Frame). Rather, it is that there may be such virtues manifest in the believers that glory will accrue to him who is ultimately responsible for these virtues. The Thessalonians will be such a bright and shining testimony to the reality of their salvation that the Savior will be seen to be the wonderful Being he is. The character in which he will be glorified is the double one of Lord (appropriate in this context so full of allusions to the second advent) and Jesus (with all its association of the human Jesus who stooped so low for us). Then there is another aspect to this glory. The Thessalonians, too, will be glorified. Their glory will result from their association with the Lord, and thus Paul speaks

---

50. The collect for Easter Day in the Book of Common Prayer expresses the thought of this passage: "We humbly beseech thee, that, as by thy special grace preventing [i.e., preceding] us thou dost put into our minds good desires, so by thy continual help we may bring the same to good effect. . . ." The thought that all our goodness comes from God is to be found in the Qumran scrolls, e.g., "For the way of a man is not his own, a man does not direct his own steps; for judgment is God's and from his hand is blamelessness of conduct" (Millar Burrows, *The Dead Sea Scrolls*, p. 388).

51. G. B. Gray speaks of the Hebrew as frequently using "name" "as almost an equivalent of the 'personality' or 'character' or nature of the person or thing named; and consequently, when a writer wishes to express forcibly the nature of a person or place, he says he will be called so-and-so, or his name will be so-and-so" (*HDB*, III, p. 478).

of their being "in" him in this connection.[52] On that day, just as he will be glorified in them on account of what they have become, so they will be glorified in him on account of what he is.[53]

Again and again Paul comes back to the great thought that Christians owe all that they have and all that they are to God. So now he adds to this picture of glory the thought that all is according to the grace of God. Grace is one of the great Christian words, and Paul uses it often (see on 1 Thess. 1:1). It carries with it thoughts of the joyous free favor of God, and of his unmerited kindness to people. This is operative in the whole process of salvation, and if it is more usual in the New Testament to find it used of the initial stages of salvation, there is no reason for thinking that it will be absent from the final stages. The glory of the last time will be due to God's grace to his people.

It seems that *NIV* is correct in its rendering of the closing words of this chapter. But since there is an article before "our God" and none before "Lord Jesus Christ," it is possible to understand the expression to mean, "our God and Lord, Jesus Christ"[54] (*GNB* mg.). However, the expression "Lord Jesus Christ" occurs so frequently that it has almost the status of a proper name. Therefore, when "Lord" is used of Jesus it is not necessary for it to have the article. This being so, it seems likely that we should understand the present passage to refer to both the Father and the Son. At the same time we should not overlook the fact that Paul does link them very closely indeed. That there can be this doubt as to whether one or both are meant is itself indicative of the closeness of their connection in the mind of Paul. He makes no great distinction between them (see further on 1 Thess. 3:11).

---

52. It is of course possible to take αὐτῷ as neuter, referring to the Name, when the translation would be "in it." Frame adopts this view, and understands ἐν "of ground." However, it is much more usual in the New Testament to speak of believers as being "in Christ" than to use the expression "in the Name" in such a connection as this. Notice that believers are said to be glorified "in" Christ, and not simply "with" him.

53. The language is that of Isa. 66:5 (LXX), but there "the Lord" is Yahweh. This is another example of the tendency of the New Testament writers to speak of the Lord Jesus in language used of Yahweh in the Old Testament.

54. Moore notes this possibility but sees a reference to Father and Son as more probable. Turner says, " 'Our Lord and God Jesus Christ' would be the correct rendering" and adds, with reference to a number of passages with this construction, "the simple grammarian may be forgiven for suspecting that special pleading has contributed to the debilitation of tremendous affirmations in the New Testament" (*Grammatical Insights*, p. 16). This may well be the case, but Turner has here reversed the order of "God" and "Lord," an alteration that is not unimportant.

2 THESSALONIANS 2

III. THE PAROUSIA (2:1-12)

A. THE DAY OF THE LORD NOT YET PRESENT (2:1-2)

1 *Concerning the coming of our Lord Jesus Christ and our being gathered to him, we ask you, brothers,* 2 *not to become easily unsettled or alarmed by some prophecy, report or letter supposed to have come from us, saying that the day of the Lord has already come.*

Paul had spoken a good deal about the second coming during his mission at Thessalonica, but it is clear that not all of his teaching had been grasped. New converts, full of enthusiasm, perhaps emotionally unstable, but as yet imperfectly instructed in the deeper things of the faith, not unnaturally went astray in some points in this important but intricate subject. Paul had had occasion to refer to the Parousia in his first letter, but this, it seems, did not clear away all doubts. He felt accordingly that he must deal with the subject again. Indeed, it forms the principal part of 2 Thessalonians. The situation had become complicated by the fact that some in Thessalonica were claiming Paul's authority for the view that the day of the Lord had already come (2:2), and it was important that this error be corrected. Our big difficulty in interpreting what he says is that it is a supplement to his oral preaching. He and his correspondents both knew what he had said when he was in Thessalonica, so there was no point in repeating it. He could take it as known, and simply add what was necessary to clear up the misunderstandings that had arisen. We find it very difficult to fill in the gaps and to catch his allusions, which are so difficult, indeed, that many and various suggestions have been put forward in the attempt to elucidate the apostle's meaning. We must bear in mind the gaps in our knowledge and not be too confident in our interpretations of this notoriously difficult passage.[1]

1 Paul begins, not by pontificating, but by making request of his friends.[2] The verb he uses is not a common one in his writings (though it is far from being an unusual word). It is appropriate to a respectful request (see the note on 1 Thess. 4:1), as is the affectionate "brothers." The subject[3] of his request is twofold, but the use of the single article shows that the coming of the Lord (see the note on 1 Thess. 2:19) and the gathering of the saints are closely connected. Indeed, they are two parts of one great event.[4] The assembly of the saints (see 1 Thess. 4:13-18) does not seem to be vitally related to the coming of the Antichrist, the subject Paul is beginning to discuss, but characteristically he includes it. It is so important, especially to his friends who had been in doubt about their loved ones who had died, and so very much a part of the coming of the Lord. "Our being gathered to him" is the "muster" (Moffatt) of the saints.[5] This may well have been something of a technical term; the cognate verb is used of the gathering of the elect (Matt. 24:31; Mark 13:27). The noun occurs again in the New Testament only once (Heb. 10:25), and there it is the assembling of believers for worship that is in mind (though it should not be overlooked that that verse also looks for the coming of the Lord). Notice the significance of "to him." It is not simply that the saints meet one another: they meet their Lord and remain with him forever (cf. 1 Thess. 4:17).[6]

1. There is a good treatment of the passage by G. Vos, *The Pauline Eschatology* (Grand Rapids, 1953), pp. 94-133.

2. ἐρωτῶμεν δέ. Paul uses the verb 4 times only (3 of which are in the Thessalonian correspondence); it occurs 62 times in the New Testament.

3. The preposition rendered "concerning" is ὑπέρ, which usually means "on behalf of." Here it is more or less equivalent to περί, but it has its own particular emphasis. It signifies something like "in the interests of the truth concerning" (Moule, "in connexion with the coming," *IBNTG*, p. 65). J. B. Lightfoot discusses these two prepositions and remarks that ὑπέρ has "a sense of 'interest in,' which is wanting to περί" (*Saint Paul's Epistle to the Galatians* [London, 1902], p. 73). This probably accounts for its use here.

4. Cf. Ward, "The *coming* and the *assembling* are united by one Greek article. Paul was thinking of one event, not two. At the climax of history the Lord will not be without his church, and his church will not be without him."

5. Deissmann notes the use of the term (ἐπισυναγωγή) for a collection of money. He thinks that it differed from the more common συναγωγή "scarcely more than 'collecting' from 'collecting together.' " He adds, "the longer Greek word was probably more to the taste of the later period" (*LAE*, p. 103).

6. J. E. Fison says about 2 Thess. 2:1ff.: "It should be faced up to for what it

2 Always, it would seem, there have been some Christians who have let their imagination rather than their reason dictate their understanding of the Parousia. This was true of the earliest days of the church, just as of more recent times. The content of Paul's appeal accordingly is that his readers should retain their mental equilibrium. He employs two expressions for the kind of weakness he wants them to avoid and to which some of them were already giving way. The first, "not to become easily unsettled," directs attention to the possibility of being caught up by a sudden excitement. The adverb "quickly" (*NIV*, "easily") does not mean "after a short period," as though pointing to their forsaking the true position soon after reaching it. Rather, it has reference to the quality of the action. Its force is "hastily," "precipitately" (cf. its use in 1 Tim. 5:22). The verb is in the aorist, which more naturally signifies a sudden action than one that is continuous. It is a verb that is often used of literal shaking; the motion produced by wind and wave, and especially violent motion. Its use of a ship driven from its mooring shows us the kind of thing Paul has in mind. He is thinking of people who lack a secure anchorage, and are readily tossed here and there.[7] *NIV*'s "unsettled" is more exactly "shaken from your mind," and the word for "mind" is one that can on occasion be near in meaning to "spirit" (as Lightfoot points out), but properly it directs attention to the reasoning faculty. For example, it is used in distinction from "spirit": "For if I pray in a tongue, my spirit prays, but my mind is unfruitful" (1 Cor. 14:14). In the present passage "mind" stands for the whole mental balance of the person (Findlay, "the regulative intellectual faculty," *CGT*). Putting all this together, then, Paul is urging his readers in the first instance to maintain the stability that will enable them to withstand any sudden shock or discovery. People taken up with advent speculations may easily take an unbalanced interest in the latest idea, and their conduct will be adversely affected thereby. But those whose views on the second coming are more stable are not easily thrown off balance.[8]

---

is, a downright apostolic condemnation of all strictly realized eschatology" (*The Christian Hope* [London, 1954], p. 162).

7. Knox's translation, "Do not be terrified out of your senses all at once" (following the Vulgate *terreamini*), is not quite what is wanted. The verb σαλεύω refers to motion rather than to terrifying. In 1 Thess. 3:3 Paul has used a different verb with a similar meaning; he strongly opposes the instability of some of the Thessalonians.

8. The preposition ἀπό, "from," adds the thought of the mind departing "from" the normal.

The second weakness is that of being "alarmed." This time the verb is in the present and points to a continuing state. Jesus used it when he said, "when you hear of wars and rumors of wars, do not be alarmed" (Mark 13:7).[9] It describes a state of "jumpiness" or of worry. Just as some are easily thrown off balance, so others can fall into a state of constant fretting. Paul wants neither of these states in his converts.

He speaks of three possible ways in which they might be affected.[10] "Spirit" (NIV has "some prophecy") must be understood in the light of the fact that the early church expected supernatural communications from time to time, for example, through the ministry of prophets (cf. 1 Cor. 14:29-30; 1 John 4:1). It means some revelation divinely communicated. Paul, of course, encouraged the right use of prophecy (1 Thess. 5:19-20), but here the content of the supposed prophecy showed that it could not have come from God. "Report" (the Greek means "word") may refer to a sermon, though the term is broad enough to cover all sorts of oral communications. Some interpreters have felt that "letter" means 1 Thessalonians, but this is far from having been demonstrated. The expression is general and might refer to that letter, or to another that Paul had written or had been said to have written, or to a forgery ("purporting to be from us," RSV). There are various possibilities. Nor is the matter rendered any easier by the following "as from us"[11] ("supposed to have come from us," NIV), for this expression, too, is rather indefinite. It indicates that Paul feared that a communication of some kind had been reputed to have come from him (and his assistants?). But he writes in general terms, and we are probably justified in inferring that he was not quite sure of exactly what had happened. Either that, or else he felt it not wise to refer to it too directly. But he is making quite clear that he accepts no responsibility

9. This is not the only place where Paul's words remind us of expressions used by Jesus. See H. A. A. Kennedy, *St. Paul's Conception of the Last Things* (London, 1904), pp. 167-68. This is more than a matter of verbal agreement; there is a unity of underlying ideas, a point that G. R. Beasley-Murray also makes in *Jesus and the Future* (London, 1954), pp. 232ff.

10. The construction, employing a threefold διά, emphasizes the means "through" which the result is brought about.

11. ὡς δι' ἡμῶν strictly means "as through us" and points to a claim that a divine communication had been made "through" God's servants. It is to be taken with all three of the preceding, which are closely linked. Paul is denying that the report emanated from a revelation made to him or from any words of his, spoken or written. Some scholars feel that it is only the letter that purports to come from Paul (BDF #425 [4] presupposes an ellipsis of γεγραμμένης), but there seems to be no good reason for restricting the application of the phrase in this way.

whatever for the report. However it had come, and however it had been attributed to him, he had had nothing to do with it. He does not want his friends to be worried by these speculations, and he completely renounces them.

The content of the particular report was "that the day of the Lord has already come" (for "the day of the Lord" see on 1 Thess. 5:2). Some commentators hold the meaning to be that the day of the Lord was on the very point of occurring. The verb, however, does not mean "to be at hand" but rather "to be present."[12] It is sometimes contrasted with verbs expressing the future idea (e.g., Rom. 8:38; 1 Cor. 3:22). Moreover, Paul could, and did, say that the Parousia was "at hand" (with a different Greek expression, Phil. 4:5). It seems that the verb ought to be given its usual sense here, rather than to have the idea of imminence imported into it. Obviously the Lord had not returned in the full sense that Paul had described in his teaching to the Thessalonians, and outlined in the First Epistle. But the day of the Lord was a complex idea. It included a number of events, as we see from the various passages of Scripture that refer to it. To say that the day of the Lord had come did not mean that it was completed and that all the glorious events associated with it had occurred. That was so obviously untrue that it needed no refutation. What it did mean was that that day had dawned. They were even then living in it.[13] This being so, the climax must infallibly be reached, and that

12. Cf. Frame, "ἐνέστηκεν means not 'is coming' (ἔρχεται I-5:2), not 'is at hand' (ἤγγικεν Rom. 13:12), not 'is near' (ἐγγύς ἐστιν Phil. 4:5), but 'has come,' 'is on hand,' 'is present.'" Later he cites Lillie as maintaining that those who favor the meaning "is at hand" do so "from the supposed necessity of the case rather than from any grammatical compulsion." Bicknell gives "is now present" as "the only possible translation of the Greek." B. B. Warfield, by contrast, uses strong language to indicate his disagreement with such views. He holds that the verb signifies "is upon us" (*The Expositor,* 3rd Series, IV, p. 37).

13. There is a sense in which Christians are even now living in the end time. The decisive victory has been won. Cf. O. Cullmann, "Just as the 'Victory Day' does in fact present *something new* in contrast to the decisive battle already fought at some point or other of the war, just so the end which is still to come also brings something new. To be sure, this new thing that the 'Victory Day' brings is based entirely upon that decisive battle, and would be absolutely impossible without it. Thus we make for the future precisely the same confirmation as we did for the past. It is a unique occurrence; it has its meaning for redemptive history in itself; but on the other hand it is nevertheless founded upon that one unique event at the mid-point" (*Christ and Time* [London, 1951], p. 141). Those in error at Thessalonica, however, were not thinking that the decisive event had occurred in its completeness, but rather that "Victory Day" had already dawned.

within a very short space of time.[14] We can easily picture the effect such news would have on those who were not well grounded in the Christian faith and who were given to excitability. Paul proceeds to show the complete falsity of such an idea.[15]

B. THE GREAT REBELLION (2:3-12)

1. The Man of Lawlessness (2:3-10a)

3 *Don't let anyone deceive you in any way, for that day will not come until the rebellion occurs and the man of lawlessness*[a] *is revealed, the man doomed to destruction.* 4 *He opposes and exalts himself over everything that is called God or is worshiped, and even sets himself up in God's temple, proclaiming himself to be God.*

5 *Don't you remember that when I was with you I used to tell you these things?* 6 *And now you know what is holding him back, so that he may be revealed at the proper time.* 7 *For the secret power of lawlessness is already at work; but the one who now holds it back will continue to do so till he is taken out of the way.* 8 *And then the lawless one will be revealed, whom the Lord Jesus will overthrow with the breath of his mouth and destroy by the splendor of his coming.* 9 *The coming of the lawless one will be in accordance with the work of Satan displayed in all kinds of counterfeit miracles, signs and wonders,* 10 *and in every sort of evil that deceives those who are perishing.*

[a]3 Some manuscripts *sin*

This is an extraordinarily difficult passage, not made any easier by the fact that its subject matter is not dealt with elsewhere. We thus have no comparable passage with which we may compare it or that we may use

---

14. Cf. the remark of Origen cited by J. Jeremias, "It may be—in view of the fact that there were people among the Jews who claimed to know from books either of the time of the destruction (of the universe) or about other secret things—that therefore he (Paul) wrote this (2 Thess. 2.1sq.), warning his followers not to believe the claims of these people" (*The Eucharistic Words of Jesus* [Oxford, 1955], p. 76, n. 1).

15. W. Schmithals and others see a reference to Gnosticism here. Against this (a) there is no real evidence that Gnosticism was as early as this, and (b) the Gnostic meaning is not a natural understanding of what Paul wrote.

to supplement it. But some things are clear. In opposing those in Thessalonica who were claiming that "the day of the Lord" had already come Paul makes it clear that that day would be marked by such outstanding happenings that there would be no danger of mistaking or disregarding its presence. Specifically he says that it will be preceded by a great rebellion of the forces of evil against God and by the appearance of a being traditionally called "the man of sin."

3 Paul is desperately anxious that his friends do not fall into error. "Don't let anyone deceive you in any way" is not only an exhortation,[16] but a reminder of the folly of being led astray in this way. The verb is a compound, the thought being that to be taken in by the kind of thing he has outlined is not only to be deceived, but to be badly deceived. The addition of "in any way" extends the possible ways of bringing about the deception. Paul objects to the conclusion. He therefore excludes all ways of reaching it.

Now we come to the great fact that proves conclusively that the day of the Lord has not yet arrived. The words "the day will not come" have no equivalent in the Greek, but they are implied. Paul's impetuous style often leaves out words that the readers may well understand for themselves, and that is the case here. There is no uncertainty about his meaning. That day will not come about until the "rebellion" takes place, and a certain evil figure, "the man of sin," has made his appearance. Since neither is yet in evidence, the argument runs, the day of the Lord cannot possibly have come. There is some difficulty with our understanding of both these expressions. What is beyond doubt is that Paul expected his allusion to be so clear to the Thessalonians that they would see the folly of their error and return to sanity. The term rendered "rebellion" is sometimes used of political or military rebellions. The characteristic thought of the Bible is that God rules. Thus the word is appropriate for a rebellion against his rule. In part "rebellion" points to this sort of thing; it includes the idea of forsaking one's former allegiance. But it is not so much forsaking one's first love and drifting into apathy that is meant, as setting oneself actively in opposition to God. Neil speaks of "a widespread and violent defiance of the authority of God." It is the supreme effort of Satan and his minions to which the word directs us.[17]

---

16. Moulton finds the tone of subjunctives like this "less peremptory than that of the imperative, as may be seen from their closeness to the clauses of warning" (M, I, p. 178).

17. This is not to deny that there will be an apostasy in the last times, and one

Paul does not speak of "a" rebellion, as though introducing the topic for the first time, but of "the" rebellion, that is, the well-known rebellion, that one about which he had already instructed them.[18]

He speaks of the rebellion coming "first" (which *NIV* omits), but he does not say what it is to precede. There can be no doubt that *NIV* is correct in supplying "that day will not come," with "that day" referring to the day of the Lord. The omission of the words shows that the writer is excited and is not paying much attention to the strict rules of grammar,[19] which adds to our difficulties. This phenomenon helps us to understand something of the importance Paul attached to the subject. It was desperately important that the Thessalonians get the thing straight. He cannot keep calm about the matter.

Associated with[20] the rebellion is the person who is traditionally known as "the man of sin."[21] The title is so universally used that it is perhaps impossible to substitute another. But "man of lawlessness" is a better reading than "man of sin,"[22] and fits in with the words used in

---

of considerable proportions (as we see from Matt. 24:10-12). All that I am maintaining is that in the present passage the emphasis is on the revolt against God rather than on the falling away from the church that will be part of the picture. Hendriksen sees in the absence of any adjective to qualify ἡ ἀποστασία an indication that practically the whole church will apostatize, but this seems to be reading a good deal into the text.

18. Lightfoot maintains that the word might apply to Christians or Jews, either of whom might be said to depart from God, but it can have no reference to Gentiles. Denney thinks that Paul is describing events in which the church is but a spectator, and that the term applies accordingly to the Jews. H. A. A. Kennedy says that the word "can only mean a revolt against God. Therefore it must take place among the people who acknowledge the true God, i.e., the Jews" (*St. Paul's Conception of the Last Things*, p. 218). Such views may be a little too confident. If the word means "rebellion" it may well apply to the rebellion of the creature against the Creator. It is thus not impossible to envisage its use with reference to others than Jews.

19. "His style is that of a speaker, not of a studied writer; such broken sentences are inevitable, and explain themselves, in animated conversation" (Findlay, *CGT*).

20. It is not certain whether the καί indicates that the rebellion and the revelation of the Man of Lawlessness are to be thought of as simultaneous, or whether the second is to follow the first. They are obviously closely connected, though not identical. "Man of Lawlessness" is of course a Hebraism signifying a lawless man, one characterized by lawlessness.

21. Knox renders "the champion of wickedness."

22. ἀνομίας is read by ℵ B 81 sah boh Marc Tert etc. and ἁμαρτίας by A D G K L P etc. Since Paul does not use ἀνομία very often, copyists would be more likely to alter it to ἁμαρτία than the reverse. Metzger also points out that γὰρ . . . ἀνομίας in v. 7 "seems to presuppose ἀνομίας here."

verses 7 and 8, whereas the traditional rendering obscures the connection of thought. However, the difference in meaning is not great; lawlessness must be understood as failure to conform to the law of God, and this is what sin is (1 John 3:4). In the last resort sin is the refusal to be ruled by God. It is the assertion of the creature against the Creator, the self against the God of grace (Best renders "man of rebellion," which well brings out this aspect; but we should bear in mind that the word is not from the same root as that which speaks of the revolt against God in v. 3). All of this fits in with the great rebellion that has just been mentioned. The individual in mind is seen against the background of the rising of Satan against the power of God.

Who is this Man of Lawlessness? A common identification is with the Roman Emperor, either as an individual or as the line of emperors. In favor of this can be urged the claim that the emperors were divine and the demand that they be worshipped. The attitude of the persecuting emperors such as Nero must have led many Christians to see in them some of the attributes of the Man of Lawlessness. But against all such identifications is the fact that Paul seems to be speaking of the last and supreme embodiment of evil, one who will make his appearance only in the last days. There seems to be no evidence that he really thought that either a present or a future Roman emperor, or the whole line of emperors, was this supreme representative of Satan.

A variant of this view is that the idea is derived from the concept of Nero redivivus. After Nero's death more than one man arose claiming to be the dead emperor, and aroused people's fears. When it became accepted that Nero was indeed dead, the expectation took shape that one day he would come back in a supernatural fashion. The suggestion is made that the present passage is not due to the apostle Paul, but to some later writer who has taken up facets of the Nero legend and woven them into his conception of the Antichrist, the Man of Lawlessness. More than one objection may be urged against this. One is that every indication seems to show that the letter is too early for it to be dependent on the Nero legend. If it is an authentic writing of Paul, then of course the Man of Lawlessness owes nothing to Nero, but in any case the thought of Antichrist in some form is very old, as Bousset has shown conclusively.[23] It does not depend on the Nero legend.

From the Reformation onward there have been those who have identified the papacy with the Man of Lawlessness (the Preface to the

23. See *The Antichrist Legend* (London, 1896).

King James Version calls the pope "that Man of Sin"). But it is difficult to think of a line of popes as constituting the Man of Lawlessness, for he seems rather to be an individual. No one would gather from reading the words of Paul that he was referring to a line of ecclesiastics. This view seems to have arisen more from hostility to the papacy than from exegetical considerations.

All attempts to equate the Man of Lawlessness with historical personages break down on the fact that Paul was writing of someone who would appear only at the end of the age; the Man of Lawlessness is an eschatological figure. Paul wrote that he will appear just before the Lord comes again, and therefore it seems futile to try to identify him. Scripture tells us that there are many Antichrists (1 John 2:18),[24] and it does not surprise us accordingly that through the ages of history many have appeared whose evil lives remind us of this or that trait of the Man of Lawlessness. But that does not give us grounds for identifying the supreme embodiment of evil with any of Satan's lesser lights along the way.[25]

Paul speaks of this figure as being "revealed," just as in 1:7 he has spoken of the revelation of the Lord Jesus. The position of the verb in the Greek gives it a certain emphasis, as does its repetition in verses 6 and 8. It indicates that the Man of Lawlessness will exist before his manifestation to the world. It may also point us to something supernatural about him, which would be natural enough, considering his close association with Satan. It seems unlikely, however, that Paul means us to understand that the Man of Lawlessness was in existence at the time he was writing (as Frame, for example, holds).

The Man of Lawlessness is further described as "the man doomed

---

24. T. F. Glasson thinks of the figure of the Man of Lawlessness as being derived ultimately from the Old Testament. In his opinion some early Christians took certain ideas from their Scripture, modified them, and produced this figure (see *The Second Advent* [London, 1947], pp. 180ff.). It is well that we bear in mind that this concept is biblical, whether we call the being Antichrist, Man of Lawlessness, Man of Sin, or anything else. There is no warrant for thinking that it was derived from current mythological speculations or from extracanonical Jewish literature (see G. Vos, *The Pauline Eschatology,* pp. 94ff.). But that does not mean that the idea was a novelty fashioned by the early church in isolation from the Master and such great figures as Paul. The teaching of Daniel was taken up by our Lord (Mark 13:14), and it is from him that it becomes Christian tradition. From the first, Christians understood that the appearing of this evil being in the end time was inevitable.

25. From the time of Theodore of Mopsuestia many expositors have held that the Man of Lawlessness is practically an "incarnation" of Satan, somewhat analogous to Christ's incarnation.

to destruction," or more literally, "the son of perdition,"[26] a description that Jesus applied to Judas Iscariot (John 17:12; see *KJV*). This type of genitive has a Hebraic twist. It denotes "characterized by" the quality in the genitive (cf. Isa. 57:4). So here it means that the Man of Lawlessness will certainly be lost. As Moffatt puts it, he is "the doomed One."

4 The description of the evil personage is continued.[27] "He opposes and exalts himself" is the translation of two participles united under a single article, which thus form a third way of describing this being. The former of the two participles might be rendered "the adversary." It is often used of Satan. In this place it does not, of course, mean Satan, but the associations of the term are evil, and it stresses the evil character of the man to whom it refers. He sets himself against God; the present participle indicates a continuing attitude: it is no passing phase. The second participle (also present continuous) deals with the exalted position the Man of Lawlessness arrogates to himself. He sets himself above "everything that is called God or is worshiped," and he can lay claim to no higher place than that. He is not content with supreme political position, but insists on having the place reserved among all mankind for the supreme object of worship. He demands religious veneration. More exactly, he insists that no god, nor anything bearing the name of God, nor any object of worship whatever[28] should be allowed pride of place. The Man of Lawlessness must be first of all.

The climax to all this is the explicit claim to deity.[29] He is to sit in the temple[30] proclaiming himself to be God. There are some interesting touches here. "So that" (for which *NIV* has "and even") is a conjunction indicating result.[31] This action is not unconnected with the preceding. It

---

26. A. Deissmann explains this as due to "an echo of LXX Is. 57:4 τέκνα ἀπωλείας" (*Bible Studies* [Edinburgh, 1901], p. 163).

27. The language resembles that in a number of passages in Daniel, notably Dan. 7:25; 8:9ff.; 11:36ff., but it is not likely that Paul was quoting. Rather, he had so often read and pondered the sacred Scripture that his language was naturally that of the Old Testament.

28. Paul uses a rather rare word, σέβασμα, which includes anything at all that can be worshipped. It is used of gods and images, but also of shrines, altars, etc. Taken in conjunction with the preceding "everything that is called God," it emphasizes the complete refusal of the Man of Lawlessness to brook any rival of any kind.

29. ὡς θεόν is read by D² F Ir^lat Eus, but this looks like an explanatory gloss.

30. Some scholars have felt that the religious associations of the Man of Lawlessness imply that he will be claiming to be the Christ, i.e., a Hebrew pseudo-Messiah. Vos has shown this to be untenable (*The Pauline Eschatology*, pp. 114ff.).

31. ὥστε.

grows out of it. "He sits" (*NIV*, "sets himself up") is the aorist infinitive pointing to the single act of taking the seat rather than the continuous action of sitting. It is in accordance with this that the preposition "in" is that naturally used of motion toward. The "temple" is the inmost shrine, and not the temple as a whole. It is not that he enters the temple precincts: he invades the most sacred place and there takes his seat. His action is itself a claim to deity,[32] and the verb "proclaiming[33] himself" seems to imply an explicit claim in so many words.

Most commentators draw attention to the attempt by Caligula to set up an image of himself in the temple at Jerusalem, an attempt that was frustrated only by his death. This took place in A.D. 40. The attempt aroused widespread horror among the Jews. It may well be that Paul has this incident in mind in writing these words, but we should bear in mind that what he says goes beyond anything Caligula attempted. The Man of Lawlessness is not pictured as setting up a statue of himself but as taking his seat in person (cf. Ezek. 28:2).

The question arises of what should be understood by "God's temple." There are passages where such an expression means the Christian church (1 Cor. 3:16-17), and some interpreters have understood this sense here. The meaning then would be that tne Man of Lawlessness makes the church his base of operations. He establishes himself there, claiming to be divine. This is a rather difficult concept (would not the church by that very fact cease to be the *Christian* church?). While the New Testament speaks of many falling away in the last days, it does not appear to envisage the church as such becoming apostate. There is, moreover, the vivid language already noted. This seems to mean that he will actually take his seat in a formal way in a sanctuary. Some commentators suggest that it is heaven that is meant (cf. Ps. 11:4). Frame, for example, sees the possibility of a reference to the ancient tradition of the Dragon that stormed the heavens. The difficulty is that Paul pictures the Man of Lawlessness as actually taking his seat in the shrine and not merely as attempting to do so. It is like our Lord's "When you see 'the abomination that causes desolation' standing where it does not belong" (Mark 13:14; the masculine participle shows that a person is in

32. E. Stauffer cites similar claims from the apocalyptic literature, such as "I am the anointed one" (*Apocalypse of Elijah* 31:40), "I am God, and before me there has been no God" (*The Ascension of Isaiah* 4:6). These are cited in his *New Testament Theology* (London, 1955), p. 215.

33. Milligan cites examples of the verb in the sense " 'nominate' or 'proclaim' to an office."

mind). Paul is certainly not saying that this evil being will conquer heaven. While the temple is not easy to identify, the best way to understand the passage seems to be that some material building will serve as the setting for the blasphemous claim to deity that the Man of Lawlessness will make as the climax of his activities.[34]

5 Paul races on with the reminder that there is nothing new in what he is saying: he had told them all this before! Frame and others speak of "a trace of impatience" here, while Findlay by contrast says that Paul "gently reproves" his readers. It is probable that neither suggestion exactly meets the case. As we have had occasion to notice before, this section is extremely lively, and throughout we get the impression that Paul was dictating animatedly with scant regard for grammatical niceties and exact balance of phrase. The previous sentence is not really finished, and his thought rushes on as he vividly recalls what he had said when he was among the Thessalonians. Although throughout most of the letter the plural is used, here Paul replaces it with the singular as he recalls what he had done in their city. What he has just written is by way of reiteration of his oral teaching. His question is framed in such a way as to expect an affirmative answer: of course, they will remember! The tense of the verb seems to imply that he had dealt with the subject often.[35] Thus he is able to content himself with the barest of outlines. Now his question obviates the need for a fuller explanation. Paul simply jogs their memory. He says, in effect, "It is as I told you before."

6 With "and now" Paul passes from a consideration of the future to the present state of affairs.[36] It is as though he were saying, "You had it all explained to you and you accepted it. Do not let some new-fangled theory alter your convictions." Once again he directs attention to a fact that was well known to the Thessalonians and on which, therefore, he has no need to enlarge. Since they knew what he was writing about, he had no need to be specific. He has accordingly left his allusion so general that

34. "Explicit, ultimate blasphemy. Not 'a god,' for all gods have been banished" (Ward).

35. The verb is ἔλεγον. The imperfect form favors the continuous sense, though, since in the case of this verb the imperfect is often used in a sense close to that of the aorist, it cannot be pressed. Most commentators favor the continuous sense.

36. Some interpreters understand καὶ νῦν as logical, marking simply the transition to a new stage of the argument. The temporal sense, "as to the present," however, seems much more to the point. *RSV* reads "you know what is restraining him now," but νῦν is surely to be taken with οἴδατε, not κατέχον (so Bruce and others); "you must now be aware" (*NEB;* though *REB* drops the "now" with "You know, too").

commentators through the centuries have been baffled as to exactly what he did mean and many conjectures have been put forward, sometimes supported by ingenious arguments. But we cannot feel at all sure that we have the clue to the situation, and it is best to face that fact. We should take notice of the conjectures that have been made by earnest and scholarly souls, for one of them may conceivably be correct. But we should maintain a reserve in what we claim for our own particular interpretation.

"What is holding him back" represents the neuter participle of a verb whose masculine participle is found in the next verse,[37] where it is rendered "the one who now holds it back." Our first problem is the meaning of the verb NIV renders "holding back." It is usually accepted that it means "hold back" or "restrain," but it can also signify "hold fast," as it does, for example, in 1 Thessalonians 5:21 ("restrain" is an impossible meaning for it there). Sometimes the verb is intransitive, when it means "hold sway"[38] (though it does not appear to have this meaning anywhere in the New Testament). While the probabilities are that the meaning assigned to it by NIV is the right one, we must not overlook the fact that our ignorance of the circumstances precludes us from ruling out the other meanings entirely.[39]

At the time the letter was written, then, some person or thing was holding something fast, or exercising sway, or restraining (presumably restraining the Man of Lawlessness). Many commentators have seen a reference to the Roman Empire, which might be referred to as neuter, or in the person of the emperor as masculine.[40] It would be dangerous to talk openly about the state or its ruler, and this oblique method is seen as the result. Those who hold such views commonly think of one of the emperors (usually Nero) as the Man of Lawlessness, whose appearance was held back by the existence of his predecessor. When the predecessor was removed the Man of Lawlessness would appear. It is difficult to carry this understanding through. There is no reason for thinking that Paul saw in any Roman emperor (Nero or any other) the Man of Lawlessness. Moreover, the Roman Empire in due course passed away without the events that Paul here associates with the End.

37. Turner regards the two as synonymous (M, III, p. 21).

38. D. W. B. Robinson has argued for this meaning (F. L. Cross [ed.], *Studia Evangelica*, II [Berlin, 1964], pp. 635-38).

39. Vos has an interesting note on the possibility of taking the verb in the sense "hold in possession" (*The Pauline Eschatology*, p. 133, n. 20).

40. Tertullian held that the passage referred to the Roman state (*On the Resurrection of the Flesh* 24).

B. B. Warfield identified the restraining power as the Jewish state.[41] The masculine "restrainer" he thought might be James of Jerusalem. Warfield was a great exegete and all his opinions must be carefully weighed, but this is one in which few have been able to follow him. It is hard to understand how the Jewish state could restrain the Man of Lawlessness (even if we accept Warfield's other idea that this was the line of Roman emperors). It is even more difficult to see the apostle James fulfilling this role.

A favorite view among many modern scholars is that Paul is here referring to some contemporary eschatological speculation. Babylonian and other myths are cited to show that many people thought that there would be a gigantic conflict between good and evil at the end of the age. Various reasons were urged for the postponement of this conflict. The suggestion is that Paul was alluding to some such idea, known to and held by the Christians at Thessalonica. This is not impossible. There is every reason for thinking that a great deal of early eschatological literature has perished, and we do not know what was in it. But that is just the point. We do not know. If Paul was alluding to some such idea, we have now no means of knowing what it was or that this is what he was doing. Under the circumstances there seems to be no point in postulating this as the solution to our problem.

Cullmann strongly opposes the view that the restrainer is the Roman Empire. He suggests that "there is a reference to the missionary preaching as a sign pointing to the end."[42] The gospel must first be preached to the Gentiles. This sounds attractive while Cullmann is dealing with the neuter "that which restraineth." But when he moves on to the masculine participle he regards it as "a self-designation of the apostle."[43] This seems most improbable. It would be an extraordinary way for Paul to refer to himself. Nothing in the passage gives countenance to the idea that he felt that he himself was holding back such a being as the Man of Lawlessness.

While not agreeing with Cullmann, others think that there must be a reference to a force for good in opposition to the evil about which Paul

41. The restraining power "appears to be the Jewish state. For the continued existence of the Jewish state was both graciously and naturally a protection to Christianity, and hence a restraint on the revelation of the persecuting power" (*Biblical and Theological Studies* [Philadelphia, 1952], p. 473; reprinted from *The Expositor*, 3rd Series, Vol. IV [1886], pp. 40-41).

42. *Christ and Time*, p. 164.

43. *Ibid.*, p. 165.

writes. Marshall argues that "it is ultimately God who will allow the rebel to be manifested only when the present opportunity of preaching and hearing the gospel is brought to an end by the removal of the angelic figure who is now in charge" (p. 199). Surely no Christian will want to quarrel with the idea that God is in charge of the whole process and that in the end it is he who will allow "lawless one" to be revealed. But the question is: Who or what is the restrainer? There is no evidence that Paul meant "the angelic figure" of whom Marshall writes.

Going to the other extreme, a number of students have identified the restrainer as some force of evil, perhaps Satan or some other evil being. Charles H. Giblin, who has a lengthy discussion of the problems of this chapter, makes some incisive criticisms of a number of suggested solutions to those problems.[44] He understands the restraining power not as opposed to the Man of Lawlessness but as a force for evil, "a present and persistent threat to faith."[45] He argues his point learnedly, but it is difficult to see in what Paul wrote a reference to a force for evil. Best "somewhat hesitatingly" takes the restraining power as evil: "That the force of evil 'possesses' or 'occupies' the present world fits suitably into apocalyptic thought" (p. 301). But he does not make clear how the removal of the force of evil now present in the world prepares for the coming of the Man of Lawlessness.

Better than any of these speculations seems to be that which favors the principle of order that restrains the working of evil. This might be referred to in the abstract as neuter, or it might be personified when it would be masculine. It might be illustrated by the system of law in the Roman Empire, which might be spoken of in the neuter or personified in the Emperor. So with other systems of law that have succeeded that of Rome. It is when law is taken out of the way that the Lawless One will rule.[46]

---

44. *The Threat to Faith* (Rome, 1967). Best, however, has shown that there are serious weaknesses in Giblin's position (Best, p. 299).

45. *The Threat to Faith*, p. 230.

46. Cf. E. Stauffer, "The civil power is set up as a bulwark against the powers of chaos, but it can only keep these powers in check, never really subdue them. The fight against them will never come to an end, and in the end it must succumb to their final onslaught" (*New Testament Theology*, p. 85). Dietrich Bonhoeffer speaks of "the restrainer" as "the force of order, equipped with great physical strength, which effectively blocks the way of those who are about to plunge into the abyss. . . . The 'restrainer' is the power of the state to establish and maintain order" (*Ethics* [London, 1956], p. 44). Bengel, too, thinks that "the civil authority" is in mind (p. 221).

But this, too, is speculation. The plain fact is that Paul and his readers knew what he was talking about, and we do not. We have not the means at our disposal to recover this part of his meaning. It is best that we frankly acknowledge our ignorance.

The important thing is that some power was in operation, and that the Man of Lawlessness could not possibly put in his appearance until this power was removed. The Thessalonians knew this. Therefore they should have known that speculations about the presence of the day of the Lord were necessarily false. Necessary preconditions had yet to be fulfilled.

An important aspect of the teaching of this whole passage is pinpointed in the expression "at the proper time." Paul is not describing some great series of events that take place in violation of the will of God, while God, so to speak, has to work out some plan as a counter. Paul thinks of God as being in control of the whole process.[47] While there are mysteries here, as there must be whenever we contemplate the workings of evil in a universe created by a God who is perfectly good, yet what is abundantly plain is that God is over all. No wicked person, be he Satan, be he the Man of Lawlessness, be he anyone else whatever, can overstep the bounds God has appointed him. The Man of Lawlessness will be revealed only as and when God permits. He is not to be thought of as acting in complete independence. Throughout this whole passage the thought of God's sovereignty is dominant. Evil is strong, and will wax stronger in the last times, but God's hand is in the process. Evil will not pass beyond its limits. God's purpose, not that of Satan or his henchmen, will finally be effected.

7 "The secret power of lawlessness" is an unusual expression.[48] The word translated "secret power" (and more usually "mystery") in the New Testament has nothing of the mysterious in our sense of the term about it (nor, for that matter, of power). It denotes rather that which is secret, which is hidden from people, and which people, for all their searching, will never find by their own efforts. Usually there is the added thought that the mystery has now been made known. It is not surprising that it is normally employed of the purposes of God in salvation and the like. The mystery involved in the gospel was not known and could not be known until God pleased to reveal it in Christ (e.g., Rom. 16:25-26). But the use

---

47. εἰς τὸ ἀποκαλυφθῆναι indicates purpose, the purpose of God.

48. A somewhat similar expression occurs in the "Thanksgiving Psalms" in the Qumran scrolls, namely, the "mystery of evil" (Millar Burrows, *The Dead Sea Scrolls* [London, 1956], p. 333).

of the term here reminds us that there are secrets as well in sin. We can never, by our own reasoning, plumb the depths of iniquity, the reason for its existence, or the manner of its working. Paul points out that even as he writes there is a secret activity of lawlessness at work. The explanation of it all is not open to us, but the fact of its being in operation is clear enough. The use of the term "lawlessness" connects it with the Man of Lawlessness. Though that individual has not yet been revealed, the principle that governs his operations is already at work on this earth (cf. 1 John 2:18). It is probable that Paul does not mean simply that evil is at work. That has always been true. It is rather "the spirit of the antichrist" (1 John 4:3) that is in mind, a special form of evil that is hostile to all that Christ stands for. We can scarcely be more specific in view of the reserve with which Paul writes. The verb rendered "is . . . at work" usually denotes some supernatural force (see the note on 1 Thess. 2:13). Here it is Satan who sets "the mystery of lawlessness" in motion.

The animated style we noted in verse 3 continues. Once again Paul rushes on without completing his sentence.[49] His point is that although the lawless principle is at work already it cannot reach its climax at present because of the restrainer. That climax will be reached only when the restrainer is "taken out of the way." This phrase is not explained. Even so it seems definite enough to exclude some suggestions as to the identity of the restrainer, for example, that which views him as the Holy Spirit (so the Scofield Reference Bible).[50] While it would be easy to think of the Spirit as restraining the forces of evil, it is impossible to envisage him as being "taken out of the way." Such an idea does not appear in Scripture.

8 It is only then, after the restrainer has been removed, that the "lawless one" will be revealed. This is the high point in the unfolding

49. The ellipse may be filled in more ways than one. Most scholars see some such sense as *NIV,* but Lightfoot gives the meaning as "Only it must work in secret, must be unrevealed, until he that restraineth now be taken out of the way." He points out that Gal. 2:10 affords "an exact parallel both to the ellipse after μόνον, and to the position of ὁ κατέχων ἄρτι before the relative word ἕως for the sake of emphasis."

50. Thomas argues for this view, citing the use of both masculine and neuter for the Spirit in John's account of the discourses in the Upper Room. He holds that "The special presence of the Spirit as the indweller of saints will terminate abruptly at the *parousia* as it began abruptly at Pentecost. Once the body of Christ has been caught away to heaven, the Spirit's ministry will revert back to what he did for believers during the OT period." But Paul does not speak of a reversion to the Old Testament pattern; he says that the restrainer will be taken out of the way. The Spirit was not "taken out of the way" in Old Testament times; indeed, he engaged in vigorous action at times (e.g., Judg. 14:6; Ezek. 37:1).

of wickedness. It takes place only in its due order. The "lawless one" is another way of referring to the personage who has already been called the Man of Lawlessness. The language is more terse, but it scarcely differs in significance. This is the third time that Paul has said that he will be revealed, and the repetition gives emphasis. This is no ordinary being making an appearance in the normal course of human events. He has supernatural associations. In the providence of God his appearance is withheld as yet. But in due course he will be "revealed" to the inhabitants of earth. It is likely that the Man of Lawlessness will have something of a career. The general impression given by the passages in Scripture that speak of the last days is that he will have a large following. But Paul's interest is not in the course of the rebellion, nor in the Man of Lawlessness as such. He puts his emphasis on the overriding sovereignty of God. He is convinced that all people and all events are in the hand of God.[51] As he contemplates the happenings of the end time, it is not with the eager eye of one who seeks to trace out in detail the course of events and follow the progress of the Man of Lawlessness. Rather, he looks with joy on the revelation of the mighty hand of God. His purpose is to meet the need of his friends, not to satisfy their (or our) curiosity. His unfolding of the picture is not with a view to providing them with a timetable of events at the end so that they will be in a position to anticipate the course of events step by step. He writes to assure them that whatever happens God is over all: God is working his purposes out and will continue to do so to the very end. The Man of Lawlessness and the great rebellion must be mentioned, but Paul's interest is not in them. His interest is in God and in the working out of God's purposes. So no sooner has he come to the appearance of the Lawless One than he proceeds to his destruction.

This destruction is to be brought about by the Lord Jesus.[52] The

51. Cf. A. E. J. Rawlinson, "The eschatological element in the Christian creed gives expression not only to the Christian conviction of the reality of the world to come, but also to the recognition (a) that the ultimate verdict upon human life and its issues is the verdict of God, (b) that the ultimate victory in the struggle between evil and good is the victory of God, and (c) that the ultimate satisfaction of the human spirit is not to be found in the sphere of things visible and temporal but in the sphere of the things eternal and invisible" (*The New Testament Doctrine of the Christ* [London, 1926], p. 123, n. 1).

52. Following the reading of ℵ A D* G P 33 1241 sah boh etc. It is possible to regard the shorter text as authentic and think of pious scribes as inserting Ἰησοῦς, but it seems more likely that it was omitted in some MSS either accidentally or in order to conform it to the prophecy of Isa. 11:4.

term "Lord" is significant and appropriate in this context, with its emphasis on the glory of him who first came in lowliness. Though he had once been despised and rejected, at the supreme moment of history he will be seen in all his glorious majesty. His splendor is brought out by the use of words reminiscent of the sacred Scripture to indicate the manner in which he will deal with the Lawless One (the passage recalls Isa. 11:4, where similar words are used of Yahweh himself). The picture is further strengthened by the ease with which the Lord will destroy this terrible being. "The breath of his mouth" will be sufficient (cf. Luther's hymn, "One little word shall fell him").

Not even an action on his part is necessary. It is enough for him to manifest himself to render the Man of Lawlessness powerless.[53] "The splendor of his coming" combines two words associated with Jesus' second advent. The former refers on one occasion to the first coming of the Lord (2 Tim. 1:10), but everywhere else in the New Testament to the second coming. It usually has some idea of striking splendor (its root meaning has to do with conspicuousness). It is a technical term for "a visible manifestation of a hidden divinity, either in the form of a personal appearance, or by some deed of power by which its presence is made known" (BAGD).[54] The latter is the usual word for Jesus' "coming" (see on 1 Thess. 2:19). The combination heightens the idea of the splendor and majesty of the Lord at that day. This has point in the present context. The Thessalonians need not fear, however illustrious evil people may

53. The verb rendered "destroy" is καταργέω. Something of the difficulty of translating this verb is seen in that *KJV* employs 17 different equivalents in its 27 occurrences. *RV* gets rid of 7 of these, but introduces 3 new renderings; to add further to the confusion, the English and American revisers do not always agree. In later translations the variety continues (I now have a list of over 80 translations that have appeared in reputable versions). The verb has the basic meaning "to render idle" (ἀργόν = ἀ + ἔργον). Thus it comes to signify "to nullify," "to rob of force and effectiveness." C. Clare Oke thinks that "our modern totalitarian word 'liquidate' is an exact equivalent" (*ET* 67 [1955-56], p. 368, n. 1). This is interesting but may be going a little too far. In the present passage the verb refers to depriving the Man of Lawlessness of all significance rather than to his destruction (which is the meaning of ἀνελεῖ).

54. The word is ἐπιφάνεια. "It adds here the idea of a conspicuous manifestation of God to help His people by His presence" (Bicknell). A. Deissmann speaks of it as "another cult-word" and gives an example of its use of the "Epiphany of Augustus" (i.e., the coming of the Emperor) (*LAE*, p. 373). Similarly, E. Stauffer cites an inscription referring to "the first year of the Epiphany of Gaius Caesar" as showing "the way the inhabitants of Cos calculated their time after the visit of a prince of the house of Augustus" (*New Testament Theology*, pp. 314-15, n. 709).

seem to be. Even the most outstanding of them all will be far outshone by the Lord of these lowly believers when he returns.

9 Paul does not underestimate the Man of Lawlessness. His confident assertions of the last couple of verses spring from his recognition of the splendor and the power of the Lord Jesus, not from any failure to appreciate the power of the opposition. He concludes his words on the Man of Lawlessness by showing that he fully recognizes his stature and the majesty he will manifest when he comes on his evil mission.

He speaks of this man as having a "coming." The word is that which has just been used of the second advent of the Lord Jesus; indeed, it is the characteristic word for that advent. This "coming" of the Man of Lawlessness is to be[55] with splendor and with power. That power is associated with Satan, whose representative he is. The verse strongly suggests that we are confronted with a parody of the incarnation. The Man of Lawlessness is not simply a man with evil ideas. He is empowered by Satan to do Satan's work. Thus it is that he comes "with all kinds of counterfeit miracles, signs and wonders." All three of these words are used of the miracles of Christ. They are probably used here for that reason. They help us to see that the Man of Lawlessness has no originality; he does no more than try to imitate what Jesus has done. The first term points to the supernatural force that actuates the miracles; indeed, in the plural it often means "mighty works" or miracles. The second indicates their character as "signs" directing attention to something beyond themselves. The third, "wonders," reminds us that miracles are inexplicable for ordinary people; they can only marvel at them. But "counterfeit" is the wrong word; the Greek means "of the Lie" *(NEB)*, and it should probably be taken with all three words. The thought is not that the miracles, signs, and wonders are pretense (cf. *RSV,* "pretended signs and wonders"), so that there is no real miracle at all. Their reality is conceded (would Satan do less?). What Paul is contending is that they are done in a spirit of falsehood. They are the miracles that befit one who seeks to deceive people, just as Christ's miracles befitted him who came to save people.

10 The melancholy catalogue of this man's wickedness continues. Whereas before Paul has been concerned with his outward, objective show, now he turns to the effect of all this on people. The Man of Lawlessness will come expressly to deceive, and he will be well equipped to do this:

---

55. Paul uses the present tense, ἐστιν, which indicates the certainty of this coming.

he will have great powers of deception. "With evil's undiluted power to deceive" (Phillips) is hardly a translation, but it conveys Paul's thought. The Lawless One will be out to lure people to their destruction. To that end he will be armed with every weapon of Satan.

The evil "deceives those who are perishing." There may be the thought here that those in Christ have nothing to fear. But the primary emphasis is on the fate of those who are deceived. The Man of Lawlessness will gain a following and be welcomed by many. But his dupes will find in the end that they have followed him to their own irreparable loss.

2. The Man of Lawlessness's Followers (2:10b-12)

They perish because they refused to love the truth and so be saved. 11 *For this reason God sends them a powerful delusion so that they will believe the lie* 12 *and so that all will be condemned who have not believed the truth but have delighted in wickedness.*

10b Paul leaves the subject of the Man of Lawlessness in the middle of this verse and turns his attention to that evil one's followers. Having said that they would perish, he goes on to the reason[56] for this, namely, their wrong attitude to the truth. "Truth" here, as elsewhere in Paul's writings, is not to be thought of simply as an abstract moral quality. It is intimately related to Jesus (cf. Eph. 4:21, "as truth is in Jesus"; John 14:6, "I am . . . the truth"). More particularly it is the saving truth of the gospel. This aspect is very marked in the present passage. Receiving it means salvation. This truth should have been received with warm affection (as everyone who has welcomed it knows). Thus Paul speaks not simply of "the truth," but of "the love of the truth," an expression found here only in the Greek Bible (*NIV* has made a verb "to love" out of the noun "love"). The whole bent of the people he is describing is away from the truth of God. They gave the truth of God no welcome (this is the force of the words rendered "refused," which are more literally "did not receive"; see on 1 Thess. 2:13). They did not receive that truth of God which is expressed in the love that brought about the gospel. This is a deliberate action. It expresses the attitude of their heart. And it is fraught with eternal consequences. The verse concludes with a clause of purpose that emphasizes the magnitude of the gift these people rejected.

---

56. "Because" is ἀνθ' ὧν. The preposition ἀντί often has the thought of correspondence, and this may well be in view here. "In requital of their refusal to entertain the love of the truth," as Findlay puts it *(CGT)*.

Other people love the truth with a view to their salvation. It was this on which those who perish had turned their backs.

11 God is not to be thought of as sitting passively by while all this is going on. Invariably the Bible pictures him as taking part in the world's drama. Indeed, the world's drama is nothing other than the working out of his purposes. He has created this universe, and set it running on his own principles. He orders the affairs of people in the way he chooses. And one of the things he chooses is that an inevitable retribution overtakes the sinner.[57] Sometimes people today refer to the inevitability of the moral law. But the Bible picture is truer. There is no self-acting moral law. There is a moral God who is operative in the working of moral law.[58] In this verse the word "God" is in an emphatic position. Paul leaves no doubt but that God himself is responsible for the action of which he writes.

There is a backward look, "for this reason." What follows is due not to any caprice on the part of God, but to the culpable failure of the people in question to welcome the saving truth that was offered to them. The certainty of the result is underlined with the use of the present tense "sends." Paul sees it before his very eyes, so sure is its coming.[59] God sends "a working of error" (*NIV,* "a powerful delusion"). The genitive is the objective genitive, meaning, as Frame puts it, "an energy unto delusion." God will send a power that will operate to bring about in them a delusion. This is further explained, "so that they will believe the lie." "The lie."[60] It is not just any lie that these people accept, but Satan's last and greatest piece of deception, the lie that the Man of Lawlessness is God. They refuse to accept the truth and they find themselves delivered over to the lie.

---

57. Cf. Moore, "Near to hand lay the answer that some are drawn of God to faith in Christ, others are attracted by Satan to allegiance to Antichrist; but to the mind schooled in the Old Testament and committed to the gospel of Jesus Christ—both certain of the sovereignty of God—this would admit of an intolerable dualism and could not for a moment be contemplated."

58. Cf. Neil, "Men start by rejecting the Gospel voluntarily; they then reach the stage when they are unable to tell what is gospel and what is fallacy. This is the powerful 'delusion' which Paul rightly regards as an Act of God."

59. The present may also carry a hint that what will take place on the grand scale when the Man of Lawlessness comes is even now at work in principle in the case of lesser people. Whenever people refuse the truth, God sends the working of error.

60. Paul uses this expression elsewhere; see the note in my *The Epistle to the Romans* (Grand Rapids, 1988), p. 90.

The principle underlying this verse is of great importance for an understanding of the moral government of the universe. From the foregoing verses it might perhaps be thought that there is a contest in which Satan on the one hand and God on the other make their moves, but with God somewhat the stronger. But Paul has a much grander conception. God is using the very evil that people (and even Satan) do for the working out of his purpose. They think that they are acting in defiance of him, but in the end they find that those very acts in which they expressed their defiance were the vehicle of their punishment. Paul has the same truth in other places. For example, he tells us that God gave certain sinners "over to shameful lusts" (Rom. 1:26). They thought that they were enjoying their sinful pleasures, but it turned out that they were receiving "in themselves the due penalty for their perversion." The same truth is found in other parts of the Bible also.[61] God is sovereign. No forces of evil, not Satan himself nor his Man of Lawlessness, can resist God's might. He chooses people's sin as the way in which he works out their punishment.[62]

12 The judicial purpose of God in thus using evil as his instrument is made clear. "That they will believe the lie" is followed by "so that all will be condemned," the construction indicating purpose. There is method in all that God does in this situation. The verb really means "judged," but in this context it surely implies condemnation (Rutherford and Moffatt both translate "doomed"). But the use of this term rather than one that simply means condemnation stresses the judicial purpose of God. His act is just.

The section concludes with a further characterization of the con-

---

61. Notably in God's putting a lying spirit into the mouths of the false prophets (1 Kings 22:23; cf. Ezek. 14:9). Similarly, an action of Satan (1 Chron. 21:1) may be ascribed to God (2 Sam. 24:1). God is sovereign, and no evil power has independent existence. God uses evil to forward his purposes, and thus, in a sense, may be said even to originate it.

62. An interesting partial parallel is to be found in the "Habakkuk Commentary" in the Qumran scrolls. The commentary on Hab. 2:12-13 begins: "This saying means the preacher of the lie, who enticed many to build a city of delusion in blood and to establish a congregation in falsehood for the sake of its honor, making many grow weary of the service of delusion and making them pregnant with works of falsehood, that their toil may be in vain, to the end that they may come into judgments of fire" (Millar Burrows, *The Dead Sea Scrolls*, p. 389). In *The Manual of Discipline* God is thought of as creating the evil spirit as well as the good (p. 374). In the closing Psalm we read, "apart from thy will nothing will be done . . . everything that has come to pass has been by thy will" (p. 389).

demned, bringing out the nature of their offense. Paul returns to their wrong attitude to the truth. Whereas previously he has complained that they had no welcome nor love for the truth, now he says that they did not even believe it. Once more he has the saving truth of the gospel in mind, but these sinners would have none of it. Paul employs a construction that is unusual with him[63] (where he has it elsewhere it is mostly in quotations) to emphasize their position. His more usual construction has the thought of personal trust, as in the case of faith in Christ. This one denotes simple credence. The dupes of the Man of Lawlessness are so blinded to reality that they do not even realize that the gospel is God's truth. So does sin blind people.

Not only have they not believed the truth, but they "have delighted in wickedness."[64] There is a sharp contrast in both parts of this clause. "Delighted" contrasts with their attitude to the truth. There was no warmth in their attitude to the gospel, no welcome, no love, no belief even. But they actively rejoiced in wickedness, they inclined toward it, they regarded it with favor and goodwill. So, too, "wickedness" is contrasted with "truth." This word has been connected with deceit in verse 10. It is a general term for all kinds of wickedness. The stark contrast reminds us that ultimately we must belong to one or other of two classes, namely, those who welcome and love God's truth and those who take their pleasure in wickedness. Those who begin by failing to accept God's good gift end by setting forward unrighteousness. Notice the way in which they become perverted. These people are not described as sinning through force of circumstances or any form of compulsion. They now find their pleasure in sin. They delight in wrong.[65] For them evil has become good.

---

63. πιστεύω followed by the dative, as in v. 11; cf. also 2 Tim. 1:12.

64. There is also an unusual construction with εὐδοκέω; this is the only place in the New Testament where it is construed with the simple dative. Elsewhere we find ἐν pointing to that "in" which the good pleasure lies. The dative will denote "inclination towards," "favor to."

65. Way's rendering, "but have actually gloated over iniquity," is probably too strong, but it brings out their delight in evil.

IV. THANKSGIVING AND ENCOURAGEMENT (2:13-17)

A. STAND FIRM (2:13-15)

13 *But we ought always to thank God for you, brothers loved by the Lord, because from the beginning God chose you*[a] *to be saved through the sanctifying work of the Spirit and through belief in the truth.* 14 *He called you to this through our gospel, that you might share in the glory of our Lord Jesus Christ.* 15 *So then, brothers, stand firm and hold to the teachings*[b] *we passed on to you, whether by word of mouth or by letter.*

[a]13 Some manuscripts *because God chose you as his firstfruits*
[b]15 Or *traditions*

It was necessary to deal with the Man of Lawlessness and his detestable enormities, but Paul's real interest lay elsewhere. The advent speculations of his Thessalonian friends had made it essential for him to say enough to set them right. That done, he turns to a more congenial subject, the divine choice of the Thessalonians to salvation. He expresses thankfulness to God for his choice of the Thessalonians for salvation, and he goes on to make this the basis of an exhortation to them to stand firm.

13 In language reminiscent of his words in 1:3, perhaps intentionally so, he says that he and his friends "ought" to thank God for them. He wants his readers to be in no doubt as to the justice of the thanksgiving he offers. So he repeats the word that indicates obligation, and this time reinforces it (as he did not do in the opening part of the letter) with the emphatic pronoun for "we."[66] The Thessalonians can after this be in no doubt that Paul thinks highly of their Christian profession. Notice the insertion of "always." His impression of the Thessalonians is of people whose Christian life is consistent. Accordingly he must be thanking God for them all the time.

He employs the affectionate address "brothers," and adds to it "loved by the Lord." The addition is not usual, though elsewhere he has used the similar expression "loved by God" (1 Thess. 1:4). There, as here, the

66. Cf. Bicknell, "In the Greek *we* is as emphatic as the language can well make it." He thinks that this is "best explained as reiterating the fact that their founders are bound to thank God for their condition in spite of the discouragement of some of their converts."

thought of election was present. Election and the love of God are connected. The perfect participle, "loved," brings the two thoughts of an action
in time past and a continuing result. This is, of course, very appropriate in
proximity to the concept of election. "The Lord," in conformity with
Pauline usage, will here denote the Lord Jesus rather than the Father. There
is probably no significance in the change from "loved by God" to "loved
by the Lord." The use of the title "Lord," however, is possibly evoked in
this context by the preceding mention of mighty ones among the evil
beings. Just as in verse 8 there is significance in referring to Jesus as the
Lord (for he is mighty to destroy the Man of Lawlessness), so here the title
is not otiose. In the face of the might of evil the Thessalonians may well
be calm, for they are beloved of the mighty Lord.

Paul thanks God because he has chosen the converts "to be
saved." "Chose" is one of a number of words used to convey the idea
of election.[67] This is the only place where it is used in this sense in
the New Testament (though it is found with this meaning in LXX[68]).
There is no one word that constantly expresses the idea of election,
but the fundamental thought remains unchanged: the salvation of
believers rests on divine choice, not on human effort. Nor was this
some afterthought on God's part. He chose them "from the beginning."
Some interpreters have thought that this means no more than from the
beginning of the mission to Thessalonica, but this is inadequate. That
this is an unusual expression in Pauline writings for "from the beginning of time" is not significant. We have just seen that Paul's election
terminology is variable, and the same goes for his expressions for time.
There are several of these without there being any real difference of
meaning,[69] and we must feel that this is no more than a stylistic

67. Thus we find ἐκλέγομαι, προορίζω, προγινώσκω, and words of more general
meaning like τίθημι (as in 1 Thess. 5:9), ἀξιόω, καταξιόω, etc. The word here is εἵλατο.
68. It is found in Deut. 26:18, and the compound προαιρέομαι in Deut. 7:6-7;
10:15.
69. He uses πρὸ τῶν αἰώνων, πρὸ καταβολῆς κόσμου, and ἀπὸ τῶν αἰώνων. The
expression here is ἀπ᾽ ἀρχῆς, which is used of the beginning of things in Isa. 63:16;
Matt. 19:4; 1 John 2:13. The variant reading, ἀπαρχήν, "as a firstfruit," is preferred
by many commentators. The meaning would be first in contrast to others yet to come,
or first in Greece. The former is not very natural, and against the latter is the fact that
the Philippians were converted before the Thessalonians. Bruce favors "firstfruits";
he rejects various views of what "firstfruits" means and appears to favor "the church
as a whole is the ἀπαρχή of mankind to God." But Paul is speaking of the Thessalonians
("you"), not the church as a whole. Both variants have good manuscript support.
Transcriptional probability may be held to favor ἀπ᾽ ἀρχῆς, for this is not a typical

variation, all the more so since it is used elsewhere in the Greek Bible in such a sense. The meaning, then, is that God chose the Thessalonian Christians from the very beginning of things. Their election was no innovation.

They were chosen for salvation (the construction indicates purpose, as in 1 Thess. 5:9). Two aspects are singled out for mention. The first, "sanctification of the Spirit" (*NIV,* "the sanctifying work of the Spirit"), takes up a thought emphasized in the first letter (1 Thess. 4:3-7). Here some expositors understand it not as the work of the Holy Spirit in the believer, but (giving "spirit" a small "s") as the sanctification of the believer's spirit. Against this we should notice that it is the whole person that is sanctified (1 Thess. 5:23), in a sanctification effected by the Holy Spirit (cf. 1 Pet. 1:2). It is more likely, then, that the expression is to be understood of the work of the Holy Spirit in making the whole person holy.[70]

"Belief in the truth" is not an easy expression. As in verses 10 and 12, "truth" is not simply an ethical quality but the truth of the gospel. It is that truth which is associated with Jesus Christ. "Belief" is better rendered "faith";[71] the expression points us to that faith in the truth of God which is the basis of the Christian life.[72] At first sight it is surprising that faith should be mentioned after "sanctification of the Spirit." It may be that we are intended to understand that this can only follow an activity

---

Pauline expression, while ἀπαρχή is. Moreover, while Paul employs the concept of firstfruits on a number of occasions, he never elsewhere connects it with election. On the other hand, he often associates election with some expression rooting it in the beginning. A further point militating against ἀπαρχήν is the absence of a qualifying genitive, which, as Frame points out, is usual in Paul's use of that noun.

70. Notice that in this verse all three Persons of the Trinity are mentioned. This is not yet the official statement of the doctrine, but it represents such an understanding of the Persons and work of Father, Son, and Holy Spirit as was bound, in the end, to give rise to the dogma.

71. The word is πίστις.

72. Cf. T. F. Torrance, "In Greek 'faith of the truth' is an awkward expression, but it is clear from the Old Testament background that for St. Paul neither *pistis* nor *aletheia* will express fully what he is after, and so he puts both words together to convey what the Old Testament means by *'emeth* and/or *'emunah*" (*ET* 68 [1956-57], p. 113). C. F. D. Moule objects that Torrance ignores the fact that "the loose genitive may be objective rather than subjective," and he speaks of his "astounding interpretation" of this verse (*ET* 68 [1956-57], p. 157). Turner also argues that this expression "can scarcely involve a subjective genitive; God has chosen us for salvation by way of our faith in his Truth" (*Grammatical Insights,* p. 110).

of the Spirit. The order may also point us to the truth that the faith being spoken of is not simply one initial act. It is a continuing habit. Or, of course, Paul may simply be calling attention to the divine and the human aspects of salvation.

14 "Whereunto" (which *NIV* omits) is to be taken with the whole of the previous expression "salvation . . . truth," and not with any one member of it. The thought is that God calls people into a state of salvation. He calls them with a view to salvation. With the idea of call Paul moves from the pretemporal election by God to his effectual calling of people in history. The idea of the divine call is a favorite one with the apostle. There are other passages where he connects it with the thought of election as he does here (e.g., Rom. 8:30). We have already seen references to God's call (1 Thess. 2:12; 5:24), in both of which there is the idea of a present call. In the present passage the call is in the past tense, which points to the time when the Thessalonians had responded to the gospel. This is made quite plain by the addition of "through our gospel." The gospel Paul and his companions had preached had been the instrument of God's call. The personal touch is to be discerned in the possessive adjective, appropriate in a passage like this where the writer is concerned to stress his care for his converts. For "our gospel" see the note on 1 Thessalonians 1:5.

Paul speaks of being called "that you might share in the glory," where we should understand "share" not in the sense of acquiring by our own effort, but of receiving as a gift (see on 1 Thess. 5:9). Paul reminds his readers that salvation is not confined to its present aspects as he moves on to the thought of future glory. The eschatological emphasis in salvation runs through these letters; clearly it was important for Paul and it was important for the Thessalonians. This glory, the apostle says, is that "of our Lord Jesus Christ." The thought that the glory of the believer is closely associated with that of the Savior is one that recurs. We have met it, for example, in 1:10 (where see note). Those who are in Christ share the glory of Christ. For them there is no other glory. Paul had earlier written of the Thessalonians as being called into the glory of God (1 Thess. 2:12). That he can here speak of the glory of Christ in a similar fashion illustrates the closeness of the relationship between the Father and the Son (cf. also Rom. 8:29-30, and for "share" see the note on 1 Thess. 5:9, where the same word is translated "receive"). It is not a usual word in this kind of context. It may be meant to stress the reality of the possession of this glory in face of the fact that some at Thessalonica all too readily became downhearted.[73]

15 "So then" represents a pair of inferential conjunctions that indicate that what follows is the logical consequence of the preceding. Paul has been pointing out something of the the evil power of the Man of Lawlessness and of the terrible things he would do. But he has also been careful to interweave with this the thought of the might of the Lord who had loved the Thessalonians and had chosen them and called them. All this means something. Paul proceeds to draw out something of its relevance to the situation in which his readers find themselves. They should not "become unsettled" (v. 2), but contrariwise they should "stand firm." His verb here is an unusual one with an emphasis on the firmness of the stand (cf. its use in 1 Thess. 3:8 and the note there).[74]

Linked with this is the injunction "hold to the teachings." The verb is used elsewhere by Paul only once (Col. 2:19, of holding fast to Christ the "Head"). It is often used in the literal sense as of holding with the hand; it then denotes a firm grip. It is used of holding the traditions of the elders (Mark 7:3, 8). The present imperative here will have the force "go on holding." "Traditions" (the margin gives the correct meaning of the word) is a word that points us to the fact that the Christian message is essentially derivative.[75] It does not originate in people's fertile imaginations but rests on the facts of the life, death, resurrection, and ascension of Jesus Christ. Paul disclaims originating these things and expressly says that the things he passed on he had himself first received (1 Cor. 15:3). For us these traditions are preserved in the New Testament. But for Paul's readers there was no such volume. For them the Christian traditions were principally those which they had received "by word of mouth." Paul also associates "letter of ours" with the spoken word; by

---

73. Denney draws attention to "the new world which the gospel created for the mind of man." The profound thoughts in these two verses were "addressed originally to a little company of working people, but unmatched for length and breadth and depth and height by all that pagan literature could offer to the wisest and the best."

74. Like the following "hold to," the verb is present imperative, signifying continuity. "Stand firm continually . . . keep holding fast" ("go on preserving," Turner, M, III, p. 77).

75. O. Cullmann has an important chapter "The Tradition," in *The Early Church* (London, 1956), pp. 59-99. He argues that the tradition that is passed on by the apostles "is not effected by men, but by Christ the Lord himself" (p. 73).

this he probably means 1 Thessalonians. He puts no difference between the authority of the written and the spoken word. Both alike were in very deed the word of God (as we see from 1 Thess. 2:13; 1 Cor. 14:37). As in the case of election (see v. 13), the handing over of the Christian message is expressed with a variety of terminology.[76] But the underlying idea is always the same. It is a message that comes from God. It must therefore be accepted with humility and transmitted faithfully. The derivative nature of the message is a reminder that people ought not to depart from it in any way. Since the traditions were not of human origin they must stand fast in them.

B. PRAYER FOR THE CONVERTS (2:16-17)

16 *May our Lord Jesus Christ himself and God our Father, who loved us and by his grace gave us eternal encouragement and good hope,* 17 *encourage your hearts and strengthen you in every good deed and word.*

As he has done in other places, Paul breaks off his argument to engage in prayer. For him prayer was of the utmost importance, and it is quite in character that he should pray as he does here.

16-17 This section begins with an adversative conjunction (which *NIV* leaves untranslated) that might well be rendered "but." Paul has been urging his friends to action. But they can do nothing effective in their own strength. Thus the apostle directs them to that one source of strength which will see them through. He does more. He prays for them, just as he did in the first letter (1 Thess. 3:11-13). The prayer is at about the same stage in the argument, and there are coincidences of language between the two.

This prayer is notable for the place it assigns to Jesus Christ. He is given the full title[77] "Lord Jesus Christ," where each word has its full weight (see on 1 Thess. 1:1 for the force of each of these). Ever since he got on to the subject of the Man of Lawlessness Paul has used every opportunity to insist on the superlative worth and might of the Savior. He is linked with the Father, and, what is unusual, he is placed before

---

76. Verbs used of delivering it include δίδωμι, παραδίδωμι, διδάσκω, γνωρίζω, παραγγέλλω.

77. It is preceded by αὐτός, which makes the expression somewhat more emphatic.

the Father. This sometimes happens elsewhere (Gal. 1:1; 2 Cor. 13:14), but the more usual practice is to place the Father first. Although the subject is in this way a double one, the two verbs "encourage" and "strengthen" are singular.[78] We have seen Paul do this in the earlier letter (see on 1 Thess. 3:11). All this combines to give the highest place imaginable to Christ. Paul is not giving a formal account of his understanding of the nature of deity, but this incidental allusion in an informal act of prayer is all the more revealing for that reason. It is clear that he made no sharp distinction between the Son and the Father.

It is not quite clear whether the clause "who loved us . . ." is to be taken only with the Father, or with both Persons. On the whole it seems more likely that it refers to the Father only (though Frame prefers the other view). Nothing much hinges on the point, for either way the acts of love and giving are divine in origin, and if they are thought of as emanating from the Father they are certainly mediated to us through the Son. Since "loved" and "gave" are both aorist participles, the probability is that they refer to definite actions. "Who loved us" will have primary reference to the divine love shown in the cross (or perhaps to election; cf. 1 Thess. 1:4). "Gave us eternal encouragement" is rather the good gift of God when he brought us into the state of salvation.

The content of the gift is encouragement[79] or strengthening (see the note on 1 Thess. 3:2). Bailey reminds us that the word "may mean the presence of a great hope" that is surely the case here. "Eternal" encouragement is particularly appropriate in this context where there is so much about the troubles of the last days. Come the Man of Lawlessness, come the Parousia of our Lord, come the Day of Judgment, come anything else whatever, their encouragement will abide. Linked with this is "good hope." This is another concept that is very much in place where the interest is so highly eschatological. The Christian hope is good, as Frame points out, both in contrast with the empty hope of those who are not believers and because it will endure till it is realized at the coming of the Lord.[80]

---

78. Cf. Lightfoot, "There is probably no instance in St Paul of a plural adjective or verb, where the two Persons of the Godhead are mentioned."

79. The optative παρακαλέσαι is apt in a prayer: "May he encourage. . . ." Burton finds this "Optative of Wishing" 35 times in the New Testament and says, "It most frequently expresses a prayer" (*MT,* 176).

80. The importance of a "good" hope should not be overlooked. J. E. Fison has reminded us that hope is a necessity for any movement that would grip people's

"In grace" is not to be taken with "hope" but with "gave" (as *NIV* makes clear by removing it from its position after "good hope" in the Greek to a place before the verb). Encouragement and the hope are both the products of the grace of God. It is because of this divine origin and backing that they are valid. The verb "encourage" has the notion of strengthening, and the noun "heart" stands for the whole of the inner life and not particularly for the emotional life as with us (see the note on 1 Thess. 2:4). With this is joined the notion of buttressing them (for the two verbs "encourage" and "strengthen" see the notes on 1 Thess. 3:2). The prayer, then, is for inner strengthening with a view to faithful Christian service. Usually when "word" and "deed" are put together in this way, "word" comes first. Possibly the order in this passage is due to a stress on the deeds that will proceed from the divine strength for which the apostle prays.

---

hearts (*The Christian Hope,* pp. 16ff.), but some of the "hope" in the modern world is illusory. The first Christians were outwardly "of all men most miserable," but they had a good hope, that sure and certain hope of the return of their Lord in glory. It transformed for them the whole of life.

2 THESSALONIANS 3

V. THE FAITHFULNESS OF GOD (3:1-5)

A. REQUEST FOR PRAYER (3:1-2)

1 *Finally, brothers, pray for us that the message of the Lord may spread rapidly and be honored, just as it was with you.* 2 *And pray that we may be delivered from wicked and evil men, for not everyone has faith.*

Paul follows his prayer for the Thessalonians with a request that they should pray for him. He was a very great apostle, but his greatness consisted not so much in sheer native ability (though he had his share of that) as in his recognition of his dependence on God. It arises out of this that he so often requests the prayers of those to whom he ministers. He did not see himself as high above them, but as one with them. He valued their intercessions and sought their prayers.

1 Thus, as he passes from the major section of this letter to that which follows,[1] he does so with a request for prayer. He puts his imperative "pray" in an emphatic position, which leaves no doubt as to the importance he attaches to it, and he puts it in the present continuous tense, so that it means "pray continually." He looks not for a perfunctory petition, but for continuing prayer (though perhaps we should not press the tense; Paul often asks people to pray for him and this may be another example of his recognition of his continuing need for prayer support). In the first letter he had requested prayer (1 Thess. 5:25). Now he specifies the objects for prayer. The first of them concerns "the word [*NIV* has "message"] of the Lord." This means the preaching of the gospel message (as in 1 Thess.

---

1. For τὸ λοιπόν see the note on λοιπὸν οὖν in 1 Thess. 4:1. It marks the transition to a new section, here from the main section of the letter.

2:13). Paul wants it to "run" ("spread rapidly," *NIV*), a piece of vivid imagery in our present verse and probably going back ultimately to "his word runs swiftly" (Ps. 147:15). It is clear that when Paul first preached in Thessalonica there were spectacular results. Many were speedily converted. It is this kind of free movement of the word of God that he has in mind. With this he couples the idea of the word's being "glorified" (*NIV,* "honored"; cf. Acts 13:48). People are led to glorify the word when they observe what it does. There may also be a glance at the idea that, when the word is operative in the way spoken of, it displays its glories before people. Both verbs are in the present subjunctive, and the significance of this continuous tense should not be overlooked. Paul is not looking for a single striking manifestation of the word, but for its continuous swift advance and its continual arousing of admiration.

"Just as it was with you" reminds us of Paul's difficulties at the time of writing. Since his departure from Thessalonica he had been compelled to leave Berea, he had had little success in Athens, and he was meeting opposition in Corinth. He had begun his work in that city by reasoning in the synagogue, but the Jews opposed him; he then concentrated on the Gentiles. He was evidently somewhat disheartened, for the Lord spoke to him in a vision to encourage him (Acts 18:1-11). He himself said that he came to the Corinthians "in weakness and fear, and with much trembling" (1 Cor. 2:3). In these difficult times he recalls the glorious days in Macedonia, days that were continuing, judging from the reports he was receiving. There is no "it was" in the Greek, and it is not required. The statement is very general.[2] Paul is probably including both the first days of the mission in Thessalonica and the days when he was writing. It is worth noting that the account in Acts 17 does not picture the mission in Thessalonica as outstandingly successful; evidently the writers of the New Testament were not concerned to highlight every success. But from this passage it is clear that the mission to Thessalonica had been very successful and that the success continued after the first preachers went on to other work.

2 The second petition is that Paul may be delivered from his enemies. Both the use of the aorist tense in the verb "delivered"[3] and

---

2. *KJV*'s "even as it is with you" limits the meaning of the expression unduly, just as *NIV* does in another direction.

3. The verb ῥύομαι is a general term for rescue, whereas verbs like "redeem" are more restricted ("redeem" = free by the payment of a price). In the Bible ῥύομαι often has the idea of deliverance with power. Milligan suggests that the use of the preposition ἀπό here, rather than ἐκ (as in 1 Thess. 1:10) lays stress "perhaps on the deliverance itself rather than on the power from which it is granted."

the article with "wicked and evil men" point to a definite situation. Paul is not asking for prayer that he might be kept safe in his constant journeys and preachings. He writes in the light of his particular situation. He writes knowing that his friends are aware of his difficulty. He looks to them to join him in prayer that he may be delivered out of it. It seems most natural to understand his enemies as those Jews who opposed his preaching (so Marshall, though Best remains dubious). We know that they dogged his steps at Corinth as they did in other places (Acts 18:5, 12ff.). His request reminds us of similar words elsewhere (Rom. 15:31).

The word rendered "wicked" (*REB*, "wrong-headed") is used of persons only here in the New Testament (it is used of things in Luke 23:41; Acts 25:5, where it is translated "wrong," and in Acts 28:6, where the rendering is "unusual"). Basically it signifies what is out of place. When it is used in an ethical sense it denotes that which is improper, and thus unrighteous ("perverse," Best). Joined with "evil" it refers to the malignant temper of those who were setting themselves in opposition to the apostle as he sought to propagate the faith.

The meaning of "faith" at the end of the sentence is not beyond dispute. The Greek word it translates may mean "faithfulness" or "fidelity." It always has this meaning when it is used of God, but never, it would seem, in the New Testament when it is used of people. Or it may mean "faith" in the sense of "trust." With the article (which it has here) it may also signify "the faith," that is, the body of Christian teaching. The first meaning is obviously unsuitable here, but it is difficult to decide between the other two. In either case the meaning is much the same in this place. There is not a great deal of difference between "Not all men believe in Jesus Christ," and "Not all men embrace the Christian faith." Both make it clear that the people opposing Paul were outside the church, and not believers. In general it seems a little more likely that we should understand "faith" rather than "the faith," for the former would lead more naturally to the thought of the next verse,[4] and in a letter as early as this perhaps "the faith" is not the probable meaning.

---

4. Notice that the πίστις that ends this verse is immediately followed by the πιστός that begins the next. Paul is fond of such wordplays. Knox tries to bring out the connection by rendering, "the faith does not reach all hearts. But the Lord keeps faith."

B. GOD'S FAITHFULNESS (3:3-5)

3 *But the Lord is faithful, and he will strengthen and protect you from the evil one.* 4 *We have confidence in the Lord that you are doing and will continue to do the things we command.* 5 *May the Lord direct your hearts into God's love and Christ's perseverance.*

Following his request for prayer for himself Paul goes on to a little prayer for his correspondents, prefaced by some words of encouragement. He has drawn attention to some of their shortcomings, and he will do this again before this letter ends. But he does not leave them in any doubt as to his confidence in them. Specifically he makes it clear that he expects them to obey the directions he has given them.

3   As so often in his writings, Paul turns away from the difficulties of people to the God on whom all must depend. He does not shut his eyes to the very great difficulties of his situation, as his request for prayer plainly shows. But he knows that the really significant factor is the character of his Lord, not the might of the enemy. His usual practice is to refer to the faithfulness of God (1 Cor. 1:9; 10:13; 2 Cor. 1:18).[5] It is quite in keeping with the whole drift of the present passage, however, for him to speak of "the Lord." From the time of the mention of the Man of Lawlessness onward Paul has been constantly referring to "the Lord." The repetition is part of the way in which he seeks to inspire his converts. The reiteration of the lordship of their Leader means a corresponding belittlement of the forces of evil. Paul emphasizes the faithfulness of the Lord as an existing reality by inserting the verb "is." Normally in Greek this verb would not be necessary in a sentence of this kind. In none of the three passages listed above, for example, where God is said to be faithful is the verb inserted. Its presence here gives emphasis and certainty to the thought. The Lord is really faithful.[6]

There are two things that he looks for the Lord to do, and it is a little unexpected that he speaks of them being done to the Thessalonians rather than to himself. He has been speaking of his own difficulties and requesting their prayers. We expect accordingly that he will go on to say

---

5. Cf. this statement from the closing Psalm of the "Manual of Discipline," "For the faithfulness of God is the rock I tread, and his strength is the staff of my right hand" (Millar Burrows, *The Dead Sea Scrolls* [London, 1956], p. 387). The Scrolls often express their authors' complete dependence on God.

6. Cf. the vision recorded in Acts 18:9-10, where the Lord encouraged Paul to continue his work at Corinth.

that he is confident that the Lord will deliver him. But the concern of the pastor for his flock rises above any personal considerations. Paul speaks of what the Lord will do for them and not of what he will do for him. First, the Lord will "strengthen" them (for this verb see on 1 Thess. 3:2). The faithfulness of the Lord means that his people will not be left to the mercy of any and every temptation that may assail them, but they will be settled in the faith.

Second, the Lord will protect them. The verb hardly calls for comment, though it is not very common in the Pauline writings. It is not joined with the verb "strengthen" anywhere else in the Greek Bible. It is not certain whether the last expression in this verse should be understood as "the evil one" *(NIV)*, or as "evil" *(KJV)*; the Greek could mean either. We have the same problem in the Lord's Prayer, and elsewhere in the New Testament. Most commentators agree that the reference to a person is probable here. It fits the context better, for the preceding chapter has been concerned with evil persons, not with the general concept of evil.[7] There is also the point made by Calvin, "I prefer, however, to interpret it of Satan, the head of all the wicked. For it were a small thing to be delivered from the cunning or violence of men, if the Lord did not protect us from all spiritual injury."

4 From the thought of the faithfulness of the Lord Paul proceeds to express his confidence, a confidence that rests in that same Lord, that his friends will do what he enjoins them. It is not clear with what we should take "confidence." The meaning may be "We have confidence in the Lord" *(NIV;* cf. Moffatt, "we rely upon you in the Lord"), or "we, in the Lord, have every confidence" *(JB)*, or "the Lord gives us confidence in you" *(GNB)*.[8] The word order favors the first view, but in the end they come to much the same. Paul is putting his trust basically in the Lord. But he is expecting the Lord so to work in the lives of his friends that they will respond to the commands laid on them. The connection of thought is not obvious, but then the connection of thought is not obvious in a number of places in this letter. It is a true letter. Paul writes to his friends as his thoughts come to him, and there is not the carefully marshalled argument of the theological treatise. These words show us something of the tactfulness of Paul. Though the things of which he speaks are not defined, it seems fairly clear that he is leading up to

7. Cf. Findlay, "The passage depicts a personal conflict, not a war of principles" *(CGT)*.

8. Cf. the similar expression in Phil. 2:24.

the injunctions of verses 6ff. He wants the Thessalonians to obey his directions, but he begins by expressing his complete and continuing confidence in them (we should not miss the significance of the fact that his verb is in the perfect). Always he loves to praise where he can. His confidence does not rest in them as people: "in the Lord" shows clearly where the basis of his certainty lies. He says that they both "are doing and will continue to do" the things in question. The emphasis is probably on "will continue to do." As Findlay points out, had he been thinking only of their present or past performances he would probably have used a verb like "know" (as he does, for example, in 2 Cor. 9:2), instead of "have confidence" *(CGT)*.

He is preparing the way for the commands that follow. The verb "command" denotes an authoritative order (see the note on the cognate noun, 1 Thess. 4:2). It is probably not without significance that this is the verb he will employ in verses 6, 10, and 12.

5 This verse has important links of thought both with what precedes and what follows. Paul has been speaking of his confidence in the Thessalonians, but it is a confidence in the Lord and what he will do in them, and not simply a confidence in people. Thus immediately after his expression of confidence he breaks into prayer. It is only as the Lord works in them that his confidence will prove to have been justified. And if the fact that he prays follows significantly on the preceding verse, the content of the prayer has an important bearing on what follows. Paul is about to deal with certain people who are idle and insubordinate. He never shirks an issue, and his directions when he comes to them are blunt enough. But it is not part of his plan to give needless offense, and the reference to the love of God is timely.[9] It reminds them that Paul speaks as one who himself owed everything to the love of God and who loved God himself, and also that they are in the same position. There should be no resentment among people whose thoughts are fixed on God's love. Similarly the reference to "Christ's perseverance" is in point when people's idleness is about to be rebuked.

"The Lord" here is Jesus; we have another indication of the place Paul accorded him in this prayer addressed to him. The verb "direct" (see on 1 Thess. 3:11) signifies the removal of all obstacles so that the

9. The Qumran scrolls often speak of the steadfast love of God. For example, in the closing Psalm in "The Manual of Discipline" we read: "on his steadfast love I will lean all the day." "As for me, if I slip, the steadfast love of God is my salvation forever" (Millar Burrows, *The Dead Sea Scrolls,* pp. 386, 388).

way is cleared. The noun "heart" (see on 1 Thess. 2:4) stands for the whole of the inner life. Paul's prayer, then, is that the Lord will lead his friends to concentrate their thinking, their emotions, and their will on the love and steadfastness to which he refers.

There is some difficulty in knowing exactly what the following expressions signify. An expression like "the love of God" might mean in Greek either God's love for us (which *NIV* chooses) or our love for God. Our first difficulty is that the logic of the prayer seems to require some such meaning as "The Lord lead you to love God," but in Paul's writings "the love of God" always seems to mean God's love for people. Lightfoot is probably right in suggesting that "the Apostles availed themselves . . . of the vagueness or rather comprehensiveness of language, to express a great spiritual truth." He goes on to suggest that the two senses are "combined and interwoven." If we may accept this, then the primary idea will be that of God's love for us, but there will also be the secondary idea of our love for him. Paul's prayer, then, will be that the inner life of his friends be so concentrated on God's love for them that this will evoke an answering love for him.[10]

Conformably to this, "the perseverance of Christ" (again *NIV* removes the ambiguity and thus half the possible meaning) will denote first the attitude of Christ, and then the answering attitude on the part of the Thessalonians.[11] "Perseverance," here as elsewhere, will denote "steadfastness" or "endurance" (see the note on 1 Thess. 1:3). The Thessalonians are being reminded of the constancy exhibited by the Master, which forms the pattern on which they should model themselves.

10. Cf. Moffatt, "It is by the sense of God's love alone, not by any mere acquiescence in His will or stoical endurance of it, that the patience and courage of the Christian are sustained."

11. Chrysostom understands the meaning as "That we should endure even as He endured, or that we should do those things, or that with patience also we should wait for Him, that is, that we should be prepared" (p. 393). *KJV* is not unlike this with "the patient waiting for Christ." But while this understanding of the text would fit in with the eschatological emphasis so marked in these letters, it is an unlikely understanding of this genitive.

251

VI. GODLY DISCIPLINE (3:6-15)

A. THE DISORDERLY (3:6-13)

6 *In the name of the Lord Jesus Christ, we command you, brothers, to keep away from every brother who is idle and does not live according to the teaching*ᵃ *you received from us.* 7 *For you yourselves know how you ought to follow our example. We were not idle when we were with you,* 8 *nor did we eat anyone's food without paying for it. On the contrary, we worked night and day, laboring and toiling so that we would not be a burden to any of you.* 9 *We did this, not because we do not have the right to such help, but in order to make ourselves a model for you to follow.* 10 *For even when we were with you, we gave you this rule: "If a man will not work, he shall not eat."*

11 *We hear that some among you are idle. They are not busy; they are busybodies.* 12 *Such people we command and urge in the Lord Jesus Christ, to settle down and earn the bread they eat.* 13 *And as for you, brothers, never tire of doing what is right.*

ᵃ6 Or *tradition*

In the First Epistle Paul had mentioned that some people would not work but were disorderly (4:11-12; 5:14), but it is evident that his brief exhortations had not produced the desired effect. He felt strongly on the matter, as we see from the fact that in this letter he devotes so much space to this problem. Next to the section on the coming of the Lord this is the longest section in the epistle. Paul is most anxious that these friends should come to their senses. It is noteworthy that he continues to treat them as friends. For all the authority that he knew he possessed, and for all the authoritative tone of some of this section, he yet bears well in mind that these are brothers. He appeals to them as such. But he uses strong words about the idlers (v. 10); laziness is never a Christian virtue.

6 Tenderness is blended with authority in this opening exhortation. Paul addresses the church as "brothers" and refers to the erring as "every brother." But his verb is the strong one he has used in verse 4. He commands; he does not simply advise. The verb is often used for the giving of military orders, and there is a military touch also in the word translated "idle," which is used of the soldier who is out of line. Moreover, Paul speaks "in the name of the Lord Jesus Christ." This is at once a reminder of the very real authority that Paul exercised and of the seriousness of any refusal to obey. Paul was not giving some private ideas of his own when he spoke "in the name."

The substance of his command is that they "keep away" from the erring. In view of verse 15 this does not mean "abstain from all interaction," but it stands for the withholding of intimate fellowship. The verb has the idea of retreating within oneself (cf. its use of furling sails). Such a line of conduct is meant as would impress on the offenders that they had opened up a gap between themselves and the rest. They had to be made to see that complete fellowship is possible only when there is complete harmony. The workers had a responsibility to the offenders. For, as Frame says, "Idleness is an affair of the brotherhood (I, 4:9-12, 5:12-14), and the brethren as a whole are responsible for the few among them who 'do nothing but fetch frisks and vagaries' (Leigh)" (on v. 11). It is an aspect of the Christian life that is but little observed today.

The offenders are characterized as being "disorderly" (*NIV* changes this to the adjective "idle") and as not following the "tradition" (see *NIV* mg.). "Disorderly" is the adverb from the same root as that which we examined in the note on "the idle" (1 Thess. 5:14). It shows us that the same people are in mind as in the former passage, and, as we saw there, that their offense was idleness. Paul speaks of the brother "that walketh disorderly" (*REB*, "who falls into idle habits"); he is speaking of a continuing practice, not of an occasional offense. In view of the fact that the day of the Lord had dawned (as they thought, 2:2) and thus the Parousia was near, they were refraining from doing any work. They would find such conduct all the easier in view of the Greek idea that labor was degrading. It was a menial occupation, fit for slaves only, not for those who were free. But this kind of conduct could not be overlooked as due to ignorance of the obligations of Christian discipleship. It was contrary to the "tradition," which indicates that Paul had given instruction on this specific point (cf. v. 10; for the word see the note on 2:15). "Received from us" shows that the particular teaching Paul has in mind is the teaching that he had given on the original visit.[12]

---

12. There is a textual problem as to whether we should read "they received" (παρελάβοσαν) or "you received" (παρελάβετε). Not much hangs on the decision, for in either case Paul is directing his readers' attention to the original proclamation. Each reading has good, though not decisive, attestation. παρελάβοσαν is favored by many scholars as the harder reading. It is possible, however, that it arose by what Westcott and Hort call "an ocular confusion" with the ending παράδοσιν in the corresponding place in the line above (*The New Testament in the Original Greek*, Introduction [London, 1907], Appendix, p. 172). In general it seems likely that παρελάβετε is to

7 By using the emphatic pronoun "yourselves" Paul stresses that his friends had all the knowledge that was necessary on this point. He was not giving them any new teaching, but simply directing their attention to what they knew quite well already.

Almost frightening is the way in which Paul continually appeals to the force of his own example.[13] Here his "ought" is a strong expression, one often translated "must." The imitation of the apostles is not optional, and Paul regards it as imperative in his converts. While we feel some diffidence today about appealing to our own example, and while we must recognize that dangers lie there, yet it remains true that no preaching of the gospel can ever be really effective unless the life of the preacher is such as to commend the message. Those who hear must feel that they are listening to one whose life shows his sincerity and the power of the message he brings (see further on 1 Thess. 1:5-6).[14]

Paul relates this general duty of imitation to the present circumstances by reminding his readers that he and his followers "were not idle when we were with you." This is a classical understatement in view of what we know of Paul's life among the Thessalonians. As the succeeding verses make plain, he had toiled hard among them, both at his trade and in preaching. His life had been highly disciplined. He had not allowed even the importance of preaching the gospel to prevent him from giving a good witness by earning his living. His behavior under those circumstances was the strongest rebuke to those who had no such excuse for not working but who nevertheless had given themselves to idleness.

8 "To eat bread" is evidently a Semitism for "get a living," not simply "get a meal," or even "meals" (cf. Gen. 3:19; Amos 7:12, etc.). Paul does not mean that he had never accepted a hospitable invitation, but that he had not depended on other people for his means of livelihood.[15]

---

be preferred. This word would lead more naturally to the οἴδατε of the next verse, where the other reading would look for οἴδασιν. Moulton thinks it "more than doubtful" that παρελάβοσαν can be accepted, since the termination is so very rare at this period (M, I, p. 52).

13. Malherbe draws attention to the fact that philosophers like Seneca held themselves up as patterns for their followers (Malherbe, pp. 52-53).

14. The expression πῶς δεῖ μιμεῖσθαι ἡμᾶς is, as Lightfoot points out, an abridgment for πῶς δεῖ ὑμᾶς περιπατεῖν ὥστε μιμεῖσθαι ἡμᾶς, "how you ought to walk so as to imitate us" (cf. 1 Thess. 4:1). The present expression, besides being more terse, puts an emphasis on μιμεῖσθαι and thus keeps the thought of imitation prominent.

15. "Without paying for it" is the translation of δωρεάν, "gift-wise," "by way of gift."

He employs a strong adversative conjunction (rendered "on the contrary") to show that his conduct was the very opposite of what he has just disclaimed. Far from being idle and imposing on others for his living, he and his friends had worked hard, constantly, and purposefully. He had made these three points in the First Epistle (see 1 Thess. 2:9, a verse very similar to the present one). Then he had been demonstrating that he was no charlatan, but that his motives in seeking to win the Thessalonians had been of the purest. Now he appeals to those same facts in putting himself out as an example to his converts. He had shown them the way a Christian ought to support himself. Paul's toil had been laborious, the conjunction of the two words he uses being emphatic. He had not shrunk from toiling through long hours ("night and day"). He had done it with the set purpose of refraining from imposing a burden on anyone.[16]

9 Characteristically Paul adds to his description of his conduct a statement of his rights.[17] He was an apostle, with all that that meant in terms of prestige and the right to maintenance. He knew that his Lord had ordained that preachers of the gospel might live from their preaching (1 Cor. 9:14; the whole passage, 1 Cor. 9:3ff., should be consulted as the fullest statement of Paul's views on this subject). Paul would never let it be forgotten that he possessed such prestige and such rights. But just as it is characteristic of him to assert that he had full rights, so is it for him to waive those rights whenever he judged that to do so would forward the cause of Christ. One such occasion had been when he preached in Thessalonica. Then his refusal to accept maintenance had demonstrated the purity of his motives and had given his converts an example. This latter point he proceeds to underline. He speaks of his friends and himself as being "a model" (for this word see on 1 Thess. 1:7), and says that their purpose was that the Thessalonians should imitate them. "To make ourselves" is literally "in order that we might give ourselves." This form of expression brings out something of the self-abasement implied in Paul's action. It reminds us of his other statement that "we were delighted to share with you not only the gospel of God but our lives as well" (1 Thess. 2:8). "Ourselves" is emphatic. They gave not only a message, but themselves. They did not only what was required, but more. They went the second mile. The Thessalonians are reminded that this was not a mere piece of pageantry or showmanship,

16. See the notes on 1 Thess. 2:9 for the force of the language employed both there and here.

17. For οὐχ ὅτι οὐκ ἔχομεν ἐξουσίαν cf. 1 Cor. 9:4, 5.

but had a very definite purpose. It was an example that they should follow. If Paul, who had the right to maintenance, had foregone that right and worked with his hands to earn his living, much more should rank-and-file Thessalonians not seek to be kept by the labors of other people.

10 Not only[18] did the apostles set an example: they embodied their teaching in a pithy precept that Paul now reproduces.[19] The origin of this precept is a matter for speculation, and the most diverse sources have been claimed. Findlay derives it from Jewish sources, others claim a Greek provenance, while Deissmann sees in it "a bit of good old workshop morality, a maxim applied no doubt hundreds of times by industrious workmen as they forbade a lazy apprentice to sit down to dinner."[20] The plain fact is that this is the oldest passage we have that contains it. Parallels have been adduced from various sources, but they lack the idea of labor as a moral duty that is the very root of the matter (they are of the "He who doesn't work doesn't eat" variety). It may have been Paul who originated the saying: it was certainly he who made it part of the Christian view of labor. The preachers kept drumming in their precept.[21] The saying emphasizes the will[22]—"If anyone *won't* work, refuses to work. . . ." The concluding clause is not a statement of fact, "he shall not eat," but an imperative, "let him not eat." Paul is giving the clearest expression to the thought that the Christian cannot be a drone. It is obligatory for him to be a worker.[23]

The importance of this to Paul is evident in many ways. There is the force of his own example, to which he has appealed in the previous verses. There is also the use of the same authoritative verb "commanded" (*NIV,* "gave you this rule") that we have already noticed (vv. 4, 6). Here it is in the imperfect tense, which indicates continuous action. Paul had repeatedly used this injunction in his teaching.

18. καὶ γάρ ("for even") should be taken in the sense "for also" or "for indeed."

19. ὅτι does not mean "that," but is ὅτι recitative introducing the words of the command (BDF #397[3]).

20. *LAE,* p. 314. Neil thinks that "It belongs to the universal realm of common sense."

21. Cf. Rutherford, "Why, when we were with you, we were always telling you that there should be only one rule, 'No work, no bread.' "

22. "Οὐ θέλω is not the mere contradictory, but the contrary of θέλω . . . not a negative supposition (εἰ μή), but the supposition of a negative" (Findlay, *CGT*). Paul is not speaking of those who cannot find work, nor of those who through injury or illness are not able to work, but of those who deliberately choose not to work.

23. Wilson quotes A. Harnack, "The new religion did not teach 'the dignity of labour.' What it inculcated was just the *duty* of work."

11 Paul comes out into the open. He has not been speaking simply in general terms, laying down precepts against some possible future need. He has in mind a definite situation. He writes to correct known errors. How he knows he does not say. The verb "we hear" is ordinarily used of hearing by the ear, and thus might well point to information received by word of mouth. But the word may be used in a wider sense, and Frame cites examples of its use for information received by letter. The present tense might indicate repeated information, "we keep on hearing." Or it could just as well be equivalent to "we have heard."[24] He does not say who the offenders are. But though his language is purposely indefinite, the impression the Greek leaves is that he knows quite well their identity; he just prefers not to say who they were. He speaks of these people as being "among you," and it may be significant that he does not say "of you." Their conduct had removed them from their full status in the church and set up something of a barrier between them and their fellows.

The offenders are characterized as "idle" (the same word as in v. 6 and the same root as in 1 Thess. 5:14, where see note). It indicates that they were loafing and not doing any work for their living. This Paul brings out further with his "They are not busy; they are busybodies."[25] This embodies a play on words that we miss in our usual translations (Moffatt's is perhaps the best attempt to reproduce it in English, "busybodies instead of busy"; cf. *REB*, "minding everybody's business but their own"). These people were not simply idle, they were meddling in the affairs of others. We may conjecture that they were trying to do one or both of two incompatible things, namely, to get their living from others, and to persuade those others to share their point of view about the second advent and so get them to stop working too.

12 Paul now interjects an exhortation directed at the offenders, though he employs a very oblique way of referring to them ("such people"). He does not say "you loafers," or even "those loafers." He uses instead an expression that means "people of this kind," "people who answer to this description." This is part of the tactfulness that we see displayed throughout this whole section. Paul leaves us in no doubt but that he reprobated their conduct, though his tone is brotherly throughout

24. For this construction with the present tense as equivalent to the perfect, see Burton, *MT,* 16. Best regards it as equivalent to an aorist (p. 339).

25. Chamberlain detects force in the compound with περί: "'I work around,' 'I overdo the matter,' and therefore 'become a busybody'" (p. 144).

the discussion. He is anxious to secure not condemnation but reconcil-iation. He wants the offenders to be won back into the fellowship of the church, and all his exhortations have this in mind. So here he addresses them in this very roundabout way. He uses the authoritative verb of commanding (see vv. 4, 6, and 10), but softens it with the addition of "urge," making a combination unique in the Pauline writings. Whereas he had earlier commanded them in the name of Christ (v. 6), now he exhorts them "in" Christ. This gives a note of authority, it is true, but they as well as Paul were in Christ. The expression has a brotherly ring, and at the same time it has the effect of drawing attention to the obliga-tions consequent on the fact that they were in Christ.

Paul urges them to work "with quietness"[26] (*NIV* paraphrases with "settle down"). The root trouble apparently was their excitability. The thought of the nearness of the Parousia had thrown them into a flutter, and this had led to unwelcome consequences of which their idleness was the outstanding feature. So Paul directs them to that calmness of disposi-tion which ought to characterize those whose trust is in Christ. They are to earn their living. Paul inserts an emphatic "their own" before bread (for the force of "eat bread" see on v. 8). These people had existed on the bounty of others. They are urged to exist on the fruits of their own labors.

13 Paul turns back to the majority of church members with an emphatic "as for you" (i.e., whatever the recalcitrant may do, you do this) and an affectionate address, "brothers." The exhortation is couched in general terms. It is broad enough to cover the whole of life, but probably has particular reference to the obligation to do everything possible to bring back the erring members.[27] Such a task is never easy, hence the exhortation not to "tire" in doing right (cf. Gal. 6:9).[28] Some commentators have felt that the majority had not been exactly tactful

26. μετὰ ἡσυχίας. The μετά marks the attendant disposition. Cf. Bicknell, quietness "probably is in contrast not to the meddlesomeness of the idle, but to the restlessness of mind that they fostered in themselves and in others." Milligan says that ἡσυχία "differs from ἠρεμία in denoting tranquillity arising from *within* rather than from *without*." The cognate verb ἡσυχάζω occurs in 1 Thess. 4:11.

27. Chrysostom relates this to the disciplining of the idle and finds a limit on withholding food: "Withdraw yourselves, he says, from them, and reprove them; do not, however, suffer them to perish with hunger" (p. 394).

28. The use of μή with the aorist (μὴ ἐγκακήσητε) implies that they had not begun to grow weary. Moulton points out that μή with the aorist subjunctive is infrequent in Paul; he finds only three genuine examples (M, I, p. 124).

toward the minority, and their impatience had only widened the breach. This may well be so, though we have no means of verifying it. If this is the case, Paul's words are more than ever in point. Calvin draws a wide moral, "however ingratitude, moroseness, pride, arrogance, and other unseemly dispositions on the part of the poor, may have a tendency to annoy us, or to dispirit us, from a feeling of weariness, we must strive, nevertheless, never to leave off aiming at doing good." Paul's word for doing good is found here only in the New Testament, though the two components that together make up the word are found as separate words several times. In accordance with the basic difference of meaning between the two words for "good" (see on 1 Thess. 5:21), the word used here will mean rather doing the thing that is right in itself, the thing that is noble, than conferring benefits (which would be the compound used in Luke 6:9).

B. THE DISOBEDIENT (3:14-15)

14 *If anyone does not obey our instruction in this letter, take special note of him. Do not associate with him, in order that he may feel ashamed.* 15 *Yet do not regard him as an enemy, but warn him as a brother.*

Paul anticipates that some of the Thessalonians may not obey his instructions, so he gives direction as to the way they are to be treated. It is most probable that it is some among the idlers that he has in mind, though his words are general enough to cover disobedience to anything he has said throughout the letter.

14 The argument takes a slightly new turn.[29] The use of the present tense, "obey," views the matter, as is common in Greek letters, from the point of view of the recipients. By the time they get to this point they have read the letter, they have heard the injunctions,[30] and any refusal to obey is present, not still future. "In this letter" is literally "through the letter." The occurrence of "letter" with the article toward the end of a letter almost always means the letter just being written. Thus

29. The conjunction δέ has left no mark on most translations, but it certainly links what follows with the preceding. It may mean no more than "and," but it is also possible that it has some adversative force, setting the person who disobeys the letter over against those who do not tire of doing right.

30. "Word" (*NIV*, "instruction"), of course, here means "command" (cf. the use of "the ten words" for the Ten Commandments).

NIV almost certainly gives us the sense of it. We should perhaps notice that some interpreters prefer to take this expression with the words that follow, giving the meaning "designate that person by letter." They understand Paul to mean that he wants to be informed in writing about such a happening. However, it is not likely that this interpretation is correct. We have already noted that the usual Greek usage is against it. So also are the word order and the general sense of the passage. Paul is telling the members of the church what action they should take, not asking for an opportunity to take action himself. "Take special note of him"[31] means more than simply "notice" him. It means "mark him out," though the means whereby this is to be done is not specified. The word was originally neutral and might mean mark out for good as well as for ill, but in time it came to have a somewhat sinister significance. It came to mean marking out for blame, as here.

The treatment of such a person is withdrawal of fellowship. This is a limited punishment compared with that laid down for the Corinthians in a more serious situation (1 Cor. 5:9-13). There, too, withdrawal of fellowship is spoken of (the verb used is the same as that here,[32] these being the only two passages in the New Testament where it occurs). But in Corinth the offense is more serious, and so is the penalty. It is specifically laid down that the Corinthians are not to eat with such a person, and that they are to put him away from among them. Here he is still to be regarded as a brother (see the very warm statement of v. 15). The treatment is primarily intended to bring him back to his rightful position. At the same time it is a punishment. He has ignored, first the teaching originally given by word of mouth, then the injunctions of the first letter and now of the second. Clearly this shows a measure of obduracy. It is no longer possible to regard such a person as being in good standing with the church. He must be disciplined.[33] Our difficulty in combining

31. Grammarians used the term in the sense *nota bene* (see MM). It meant more than just a passing notice, and implied serious attention.

32. συναναμίγνυμι is an expressive double compound, with a meaning like "mix up together with."

33. There are many examples in the Qumran scrolls of the withdrawal of fellowship, especially in "The Manual of Discipline." Exclusion for varying periods is the penalty for a number of offenses; one that is not without its interest runs: "One who lies down and goes to sleep during a session of the masters [shall be punished] thirty days" (Millar Burrows, *The Dead Sea Scrolls,* p. 380). A curious provision in the two-year punishment of a traitor is that he may not "touch the sacred food of the masters" during the first year, while "during the second he shall not touch the drink of the masters" (p. 381).

the two thoughts of withdrawing fellowship and treating the person as a brother should not blind us to the fact that Paul expected the church to be capable of both at once. Neither could be neglected.

The purpose of this discipline is "that he may feel ashamed." Always Paul has in mind his repentance and reinstatement. Findlay draws attention to the fact that the verb is in the passive (as it usually is in the New Testament), with the meaning "to be turned in (upon oneself)" (*CGT*). It is this process of reflection on the enormity of one's actions that Paul wishes to see effected in the unruly.

15 Paul's thought that the offender must still be regarded as a brother now becomes explicit. The "yet" of *NIV* should probably be omitted. While it could possibly be understood from the Greek[34] it is more natural to take the connective as meaning simply "and." The point is that Paul is not contrasting the behavior outlined in this verse with that in the previous one, but carrying on a consistent line of thought. Throughout this whole section he aims at having the dissident reclaimed in a spirit of love. The actions enjoined in verse 14 are just as kindly intentioned as those in this verse.

It is noteworthy that Paul puts the injunction not to treat the offender as an enemy before that to admonish him. He is eager to protect the brother's standing, and to be sure that what is done to him is done from the best of motives and secures the desired result. The enforcement of discipline is a difficult matter, for it is easy for people to become censorious and unnecessarily harsh in the process. Paul's words are directed against any such eventuality. His "but" between the two clauses of this verse is a strong adversative. They are to be far from treating the offender as an enemy. The verb contains the idea of a rebuke for wrong-doing, but Paul always uses it with a certain tenderness.[35] It is the rebuke of a friend. It is most appropriate here with its combination of the two ideas of a steady refusal to have any truck with the evil thing and a genuine concern for the well-being of the wrongdoer.

34. Taking καί in the sense of καίτοι.

35. The verb is νουθετέω, for which see the note on 1 Thess. 5:12. Cf. its use in 1 Thess. 5:14

VII. CONCLUSION (3:16-18)

16 *Now may the Lord of peace himself give you peace at all times and in every way. The Lord be with all of you.*
17 *I, Paul, write this greeting in my own hand, which is the distinguishing mark in all my letters. This is how I write.*
18 *The grace of our Lord Jesus Christ be with you all.*

Paul brings the letter to a close in his normal fashion. He stresses the peace that he prays will come to his correspondents from the Lord of peace, and concludes with his habitual prayer for grace. But in between he has an unusual section in which he explains his habit of authenticating his letters by writing a little in his own handwriting. Apparently he did this constantly, but he does not normally explain what he was doing.

16 Paul usually has a short prayer[36] toward the close of his letters, and it not uncommonly includes a reference to "the God of peace." Because of this it is probably wrong to place a great deal of emphasis on the occurrence of "peace" just here. Yet at the least we may notice that it is appropriate immediately following his references to the unhappy division in the church. The Lord they serve is a Lord of peace, and those who serve him should likewise be characterized by peace. At the same time we must bear in mind that peace in the Bible is not simply the absence of strife (see on 1 Thess. 1:1). It means prosperity in the completest sense, and its association here with the Lord is a reminder that such a state comes only as the gift of God.

Though a prayer with a reference to "the God of peace" is common in Paul, one mentioning "the Lord of peace" is not (the expression is found here only in the New Testament). "Lord" with Paul usually means Jesus Christ, and there is every reason for thinking that it is Jesus who is in mind here. The "himself" gives it a certain emphasis, as is the case elsewhere in these epistles. The entire expression is a reminder to the Thessalonians that the solution to the problems before them, including those of the idlers and disobedient, rested not in their own efforts, but in the help that the Lord would bring them.[37] "At all times" is not quite

---

36. Moule regards the verb here as an optative "of prayerful expectation" (*IBNTG*, p. 136). There are similar optatives in 1 Thess. 3:11, 12; 5:23; 2 Thess. 2:17; 3:5.

37. Cf. Lightfoot, "The disjunctive particle δὲ is slightly corrective of the preceding. It implies: 'Yet without the help of the Lord all your efforts will be in vain.' "

the force of the Greek, which is rather "continually" (as Moffatt renders it). The thought is not that of a peace that comes on a series of occasions, but that of a peace that is unchanging. It abides continually. The thought of a peace that is present no matter how the circumstances may change is contained in the following "in every way." "Way" literally means "turning." It has within it the idea of the manner in which conditions alter. No change in that which is outward can interfere with the Christian's deep-seated peace. His peace is not a matter of equilibrium with the tensions of the outward. It is the gift of the Lord, and comes independently of outward circumstances.

This is put in another way when Paul prays, "The Lord be with all of you." The Christian's peace is never independent of the Lord. It is the gift of the Lord, and it is impossible apart from him; indeed, it is the very presence of the Lord. It is only as the Lord is in the heart of the believer day by day that he knows this peace. It may be an example of the way Paul enjoyed it that he puts "all" at the end of his prayer. There is no resentment against those who disobey his injunctions. He prays for all the Thessalonians, those who were out of step as well as those who were in perfect harmony with him.

17 As the letter draws to its close, Paul explains the method he employs to authenticate his writings. It seems to have been his custom (as with most people of antiquity) to dictate his correspondence while an amanuensis wrote down what he said (in Romans we even read of Tertius, "who wrote down this letter," Rom. 16:22). The apostle would take the pen himself, however, toward the close of the letter and write a few lines himself; his own characteristic handwriting would show that the letter came from him (cf. *GNB*, "With my own hand I write this"). The stage at which Paul took the pen seems to have varied. He wrote quite a few verses at the end of Galatians (Gal. 6:11), but shorter passages in other letters (1 Cor. 16:21 and Col. 4:18 are other places where he draws attention to what he was doing). It is possible that in the case of a short letter like that to Philemon he wrote the whole (Phlm. 19). We do not know why he drew attention to the autograph on some occasions but not on others. There is no reason for thinking that he penned his salutation only in the cases where he specifically calls attention to it. He tells us here that it was his custom "in all my letters." Deissmann has drawn attention to an interesting example of this practice when he reproduces a letter from a gentleman called Mystarion to a priest.[38] The

38. *LAE*, pp. 170-72.

letter is written in one hand, but the final greeting and the date are in another hand. There is no reasonable doubt that this latter is the hand of Mystarion himself. The interesting thing is that Mystarion says nothing about this. He just does it. If we had only a copy of his letter, and not the original itself, we would not know what had happened. And what Mystarion did, so also did Paul the apostle.

Paul proceeds to tell us that this is his customary "mark," that is, means of authentication. This is the way he shows that his letters are genuine. Some exegetes have thought that this mark shows that this is the first letter Paul wrote to the Thessalonians; such a statement would be necessary in a first letter, they maintain, but not after that. This, however, is to go too far too fast. Paul may well have simply followed his normal practice in his first letter. Later people were not certain about a letter that purported to come from Paul (2:2). Was it really from the apostle? To answer such questions he now makes his practice clear. They may know that this letter is authentic because they can recognize his handwriting. And since this is his normal practice, they have a test that they can apply to every letter that claims to come from Paul. Incidentally, the way he puts it, "the mark in all my letters," makes it seem as though he wrote other letters that are now lost. "This is how I write" probably means "This is what my writing is like," rather than "This is my custom" (cf. Knox, "This is my handwriting").

18 The letter concludes in exactly the same fashion as the first (see the notes there), with the exception that the word "all" is added. Twice in the last three verses we have seen this reference to the whole membership, and we can only feel that Paul's tenderness for his entire flock carries through to the end. He has had some hard things to say about those who were offending, but he closes on an inclusive note. *All* his friends were included in his final prayer.[39]

39. That is, if we assume that the addition of "all" is significant, and is included in view of the specific disturbances noted earlier. This assumption is likely, but we should notice that Paul could use a similar expression in Rom. 15:33, where no such inference is to be drawn. At the very least we can say that nobody is excluded.

GENERAL INDEX

265

INDEX OF AUTHORS

269

270

INDEX OF SCRIPTURE REFERENCES